Basics and Beyond

Paragraph and Essay Strategies

Margaret van Dijk
Centennial College

Prentice
Hall

Toronto

DEDICATION

To Peter Dyson, a dear friend and a great teacher
To Maarten — Master Scanner and Helpmate Extraordinaire

National Library of Canada Cataloguing in Publication Data

van Dijk, Margaret, 1949–
   Basics and beyond: paragraph and essay strategies

Includes index.
ISBN 0-13-090909-2

   1. English language—Rhetoric. 2. Report writing. I. Title.

PE1408.V35 2002   808'.042   C2001-904286-8

0-13-090909-2

Vice President, Editorial Director: Michael J. Young
Acquisitions Editor: Marianne Minaker
Executive Marketing Manager: Christine Cozens
Signing Representative: Lenore Taylor
Executive Developmental Editor: Marta Tomins
Production Editor: Tammy Scherer
Copy Editor: Claudia Forgas
Production Manager: Wendy Moran
Page Layout: Janette Thompson
Art Director: Julia Hall
Cover and Interior Design: Amy Harnden
Front Cover Image: Dia Max / FPG

1 2 3 4 5 06 05 04 03 02

Printed and bound in Canada.

Contents

Preface   ix

Acknowledgments   xii

Part 1: Active Reading and Beyond   1
Working Together   1

Chapter 1   Active Reading   4
Active Reader Program   5
Another Reading Strategy: P3SE Formula   6
Reading 1: "Summer Barbecues" by John Fitzgerald   8
Reading 2: "Dining Out" by Joe Campbell   11
Etymology   14
Reading 3: "Know Thyself" by Daniel Goleman   20
Reading 4: "After Breathalyzer, A Sleepalyzer?" by Michael Filosa   22
Reading 5: "Looking Back on the Exxon Valdez" by Greenpeace   27
    Review and Remember: Remembering Assigned Readings   31

Chapter 2   Context and Comprehension: Personal Narratives   32
Reading 1: "The Unsinkable *Titanic*"   34
    "The *Titanic*: A Fireman's Story, 15 April 1912—Harry Senior"   34
    "The *Titanic:* From a Lifeboat, 15 April 1912—Mrs. D. H. Bishop"   36
Objective or Subjective?   40
Reading 2: "New Directions" by Maya Angelou   41
Spelling   43
Word Recognition   43
Reading 3: "Mum's Snake" by A.B. Facey   49
Reading 4: "Wounded by a Fascist Sniper, 20 May 1937" by George Orwell   56
Reading 5: "My Family Life" by Catherine Gildiner   65
    Review and Remember: Context and Comprehension, Subjective
    and Objective   70

Chapter 3   Vital Information and Vital Language   71
Summary Writing: Focusing on the Essential   72
Reading 1: "On the Line" by Solange De Santis   75
Reading 2: "Resolving a Weighty Matter" by Deborah King   82
Figurative Language, or Language with Life   85
    Figures of Speech   86

Reading 3: "Culture Jamming: Ads Under Attack" by Naomi Klein   90
Reading 4: "To Die a Martyr's Death" by Ken Wiwa   98
    Ken Saro-Wiwa's Last Words   105
    Review and Remember: Summary Writing and Figurative Language   106

Chapter 4   Power Reading   107
Reading 1: "You Can Make a Difference" by Richard Johnson   108
Slave Narratives   113
    Interesting Facts in the History of Slavery   114
Reading 2: "The History of Mary Prince, a West Indian Slave",
related by herself   114
Reading 3: "I Tried to Kill My Pretty Sister" by Hester Lacy   121
Reading 4: "The Cult of Mao" by Jung Chang   127
    Review and Remember: Power Reading   134

Chapter 5   Critical Reading and Thinking   135
Reading 1: "Equipped to Make Her Own Way" by John Stackhouse   137
Reading 2: "Our Environmental Shame" by David Suzuki   142
Reading 3: "Men are Different" by Steve Connor   148
Reading 4: "John Kenneth Galbraith's World Tour" by John Kenneth Galbraith   157
Word Recognition   160
Paraphrasing   162
    Review and Remember, Part 1: Critical Thinking and Comprehension   169

Part 2: Interactive Critical Thinking   171

Chapter 6   Getting to the Point   172
Steps to Becoming a Clear Communicator   174
Step 1: Think Before You Write, *or* It's the Thought that Counts   174
Step 2: Support Your Views   177
Step 3: Ask Questions and Find Answers   183
Step 4: Be Specific—Avoid Vague Generalizations   189
Step 5: Find a Focus   194
Step 6: Make a Clear Point about Your SPC Subject   196
Step 7: Use All Available Resources and Get Plenty of Input   201
Step 8: Introduce Your Topic with Impact   203
Step 9: Craft Your Conclusion   207
    Famous Last Words   210
Step 10: Convince an Audience   212
Step 11: Plan an Essay   215
Reports or Commentary on Current Issues   217
    Review and Remember, Part 2: Strategies for Communicating Clearly   222

Part 3: Practising Paragraphs   223

Chapter 7   Topic Sentences: The Audience, the
Micro-subject, and the Point About It   224
The Audience: Who is going to read your writing?   225

The Micro-subject: What exactly are you going to write about?   227
    Make Things Clear   228
The Topic Sentence: Stating the Point about Your Subject   232
    Examples of Topic Sentences   233
        Review and Remember: Topic Sentences   246

**Chapter 8   Outlines: The Proof, the Support, and
the Way to Convince Your Readers   247**
Outline of Support   248
    Examples of Outlines of Support   248
    Specific Data   250
    Signal Phrases for Introducing Quotations   250
    What support would you provide?   252
        Review and Remember: Strong Support Systems   265

**Chapter 9   Coherence: The Reminders, the Glue,
and the Ways to Avoid Coming Unstuck   266**
Constant Reminders   267
Transitional Expressions   268
    Transitional Expressions that Glue Points Together   269
Attitudinal Markers   270
    A Note about the Personal Point of View   270
    Review and Remember: Coherent Writing   276

**Chapter 10   Other Modes of Discourse: Some Versions
of the Paragraph   277**
Rhetorical Modes   278
    Description   278
    Process, or "How to" Instructions   282
    Comparison and Contrast   285
    Definition   288
    Classification   290
    Cause and Effect   292
        Review and Remember: Rhetorical Modes   295

Chapter 11   Essays   296
The I-Frame   299
    The I-Frame for a Paragraph   299
The Formula Five Essay   306
Quoting for Support   311
Using Research Material   312
    A Note About Plagiarism   314
    A Word about the Web   316
    Documenting Electronic Resources   317
        Review and Remember, Part 3: A Strong Paragraph or Essay   320
Sample Student I-Frame Paragraphs   320

Part 4: Celebrating the Sentence and other
         Grammatical Necessities   325

Chapter 12   Clear Sentences: The Basics   326
Subjects   328
Verbs   331
Subject-Verb Agreement   343

Chapter 13   More about Sentence Structure   352
Sentence Fragments   353
Run-on Sentences   360

Chapter 14   The Sick Sentence   369
Modifiers   370
Parallel Structure   375
Pronoun Reference   381
    Indefinite Pronouns   382

Chapter 15   Mainly Mechanics   388
Punctuation   389
    Overview of Punctuation   389
    The Comma   390
    Where to Use a Comma   391
    Where Not to Use a Comma   393
        For Fun   393
    The Apostrophe   395
    Capitalization   400
    Semicolons and Colons   402
Spelling   407
    Spelling Rules   408
    Word Confusions   412
        Review and Remember, Part 4: Syntax and Mechanics 428

Works Cited   431

Answer Key   435

Index   448

Steps to Success Boxes

Nine Steps to Becoming an Active Reader	5
How to Write a Good Summary	73
Avoiding Generalizations	190
Audiences and Micro-subjects	232
Description Techniques	279
Process Writing Techniques	283
Comparison-and-Contrast Techniques	286
Definition Techniques	289
Classification Techniques	291
Cause-and-Effect Techniques	293
Expository Writing	298
Conclusions	298
Quoting within a Paragraph	312
Subjects	328
Verbs	332
Subject-Verb Agreement	344
Clauses	354
Avoiding Sentence Fragments	355
Avoiding Run-on Sentences	361
Modifiers	371
Avoiding Faulty Parallel Structure	376
Avoiding Pronoun Problems	382
The Comma	391
The Apostrophe	396
Capitalization	401
Semicolons and Colons	403
Spelling	407

Preface

Basics and Beyond is a practical Canadian textbook developed in the classroom to meet the needs of many first-year college students. It avoids much of the semantic baggage and old-fashioned approaches of traditional composition texts, but still concentrates on the traditional writing skills students need for their professional lives.

The book begins with readings. Most teachers begin with assigned readings in order to stimulate critical thinking and analysis of ideas. Responses to the readings here are designed to help students master the skills needed for planning and writing clear, correct, coherent comments on a topic. Clear thinking is essential for clear writing. Throughout the book, students are encouraged to think in some depth about ideas before writing.

This text offers students and teachers variety and choice. The readings are general rather than vocational, designed to appeal to students enrolled in many different programs and from many different backgrounds.

Written responses to the readings tend to be short, because students need practice with developing clarity of expression in short pieces before moving to the longer essay. The writing section focuses on the paragraph. Throughout, review boxes offer a succinct summary of reading and writing strategies. Each part ends with a *Review and Remember* box for review of the key points of its chapters. As with physical exercise, it's a good idea to start small. From the beginning, students begin with warm-ups and move on to build strength and flexibility in their writing.

Flexibility is stressed. Teachers may decide to begin with grammar in Part 4 (Celebrating the Sentence and other Grammatical Necessities), or developing thinking skills for writing in Part 2 (Interactive Critical Thinking). They will select the part that suits their teaching approach and their personal needs. *Basics and Beyond* allows for choice and encourages flexibility.

This book has four parts. In the first three parts, the focus is on the *essences* of discourse. In Part 4, the focus is on the *accidents* of discourse.

Throughout the text, the exercises and instructions are not of the cookie-cutter variety. They vary. They are intentionally inconsistent. Students learn to read the instructions carefully and focus on key words. This textbook gives students plenty of practice in interpreting and following differently phrased instructions.

Answers are provided for only some exercises, which are indicated by an asterisk in the text. In line with current practice, some exercise answers are found for only odd or even numbers. This practice ensures that students who turn straight to the Answer Key will still have a challenge. Teachers may also wish to assign unanswered exercises as test opportunities.

This book is accompanied by an Instructor's Manual. It contains multiple-choice test material, additional exercises, possible answers and comments for selected readings, suggested instructional strategies, some ESL material, and study guides. It also offers two light-hearted surveys for teachers and students on their teaching and learning styles.

Part 1: Active Reading and Beyond

This part offers five chapters of readings of increasing difficulty. Most readings are followed by:

Word Recognition—exercises on word use

Recall—questions to test basic memory and comprehension

Review—questions to provoke more analytical thinking

Response—activities for individual or collaborative writing, or oral presentations, that encourage critical response and creative analysis

Part 2: Interactive Critical Thinking

This part looks at pre-writing and is designed to develop the thinking skills needed for clear writing. Exercises on topical themes encourage focusing, planning, introducing, supporting, and concluding.

Part 3: Practising Paragraphs

This part helps students learn to organize their ideas more formally. They review and reinforce the skills introduced in Part 2 with more formal attention to basic writing skills. Chapter 10 introduces the traditional rhetorical modes still used by many English teachers. Chapter 11 looks at the essay.

Learning how to organize ideas teaches students to give evidence for what they say, to avoid irrelevant data, and to avoid ambiguity. They need these skills regardless of what professional field they are in. In a world that needs clear thinking and clear writing, these skills are invaluable.

Part 4: Celebrating the Sentence and other Grammatical Necessities

This part deals with basic grammar instruction. While some critics may tell us that studying formal grammar produces no significant improvement in student writing and has no useful place in our post-industrial world, English teachers know that students like to have some grammatical tools for editing and correcting their writing.

With some understanding of basic grammar and usage, students learn to think of the image their writing presents, to be aware that they are often judged (even if unfairly) by their writing errors, and to think of the readers' response to their prose. They learn not to leave readers puzzled, insecure, or uncertain.

The Strengths of this Textbook

No matter what pedagogical approach, teachers will find they can use the material in this textbook to help their students develop confidence in writing. Why? Because the material is the result of many hours in the classroom, and

- It avoids the textbook chill of much instructional material.
- It offers a practical response to student learning and pedagogical styles.
- It focuses on critical thinking, reasoning, and basic writing needs for employment.
- It encourages students to try out new ideas in non-threatening classroom exercises.
- It allows plenty of interaction with both teacher and fellow students, so students participate fully in their learning enterprise.
- It makes students want to improve their writing.
- It acknowledges the presence of deadlines and audience expectations.
- It contains topical, engaging, accessible readings and exercises.
- It is relatively brief and not too heavy.
  Pedagogues from every school of thought will find something here.
- Formalists will find structure and grammar are covered.
- Expressivists will find personal growth and creative thinking are encouraged.
- Rhetoricists will like the balance between written expression and critical thinking.

- Perfectionists will find that the emphasis on process and production prevents them from floundering in a rhetorical swamp.

For academics in the college classroom — whether seasoned classroom teachers, confident with their teaching habits and at ease with a multicultural audience, or recent graduates, confident discussing Derrida and at ease with heuristics, hegemony, and hermeneutics — this textbook's wide-ranging content, its sensitivity to learning styles, and its stress on the importance of collaborative learning and teamwork will be valued. Its liveliness and practicality will not only be a relief, but will reinforce many of the current theories and philosophy of rhetoric. Best of all, it will constantly remind all teachers that everything that happens in the English classroom is important.

Acknowledgments

I wish to thank many colleagues and friends from both northern and southern hemispheres for their generous support and encouragement over the years. I am especially grateful to Jack David, Jianghai Mei, and John Redfern for getting me going, and to Michelle Buuck for her analysis and encouragement. Sheila Docherty, Lucy Valentino, Paul Saundercook, Martha Finnegan, Rhonda Sandberg, and John Edward Stowe have all been helpful.

Many people at Pearson Education Canada have given me practical, patient, and gracious assistance. Thank you to Michael Young, Marta Tomins, Claudia Forgas, and Tammy Scherer. As well, without the literary criticism, thoughtful suggestions, and moral support of Linda Cook, Maria Victor, Jane Scott, and my family—Maarten, Beatrice, and Pieter van Dijk—this book might never have been completed.

Any faults, errors, omissions, defects, or limitations in this textbook are entirely my responsibility. Any strengths, wisdom, discernment, or *jeu d'esprit* come not only from having wonderful colleagues and friends but also from hours in front of the blackboard, in front of thousands (well, maybe hundreds) of tolerant and resigned students, honing my craft. As T.S. Eliot might have said, "I have measured out my life in chalk." This book is the result of all of those years and input.

Part 1

Active Reading and Beyond

Working Together

Introduction to Collaborative Writing

Throughout this book you will often be asked to work in groups. When working in any kind of group, it is helpful to apply the principles of parliamentary procedure. They took hundreds of years to develop and we are accustomed to them. These principles should be respected and followed in all group discussions.

What are the basic principles of parliamentary procedure?

- The will of the majority shall prevail.

- The minority has the right to be heard.

- Business shall be conducted in an orderly fashion.

One of the first things to remember when joining a group is *don't panic*. Other members of the group probably know as much (or as little) as you do about the subject under discussion. The purpose of the group is to

- get organized
- share ideas
- produce results

In group efforts, the process often determines the product. That means the way you work together can be as important in determining the success of the result as the expertise and background of group members. Whether the results of group work are a meal for a group of campers, a proposal for job action, a report on company policy, or a checklist for market research, success will be yours if you make good use of your resources and time.

Productive group work anywhere depends on

1. a clear task

2. thoughtful use of available resources

3. an efficient process

1. A Clear Task

In this book, the tasks are usually outlined, but sometimes in other courses, or in your field of employment, you will have to define a topic or task more clearly before you begin.

Get into the habit of asking yourself *what, why, how, what kind of, where* and *when* before beginning a task. Sometimes these questions are useful, and they may lead to a clearer sense of what is involved in the assigned task. Always know what it is you are being asked to do, and don't be afraid to ask more questions for clarification. Are you being asked to reach *a decision*, to make *a presentation*, or come up with *a recommendation*? Maybe you have to prepare a report, plan a project, or suggest a series of actions. Begin only when you are clear on

- what is required
- your deadline

You wouldn't go to a party without knowing where it is and what sort of party it is before leaving the house. The same applies to an intellectual event, or a party of ideas.

2. Thoughtful Use of Available Resources

In this book, the first resource is the assigned reading and the second is your response to it. Every group member will have a different response. That means the people in the group and the information they share will be key resources. Resources for most tasks usually include people and information, but they may also involve time, materials, money, equipment, and energy.

To make the most of the resources in your group, always try to

- learn the name of each group member
- listen to each group member
- respect and value each response
- speak clearly and slowly
- take notes of what is covered
- nod, smile, and show approval as often as you can

3. An Efficient Process

In this book, you are often given suggestions on how to manage your time and resources. Where you are not, be sure to note the time available and the specific results to be achieved in that time. Allot the available time to the different parts of the task.

Always leave sufficient time to organize your material into its final presentation format. Whether you use this time to review material, check for errors, proofread, or organize speakers and their delivery depends on the actual task. Be sure to

- allow adequate time for every part of the task, leaving more time for the most important topics, not necessarily the most difficult ones
- review frequently to avoid wasting time with frustration, irrelevancy, and misunderstanding
- be aware of the deadline
- follow the rules of parliamentary procedure

CHAPTER 1

Active Reading

This chapter has five short readings for comprehension, analysis, and response.

By the end of this chapter, you will be able to

- use the Nine-Step Active Reader Program to approach assigned readings

- understand how to **predict, skim, scan, specify, and evaluate (P3SE)** written passages

- note key information in a reading, such as the title, the introductory and concluding sections, the key ideas, and the specific points used to support those ideas

- examine word use and structure

- understand how important a dictionary and word recognition are in developing literal comprehension

STEPS TO SUCCESS

Nine Steps to Becoming an Active Reader

1. Note the title and writer of the reading.

2. Note any biographical data, commentary, or explanation given as an introduction to the reading.

3. Read the introductory section of the reading more than once.

4. Read the entire passage, noting any unfamiliar words or expressions.

5. Use a dictionary to discover the meanings of words or expressions you cannot guess from context.

6. Re-read the assigned reading, noting how unfamiliar vocabulary is used. Read it aloud once or twice.

7. Stop and think about what you have read. Consider your reaction to the material. How do you feel about the ideas expressed? Do you agree? Disagree?

8. Note the specific data the writer uses to support key ideas.

9. Review the reading, paying particular attention to the introduction and conclusion.

At college and in your professional life, you will read a lot. Many of the texts you are expected to read may be quite complex and demanding. Do not despair. While you may find the amount of assigned reading overwhelming at first, with practice you'll discover techniques and strategies for effective and efficient reading.

Active Reader Program

If you follow the Nine-Step Active Reader Program in the Steps to Success box above, you will develop good reading habits. The techniques and strategies suggested there will take you successfully through college. Use the program every time you read, until you follow it automatically. Remember that it takes 3 weeks to develop a habit. Try the Nine-Step program for 21 days at least, in all your college readings.

Another Reading Strategy: P3SE Formula

If you find nine steps too many, you might prefer the **P3SE Formula;** that means **predict, skim, scan, specify, and evaluate.**

1. Predict What the Reading Will Cover.

Ask yourself, What's this going to be about? Get into the habit of guessing from clues given in the title, the introductory material, or even the writer's name, if it's well known.

For example, if a title is "Summer Barbecues," try to **predict** what the reading might deal with. Is the reading likely to be about eating alone, about roast duckling in plum sauce, or about sitting up straight at a long, white-clothed formal table, minding your manners? No. If a title contains the words *breathalyzer* and *sleepalyzer,* could it be about alcohol and sleep in association with driving?

Your predictions will give you some sense of what you are going to read. They might even whet your appetite, making you keen to read what a writer has to say about the assigned subject. Dream on, or at least dream about the reading to come, and what it will tell you.

2. Skim, Scan, and Specify. What do these 3 S's mean?

First, they mean you read, or **skim,** through the text quickly to get the general meaning. Notice the introductory section and the conclusion in particular. This stage is also known as the *browse function.*

Second, you **scan** a reading, going through the text again a little more closely, noting any words you cannot guess from the way they are used, and looking at the key points and examples. If you cannot guess what new words might mean from context clues, use a dictionary. Notice carefully how unfamiliar words are used in the reading before moving to the third S. This is a good time to read some parts of the reading aloud, practising the new vocabulary.

Third, **specify** means you look even more closely at specific supporting details and ideas, as well as noting how new words are used. Specifying requires a more careful reading, not a quick overview. You look at any specific points made by the writer at this stage.

3. Evaluate the Text.

You have grasped what the reading is about. You have noted the key ideas and how they are presented. Now it is time to think about what the writer is saying, and what you think of the writer's ideas, and **evaluate** the material.

Notice that you consider what the writer *is saying*, not what the writer *said*. When we talk about a text, the words are alive on the page, not dead and buried. They exist in the present. We use the present tense when we talk or write about a written passage, an essay, or a book.

Evaluating a reading means responding to the text. What do you think of this reading? What do you think of the ideas you have just come across?

You don't have to like what you read, you don't have to agree with what the writer says, but you do have to think about the reading and your reaction to it. No blind emotional responses to a reading are allowed at college. Save them for rock concerts and motivational rallies. At college, and in the workplace, you have to be able to analyze your response.

So if you say to yourself, *this is boring,* you have to be able to say why. What makes the reading dull? The long words? The silly ideas? The examples? The conclusion? Or the fact that you would rather be jogging or watching television? Try to think more deeply about the material. Your response can tell a listener a lot about you as a person.

When thinking about a reading, ask yourself *who* the writer is talking to and *what* the writer is communicating. In other words, decide what **audience** the writer is trying to reach and what the **purpose** of the reading is. Ask yourself

> *What is it about?*   (purpose, ideas, content)
>
> *Who would want to read it?*   (audience)

Then ask yourself, what is interesting, boring, exciting, irritating, unusual, or inspiring about the reading? Why do you think so? Does the writer know what he or she is talking about? Why do you think so? Ask yourself

> *What do I think of it? Why?*   (critical evaluation, analysis)

Every time you consider what any writer is saying and why you have responded to a reading in a certain way, you are participating more fully in the social world.

Every time you become aware of the key points of a reading and think about them, you are opening the doors of perception.

Every time you question what you read and every time you reach conclusions, you are exercising your mind, keeping your neurotransmitters active. You are developing your intellectual muscles and avoiding neural atrophy.

Reading with analytical or critical thinking helps you participate more fully in the cooperative social action that keeps a developed society running smoothly. You are part of a developed society. You are also part of its social action. Keep that thought in mind as you read.

Whether you choose the Nine-Step Active Reader Program or the P3SE Formula, with critical reading and thinking, you are entering a new stage of perceptual awareness. You are learning to examine ideas and your personal response to them. You are using critical thinking skills and becoming a mature, thoughtful, and informed reader.

Reading is a stimulus to thinking. Thinking comes before writing. Read on . . .

READING 1

Summer Barbecues

by John Fitzgerald

1   Along with sneakers and shorts, sunny skies and warm weather, few things are as evocative of summer as the rites of barbecuing. The hiss and smoke and sizzle, and the all-round commotion make it always a special event. It's one of the rare times of the year when the whole family can get involved in the business of cooking. That goes especially for the male of the species, some of whose members have been known to restrict their activities other-wise to the grand gesture of carving the Christmas turkey.

2   For some men barbecuing can be obsessive as well, something with its own rules and rewards. Writer and beer expert Stephen Beaumont recalls growing up in Montreal with a father who insisted on barbecuing year round, no matter what the weather. His eagerly awaiting family also appreciated the results.

3   Although obviously not restricted to men, barbecuing can be a truly communal activity, one which is outdoorsy, usually fuss-free, and accomplished without the inevitable round of cutting, chopping and measuring. Going beyond the simple labours of grilling burgers or chops, however, does take a little effort, but the results are well worth it.

John Fitzgerald, ed., "Summer Barbecues," *Gusto,* 1.4, Summer 1995

Recall

Try to respond to the following activities from memory, where appropriate.

1. Dictate any sentence from the article to a partner to check aural skills, spelling recall, sensitivity to punctuation, and verb forms. For example, have your partner write "The hiss and smoke and sizzle, and the all-round commotion make it always a special event." Then, it's your partner's turn.

2. Who wrote this article? When was it published?

3. Quickly recall and express the subject. Then in one sentence, in your own words, state what this article is about. Begin with the writer's name and say what his main point is.

4. What does the writer mean when he says that barbecuing can be "a truly communal event," and that it is "evocative of summer"? Explain in your own words.

5. What sort of audience does the writer seem to be expecting? What makes you think so?

6. If an activity is obsessive, what is it?

7. How many *s*'s are in *obsessive*?

8. What point does the writer make about the male of the species?

9. Which words or expressions do you remember most after reading this article? Why? Make a list of at least three words or expressions which you will try to use yourself.

10. What is the writer's conclusion?

Review

Answer the following questions.

1. What is the difference between a *rite* and a *right*?

2. What do we call words with the same sound, but with a different meaning, like *weather* and *whether*?

3. What do you usually associate with the word *rite*? Why do you think John Fitzgerald uses this word in the first paragraph?

4. Why would Fitzgerald use words like *hiss, smoke,* and *sizzle*?

5. Which of the following are facts?

    a. Stephen Beaumont thinks beer is great.

    b. Stephen Beaumont grew up in Montreal.

    c. Stephen Beaumont's father liked baking in winter.

    d. Stephen Beaumont is a male of the species.

    e. Stephen Beaumont's father liked barbecuing year round.

6. Why doesn't Fitzgerald need to use many facts in this article? Explain.

7. If you "go beyond" something, what do you do?

8. Who might be reading the magazine *Gusto* where this editorial was found? For example, would the reading audience be educated? Would they be interested only in celebrities, in computer games, or in food? What could be the subject of this magazine?

    (Note: the word *gusto* comes from the Latin word for taste. If you do something "with gusto," you do it with zest, with great enjoyment.)

9. Do you think Fitzgerald's chief purpose is to inform, persuade, introduce a topic, or make people laugh? Give one reason for your answer.

10. What do you think of this reading? Does it do a good job of introducing the joys of barbecuing? Give reasons.

Response

Respond to *one* of the following topics in small groups. This activity may involve a timed group discussion with an oral response or a brief comment written collaboratively. Deadlines are encouraged. Time suggested: 15 to 30 minutes.

Topics

1. Prepare a statement about the joys or sorrows of barbecuing. Focus on a specific kind of barbecue. Give details about the food, the smell, the weather. Use names, colours, and at least three expressions from the article.

2. Discuss why barbecuing tends to appeal to the male of the species more than regular cooking. Think about the specific activities and duties involved in each, and their appeal.

3. Are you obsessive about anything in summer? Discuss summer obsessions, like getting or avoiding a tan, swimming 100 m every morning, buying a new bikini, going on picnics.

    Together, write a short statement about, or explain orally, the sort of obsessions that go with hot weather, what brings them on, and what effects they have. Use words from the article as much as possible, and give specific examples.

READING 2

Dining Out

Sharing the dining area with ants, dogs, and birds

by Joe Campbell

---

1 At the first sign of spring, North Americans by the millions can't wait to indulge in that fair weather custom of cooking dinner in the back yard.

2 I'm not one of them.

3 I like my back yard and I like eating. I also like the theatre and I like sleeping. But I don't go to the theatre to sleep. I can't see why I should go to the back yard to eat.

4 How so many of us could be hoodwinked into believing that food tastes better outside than it does inside is beyond me. I certainly don't believe it, and I don't think many others would if it weren't an international mania to sit out on the grass, where the dogs have been, and bolt salad and steak under the trees, where the birds are. They think they're getting back to nature, like the sunbathers who lie out in the open until they've burned themselves. I think sunburn is nature's way of getting back at them. But they do it in droves every year, particularly on weekends and vacations, when they should be recreating.

5 People cheerfully turn their backs on sanitary kitchens and intimate dining rooms with immaculate table cloths and comfortable chairs; they expose themselves to the elements, the insects, and the neighbours. They do it because they think that sitting cross-legged by an ant hill with a chunk of charred meat in their hands is the thing to do. They think it gives them status. What's more, they think they like it. They think they enjoy feeling the smoke in their eyes and the dew clear through to their underwear and the wind blowing ashes in their mouths, while the neighbours peer through the hedges and clear their throats.

6   They could just as easily do it inside. They could put sand in the pepper shaker, a low-horsepower fan in the centre of the table and a smudge pot underneath it.

7   But they wouldn't hear of it. It's not the thing to do. There's no status in it.

8   Many aren't content to do it in the semi-privacy of their back yards. They go out and do it on public property in parks and playgrounds, where perfect strangers can watch them. Others get into their cars and drive hundreds of miles to do it in places they may not have seen or heard of before. The farther they go to get back to nature, the more unnatural they become.

9   In the parks they sit on benches at picnic tables; at the resorts they rent cottages with refrigerators, stoves and television sets, not to mention pantries and freezers that they stock with canned goods and frozen foods. They call this roughing it.

10   Every year I get talked into doing it a time or two. I go out into the back yard and suffer with the rest of them. But I refuse to pretend that I like it. I refuse to disparage thousands of years of culinary progress and propose that the Cro-Magnon man was a better cook than my wife.

11   Don't get me wrong. I love the great outdoors. I think it's one of the best places you could find for hunting and fishing, and I wouldn't want to ski or play golf anywhere else. But eating outdoors is something else again. That's what the cavemen dug caves to get away from; that's what made the barbarians barbarous. I must look up the etymology of that word barbarous. I wouldn't be at all surprised if it came from the same root as barbecue.

Joe Campbell, "Seared meat, smoke and status," The Globe and Mail, 24 May 1999, A22

Vocabulary

hoodwinked (para. 4): tricked; deceived

droves (para. 4): great numbers of animals or people; people acting as a herd

disparage (para. 10): put down

etymology (para. 11): the study of a word, where it came from, and the development of its meaning over the years

Exercise 1.1

Find the following expressions in the article:

    hoodwinked into believing

    bolt salad and steak

    getting back to nature

    getting back at them

    they do it in droves

    recreating

    expose themselves to the elements

    the thing to do

    clear their throats

    roughing it

    culinary progress

    the great outdoors

Choose *four* of the above expressions. What do they mean? Look at where they appear in the article. Also, look at how they are used in **context,** the part in the article where a specific word or expression occurs. Do any other words or expressions nearby help you guess their meanings?

Try to explain what each expression means, in writing or orally, to someone who has English as a second language. To give someone a clear idea of the meaning, try using verbal pictures and examples from daily life.

Spelling

Can you spell these words correctly? Give a partner *seven* of the following words to spell. Say the word clearly once, paying attention to the consonants, and then repeat the word, using it in a short sentence or as it is used in the article. Say the word only once more if necessary. This is a quick test of spelling, listening, and speaking skills. Your partner will then test you.

barbarian	pantries
clothes	particularly
cloths	roughing it
comfortable	steak
dining	surprised
intimate	unnatural
neighbours	vacation

Etymology

In his article, Joe Campbell says he must look up the etymology of the word *barbarous*. He suspects it comes from the same root as *barbecue*. He's wrong, in fact. If you look in a dictionary, you will find that *barbecue* comes from Haitian Creole *barbacòa*, a wooden frame on posts, while *barbarous* comes from Greek *barboros*, meaning foreign, rude, and not like a Greek. Interestingly, the word *barbarous* was often used by the ancient Greeks to refer to incorrect speech or expression.

What does Campbell mean, then, by wondering if a word comes "from the same root"? The root of a word is exactly that. It is the essential part of the word, the base that provides the support for prefixes and suffixes. In English, words come from many roots or bases. English, with words from Greek, Latin, French, German, Norse, Arabic, Bantu, Urdu, Hindi, and Turkish, to mention only some roots, is a truly multicultural language.

A prefix is a word or letters at the beginning of a word.

A suffix is a word or letters at the end of a word.

Look at the word *autograph*. It is made up of the prefix *auto,* meaning self, and *graph,* meaning write. What other words do you know that contain *auto* and *graph*? How about *automobile, automatic, biography, autobiography, graphic, oceanography*?

If you learn to recognize the root, prefix, or suffix of a word, you have a key to unlocking the word's meaning. If you know, for example, that *tele* comes from Greek and means at a distance, and *phon* means voice, you can see where the word *telephone* comes from.

Exercise 1.2

A. Work out the meaning of the boldface groups of letters listed below. For example, *path*, the root of *pathetic, empathy*, and *sympathy*, must have something to do with feelings like pity or tenderness. In fact, *pathos* comes from the Greek word meaning passion or suffering.

B. Write *two* more words using the prefix, suffix, or root found in the words listed.

auto automatic _____

bio biology _____

contra contradict _____

cred credible _____

dis disapprove _____

ex ex-boyfriend _____

homo homonym _____

morte postmortem _____

trans transatlantic _____

un unpleasant _____

Recall

Choose the best answer.

1. What idea does Joe Campbell introduce to us with his comment, "I'm not one of them"?

    a. He is not happy with his wife's cooking.

    b. He hates driving hundreds of miles to parks and playgrounds.

    c. He is not keen on sunbathing.

    d. He thinks eating outdoors is unnatural.

2. Another title for this article could be

    a. My Wife's Cro-Magnon Cooking

b. People in Saskatchewan Are Strange

c. Roughing It in the Bush

d. Barbarians at the Barbecue

3. The international mania Campbell refers to is

a. renting cottages at the beach with refrigerators, stoves, and televisions

b. driving long distances to be amongst perfect strangers

c. eating outdoors on weekends and while on vacation

d. getting back to nature to enjoy hunting and fishing

4. According to Campbell, people leave their clean and sanitary indoor surroundings to eat outdoors because

a. they are conforming to a wish for status

b. they feel they will gain social approval from avoiding canned goods

c. they fear the effects of culinary progress

d. they like having their neighbours peer at them

5. From this article, you can tell that Campbell likes

a. getting back to nature at the first sign of spring

b. eating in front of perfect strangers

c. eating his wife's cooking indoors

d. eating dinner in the backyard in summer

6. Campbell uses the idea of sand in the pepper shaker to show readers how

a. in Canada, social approval is gained from putting up with inconveniences without complaining

b. easy it is to gain a feeling of discomfort and inconvenience while eating

c. to be like the rest of Canadians at the table

d. to get a recreational effect in front of the neighbours

7. People avoid comfortable chairs as soon as the warm weather comes, according to Campbell, because they

a. think they enjoy getting away from ease and returning to nature

b. are not content with their furniture

c. have a deep-seated urge to sit cross-legged on an anthill

d. prefer to be unnatural when the sun shines

8. Which statement best expresses Campbell's main idea?

a. No one can convince me that eating and drinking outdoors is not better than hunting and fishing.

b. No one can convince me that eating and drinking outdoors is fun.

c. No one can convince me that eating outdoors makes us look like cavemen.

d. No one can convince me that eating and drinking outdoors is uncivilized.

9. "But eating outdoors is something else again." Campbell's statement means that barbecues are

a. a specific barbaric activity avoided in Saskatoon

b. not as remarkable as fishing or hunting

c. nothing like hunting, fishing, skiing, or golfing

d. to some extent, an undefined pleasure

10. Campbell's article shows that he

a. knows a lot about the behaviour of barbarians

b. believes that civility is not a sign of weakness

c. is confused about the attractions of barbecues in the great outdoors

d. has specific reasons for his arguments against barbecues

Review

Answer the following questions. You will find your answers to the material in the preceding Recall section useful. Get into the habit of using all the information available in the readings and follow-up questions for other test questions.

1. How does Joe Campbell feel about barbecues and the great outdoors? How do you know? Give reasons.

2. What two reasons does Campbell give for the popularity of barbecues?

3. What does Campbell think is an international mania?

4. What are five things Campbell hates about barbecues?

5. How does Campbell feel about eating outdoors? Use some of the details from Question 3 and explain in one sentence.

6. "The farther they go to get back to nature, the more unnatural they become." What does Campbell mean by this statement? When do people become more unnatural? What details does he use to support this idea?

7. Why does Campbell compare neighbours with perfect strangers? What point is he making with this comparison?

8. What do people consider "roughing it" according to Campbell?

9. Campbell refuses to disparage thousands of years of culinary progress. Why does he say that?

10. Why does Campbell mention Cro-Magnon man?

Response

Respond to *one* of the following activities in small groups.

A. Prepare for a debate on the pros and cons of barbecues. Prepare arguments for each side. Make a list of points for and against barbecues and the appeal of eating outdoors. Use as many specific details as possible to support each point.

Note how Joe Campbell creates the scene with details like charred meat, anthills, insects, smoke in their eyes, dew through their underwear, and the wind blowing ashes in their mouths. What details can you come up with for your debate? Choose details from the readings on barbecues here or from your own experience. Use specific names and places as much as possible.

Your teacher may ask for a debate or may simply ask your group to present an argument for one side. Knowing what the other side, the opposition, might say often helps you counteract their argument more strongly. Get into the habit of thinking what someone opposed might say about your topic at any time, and prepare to respond to the opposition.

OR

B. Prepare a response to one or two of the following topics. Each group member will

- write a short individual answer after 10 minutes of discussion
- proofread and edit each other's work so that each written response clearly reflects the main point of the discussion
- put the name of each group member at the top of each page, with the date

Your teacher will collect *one* random written answer only from each group. It could be yours, so record carefully and correctly. It could be your partner's, so check spelling, punctuation, and clarity.

Topics

1. "... they do it in droves ... when they should be recreating." Here, Joe Campbell uses the verb *recreate*, which means to make new again, to give fresh life to, in its basic form. Recreation is supposed to give fresh mental and physical life to people.

   What are the best ways for students to become renewed, to gain fresh life? What would you include in a recreation program for college students that would refresh them physically and mentally? Give reasons for your choices.

2. "People cheerfully turn their backs on sanitary kitchens and intimate dining rooms with immaculate table cloths and comfortable chairs." Note the way the writer presents this picture and then a contrasting one.

   Prepare a brief description of the joys of eating outdoors compared to eating in fast-food restaurants. Use specific examples to create a picture of each place.

3. What makes barbarians barbarous? The writer suggests (facetiously, perhaps) that eating outdoors was the cause of barbarism in the time of cave dwellers. (*Facetious* means intending to be amusing, playful.) You know, today some people can act like barbarians, even if they don't live in caves. When are people in the twenty-first century likely to be barbaric?

   Write a brief description of an incident of barbaric behaviour you have observed or discussed recently. Mention the exact location and indicate the cause. End with your feelings about this behaviour.

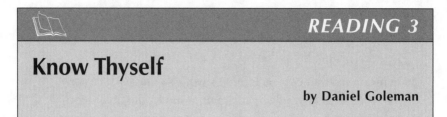

READING 3

Know Thyself

by Daniel Goleman

1   A belligerent samurai, an old Japanese tale goes, once challenged a Zen master to explain the concept of heaven and hell. But the monk replied with scorn, "You're nothing but a lout—I can't waste my time with the likes of you!"

2   His very honour attacked, the samurai flew into a rage and, pulling his sword from his scabbard, yelled, "I could kill you for your impertinence."

3   "That," the monk calmly replied, "is hell."

4   Startled at seeing the truth in what the master pointed out about the fury that had him in its grip, the samurai calmed down, sheathed his sword, and bowed, thanking the monk for the insight.

5   "And that," said the monk, "is heaven."

Daniel Goleman, *Emotional Intelligence* (New York: Bantam Books, 1995), 46

Vocabulary

samurai (para. 1): one of an exclusive group of Japanese warriors

Zen master (para. 1): a teacher and guide who has reached the highest level of harmony in a form of Buddhism that emphasizes meditation and spiritual peace

lout (para. 1): a badly behaved loudmouth; a rude brat

scabbard (para. 2): sword holder or cover

impertinence (para. 2): not showing proper respect; talking back rudely

the fury that had him in its grip (para. 4): taken over by wild rage; out of control

Recall

Try to answer the following questions from memory.

1. Where does this event take place? When?

2. Who are the people involved? Describe each one briefly.

3. Why did the samurai lose his temper?

4. How did the Zen master react to the samurai's threat?

5. What did the samurai learn?

Review

Tell the story in your own words to a partner. If you have trouble getting started, try beginning with "Once upon a time . . ." Be sure to use the information you came up with in the preceding Recall section.

Tell the story dramatically if you can, showing the difference between the Zen master and the samurai with your voice and actions. The whole class might like to hear the most confident and dramatic retelling of the story.

Response

Respond to *one* of the following topics in pairs or groups of three.

Topics

1. Why do you think this reading is called "Know Thyself" (a quotation from the Greek philosopher Socrates)? Think about the difference between being unconsciously caught up in a feeling and being aware that you are caught up in a feeling. Use examples from your own experience to illustrate your answer. Prepare a half page (four to six sentences) explaining what the expression *know thyself* means.

2. Discuss the idea of heaven and hell. Try to come up with a story or examples from your own experience to support your point. After your discussion, choose the story or examples that best describe heaven and hell.

   Together, write a brief definition of heaven and hell (about a half page, or four to six sentences), using ideas from your discussion. Read your final draft aloud to each other, and revise sentences for clarity before handing in your definitions.

READING 4

After Breathalyzer, a Sleepalyzer?

by Michael Filosa

1   In many countries, a blood-alcohol concentration (BAC) of 0.05% is regarded as hazardous for driving a motor vehicle. It is a matter of common experience that fatigue, such as that brought on by sleep deprivation, can also affect driving performance. Two scientists in Australia and New Zealand compared the decline in performance brought about by fatigue with that resulting from alcohol by testing 37 volunteers doing tasks that required speed, accuracy, and memory. Each volunteer did these tasks with different amounts of alcohol in their blood and then, at a later time, under different amounts of sleep deprivation.

2   The findings indicate that 17 to 19 continuous hours without sleep produced decreases in performance levels that were equivalent to that produced by a BAC of 0.05% and therefore incompatible with the safe operation of a motor vehicle. Longer periods without sleep reduced performance to levels equivalent to BAC of 0.1%.

3   A study at Ontario's Queen's University used a computerized driving simulator to test the combined effects of fatigue and alcohol. It was found that the decrease in driving performance was greater than under either condition alone. Furthermore, the subjects were unable to accurately judge the degree of the decline in their driving impairment. A question raised by these studies: Should drivers without sleep for 18 hours or more be restricted by law from operating motor vehicles? Something for the Toronto R.I.D.E program to contemplate.

Michael Filosa, "After breathalyzer, a sleepalyzer?" In *Wellness Options*, February & March 2001, Volume 1 No 2, 32. Adapted from *Journal of Sleep Research* 9 (2000): 233 in *Occupational and Environmental Medicine* 57 (2000): 649

Word Recognition

Select the correct word form for each of the following sentences. Decide if you need a noun, verb, or adjective, and choose accordingly.

1. **drive, driving, driven, drove, driver, droves**

    a. Simone has not _____ such a long way in snow before.

b. The teenagers came in _____ to see their favourite singer perform at the Skydome.

c. Going over 17 continuous hours without sleep will always affect your _____ performance.

d. Stephen slammed the car door shut and _____ off suddenly, leaving Simone alone at the side of the road.

e. It is dangerous to _____ a motor vehicle with a blood-alcohol concentration of 0.05%.

2. **restricted, restful, restrict, restrain, results, result**

a. After spending so long at the lab, Maria was annoyed that she had to wait so long for the _____ of her blood tests.

b. Many doctors believe that use of those drugs should be _____, so people do not have easy access to them.

c. The bodyguard tried to _____ the angry rock star so he could not punch the intrusive fan.

d. Bad behaviour at rock concerts will _____ in many restrictions on fans.

e. Her parents did not try to _____ her because they knew she wanted to go to the concert so much.

3. **deprive, deprivation, decline, deprived, depraved, depression**

a. Roberta Bondar says you get less sleep in space than on Earth because you are working so hard, but even so, she did not feel _____ of sleep.

b. Most studies of sleep _____ in humans were done more than 30 years ago.

c. People who have sleepless nights, people with insomnia, often suffer from anxiety or _____.

d. Your standards of driving, use of memory, and accuracy of response will _____ if you do not get enough sleep.

e. A police officer will _____ you of your licence if he or she thinks your driving is impaired.

4. **performance, performing, perform, perfection, perfect, perfectionist**

a. Fatigue resulting from sleep deprivation will prevent you from _____ safely at the wheel of a car.

   b. For the first time, Raoul badly wanted to _____ his own composition at the concert.

   c. His sister was surprised because he had always been such a _____; he was convinced that nothing he wrote was ever good enough for the public.

   d. Drinking and fatigue combined cause a serious decline in driving _____.

   e. "Nobody is _____," said the old millionaire at the end of *Some Like It Hot,* when Daphne told him she was really a boy.

5. **accuracy, accurately, accurate, accused, accustomed, account**

   a. The figures announced at the press conference were not _____, so no one really knows how many people were killed in the earthquake.

   b. Many politicians have _____ the country's president of lying about the death rate to hide the true horror of the disaster.

   c. People in that small country are _____ to frequent changes in presidents.

   d. No one can predict with _____ when another earthquake will hit the country.

   e. Most drivers are unable to judge _____ when their driving is impaired.

Recall

Try to answer the following questions from memory.

1. What does the abbreviation BAC stand for?

2. What does ". . . a (BAC) of 0.05% is regarded as hazardous for driving" mean? Explain in your own words.

3. Read the following words quickly. Jot down only *five* key words from the article.

brain	insomnia	energy	transport
fatigue	depressed	bacteria	restricted
cabins	drugs	disorders	sleeplessness
contemplate	significant	collapse	decline
deprivation	sleep	driving	study

4. Which statement best expresses the main idea of paragraph 1?

   a. Everyone knows that sleep deprivation affects tasks requiring speed.

   b. Alcohol and fatigue cause a decline in driving performance Down Under.

   c. Sleep-deprived volunteers cannot undertake tasks with alcohol in their blood.

   d. Fatigue resulting from sleep deprivation can affect driving performance in the same way alcohol levels in the blood can.

5. Decide whether the following statements are true or false. Try to do so without referring to the article.

   a. In Ontario, the Queen's University study subjects could not make accurate judgments after they used computerized driving simulator tests.

   b. Speed, accuracy, and memory suffer only after 37 hours of sleep deprivation.

   c. In many countries, a blood-alcohol concentration of 0.05% is considered incompatible with the safe operation of a motor vehicle.

   d. In New Zealand, scientific tests of 37 drivers showed sleep-deprived drivers cause more accidents than drunk drivers.

   e. In Ontario, drivers without sleep for more than 18 hours are restricted by law from operating motor vehicles.

Review

Answer the following questions.

1. What do many countries consider hazardous when it comes to driving a motor vehicle?

2. What did the scientists in Australia and New Zealand compare?

3. Why did the scientists test the volunteer drivers' speed, accuracy, and memory?

4. What were the results of the tests done in Australia and New Zealand? Explain in one sentence.

5. What did the scientists test to show the decline in performance brought about by alcohol and fatigue?

6. How much sleep deprivation does it take to get a decline in performance equal to a blood-alcohol concentration of 0.05%?

7. When the combined effects of alcohol and sleep deprivation were tested at Queen's University, what did the study find? Answer in one sentence, if writing.

8. According to the study at Queen's University, how did the subjects involved judge their own driving?

9. What does the title of the article mean?

10. What important point does the writer make in his conclusion?

Response

Respond to *two* of the following topics in small groups. Your teacher may ask for a short individual written response instead.

Topics

1. Decide what the main point of the article is and what you think of this point. Write out the main point in one or two sentences. State your group's response to this point in one clear sentence. Give a list of reasons for your views, with specific examples, if possible. Conclude by restating your group's response in different words. Length: about one page, double-spaced.

2. Discuss the amount of sleep each of you gets each night. Think about the effects of your sleep patterns on your driving and academic performance.

   Prepare a statement for fellow students offering advice on sensible sleep behaviour while at college. Use at least three specific examples to support your advice. Consider ideas like naps, bedtime routines, regular habits, hours of sleep, exercise during the day, warm feet, reflecting on the mistakes of the day, and plans for the next day. Length: about one page, double-spaced.

3. Prepare advice on "How to have bad dreams." Be as outrageous as you want to be, but be specific. Use as many names and examples as possible. Consider some of the ideas suggested in Topic 2 above. Begin with a general statement and conclude by reinforcing that statement. Length: about one page, double-spaced.

READING 5

Looking Back on the Exxon Valdez

by Greenpeace

1   Shortly after midnight on March 24, 1989, the tanker Exxon Valdez ran aground on Blight Reef in Alaska's Prince William Sound, spilling 11 million gallons of crude oil. Within days, approximately 700 miles of Alaskan and British Columbian coastline were covered in oil.

2   The spill killed over 3,500 sea otters and over 300,000 seabirds.

3   After 10 years, only two species of wildlife, bald eagles and river otters, are considered to have recovered from the spill's effects. Harbour seals, three species of cormorants, harlequin ducks, pigeon guillemots and a family pod of killer whales are still listed as "not recovering."

4   The Exxon Valdez disaster was not an isolated event. It was just one in a series of ongoing major oil spills that have wreaked havoc across the world.

5   "These spills are just one source of pollution and environmental damage resulting from oil exploration and development," said Steven Guilbeault, Greenpeace climate and energy expert.

6   "After years of concern over the impacts of oil pollution on marine and coastal environments, attention is turning to the fact that fossil fuels such as oil and gas are affecting the climate and the entire planet."

7   British Petroleum has begun construction of the first offshore oil rig in the Arctic just north of the Alaskan coastline. This project, known as Northstar, will use a pipeline buried beneath the Arctic Ocean to transport the oil to southern Alaska for shipping.

8   A major spill from Northstar could prove disastrous for the biologically-rich Arctic ecosystem. It would imperil endangered bowhead whale populations and threaten subsistence hunting by the Inuit communities. It could also kill large numbers of polar bears, ringed seals and sea ducks.

9   "The only way to ensure that tragedies such as the Exxon Valdez are not repeated is for the industrialized world to wean itself off its dependence on fossil fuels," said Guilbeault. "Greenpeace is working to promote the use of renewable energy sources such as wind and solar power and to end government subsidies to the oil and gas industries."

Greenpeace, "Looking back on the Exxon Valdez," *Greenlink,* 7: 2 Spring/Summer 1999, 3.
Courtesy of Greenpeace Canada (www.greenpeace.ca).

Word Recognition

Do you understand the meaning of the following words or expressions from their location in the article? You hear many of these terms used every day. Can you explain what they mean in your own words?

crude oil	cormorants	isolated event
offshore oil rig	imperil	renewable energy sources
fossil fuels	subsistence hunting	government subsidies
ecosystem	wreak havoc	wean itself

Vocabulary

crude oil (para. 1): the natural, unrefined form of petroleum

wreaked havoc (para. 4): caused destruction

fossil fuels (para. 6): fuel coming from organisms of a past geological age

ecosystem (para. 8): biological community where organisms interact and work together with their environment

imperil (para. 8): endanger

subsistence hunting (para. 8): hunting for only the necessities to sustain life; killing wild animals for only one's family and immediate community

wean (para. 9): to get a baby to give up milk gradually; in a gentle way, to get people to break a habit

Exercise 1.3

Using expressions from the article, as well as your own words and ideas, complete the following statements. Be careful with your verbs.

1. The best way to prevent such tragedies _____.

2. One source of pollution today _____.

3. What I think is most important for helping the environment today _____.

4. All of these oil spills _____.

5. Harbour seals, cormorants, and harlequin ducks
    _____.

6. The project known as Northstar _____.

7. The subsistence hunting of the Inuit communities
    _____.

8. After years of concern over the effects of oil pollution
    _____.

9. Major spills from a project like Northstar _____.

10. Our dependence on fossil fuels _____.

Recall

Try to answer the following questions from memory.

1. What happened on March 24, 1989?

2. What exactly was the Exxon Valdez?

3. List three results of the Exxon Valdez oil spill.

4. Who is Steven Guilbeault?

5. What project is British Petroleum working on and where?

6. What will this project do?

7. What are two renewable energy sources?

8. What could be disastrous for the Inuit communities in the Arctic?

9. What wildlife would be endangered by a major oil spill in the Arctic?

10. What is the industrialized world too dependent on, according to Steven Guilbeault?

Review

If writing your answers to the following questions, answer briefly in about two sentences.

1. What does the title of this article mean? Explain.

2. Why are renewable energy sources important?

3. What are fossil fuels and how do they affect the environment?

4. What has been wreaking havoc across the world according to this article? Why?

5. Why are coastlines vulnerable environments?

6. Why do the Inuit communities in the Arctic feel threatened?

7. How can we protect our environment more?

8. What can we do to avoid tragedies like the Exxon Valdez oil spill in future?

Response

In small groups, prepare a short comment on *one* of the following topics. Begin with a general statement of response. Conclude by reviewing the main point of your statement of response. Your comment may be written or oral. Each group may be allotted a different topic.

Topics

1. If you were in charge of climate and energy issues at Greenpeace, what would you propose to avoid another oil spill tragedy? Prepare a short policy statement.

2. Prepare a statement for British Petroleum, explaining your concerns about its project, Northstar. Remember that you can always send a letter to the company.

3. Explain how you would encourage people to avoid reliance on fossil fuels. Prepare a press release on the subject. (You might consider electric cars, ethanol, solar power, and other renewable energy sources.)

4. Give your views on organizations like Greenpeace and Pollution Probe.

Success in reading, like success in anything, comes from practice. Once you understand the vocabulary used, know how to focus on the main points, can recall main points and supporting data, review the ideas, and evaluate your response to them, you are a successful reader. Be consistent and use the Nine-Step Active Reader Program or the P3SE Formula on a regular basis. Just do it. Then you will take the *d* from in front of *read* when it comes to assigned readings at college.

REVIEW AND REMEMBER

Remembering Assigned Readings

1. Build your reading stamina by recalling the main ideas of short readings in sequence.

2. Decide what each short reading is about. Tell yourself what the main idea is, in your own words.

3. Review each section in the reading—beginning, middle, end.

4. Read each section aloud slowly, listening to what you are reading.

5. Consult any reference material needed, if you have not already done so, in your initial preparation. Do you still need a dictionary, or an encyclopedia, the Internet, or a biographical dictionary?

6. Note what the main subject is and think about the writer's purpose in writing.

7. List any supporting points used.

8. Review the introduction and conclusion.

9. Try telling someone else, or your cat or the mirror, what you have just been reading and what you thought of the ideas. Explain with as much supporting detail as possible.

CHAPTER 2

Context and Comprehension:

Personal Narratives

This chapter has five readings for comprehension, analysis, and response.

By the end of this chapter, you will be able to

- further practise the predicting, skimming, scanning, specifying, and evaluating skills of Chapter 1

- identify a writer's purpose, point of view, and possible readers

- use context clues to develop your vocabulary

- differentiate between *objective* and *subjective* writing

- connect more easily with the minds and hearts of other people from other times through their writing

Personal narratives and historical perspectives give you a broader understanding of purpose and audience. In this chapter, you are encouraged to respond to the use of telling details and to the power of narrative in records of human responses to dislocating situations.

Everyone has a story to tell. Everyone's life is a story with a beginning, a middle, and an end. Some stories, though, are more interesting than others.

Narratives tell a story. A good narrative well told will keep readers reading, even if they already know what happens. All narrative writing has a purpose. Narratives state what happened but they tell what happened for a reason. Those reasons affect the choices writers make about what to include in the narrative. Writers may choose to describe an event in a straightforward way or they may choose to entertain readers. Narrative writers may wish to explain something that happened in their lives. They may wish to examine why something happened, or they may expect readers themselves to work out why it happened. They may want readers to understand their personal version of a situation, issue, relationship, or event. Often writers write to set the record straight or, for therapeutic reasons, to unload guilt or justify an action. Readers can usually decide why a writer is telling a story.

Personal narratives, stories about people's lives, depend on what writers choose to tell their readers. Specifically, they depend on

- the writer's purpose
- the writer's point of view
- the specific details chosen to communicate that point of view
- the writer's understanding of reader expectations

Think about your version of a breakup or a divorce, and compare it with another person's version. The two versions are never the same. Why? It all depends on the angle, the perspective of the person narrating the story.

Your perspective is your view of an event, a situation, an experience. That perspective, or point of view, depends on many things: culture, education, age, income bracket, race, gender, social class, language background, political and religious beliefs, experience, ideology, family background, and the physical and psychological environment.

When you read the narratives that follow, think about what seems to be important to their writers. *What* do you remember after reading the selection? *Why?* Your answers to those two questions are important.

READING 1

The Unsinkable *Titanic*

The "unsinkable" Titanic *had double bottoms and 16 watertight compartments in her hull. She was the largest ship afloat at the time, and believed to be the safest, described by some as a "gigantic lifeboat." The* Titanic *had only 1,178 lifeboat spaces for the 2,224 people aboard. When she sank, over 1,500 lives were lost—a high proportion of them steerage passengers. The following personal narratives of two survivors appeared orginally in* The New York Times *on April 19, 1912.*

The *Titanic*: A Fireman's Story, 15 April 1912

Harry Senior

1   I was in my bunk when I felt a bump. One man said, 'Hello. She has been struck.' I went on deck and saw a great pile of ice on the well deck before the forecastle, but we all thought the ship would last some time, and we went back to our bunks. Then one of the firemen came running down and yelled, 'All muster for the lifeboats.' I ran on deck, and the Captain said, 'All firemen keep down on the well deck. If a man comes up I'll shoot him.'

2   Then I saw the first lifeboat lowered. Thirteen people were on board, eleven men and two women. Three were millionaires and one was Ismay [J. Bruce Ismay, Managing Director of the White Star Line; a survivor].

3   Then I ran up on to the hurricane deck and helped to throw one of the collapsible boats on to the lower deck. I saw an Italian woman holding two babies. I took one of them, and made the woman jump overboard with the baby, while I did the same with the other. When I came to the surface the baby in my arms was dead. I saw the woman strike out in good style, but a boiler burst on the *Titanic* and started a big wave. When the woman saw that wave, she gave up. Then, as the child was dead, I let it sink too.

4   I swam around for about half an hour, and was swimming on my back when the *Titanic* went down. I tried to get aboard a boat, but some chap hit

me over the head with an oar. There were too many in her. I got around to the other side of the boat and climbed in.

John Carey, ed., *The Faber Book of Reportage* (London: Faber and Faber, 1987), 434–35

Vocabulary

steerage (introduction): the lower decks of a ship for passengers paying the lowest fares, usually overcrowded; today, this expression is often used to refer to economy class seats on airplanes

forecastle (para. 1): part of the upper deck of a ship; the forward part nearest the bow

muster (para. 1): summon or assemble; gather together

Recall

Try to answer the following questions from memory after reading the passage at least twice. Follow the nine-step Active Reader Program or the PS3E Formula presented in Chapter 1.

1. Where was Harry Senior when the *Titanic* hit the iceberg?

2. What did Senior see when he went on deck?

3. Why did Senior return to his bunk?

4. What did the captain say to the firemen?

5. What facts did you learn about the first lifeboat lowered?

6. What did Senior do for the Italian woman?

7. What made the Italian woman give up?

8. Where was Senior when the *Titanic* went down?

9. What happened to Senior when he first tried to climb on board a lifeboat?

10. How did Senior finally get on board a lifeboat?

The *Titanic:* From a Lifeboat, 15 April 1912

Mrs. D. H. Bishop

1   We did not begin to understand the situation till we were perhaps a mile or more away from the *Titanic*. Then we could see the rows of lights along the decks begin to slant gradually upward from the bow. Very slowly the lines of light began to point downward at a greater and greater angle. The sinking was so slow that you could not perceive the lights of the deck changing their position. The slant seemed to be greater about every quarter of an hour. That was the only difference.

2   In a couple of hours, though, she began to go down more rapidly. Then the fearful sight began. The people in the ship were just beginning to realize how great their danger was. When the forward part of the ship dropped suddenly at a faster rate, so that the upward slope became marked, there was a sudden rush of passengers on all the decks towards the stern. It was like a wave. We could see the great black mass of people in the steerage sweeping to the rear part of the boat and breaking through into the upper decks. At the distance of about a mile we could distinguish everything through the night, which was perfectly clear. We could make out the increasing excitement on board the boat as the people, rushing to and fro, caused the deck lights to disappear and reappear as they passed in front of them.

3   This panic went on, it seemed, for an hour. Then suddenly the ship seemed to shoot up out of the water and stand there perpendicularly. It seemed to us that it stood upright in the water for four full minutes.

4   Then it began to slide gently downwards. Its speed increased as it went down head first, so that the stern shot down with a rush.

5   The lights continued to burn till it sank. We could see the people packed densely in the stern till it was gone . . .

6   As the ship sank we could hear the screaming a mile away. Gradually it became fainter and fainter and died away. Some of the lifeboats that had room for more might have gone to their rescue, but it would have meant that those who were in the water would have swarmed aboard and sunk her.

John Carey, ed., *The Faber Book of Reportage* (London: Faber and Faber, 1987), 436–37

Recall

Try to answer the following questions from memory.

1. Where was Mrs. Bishop when the *Titanic* went down?

2. When did Mrs. Bishop begin to understand that the *Titanic* was sinking?

3. What did the lights on board indicate to the people in the lifeboats?

4. Why were the changes on board hard to perceive at first?

5. How long did the *Titanic* take to sink?

6. What fearful sight did Mrs. Bishop see from the lifeboat?

7. Why was it possible to see exactly what was happening on board the *Titanic*?

8. Why did the deck lights keep disappearing?

9. What noise could be heard as the ship sank?

10. Why didn't the people in lifeboats go to the rescue of those in the water?

Review

Harry Senior's and Mrs. Bishop's Stories

Answer the following questions.

1. Why are the details in Harry Senior's story about the first lifeboat lowered significant?

2. Why would the captain threaten to shoot any fireman who came on deck in Senior's story? What impression do you get of the captain from this command? Give reasons.

3. What impression do you get of Harry Senior? Why?

4. What impression do you get of Mrs. Bishop from her story? Explain briefly with reference to her story.

5. What is the effect of the details about the lights and the angle of the ship mentioned by Mrs. Bishop?

6. What details in Mrs. Bishop's story help convey the terror of the people trapped on board the *Titanic*?

7. What differences in language, style, choice of words, and details do you notice between Harry Senior's and Mrs. Bishop's stories? What do these differences reveal about their possible ages, education, gender, income brackets, social class, or concern for others? What points would you make in a brief description of each?

8. Who would be reading these stories? What sort of audience are they for?

9. Why do people want to hear survivors' stories?

Response

The following topics are suitable for collaborative writing in small groups or as decided by the teacher. Be sure that each member of the group gets a chance to contribute to the discussion and the response, whether written or oral.

Topics

1. Consider the idea of *hubris* in relation to the *Titanic*.

   Hubris means overbearing pride or arrogance, insolence, presumption, arrogant pride in one's own abilities or achievements, going beyond one's abilities, and making a fool of oneself. The ancient Greeks regarded hubris as an evil force in human beings, a human pretense of being as great as the gods. Hubris tended to result in a person's downfall or disaster for everyone involved. The *Titanic* was considered to be a great technological achievement, capable of facing any Atlantic storm.

   Prepare a short comment on what we can learn today about hubris and human behaviour from the story of the *Titanic*.

2. Consider the idea of *status quo* in relation to the *Titanic*.

Status quo means the way things are in society, the accepted norms, existing conditions at a particular time. One of the accepted beliefs in 1912, and still today, is the idea of "women and children first." The idea that women and children deserve the first chance to flee a sinking ship is a belief that presumably shows the human need to allow the human race to survive, and the desire to look after the vulnerable amongst us.

Look at Harry Senior's description of the people on board the first lifeboat. Why do you think he mentions them so specifically? What does he reveal with his choice of details here? Prepare a short comment on what we can learn today from the survivors of the *Titanic* disaster.

3. Many mistakes were made on the *Titanic*. What do you think you might have done to avoid panic on board?

Prepare a list of instructions that might have allowed more people to survive. Think about some of the criticisms made about the behaviour on board that night. For example, people often wonder why the strong oak doors and other wooden features were not wrenched loose to make rafts. People wonder why the first class passengers were allowed to take up valuable time using the ship's telegraph system to telegraph their friends in New York, explaining that they would be arriving late. Also, if there is not enough room in a lifeboat, most sailors are trained to take turns at being in the water and being on board, while waiting to be rescued. What would you have done?

Write about the *Titanic*

Answer the following questions.

1. Why do you think people are still so fascinated by the *Titanic*?

2. What do you find so interesting about the story of the *Titanic*?

3. What can we learn from the story of the *Titanic*?

4. Imagine the scene on board that night. Describe it, as if you were one of the people on board, like Harry Senior or Mrs. Bishop. Choose your angle and mention exactly where you were and what struck you most. Obviously, you survived to tell your tale.

Objective or Subjective?

You know what objective tests are. Multiple-choice, true-false, matching, and completing tests are all objective. All you have to do is select the correct answer. Sometimes a machine marks the test. No emotions are usually involved in answering or marking objective tests.

Subjective tests, on the other hand, require decisions and judgments. They require you to demonstrate an understanding of assigned material. They require reasoning and interpretation.

Objective means *not* concerned with the ego, without any obvious bias. Objective writing tries to eliminate personal response and keep to the facts on the subject. Remember, facts can be tested. Business and scientific writing, case observations, and reports should be as objective as possible.

Subjective means concerned with *self*. (Remember the *s*.) Subjective writing is personal, often revealing the writer's emotions, beliefs, and attitudes to the subject. Subjective writing gives opinions. Not everyone may agree with them.

Exercise 2.1

Which of the following statements are subjective? Which statements are objective?

1. Twenty-six per cent of Canada's population uses drugs and tobacco.

2. Pierre Trudeau was the wisest prime minister Canada ever had.

3. *Titanic* was the best movie ever made.

4. My aunt saw *Titanic* six times, and my sister saw it nine times.

5. In 1999, Robert Mundell, who grew up in small-town Ontario and British Columbia, was awarded the Nobel Prize in Economics.

6. At least 20 companies in the Vancouver area deliver organically grown fruit and vegetables to the door.

7. Organically grown fruit and vegetables often look deformed.

8. Shania Twain's parents died when she was 21.

9. Shania Twain is Canada's sexiest export.

10. The *Titanic* had 2,224 people on board and only 1,178 lifeboat spaces.

Did you come up with six objective and four subjective statements (#2, #3, #7, #9)? Easy?

If you can distinguish between value judgments and measurable facts, you will be able to determine whether to use an objective or subjective approach in your own writing. Both objective and subjective writing are fine. The writer's attitude to the subject will determine whether the approach is subjective or objective. When you write, the purpose of your writing will determine your approach.

An essay may be subjective. A report must be objective unless otherwise instructed. Ask your teacher if you can use the first-person pronoun I in your writing, or if a more objective approach is necessary. Consider the context of an assignment before deciding whether an objective or subjective approach is best. What is the assignment's purpose? How will it be used?

The readings in this text are mostly subjective. Get into the habit of asking what is objective, measurable data in your reading, and what is subjective, or personal truth. Both kinds of writing are valuable. It is important to know which kind is needed for a particular context.

READING 2

New Directions

by Maya Angelou

Maya Angelou, writer, actor, dancer, newspaper editor, civil-rights activist, and poet, grew up in Arkansas. She wrote about growing up in her famous book I Know Why the Caged Bird Sings *in 1970. Besides being a well-known speaker and performer, she has written many books, television specials, and poetry.*

1   In 1903 the late Mrs. Annie Johnson of Arkansas found herself with two toddling sons, very little money, a slight ability to read and add simple numbers. To this picture add a disastrous marriage and the burdensome fact that Mrs. Johnson was a Negro.

2   When she told her husband, Mr. William Johnson, of her dissatisfaction with their marriage, he conceded that he too found it to be less than he expected, and had been secretly hoping to leave and study religion. He added that he thought God was calling him not only to preach but to do so in Enid, Oklahoma. He did not tell her that he knew a minister in Enid with

whom he could study and who had a friendly, unmarried daughter. They parted amicably, Annie keeping the one-room house and William taking most of the cash to carry himself to Oklahoma.

3   Annie, over six feet tall, big-boned, decided that she would not go to work as a domestic and leave her "precious babes" to anyone else's care. There was no possibility of being hired at the town's cotton gin or lumber mill, but maybe there was a way to make the two factories work for her. In her words, "I looked up the road I was going and back the way I come, and since I wasn't satisfied, I decided to step off the road and cut me a new path." She told herself that she wasn't a fancy cook but that she could "mix groceries well enough to scare hunger away from a starving man."

4   She made her plans meticulously and in secret. One early evening to see if she was ready, she placed stones in two five-gallon pails and carried them three miles to the cotton gin. She rested a little, and then, discarding some rocks, she walked in the darkness to the saw mill five miles farther along the dirt road. On her way back to her little house and her babies, she dumped the remaining rocks along the path.

5   That same night she worked into the early hours boiling chicken and frying ham. She made dough and filled the rolled-out pastry with meat. At last she went to sleep.

6   The next morning she left her house carrying the meat pies, lard, an iron brazier, and coals for a fire. Just before lunch she appeared in an empty lot behind the cotton gin. As the dinner noon bell rang, she dropped the savors into boiling fat and the aroma rose and floated over to the workers who spilled out of the gin, covered with white lint, looking like specters.

7   Most workers had brought their lunches of pinto beans and biscuits or crackers, onions and cans of sardines, but they were tempted by the hot meat pies which Annie ladled out of the fat. She wrapped them in newspapers, which soaked up the grease, and offered them for sale at a nickel each. Although business was slow, those first days Annie was determined. She balanced her appearances between the two hours of activity.

8   So, on Monday if she offered hot fresh pies at the cotton gin and sold the remaining cooled-down pies at the lumber mill for three cents, then on Tuesday she went first to the lumber mill presenting fresh, just-cooked pies as the lumbermen covered in sawdust emerged from the mill.

9   For the next few years, on balmy spring days, blistering summer noons, and cold, wet, and wintry middays, Annie never disappointed her customers, who could count on seeing the tall, brown-skin woman bent over her brazier, carefully turning the meat pies. When she felt certain that the workers had become dependent on her, she built a stall between the two hives of industry and let the men run to her for their lunchtime provisions.

10   She had indeed stepped from the road which seemed to have been chosen for her and cut herself a brand-new path. In years that stall became a

store where customers could buy cheese, meal, syrup, cookies, candy, writing tablets, pickles, canned goods, fresh fruit, soft drinks, coal, oil, and leather soles for worn-out shoes.

11   Each of us has the right and responsibility to assess the roads which lie ahead, and those over which we have traveled, and if the future road looms ominous or unpromising, and the roads back uninviting, then we need to gather our resolve and, carrying only the necessary baggage, step off that road into another direction. If the new choice is also unpalatable, without embarrassment, we must be ready to change that as well.

Maya Angelou, "A New Path For Annie," from *Wouldn't Take Nothing for My Journey Now*. Copyright © 1993 by Maya Angelou. Used by permission of Random House, Inc.

Spelling

Maya Angelou is an American and her writing uses American forms, in vocabulary and spelling. She writes *savors,* while in Canada, we write savou*r*s. Angelou writes that the workers came out of the gin "looking like *specters.*" In Canada, where we use the metric system of measurement, and what American humorist Dave Barry calls "metric spelling" too, we write *spectre,* just as we write *centre, metre.* (But we would write World Trade *Center* because that is the place name, and we show respect by getting the name right.) Canadians also write *travelling* with a double *l,* even if computer spell checkers don't like it.

In today's global world, most Canadian writers demonstrate their pride in being Canadian and maintain their national identity in writing by using Canadian spelling. Other Canadian writers shrug off Canadian spelling and opt for American spelling. It is a good idea to follow Canadian spelling in Canada, especially if you work in the media, unless told that spelling style does not matter. Be aware of the differences between both spelling styles. Ultimately, it is more important to write clearly, coherently, and correctly so all readers on both sides of the border can understand what you've written.

Word Recognition

You can often discover the meanings of words from their context. What is *context*? Context is simply the place in a text where a word or expression is found. It is the location of the material. You may have heard that the three most important factors in determining the price of real estate are location, location, and location. The same is true for language. The most important factor for determining the meaning of a word is its location. Words take on different meanings according to their location, or context.

Think of the different places you could find the word *tough*—tough cookie, tough times, tough meat. The context would show the meaning. After all, the words "Go jump in the lake" mean one thing in a donut shop and another on the shores of a lake.

When you read an unfamiliar word, its context can help you understand that word. Guessing the word from context means you do not have to use a dictionary immediately. As a child, you learned most words from context. You did not consult your mother or a dictionary for every new word.

The same is true today when you read. Keep on reading and think about the context of new words or words used in a new way. Usually, the location of the word gives a clue to its meaning. Such clues are called *context clues*.

For example, Maya Angelou writes that the workers "spilled out of the *gin*, covered with white *lint*, looking like *specters*." Do you think the workers fell out of a bottle of liquor, covered with white flowers looking like sparrows? No. You guessed that the cotton gin she is talking about is some kind of factory, a hive of industry like the lumber mill, but for manufacturing cotton. Indeed a cotton gin, originally the en*gin*e that separated the cotton from its seeds, became the word used for the factory itself where cotton was processed. Someone covered with white lint probably looks like some kind of spirit or ghost. If you don't know what lint is, then maybe you need to do more of your own laundry . . .

In the store that grew out of Annie Johnson's stall, you could buy "writing tablets." Do you think you would swallow those tablets? If "the future road *looms ominous* or unpromising," do you think it offers favourable omens or does it threaten bad luck?

Save time when you read by being a detective. Be alert for context clues.

Recall

Choose the best answer. Try to make your choice based on context clues. Look at how the words are used in the reading. Practise developing your word sense before using a dictionary.

1. "... he conceded that he too found it to be less than he expected ..." William Johnson's attitude to the marriage is that

   a. he is superior to his wife, and she needs to treat him with more dignity

   b. his expectations were quite different from Annie's

   c. he feels much the same as Annie does, and agrees with her about married life

   d. he is proud of their partnership and what they have achieved together

2. "They parted amicably, Annie keeping the one-room house ..." The couple then

   a. split without tension in a friendly way, and Annie kept her dwelling place

   b. disintegrated, with Annie maintaining an illusion of control

   c. decided that matrimony was a lethal experience, but William had no right to their abode

   d. allowed Annie to initiate divorce proceedings

3. "She made her plans meticulously and in secret." Annie Johnson

   a. proposed a detailed scheme for survival in a concealed spot

   b. discarded previous arrangements in favour of working on a steady path

   c. worked out what to do on her home territory using espionage

   d. made arrangements precisely and carefully without telling anyone

4. Annie could be described as a

   a. stubborn political activist whose will triumphed over all racist and sexist prejudice in Arkansas in 1903

   b. strong and determined woman who had a life plan and showed courage in finding a new direction in life

   c. beautiful young mother who found herself alone, lost in a dark forest in life, loaded with unnecessary baggage

   d. single parent whose ability to assess the weight of stones and rocks made workers forget their lunch

5. After her marriage to William ended, Annie did not want to

    a. labour at cleaning house for someone else and be unable to take care of her adored children

    b. become a drudge and forget how to warm savoury food in a metal pan for her babies

    c. work as an amateur in other people's kitchens without her children near

    d. fry chicken and sort groceries for any other woman

6. "... she dropped the savors into boiling fat and the aroma rose and floated over to the workers ..." Here, Annie is

    a. combining ingredients to make workers dream of home cooking, their mothers, pinto beans, and biscuits

    b. transporting raw but fragrant spices to the iron brazier through the air

    c. cooking chicken and onions in fat before wrapping them in newspapers

    d. using the pleasant smell of hot food to excite the palates of the workers

7. After her first few days of selling pies, Annie made sure

    a. her pies were made over medium-hot coals so the flavour never varied

    b. she never agitated her customers by placing stones in her brazier on balmy spring days

    c. she never failed to turn up and turn over the meat pies

    d. she was never unsuccessful whether the weather was hot or cold

8. In later years, Annie

    a. directed her enterprise so that instead of Annie going to the workers, the workers came to Annie

    b. made her pies with corn syrup, meat, and cheese and sold them from a stall on the dirt road

    c. was sure that when the workers swarmed from their hives, they would wear out their shoes' leather soles seeking her new road

d. offered only hot pies, not cooled-down ones, at all locations for three cents

9. When we assess the roads that lie ahead, we

    a. take the easiest route to get to our destination without effort

    b. evaluate which flavours are the best to swallow in life

    c. resolve to become better informed about travel plans

    d. analyze and think about the pathways open to us in life

10. "If the new choice is also unpalatable," says Maya Angelou, "without embarrassment, we must be ready to change that as well." She means

    a. if a new menu tastes bitter, without shame, add sweeter ingredients so another flavour emerges

    b. always invest in all new enterprises unselfconsciously

    c. avoid all prophetic road signs on the pathway of life and choose the road less travelled

    d. don't be afraid to discard a bad choice and try another one

Review

Answer the following questions.

1. What sort of life did Annie Johnson have at the beginning of this reading? Describe her situation in one or two sentences.

2. What happened to Annie's husband?

3. Annie decided to make "the two factories work for her." How did she do that?

4. What skills did Annie have? List at least three.

5. How did she do her research for her new job?

6. On her first day, what did Annie take with her to the cotton gin?

7. What did Annie do when she reached the cotton gin?

8. What effect did the aroma coming from Annie's cooking have on the workers?

9. How did Annie arrange her business hours and locations? Explain with reasons in two sentences.

10. What could Annie's customers always count on?

11. How did Annie's business expand?

12. Why does Maya Angelou tell the story of Annie Johnson? What does she want us to think about? (This could be answered in a half page.)

Response

In small groups or individually, prepare a brief oral or written report on at least *one* of the following topics. Any member of the group should be prepared to present the group's response to the rest of the class after 20 to 30 minutes, so allot your time wisely and take clear notes.

1. Begin with a clear statement of your response to the topic, stated in one to two sentences only.

2. Give reasons for your point of view. Use examples from your own life or from your community, as well as from the reading to support your views.

3. Conclude by reinforcing the point you made at the beginning, using different words as much as possible.

Topics

1. Maya Angelou writes that Annie Johnson not only had a disastrous marriage, but also suffered from the burdensome fact that she was a Negro (note the capital *N*). Today we would call her African-American.

    Language reflects society and social changes in attitude. The respected African-American academic Professor Henry Louis Gates, Jr. emphasized the way language reflects social change when he pointed out that his great-grandfather was a "nigger," his grandfather was a "Negro," his father was "coloured," he is "Black" and his son is "African-American."

    Think about other language and attitude changes that Annie Johnson might notice today if she was starting a business. Think about today's attitudes towards women, single parents, and people of colour. How might the cotton-gin workers have described Annie then? Would their descriptions today reflect a change in attitude? Give reasons and examples in your response.

Prepare a comment on the way language reflects social change, focusing on sexist attitudes, as well as racist ones. For example, consider one student's complaint that a daisy will never earn as much as a buck.

2. Why did Annie Johnson succeed in her business? What qualities did she have that all entrepreneurs or employees need? What objective data did she assess in setting up her business? Prepare a brief report on how Annie offers an important example and role model for all people wanting to be a success in their jobs.

3. Annie Johnson's story takes place in 1903. What relevance does it have for us today? Explain.

4. What advice would you give to someone who needs to make a change in his or her life? Do you have any stories to tell, like the story told by Angelou? Begin with the story and end with your advice, the way Angelou does.

5. Tell a story of someone famous whose life is an inspiration and end with a comment similar to the last two paragraphs of Angelou's story here. Make clear what you want readers or listeners to understand after hearing this story.

READING 3

Mum's Snake

by A.B. Facey

Albert Facey, born in 1894 in the wheatbelt of Western Australia, had a difficult life, but triumphed over all its obstacles and challenges. He considered his life a fortunate one. His father died before he was 2. He was deserted by his mother and raised by his grandmother until he was 8 years old, when he was sent out to work.

Albert Facey had no formal education. He taught himself to read and write. His book, A Fortunate Life, *about his life was published in 1981. He died in Perth, Australia, in 1982. In this excerpt, Bert is 12 years old and working for Mr. and Mrs. Phillips, who asked him to call her Mum. He had to work hard, but he liked the Phillips and said they treated him as if he were their own son. At the time of the excerpt, Bert and Frank (Mr. Phillips) are busy clearing a firebreak about half a mile from the house.*

1   Mum had an arrangement to give us an idea when it was lunch-time. She would peg a white tea towel on the clothes line near the house at ten minutes to midday. By the time we got home and had a clean up, lunch would be ready.

2   One day, at the signal, we started walking towards the house. We were about fifty yards away when we heard Mum let out a terrible scream. She came running out of the lavatory holding up her dress with one hand and clutching her bottom with the other. She was yelling out loudly, 'I've been bitten by a snake!' Frank and I ran to her and helped her inside the house. Frank took her into the bedroom and told me to run over to the Connors' place and get Jack to bring his horse and sulky to take Mum to the doctor. It was a little over two miles to Jack's and I ran all the way. It was a very hot day and I was done in when I got there. It took me a few minutes before I could explain what had happened.

3   Jack wasn't long putting the horse in the sulky and we drove back. Mum was crying when we got there. Frank told Jack that the snake bite was very distinct and he had cut it with a razor and sucked out as much blood as he could.

4   Mum looked very pale and was badly shocked. After giving me some quick instructions as to what to do while they were away, they set out to get Mum to the doctor in Narrogin as soon as possible. Jack's sulky horse was a beauty, one of the best in the district, and although Frank and Jack were at loggerheads over the boar, they had forgotten about it with the crisis in hand. The trip to Narrogin would take them all afternoon and well into the night.

5   After they had gone I got a nice handy stick, about four feet long, and went into the lavatory after the snake. This lavatory was mainly used by Mum; I never used it and Frank only sometimes. It was made of galvanised iron and had a small hole cut out at the back to allow Mum to slide the pan in. (The pan was an old kerosene tin cut off to fit.) A bag was hung onto the back wall to cover the hole. With the stick I approached the lavatory, carefully looking in and around, but I couldn't see any sign of the snake. I lifted the bag up very slowly (I was scared stiff), then I heard something move. Quickly I dropped the bag and jumped back. Then all was quiet again. I lifted the bag once more. This time I noticed some feathers, and as I lifted the bag further, more feathers came into view. All at once I knew what had bitten Mum. It wasn't a snake and all my fears turned to mirth. In fact, I almost lost control of myself with laughing.

6   Mum's snake was a hen. The hen had made a nest close to the pan to lay her eggs and Mum hadn't noticed her. She didn't mind Mum sitting on the lavatory at first, but when she went broody—a hen can be placid while laying and vicious when broody— she had decided to peck Mum on the bottom.

7   Mum was very frightened of snakes and also terribly frightened of dingoes. She wouldn't venture outside on her own, except in special circumstances.

8   They were away for nearly four days. When they came home Mum seemed jolly and didn't show any ill effects from the shock she'd had. I asked her how she was and she said that the doctor had said he didn't think it was a snake that had bitten her and if it was it wasn't poisonous. She asked if I'd looked around the lavatory for the snake and I said that I had and that I had found the thing that had bitten her. I said that it was still in the lavatory and I offered to show it to her.

9   We went to the lavatory and I lifted up the bag. She looked under and exclaimed, 'Good God. No!' She said that the doctor had said it looked like beak marks but it never occurred to her that a hen might have done it. She stood for a while and seemed to be thinking, or working something out in her mind. Then she suddenly said, 'Did you have any visitors while we were away or see anyone?' I said, 'No.' 'Well,' she said, 'don't you say anything, not even to Frank or anybody, about this. If you do I'll be the laughing stock of the district.' She said, 'Bert, I love you, but if you tell anyone about this I'll kill you.' I promised not to tell anyone. Nothing more was said about the 'snake bite'.

A. B. Facey, *A Fortunate Life* (Victoria, Aus.: Penguin Books, 1981), 68–69

Word Recognition

Many of the words and expressions used in the reading may be unfamiliar, but their context offers many clues to their meaning. You should have no trouble guessing what they mean from looking at their location in the text.

For example, the reading refers to a "horse and sulky." You know that if your girlfriend is *sulky*, she will probably be silent, full of resentment, not nice to be near, no fun at all. Did Bert Facey run all the way to the neighbour's to get a grumpy person? No, obviously a horse and sulky is more likely to be some kind of horse-drawn wagon or carriage. A dictionary tells you that a *sulky* is also a light two-wheeled vehicle, pulled by only one horse. The context alone would indicate that meaning.

However, an expression like "at loggerheads" might puzzle you. A *loggerhead*, your small dictionary may tell you, is a kind of turtle, or an idiotic person, or an iron tool used for heating hot liquid. At sea in the old days, on whaleboats, it was the name given to a post for a harpooned whale to be tied up to. Do any of those meanings fit the context here of Frank and Jack being at loggerheads over the boar? No, obviously the meaning given in a bigger dictionary of the expression *at loggerheads* as arguing strongly, quarrelling, and trying to prove the other wrong is more suited to this context.

Exercise 2.2

Look at the way the words and expressions listed below are used in the reading. Try to guess their meanings from the context (consult a dictionary only if necessary). Then, write the appropriate word or expression in each sentence.

lavatory	broody
galvanised iron	mirth
done in	vicious
crisis in hand	laughing stock
placid	kerosene tin

1. After arranging for babysitters, spending 2 hours with her personal trainer, and singing at the concert, Céline felt quite _____ when she finally got home.

2. The appearance of Angelina's bodyguards looking like three well-dressed gorillas, combined with her hobnailed leather garments, made her a _____ at the Academy Awards.

3. The disappearance of small birds across the metropolitan area shows there is a _____ with persistent organic pollutants, or POPs.

4. People who grew up in the Caribbean might say that the clatter of gentle rain on a roof of _____ can be very soothing.

5. When a storm blows up, and the pounding of the rain and the roaring of the wind make the weather seem _____, it's time to get nervous and hope that no hurricane will remove the roof.

6. It is difficult to remain calm and be _____ when the roof blows away.

7. Sanjit did not think it was funny to get a phone call from his Grade 6 girlfriend, accusing him of cheating on her, so he could not understand Muna's _____, and was furious when she collapsed with laughter.

8. On farms in the old days, a _____ had many uses, in spite of its strong smell.

9. Some empty tins were used as targets for shooting practice, others for storage, and some for the outdoor _____, when there was no indoor plumbing.

10. It's not just hens who get moody and act strangely when _____; my sister, Demi, offered to pose naked for magazine covers when she was pregnant with her twins.

Recall

Try to answer the following questions from memory.

1. What did the white tea towel signify to young Bert Facey and Frank Phillips?

2. What did Frank and Bert see and hear, as they walked towards the house on the day in question?

3. What did Frank and Bert do immediately?

4. What instructions did Frank give Bert next?

5. How far did Bert have to run for help?

6. Why did Bert run to the Connors' place?

7. What did Frank do while Bert went for help?

8. What did Bert discover when he went to find the snake?

9. How was Mum when she returned home from Narrogin?

10. What did Mum worry about when she saw what had bitten her?

Review

Choose the correct answer.

1. When Bert Facey was 12 years old, he lived

    a. in a small town called Narrogin in Western Australia

    b. with his mother and father on a large wheat farm in Western Australia where fires were common

    c. just over two miles from the Connors in Western Australia

    d. half a mile from an outhouse made of galvanised iron

2. Mum screamed because

    a. she was terrified of going to the lavatory outside because of the dingoes and snakes

    b. it was a very hot day, the lavatory was dark, and she saw something inside the lavatory move

    c. she was afraid of the boar attacking her, and that Jack and Frank would remain at loggerheads

    d. she was worrying about what the people in the district would think of her toilet arrangements

3. "... and although Frank and Jack were at loggerheads over the boar, they had forgotten about it with the crisis in hand." This statement shows that the people of the district

    a. had so many disputes about water that they were digging as many deep holes as possible all over their farms

    b. understood how crucial it was to get hold of the right tools when faced with a problem in a lavatory, even if they were fighting with their neighbours

    c. when faced with snakes, dingoes and water restrictions, would all work together to build a boar, sharing iron tools and logs

    d. would pull together in a time of acute danger and overlook differences of opinion

4. Bert suggests that Mum was bitten because hens

    a. are vicious and anxious when it rains, no matter what time of the year

b. do not get angry easily when they are producing eggs regularly, but will behave differently when they are hatching eggs

c. are, like most birds, bold and ready to fight when protecting their young

d. are not to be trusted when the sky darkens and their enclosure heats up

5. Mum threatened to kill Bert if

a. he told anyone how ridiculous she looked running from the lavatory clutching her bottom

b. he told visitors about her fear of dingoes and poisonous snakes

c. her personal reputation in the district was linked to the lavatory in any way

d. the story of the snakebite made her look ridiculous

6. The trip to Narrogin shows that people like the Phillips and the Connors, living on farms in the wheatbelt of Australia at that time,

a. travelled to town in a horse and sulky rather than by foot in the extreme heat

b. had to drive a horse and sulky to get to a town with hotels and a railway station

c. lived far away from schools, doctors, and other amenities

d. faced dingoes, kangaroos, snakes, and possums every day

7. Mum would not "venture outside on her own, except in special circumstances." This means that Mum

a. almost lost control of herself if she ever saw a dingo or a snake

b. only went into town and visited around the district under certain conditions

c. never dared to go to the bathroom alone for fear of the wildlife

d. was afraid to go out all by herself, and only did so on certain occasions

8. In your own words, in about three sentences, explain why Bert laughed when he saw what had bitten Mum.

9. Explain Mum's reaction to Bert's discovery.

10. Briefly describe the conditions Bert lived in at the Phillips' home.

Response

Respond to *one* of the following topics with a partner or in groups of three. If your teacher does not assign a specific activity, try to choose one that no other group is doing. Be prepared to present the best response to the entire class or to write about it in one page.

Topics

1. In your own words, tell your partner or the group the story of "Mum's Snake." Listen to your partner or each person in the group. Decide which version comes across best and jot down at least two reasons why. For example, is it the order of events, the details remembered, the vocabulary, the tone of voice, or use of dramatic pauses? Then, list the reasons for the success of this version, and note the details used, explaining what worked and why.

2. You want a group of high school students to hear this story. What will you tell them first? Why? Explain your choice with reasons and examples. If you can, use examples and details that come from other stories or movies that have worked with such an audience.

3. Each of you will describe an incident where you, or someone you know, became even briefly "the laughing stock" of your community. This community could be a classroom, school, church, shop. Select the best answer from the group for your final version. Add vivifying details to make the story interesting. Tell the story to the class. Anyone in the group can be the narrator of the story.

READING 4

Wounded by a Fascist Sniper, 20 May 1937

by George Orwell

George Orwell (1903–1950) is known to many students as the writer of Animal Farm *and* 1984, *but those are only two of his books. Celebrated for his plain style and his sensitivity to ordinary people, he writes about many sub-*

jects ranging from his days in colonial service in Burma to his days in poverty in Paris and London; from his time visiting areas of mass unemployment, poverty, malnutrition, and despair in the north of England in the 1930s to his experiences in Spain and the Second World War.

This excerpt is from Homage to Catalonia, *describing the time Orwell spent fighting for democracy against dictatorship in Spain. At the end of 1936, Orwell went to fight for the International Brigade in the Spanish Civil War. More than 1,500 idealistic young Canadians also volunteered to fight in this civil war, far from home, and more than half of them did not return. Norman Bethune and Ted Allen are two of the best-known Canadians who fought in the Spanish Civil War.*

1   I had been about ten days at the front when it happened. The whole experience of being hit by a bullet is very interesting and I think it is worth describing in detail.

2   It was at the corner of the parapet, at five o'clock in the morning. This was always a dangerous time, because we had the dawn at our backs, and if you stuck your head above the parapet it was clearly outlined against the sky. I was talking to the sentries preparatory to changing the guard. Suddenly, in the very middle of saying something, I felt—it is very hard to describe what I felt, though I remember it with the utmost vividness.

3   Roughly speaking it was the sensation of being *at the centre* of an explosion. There seemed to be a loud bang and a blinding flash of light all round me, and I felt a tremendous shock—no pain, only a violent shock, such as you get from an electric terminal; with it a sense of utter weakness, a feeling of being stricken and shrivelled up to nothing. The sandbags in front of me receded into immense distance. I fancy you would feel much the same if you were struck by lightning. I knew immediately that I was hit, but because of the seeming bang and flash I thought it was a rifle nearby that had gone off accidentally and shot me. All this happened in a space of time much less than a second. The next moment my knees crumpled up and I was falling, my head hitting the ground with a violent bang which, to my relief, did not hurt. I had a numb, dazed feeling, a consciousness of being very badly hurt, but no pain in the ordinary sense.

4   The American sentry I had been talking to had started forward. 'Gosh! Are you hit?' People gathered round. There was the usual fuss—'Lift him up! Where's he hit? Get his shirt open!' etc., etc. The American called for a knife to cut my shirt open. I knew that there was one in my pocket and tried to get it out, but discovered that my right arm was paralysed. Not being in pain, I felt a vague satisfaction. This ought to please my wife, I thought; she had always wanted me to be wounded, which would save me from being

killed when the great battle came. It was only now that it occurred to me to wonder where I was hit, and how badly; I could feel nothing, but I was conscious that the bullet had struck me somewhere in the front of my body. When I tried to speak I found that I had no voice, only a faint squeak, but at the second attempt I managed to ask where I was hit. In the throat, they said, Harry Webb, our stretcher-bearer, had brought a bandage and one of the little bottles of alcohol they gave us for field-dressings. As they lifted me up a lot of blood poured out of my mouth, and I heard a Spaniard behind me say that the bullet had gone clear through my neck. I felt the alcohol, which at ordinary times would sting like the devil, splash on to the wound as a pleasant coolness.

5   They laid me down again while somebody fetched a stretcher. As soon as I knew that the bullet had gone clean through my neck I took it for granted that I was done for. I had never heard of a man or an animal getting a bullet through the middle of the neck and surviving it. The blood was dribbling out of the corner of my mouth. 'The artery's gone,' I thought. I wondered how long you last when your carotid artery is cut; not many minutes, presumably. Everything was very blurry. There must have been about two minutes during which I assumed that I was killed. And that too was interesting—I mean it is interesting to know what your thoughts would be at such a time. My first thought, conventionally enough, was for my wife. My second was a violent resentment at having to leave this world which, when all is said and done, suits me so well. I had time to feel this very vividly. The stupid mischance infuriated me. The meaninglessness of it! To be bumped off, not even in battle, but in this stale corner of the trenches, thanks to a moment's carelessness! I thought, too, of the man who had shot me—wondered what he was like, whether he was a Spaniard or a foreigner, whether he knew he had got me, and so forth. I could not feel any resentment against him. I reflected that as he was a Fascist I would have killed him if I could, but that if he had been taken prisoner and brought before me at this moment I would merely have congratulated him on his good shooting. It may be, though, that if you were really dying your thoughts would be quite different.

6   They had just got me on to the stretcher when my paralysed right arm came to life and began hurting damnably. At the time I imagined that I must have broken it in falling; but the pain reassured me, for I knew that your sensations do not become more acute when you are dying. I began to feel more normal and to be sorry for the four poor devils who were sweating and slithering with the stretcher on their shoulders. It was a mile and a half to the ambulance, and vile going, over lumpy, slippery tracks. I knew what a sweat it was, having helped to carry a wounded man down a day or two earlier. The leaves of the silver poplars which, in places, fringed our

trenches brushed against my face; I thought what a good thing it was to be alive in a world where silver poplars grow. But all the while the pain in my arm was diabolical, making me swear and then try not to swear, because every time I breathed too hard the blood bubbled out of my mouth.

> George Orwell, "The Spanish Civil War: Wounded by a Fascist Sniper, near Huesca, 20 May 1937," from *Homage to Catalonia* (Copyright © George Orwell, 1937), by permission of Bill Hamilton as the Literary Executor of the Estate of the Late Sonia Brownell Orwell and Secker & Warburg Ltd. In John Carey, ed., *The Faber Book of Reportage* (London: Faber and Faber, 1987), 521–23.

Word Recognition

Look at the context in which unfamiliar words occur in the following sentences before looking them up in your dictionary. Can you guess the meaning of the words in italics from their context?

- It was at the corner of the *parapet*, at five o'clock in the morning.

- I was talking to the *sentries preparatory* to changing the guard.

It is not hard to guess what is happening in these sentences. Save time and look up only the words that keep you guessing, words that give you no clues.

> **parapet:** defensive wall or fortification; protective barrier at the edge of a balcony or roof
>
> **preparatory:** preparing to; getting ready to
>
> **sentry:** a guard at a special place (post); keeping watch
>
> **Fascist:** a person who follows a dictatorship or system of government of the extreme right with unreasoning devotion, never tolerating any opposition to the extreme views of the fascist system
>
> **diabolical:** fiendish; coming from the devil

Word meaning changes according to context, as you know. It also changes according to how a word is used in a sentence, according to its part of speech. For example, a word like *guard* can be a noun. As a noun, it names a person protecting someone or something from harm, or it names an object used to protect parts of the body.

Guard can also be a verb, meaning the actual action of protecting from harm, keeping watch over. A security guard *guards* someone or something. Remember that a verb is always directed by a subject, such as I, we, you, he, she, it, they: *he* guards, *we* guard, *they* guard. Also you can *change* guard, *mount* guard, *stand on* guard, *be on* guard or *off* guard.

Then there are other uses of the word, growing out of its original meaning. A *guarded* reply to a question is one where the person is cautious, not giving too much information away. In this context, *guarded* is an adjective. A *guardian* is someone who takes care of someone else, usually the legal protector of a young person.

Now think of the different meanings for the word *watch*. How can it be used as a verb? As a noun? Note that the context determines its grammatical function and label.

Exercise 2.3

Choose the correct word form for each sentence. Look at the following words and think about their different forms. Use singular or plural forms and appropriate verb tenses as necessary. Note: Some words may be used more than once.

1. **conscious, conscience, conscientious**
   "I was **conscious** that the bullet had struck me somewhere in the front of my body."

   a. Even though a bad hair day is annoying, I try not to be too _____ of how my hair looks all the time.

   b. Although she did not think she had strict moral views, Sandrine found that her _____ made her tell the principal what had happened.

   c. Dino's high grades and his clever time management show that he is a _____ student.

   d. Gobbo thinks that _____ makes cowards of us all.

   e. Sometimes it seems as though my boyfriend is from a different planet, because he is just not _____ of how he comes across to other people.

2. **thought, though, thorough**
   "I **thought,** too, of the man who had shot me. . ."

   a. Jennifer was _____ in her preparations for the wedding.

   b. She did not invite her mother, _____.

   c. The _____ of the gulf between her and her mother makes her sad.

d. Jennifer _____ about how her mother struggled after giving up her career, and decided she would never do the same.

e. Has she ever _____, _____, about making a conciliatory gesture to ease the gulf between them?

3. **terminal, term, terminate, termite**
   ". . . no pain, only a violent shock, such as you get from an electric **terminal**. . ."

   a. Jennifer hopes that her relationship with Brad is a lasting one because she does not want it to _____ in a divorce.

   b. The sound of the mere _____ "divorce," is enough to send shudders through her.

   c. After hearing that her grandfather had _____ cancer, Alisha took the next plane to Jamaica.

   d. When Joe saw the bus leaving the _____, he knew he had to phone his mother and explain he would be late.

   e. The wood shavings under the wardrobe are a sign that the furniture has been attacked by _____.

4. **suit, suite, suitable**
   ". . . at having to leave this world which, when all is said and done, **suits** me so well."

   a. The next _____ is where you will find the dentist's office.

   b. When deciding on your monthly contribution plan for your RRSP, always choose one that _____ your income and family status.

   c. If you have nothing _____ to wear to the party, come and look at the clothes Zsa Zsa has decided to throw away.

   d. Now that the company has decided that all employees will wear "business casual" in summer, Tyrone does not know what to do with all his light _____.

   e. The stair climber _____ her need to build endurance and stamina, and to burn body fat.

5. **dying, dyeing, quiet, quite**

". . . if you were really **dying** your thoughts would be **quite** different."

a. Sylvia said she was _____ the eggs in different colours.

b. Although he is fit and plays every day on an outdoor rink, Alexander felt _____ tired after that on-ice training session.

c. Vesna was _____ to go to the fancy dress party at Spadina House.

d. She became unusually _____ when she saw the huge crowd of people gathered in the reception room.

e. As soon as she saw her grandfather's tired face, Alisha realized that he really was _____ and might not last the night.

Exercise 2.4

Use *five* of the words in the list below in *two* different word forms in sentences which clearly show their meaning.

Example: *shock*

Sentence 1: I had such a shock when I saw Dracula's staring eyes and pointy teeth, my hair stood on end. (*shock* as a noun)

Sentence 2: She shocks her aunt with her tight, low-cut clothes and her comments about marrying only for money. (*shock* as a verb)

breathe: ". . . every time I breathed too hard . . ."

bubbled: ". . . the blood bubbled out of my mouth."

bumped: "To be bumped off, not even in battle . . ."

clean: ". . . the bullet had gone clean through my neck."

experience: "The whole experience of being hit . . ."

fuss: "There was the usual fuss . . ."

going: "It was . . . vile going, over lumpy, slippery tracks."

outlined: ". . . it was clearly outlined against the sky."

pain: ". . . The pain in my arm was diabolical . . ."

please: "This ought to please my wife . . ."

Recall

Try to answer the following questions from memory.

1. After being hit by the bullet, what were the immediate sensations George Orwell had?
2. Why did Orwell feel a vague satisfaction?
3. When did Orwell speak and what did he ask?
4. How did the alcohol feel?
5. Why did Orwell think he was done for?
6. What was Orwell's second thought on assuming he had been killed?
7. Who did Orwell eventually begin to feel sorry for and why?
8. Why did the pain reassure Orwell?
9. How did Orwell feel about the silver poplars?
10. Why did Orwell try not to swear?

Review

Answer the following questions in your own words and in complete sentences.

1. What is George Orwell's purpose in writing about being shot?
2. Why was five o'clock in the morning a dangerous time?
3. What does Orwell mean when he says ". . . it was the sensation of being *at the centre* of an explosion"? What details help him explain his point here?
4. Why do you think Orwell had "no pain in the ordinary sense"?
5. Describe briefly Orwell's attitude to being shot. What infuriated him?
6. Why did Orwell feel no resentment against the man who shot him?
7. What do Orwell's points show us about the experience of being on the battlefield?
8. How did Orwell know he was not dying?
9. What do you learn about the other men fighting alongside Orwell from this reading?

10. What objective data do you learn about being shot from Orwell's reading? What subjective details does he use to tell about his experience?

Response

Respond to at least *two* of the following topics, but not to two consecutive topic numbers. Undertake this activity in small groups or individually.

A. Prepare a clear topic sentence presenting a summary or the focus of your views. (Topic sentences make clear the idea that will be developed in the paragraph.)

B. Then, prepare a question that will lead into the topic sentence and begin your response by answering the question. In your answer, show how you reached this idea. Answers may be presented orally or in writing.

Topics

1. "The meaninglessness of it!" writes George Orwell. What do you think he means? Explain briefly in your own words.

2. How do you think you might you feel if facing death from a bullet? Give reasons.

3. Special effects in movies give us an idea of how gunshot wounds might look. After reading Orwell's account, do you think the bloody effects loved by Hollywood are realistic, or do they avoid realism? Why?

   Explain, and conclude with a statement on your views regarding blood and gore in movies, with reasons for those views. Use details from movies like *Saving Private Ryan*, if you can.

4. Orwell was fighting the Fascists in Spain in 1937, when he was hit in the middle of the neck by a bullet. Thinking about the man who had shot him, he ". . . reflected that as he was a Fascist I would have killed him if I could, but that if he had been taken prisoner and brought before me at this moment I would merely have congratulated him on his good shooting."

   Do you think the writer's response is a normal one? How do you think you might feel about someone who wounded you in a similar situation? Explain your response.

(The movie *Land and Freedom* by acclaimed director Ken Loach gives a fascinating picture of the idealism of young men like Orwell at that time, and of the conditions and confusion of the Spanish Civil War. The award-winning Spanish movie *Butterfly* shows the situation from the point of view of a child. The Fascists won that war.)

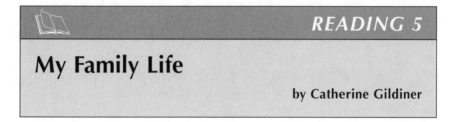

READING 5

My Family Life

by Catherine Gildiner

In her memoir Too Close to the Falls, *Catherine Gildiner, a well-known Toronto psychologist who also writes for* Chatelaine *magazine, describes growing up in the fifties in Lewiston, New York, just south of Niagara Falls. Gildiner, then Cathy McClure, had an unusual family life. Her book captures the quality of this life and the quality of small-town life in the fifties. In the chapter about her mother, Gildiner tells us that in her entire childhood, she never remembers her mother making a meal. In the following excerpt, she explains how her mother coped with one of the social demands of life in Lewiston.*

1　In those days, in Lewiston, at any rate, people didn't seem to make formal arrangements to visit one another; they simply dropped in unannounced. My mother had a system for such spontaneous occurrences. Whenever headlights hit the curtains of the picture window, we all had to drop to the floor in hopes that they hadn't already seen our shadows. When the company rang the doorbell, the dog would bark furiously, growling and biting the throw rug in the hail, shaking it mercilessly as though to warn the visitor what might happen to him. When Mother yelled, "Hit the floor!" we'd all lie prostrate until the caller gave up and left. Sometimes the more tenacious visitors would go around to the back door and we'd hear them say in a bewildered tone, "All the lights are on, or "The car's in the driveway." When they left, my mother would say, "Thank God," and my father and I shared her relief.

2　　A number of years later, the day after he died of a brain tumour, some robbers read about my father in the obituary section of the paper and broke into the house to steal things. The police who came to our house explained that this is a common scam because valuables are unattended and everyone is supposed to be at the funeral home at the times announced in the paper. My mother, who had returned home for her headache pills minutes before the robbers arrived, was, of course, well-hidden behind the couch by the time the robbers got in and she was never detected. She wrote down what each of them said, got their car licence number through a slit in the curtain, and was later able to identify all of them. The police were amazed she could have hidden so quickly and that she was so self-possessed. Little did they know she found them no more frightening than anyone else who may have dropped in.

3   Once in a while on the way home after Sunday mass and brunch, my father, the gregarious type, would suggest dropping in on some acquaintance, since we were already dressed in our Sunday best, but Mother would remind him that if we dropped in on them, then they would drop in on us, and it would be never-ending, and we'd have no one to blame but ourselves. She explained that one had to have refreshments for people when they dropped in, and we couldn't provide any. Seeing the wisdom of this, we drove home to pursue our individual interests. When my father, on rare occasions, suggested calling people and then going over to visit them, Mother said she'd like to go except that Willie, our dog, always chewed my father's electric blanket if we left him for more than an hour.

4   My mother and father invariably treated each other with politeness. They never contradicted each other and their mutual agreement never seemed strained or an uneasy compromise. (When my friends' parents disagreed mildly about when they should leave for their cottage, I was sure they were headed for a divorce.) I had never met anyone who was divorced; nuclear-family meltdown was still two decades away. The only people who got a divorce in the 1950s that I had even heard of were Debbie Reynolds and Eddie Fisher. Even that wasn't a real divorce; it was Hollywood filtered through *Silver Screen*. Liz Taylor stole Eddy while she was crazy with grief because her own husband, Mike Todd, died tragically in a plane crash. Poor Debbie was left to climb the walls with Donald O'Connor.

5   Father called Mother at three-thirty to see if she was enjoying her day and if I had gotten home from school safely. She routinely put on lipstick and changed her dress before my father came home and insisted that I put on a clean tee-shirt. Every time he walked in the door she acted relieved, as though he had returned from a dangerous journey.

Catherine Gildiner, *Too Close to the Falls* (Toronto: ECW Press, 1999), 65–67

Word Recognition

Find the following words in the reading and note how they are used.

> **spontaneous:** unplanned; on the spur of the moment
>
> **prostrate:** lying down flat; prone on the ground (never confuse with *prostate*, a gland found in male mammals—remember the *r* in prone and prostrate)

tenacious: refusing to give up; holding on firmly

bewildered: lost and confused

obituary: death notice in a newspaper

self-possessed: self-controlled; poised

gregarious: sociable; enjoying the company of other people

nuclear family: a father, a mother, and their children only. It is not a blended family, not a single parent family, not an extended family, but one small unit

Exercise 2.5

Match the words or expressions in Column A with the closest synonyms (words that have a similar meaning) or expressions in Column B. Note: There are more choices than necessary in Column B.

Column A
1. tenacious
2. dropping in on
3. an uneasy compromise
4. meltdown zone
5. routinely
6. in a bewildered tone
7. formal arrangements
8. spontaneous occurrences
9. brain tumour
10. mercilessly

Column B
a. sticking firmly to one's principles
b. an awkward, uncomfortable effort to reach an agreement acceptable to two different sides
c. a sudden mental lapse
d. without pity
e. in a regular way; as standard procedure
f. events organized by strict rules and conventions
g. a place of disaster; the overheated centre of a nuclear disaster
h. a complete disregard for social conventions or rules
i. sounding puzzled
j. events taking place on impulse; not planned
k. a neural cell causing fever and sudden red hair growth
l. visiting people without calling beforehand
m. a growth in the grey matter

Recall

Try to answer the following questions from memory.

1. What did the people in Lewiston in the fifties do when they wanted to see each other?

2. What happened in the McClure house when unexpected visitors rang the doorbell?

3. What bewildered some visitors after no one answered the door?

4. What did Willie do if they left him alone too long?

5. What happened on the day of the funeral for Catherine Gildiner's father?

6. What information was Mother able to give the police when the house was robbed?

7. What reasons did Mother give for not dropping in on other people?

8. How many divorced people did Gildiner know at that time?

9. What did Mother always do before her husband arrived home from work?

10. How did Mother react to her husband's homecoming each day?

Review

Answer the following questions.

1. Why did Mother yell, "Hit the floor!" when visitors rang the doorbell?

2. Why were the police amazed at Mother's self-possession after being robbed?

3. Why was her daughter not amazed?

4. "Seeing the wisdom of this, we drove home to pursue our individual interests." What does this statement mean? What does it show about the family?

5. How do you know that Catherine Gildiner's mother and father were quite different in their personalities?

6. Gildiner's parents always treated each other with courtesy and respect. How do you know?

7. Was divorce common in the fifties? What was Gildiner's approach to divorce at that time?

8. What made Gildiner sure people were headed for divorce? Why?

9. ". . . it was Hollywood filtered through *Silver Screen*." The italics show that *Silver Screen* is a title. What might it be the title of? What does Gildiner mean by this statement?

10. What does Mother's behaviour towards her husband show about her and her attitude to marriage?

Response

The following topics are for collaborative or individual writing assignments. Respond to *one or more*. Where possible, try to use names and details from popular culture as well as your own experience to support your points.

Topics

1. Complete the sentence and then support the points you make with specific evidence. Note: You do not have to write about your real family.

    "Coming from a family like mine, a family of _____, means that I will never forget_____."

    In the first part of the sentence, briefly establish the kind of family you mean here—it could be of a particular ethnic or religious background; it could be a family of bikers, actors, musicians, fisherfolk, beauty queens, social activists, or kind-hearted, sensitive men and women. In the second part of the sentence, describe an attitude to visitors, a particular event, food, anything you like.

2. Catherine Gildiner's mother created a particular atmosphere in her household. How would you describe the household from the evidence given here? What do you think of this atmosphere? Explain with reasons.

3. Gildiner says that as a child she had never met anyone who was divorced. Few school-age children could say this today.

    What do you think of today's attitude to divorce, compared with earlier attitudes? Do you think people are more realistic, or happier these days? Why? Give reasons and references in your answer. Use evidence from your own observations as much as possible.

By now you have been taken into many different worlds and many different experiences. Each reading though, no matter whether from a *Titanic* survivor in New York, the Southern United States, Australia, Spain during the Spanish Civil War, or Lewiston, New York in the fifties has one purpose: to make an experience clear to a reader. Each writer's style and story is quite different. As you read, think about how the writer talks to you with a particular voice, with a subjective tone.

REVIEW AND REMEMBER

Context and Comprehension
Subjective and Objective

1. Active readers are aware that writers have a purpose and an audience.

2. Active readers use context clues to help them predict the meaning of unfamiliar words.

3. Active readers know when writers are downplaying the personal and being **objective.** They know when and how to focus on the objective in their own responses to events.

4. Active readers know when writers are using personal judgments, emotions, or beliefs, and are being **subjective.** They know when to be subjective in their own writing.

CHAPTER 3

Vital Information and Vital Language

This chapter has four readings for comprehension, analysis, and response.

By the end of this chapter, you will be able to

- demonstrate stronger critical thinking skills

- focus on key ideas and write summaries to show comprehension skills

- recognize and use figurative language

- connect more easily with the minds and hearts of other people from other times through their writing

Are you now an active reader? How are your reading habits? When you are asked to read material at college, no matter what the subject, do you always follow the Active Reader Program? Do you follow these steps?

1. Note the title and writer.

2. Note any biographical data given, observing when and where the writer lives or lived, for example.

3. Read the introductory section more than once.

4. Note how unfamiliar words are used and try to guess them from context before using a dictionary.

5. Use a dictionary to discover the meanings of words or expressions you cannot guess from context.

6. Re-read the assigned reading, noting how unfamiliar words are used.

7. Think about your reaction to the ideas and information in the material.

8. Note any specific data used to support key ideas.

9. Review the assigned reading before class.

Or do you follow the P3SE Formula? Are you in the habit of predicting what a passage is about, of skimming, scanning, specifying, and then evaluating it? Do you regularly think about the writer's *purpose* and the *audience* the writing is intended to reach?

Reading for study is quite different from reading for pleasure. Both are important and both can be enjoyable, but the neural exercise is different in each case. The reading you do at college is to analyze ideas or extract information. Sometimes you are asked to summarize a reading. Then you have to restate the information briefly in your own words and present it coherently.

Summary Writing: Focusing on the Essential

What is a *summary*?

A summary is a shorter version of something. It contains essential data only. A summary has no opinions of your own and is concise. Being able to summarize is an important skill because it shows that you

• have grasped the key ideas of a reading or event

- know what is essential to communicate

- can use your own words, and not rely on those of others

- can communicate clearly, correctly, and coherently

When someone summarizes something, choices have to be made. The main idea has to be determined. Unimportant data has to be deleted. Therefore, the person summarizing has to decide what is important and what can be omitted. That decision can be very influential.

News writers, health professionals, scientists, engineers, travel writers, professors, and managers are a few of the people who have to be able to summarize. They have to decide what to include and what to omit in news bulletins, medical reports, community service records, business reports, lectures, and such. Their ideas of what is important can have consequences. Their choices can affect lives and attitudes.

There's too much information out there for many people. The ability to focus on essentials and make them plain to others is part of most jobs. A professional has to be able to zoom in on essentials, to understand the substance, not just notice the style. That's why it's important to develop your summarizing skills at college.

To write a good summary, you must first understand what you have read and then synthesize the information. *Synthesize* means to combine the most important points and present them in a coherent statement.

First, develop good reading habits. Analytical reading is essential for writing good summaries. Then follow the suggestions in the Steps to Success box. You will discover that summary writing is easier than you think.

STEPS TO SUCCESS

How to Write a Good Summary

A summary is a much shorter version of the original material, written in your own words. A summary *does not* reveal your feelings about the subject matter.

Pre-writing

1. Read the passage to be summarized at least two times.

2. Note the title, the writer, and the key point in any introductory material given on rough paper.

3. Ask yourself what the passage is about. Find the central point. It will usually be indicated in the opening section, but may not be stated directly. Write what you think it is in one sentence, in your own words on rough paper.

4. What are the words, expressions, or concepts that occur most? Underline them.

5. List key details supporting the central idea of the passage.

6. Re-read the introduction and the conclusion.

7. Without looking at it, ask yourself again what you remember about the passage. Jot down two or three points you remember. Compare them with your previous notes.

Writing

1. Introduce your summary by citing the writer and, if possible, the title of the passage. If you have the space and it seems important, mention briefly where the information comes from.

2. State clearly and briefly what the passage is about in one sentence.

3. Put away the original and write your summary from your notes.

4. Avoid using most of the examples, illustrations, or lively details used by the writer. Keep to the main points only.

5. Use your own words.

6. Keep to the present tense.

7. Avoid any mention of your feelings about the subject.

8. Keep to the order of the original as much as possible.

9. Avoid unnecessary words or expressions. Be economical with your words.

10. Conclude briefly, reinforcing the writer's conclusion.

Post-writing

1. Have you told readers who the writer is and what the subject of the passage is?

2. Do you need to mention any location, setting, or time period?

3. Have you used the present tense?

4. Have you begun and concluded clearly?

5. Is your summary short?

6. Have you mostly used your own words? (No direct quotes are permitted.)

7. Does your summary make sense? Is it coherent?

Summary Writing Exercise

Choose *three* of the readings in Chapter 1. Follow the How to Write a Good Summary steps, and write a one-sentence summary for each. Decide what is most essential before you begin writing. Share your summaries with a partner. Decide which sentences cover the readings most clearly.

READING 1

On the Line

by Solange De Santis

Solange De Santis, a journalist, took a job installing insulation panels at a dying General Motors van plant near Toronto. She took the job to find out what life on an assembly line was really like. Her 18 months of research and investigation were painful and demanding, but she discovered a lot about working with fibreglass, and about herself. In this excerpt from her book about the experience, Life on the Line, *she describes her first day alone on the job.*

1   "Hi, Sally!" My first day on the line it seemed I had become Sally. I liked that; it sounded jaunty. Rosie the Riveter, meet Sally the Autoworker. Sally was a calmly efficient factory worker, who probably bounced around in a ponytail or wore a long braid down her back. She certainly wasn't this awkward 36-year-old journalist who kept her dark-brown hair in a short, wash-and-run cut, an introvert by nature with a tendency to gain weight, who would be happy to spend all her life reading books.

2   My trainer, Caitlin, suggested I watch her first, so I sat cross-legged on a pile of boxes next to the worktable as she carried two panels of stiff material—fibreglass insulation for the engine compartment—over to a van moving slowly down the line. She bent over the front, whisked one piece in, then the other, and secured them with a big black clip. Caitlin then grabbed a black plastic vent, leaned into the van on the driver's side and secured it into the dashboard base with a clip and a screw. She then changed bits on the drill gun and affixed three screws that secured a piece of plastic to the metal of the engine compartment. The job looked impossibly complicated.

3   We decided that I'd do insulation only for the next 10 vans (everybody called them trucks, I soon learned), while she took care of the vent-screw combination. Caitlin waltzed along, zapping vents in trucks, strolling back to the worktable to read The Toronto Sun. I never stopped. As soon as I finished wrestling with one set of insulation/clip, it was time for the next.

4   I was stiff, clumsy and completely out of my element. I fantasized that at any moment a couple of General Motors of Canada officials would materialize. "Yup, that's her, all right." "OK, we found you; the jig's up. Come with us." Other workers would gather, forgetting their jobs. An official would turn to them. "Impostor. White-collar worker. Third one this week."

5   My second day with Caitlin went much like the first. I discovered fibreglass was a bitch to handle. It stung; the glass fibres were stuck on my hands; they snuck up my nose. My jeans and sweatshirt were covered with it. I hated to put on my jacket, because that would press the fibres into my skin as I sat in the car. I couldn't wait to get home and strip off the filthy garments.

6   On the third day, I arrived about 15 minutes early and learned I'd be on my own, without Caitlin. The body shop had started a half-hour before us, at 6:30 a.m. Across the aisle, the 13 huge welding robots swung into action. Bang! Bam-boom-chukka-bang-boom! Bang! Bam-boom-chukka-bang-boom!

7   Our part of the line started and the vans began their stately procession. I went over to the stack of boxes, picked up a black plastic vent and shoved it into the plastic base of what would become the dashboard. I reached into my apron, grabbed a little clip, got the gun and took a screw out of the apron. Zap, I secured the vent. Then I changed bits on the gun and fumbled for three screws. Placed a screw on the gun bit, leaned in and screwed it into a hole in the plastic. One, two, three. Oops, the third one was tough. I used both hands to push it in and heard the grinding sound that meant it'd gone through the metal. One job done.

8   The van was at the end of my job station. Time for the next one. Insulation, clip. Vent, clip, screw. Screw, screw, screw. Insulation, clip. Vent, clip, screw. Screw, screw, screw. I struggled with each part of the job, always keeping my eye on the pillar marked D22—the end of my job station. I was supposed to get the job done between D21 and D22, which had a parts list affixed to it with funereal black tape. Rats! The panels wouldn't fit in the next one. Something seemed stuck. I was draped over the front of the truck, stepping backward, trying to get this itchy fibreglass thing into position and it just wouldn't go. Damn, damn, damn, the Pillar of Doom was looming. I was breaking out in panic sweat. I would just have to leave the edge sticking out like that. I supposed somebody would see it and fix it if our repairman missed it. I hustled around to the side, grabbed a vent and dropped a screw. Oh, jeez, almost up to the pillar. Changed the bit, now the three screws. I grabbed five, dropped a couple. None of them went in easily, and I had to use two hands on all. I was a step or two past the pillar, and the next job was more than halfway through my job station.

9   Jesus, it was hot. I kept falling behind. The insulation was awkward, I missed the big-clip bracket and lost precious seconds feeling for it, dropped screws, dropped the little clips. The more perspiration ran down my face,

the more nasty, yellow fibreglass wisps stuck to me. They were embedded in my rough-weave white cotton gloves, jeans and T-shirt.

10   Balthasar, our genial Hispanic repairman, came along to see why so many of my screws were loose when they arrived at his workstation, midway through the Trim 2 department.

11   "Hey, sweetheart, what's the matter here? You don't like doing the screws?"

12   "No, well, I don't know, Balthasar, maybe the holes aren't lined up."

13   "Uh-huh. Hey, George." He motioned to a fellow who didn't seem to have anything to do. "Help Sally with these screws. She's not strong enough."

14   Oh. But that couldn't be it. Nobody could be strong enough to push those things through metal. George grabbed a vent and the gun, secured it and then started the three screws. Crunch, crunch, crunch, in they went. I didn't believe it. What was the secret?

15   After lunch came the hump—two hours until second break. It seemed like an eternity. For the first two hours of the day I was relatively fresh, but these were bastards. My arms were sore, my chest bone was bruised and my legs felt like wobbly plant stems. Tightening those screws was such an effort that I was grunting with nearly each one. Sweating like a pig again too, even with the fan on. Insulation, clip. Vent, clip, screw. Screw, screw, screw.

16   I was determined not to get help. It was embarrassing enough having to grunt and struggle over nearly every job while everyone else seemed so competent. I was going to gut this thing out myself I knew it would end at 3:30 p.m. I just had to keep going, going. But God, I wanted to sit down so badly and there was just no letup. I tried to bargain with it. "C'mon, line, one little stop, OK? How about it? Just stop. Stop, please stop. One minute, all right? I just need a minute to sit down. Stop, for Christ's sake, stop." I had taken off my watch and put it on the worktable. For one thing, the glass fibres worked under the watchband and stung like crazy. For another, I just didn't want the temptation of looking at it every two minutes.

17   Gotta keep going, gotta keep going. My arms and chest were so sore now that sometimes my eyes filled with tears when I was bent over the front of the van. But I figured it was OK, nobody could see, since I had my head under the hood.

18   I kept checking my watch. One o'clock. One-fifteen. One-twenty. Only five more jobs. One-thirty I was behind, as usual, so I was still working when the line stopped for second break. I finished the job and dragged over to my throne of boxes. I did not look at a newspaper or book. I just sat. No sooner had I sat down than the line started again—that's how fast the 23 minutes seemed to fly. My feet ached and I was making my body move by sheer willpower. "Running on fumes" took on a whole new meaning. Everything hurt, but I picked up insulation panels, affixed clips and strug-

gled with the demon screws. My eyes glazed. I couldn't talk; I couldn't think. I could only will myself to move.

19   Final half-hour. Just 30 minutes, 15 jobs to go. I worked away, determined to get through. At last the line stopped. I finished the last job half a minute or so past 3:30 and that was it. I stripped off the fibreglass-encrusted gloves and dropped them in the garbage.

20   My aching legs were definitely not attached to my body; they were stomping through the plant by some other motor. I walked through the back gate and found my brown Ford Tempo. I unlocked the door and creakily lowered myself into the driver's seat, shaking with fatigue. I could barely grip the steering wheel. Shifting gears was painful. As I pulled onto the Don Valley Parkway, I sobbed from exhaustion. "I don't know how I can do this; it's just too hard," I wept.

21   Next morning I crossed the parking lot at 6:40 a.m., unwilling to believe I was going to submit again to this torture. A woman I vaguely recognized said hi and asked how I was doing.

22   "Well, yesterday was my first day alone on a job and it was pretty rough. I was so beat I burst into tears on the way home," I admitted sheepishly.

23   "Oh, are you kidding?" she exclaimed. "My husband cried after his first day. Don't worry, everybody cries."

Solange De Santis, "On the Line," *Chatelaine,* June 1999, 67–70. From *Life on the Line: One Woman's Tale of Work, Sweat and Survival* by Solange De Santis (Doubleday, 1999). Reprinted with permission.

Word Recognition

Solange De Santis often uses slang in this reading. Slang is the language everyone hears on television sitcoms, in the malls, on the streets, and in the parking lot. It is cool language, but it is not standard English. The fashionable words of slang change frequently and are very impermanent.

You would not use slang for writing on the job. Slang has no place in reports or letters. It may occasionally be used in essays and articles if the context seems to demand a sense of being up-to-date and hip. The subject matter determines whether the use of slang is appropriate. De Santis uses slang here mostly in reporting the speech of the people at the plant, or at other times, to convey a sense of being extra alert, sharp, and on-the-ball.

Vocabulary

Rosie the Riveter (para. 1): a poster girl auto-worker used in World War II to encourage women to work in factories while men were away fighting

materialize (para. 4): become visible; able to be seen

the jig's up (slang) (para. 4): the game is up; someone's been found out; the joke is discovered

impostor (para. 4): a person pretending to be someone else

zap (slang) (para. 7): attack; hit

funereal (para. 8): dark and dismal (pronounced with the stress on the second syllable, funEARreal)

genial (para. 10): kind and cheerful; warm

the hump (slang) (para. 15): the worst part (as in *over the hump*)

competent (para. 16): having the ability to do what is needed for the job

stomping (para. 20): walking or dancing with heavy steps

Exercise 3.1

Dictate *five* of the following words and *three* of the following sentences to a partner. Compare your answers. Check punctuation as well as spelling.

1. bruised	6. sheepishly
2. competent	7. stately procession
3. insulation	8. affixed to it
4. no letup	9. funereal black tape
5. sheer willpower	10. genial

1.   She bent over the front, whisked one piece in.

2.   Impostor. White-collar worker.

3.   So many of my screws were loose.

4.   I didn't believe it.

5.   The panels wouldn't fit in the next one.

6.   George grabbed a vent and the gun.

7. I couldn't wait to get home and strip off the filthy garments.

8. The job looked impossibly complicated.

Recall

Try to answer the following questions from memory.

1. Who wrote "On the Line," and what is her usual job?

2. Who is Sally the Autoworker?

3. What did De Santis first watch Caitlin do?

4. What tools did Caitlin use?

5. What did De Santis discover on her second day? (Use your own words in your answer.)

6. What did De Santis wear to work?

7. What was "the hump" after lunch?

8. Name three parts of the body mentioned by De Santis. Why did she mention them?

9. What did De Santis throw in the garbage at the end of her shift?

10. What did De Santis learn from the woman in the parking lot?

Review

Answer the following questions.

1. What exactly was Solange De Santis doing? Explain in one sentence.

2. Describe how De Santis felt at the beginning, in three to four words. What images did she use to describe how she felt?

3. Why did De Santis call pillar D22 "the Pillar of Doom"?

4. Why did De Santis take off her watch?

5. How did De Santis spend her break on her first day alone on the job?

6. What are the three activities that made De Santis' eyes glaze?

7. Why did De Santis later say her "legs were definitely not attached to [her] body"?

8. How did De Santis feel as she pulled onto the Don Valley Parkway?

9. How did De Santis feel the next morning as she crossed the parking lot?

10. What is the effect of the comment made by the woman in the parking lot at the end of this reading? What does it make you realize?

Summary Writing Exercise

In three to five sentences, summarize what this reading is about.
Include the following information in your summary:

1. the name of the writer and the title of her book

2. the name of the place where the writer worked on the line

3. the name of the tools the writer used and the material she worked with

4. the writer's feelings during and after the first day

Response

In small groups, discuss horrible jobs you have had. Describe what it was like the first day on the job. Jot down any experiences or details from the discussion that you find interesting, shocking, or moving.

Now prepare one of the following reports or presentations making use of this material. This will be a combined effort. Make creative use of each other's experiences, but write or speak about one generic experience in your response.

1. Prepare a description of a bad first day at a job.

    • Make clear the location.

    • Make clear what you were expected to do.

    • Establish a time frame.

    • Describe your feelings (try to use images).

    • End with a comment from a co-worker.

2. Prepare some suggestions and advice for a new worker at a particular job.

    • Make clear the location.

- Make clear what activities are expected.

- Keep your material chronological.

- Include advice about activities on breaks.

- Indicate causes of stress.

- End on a positive note.

3. Describe what you learned about yourselves from jobs that were physically demanding, or jobs you hated. Be selective in your choice of details to support your descriptions.

- Describe briefly some of the surroundings you worked in.

- Describe exactly what your tasks were.

- Describe in detail your physical response to the work.

- Compare how co-workers handled the demands.

- Examine your psychological state and what you learned about yourself.

- Conclude with a comment on what you can learn about yourself from such an experience.

 READING 2

Resolving a Weighty Matter

by Deborah King

Deborah King is an editor at The Globe and Mail. *She writes that if she were an alcoholic or drug addict, there would be programs to help her, but compulsive overeating can be equally dangerous. Now it's time to look at the issues she's tried to smother with food.*

1 I cannot remember a time when I did not think I was fat.

2 Yet, for almost half of my 44 years, family photos prove that I was of "normal" weight.

3 As I begin another attempt to beat the yo-yo dieting cycle that has helped to qualify me for the medical term "morbidly obese," I realize that the battle must be fought on more than one front—not just physical, but emotional and mental.

4   I have the disorder known as compulsive overeating. It's less well-known than its cousins, bulimia and anorexia, but just as deadly. The difference is that sufferers don't purge the food they binge on, or starve themselves into walking skeletons. We just binge—when we're tired, angry, happy, frustrated, bored, stressed, sad, anxious.

5   And it shows in the fat our bodies amass.

6   My earliest memory of hating my body size dates from the age of 10. I tried on skirts before school in the morning and judged in the bathroom-door mirror whether they made me look fat from the back or not. The ones that I thought did went back in the closet.

7   I had a horror of looking fat. I can come up with two hypotheses for this. One was that a girl in my grade 5 class was teased and rejected by many kids for being overweight. With the cruelty of children, we put Xs on our hands in ink to protect us from "fleas" in case she accidently touched us. As we grew older, the shunning became more sophisticated: Tales were told that she was "fast" with boys and let them take liberties.

8   The other possibility lies in sibling rivalry. I am the eldest of four sisters, but it was the one closest in age to me that I wanted to be like. She was considered dainty, delicate, pretty. I was the clever one, who got glowing comments from teachers on report cards full of top marks.

9   But I wanted to be the pretty one. When strangers marvelled at how I looked like my father, I would retort, "But I don't smile like him."

10   I can remember someone telling my mother when I was about eight that my sister, who was then six, would one day be able to wrap boys around her little finger, and I felt horribly jealous.

11   Perhaps my conviction that my body was too big began then. In my teens, I tried every fad diet I could. Forget that I looked fine in a size -10 or size - 12 pair of pants. I wanted to be a size 5 like my sister. So, there was the hard-boiled egg diet, the one-meal-a-day diet, the banana diet, the fruit diet, the vegetable diet, the protein diet. Being told I was attractive wasn't enough—I wanted to be beautiful.

12   I got myself down to just above 100 pounds (I'm five foot) and thought I looked wonderful. Of course, I often felt dizzy or hungry, but you can't have everything. Then my boyfriend at the time casually told me, after I had spent weeks starving myself, that I'd never have the perfect body for a bikini. So I ate a chocolate cake as a show of defiance. Instead of dumping him, I spent months alternately trying to be what I thought he wanted and binge-eating to muzzle my emotions.

13   We broke up a year later because, irony of ironies, he thought he'd like to date my sister.

14   That declaration sent me into depression that turned my small binges into large ones. I was away at university, and any spare change I could scrape together went for junk food, lots of it.

15   I hoarded food and ate in secret, when my roommate was out. I skipped classes and began to withdraw from campus social life. I switched schools, changed courses and moved home in a desperate search for happiness.

16   It wasn't until my final year of journalism school, in 1976, that I was able to drop the pounds I'd packed on. The only problem was, I did it by a form of starvation diet until I had lost 40 pounds over the summer.

17   Now the cycle had me in its grasp. Over the years and through the tribulations of marriage, career, children and family finances, I lost and regained weight depending on whether I was eating to avoid things in my life or desperately dieting to try to make things better. I hated how I looked but couldn't break free of my addiction to food and my despair that, even at my so-called ideal weight, I would never be pretty enough. I tried Weight Watchers and Overeaters Anonymous. For a while, they helped, but they were not enough.

18   Now, I begin the fight again. This time, I carry additional baggage—not only more than 150 pounds to lose, but the burden of adult-onset diabetes. The disease, which some are calling an epidemic among baby boomers, is the result of my weight, and that makes me feel guilty. And the guilt extends to my husband and children, whom I feel I have let down—despite their constant support—through all the energy, time and money I have spent on my weight problem.

19   But I do have some hard-won knowledge to help me. I know I can't do it alone and need professional counselling. If I were an alcoholic or drug addict, there would be many programs to help. Eating disorders lag behind in this area. And any treatments or programs that do exist can be expensive. Company health plans, including mine, provide financial help for treating alcohol and drug abuse, but not eating disorders.

20   I also know I must deal with issues in my life that I have tried to smother with food. I have to confront my demons and learn to accept myself for who and what I am, not for who I might have wanted to be. And I know I will need patience, both in terms of time and how I treat myself.

21   This time, I don't want to fall into the same holes on the same path. I'm finally going to try a new route. And I'm going to have help reading the map.

Deborah King, "Resolving a Weighty Matter," The Globe and Mail, 19 May 1998, A20

Vocabulary

morbid (para. 3): indicating disease; psychologically unhealthy interest in unpleasant things

purge (para. 4): empty the bowels; get rid of

amass (para. 5): heap up; collect

hypotheses (para. 7): possibilities to investigate; statements or ideas to be proved; suggestions made as a basis for reasoning

shunning (para. 7): avoiding; keeping away from

take liberties (para. 7): indulge in improper behaviour

muzzle (para. 12): keep under control; stop something

irony (para. 13): the opposite of what is expected

tribulation (para. 17): something causing pain, misery

confront (para. 20): come face to face with; examine closely

Figurative Language, or Language with Life

Deborah King's sister "would one day be able to wrap boys around her little finger."

Deborah King spent months binge-eating "to muzzle" her emotions.

Now she doesn't "want to fall into the same holes on the same path."

She is "finally . . . going to have help reading the map."

Could Deborah King's sister really pick boys up and twist them? Did King wear straps or wires over her head to stop feeling depressed? Is she walking on a dangerous path? What map is she reading?

Readers know that King is not speaking *literally* when she uses the expressions quoted above. They know she is not using the words in their most basic sense, but instead, is creating pictures. In these statements, she is using words imaginatively, or *figuratively.*

If writers wish to make something clear and vivid to their readers, they will often create a picture for us, a picture in words. They appeal to our sense of sight. They can also appeal to our other senses: sound, touch, smell, taste. Writers using imaginative comparisons and going beyond plain, straightforward statements are using figurative language. Figurative language captures the imagination and usually leaves readers with a clearer sense of what is being discussed, more than a simple matter-of-fact explanation will. Try to make some imaginative comparisons in your own writing.

Look for figurative language in your reading. This language includes imagery, metaphor, simile, allusion, and personification. These figures of speech allow readers to read more perceptively.

FIGURES OF SPEECH

Imagery—Writing that appeals to our senses by creating pictures in our minds or recalling sounds and smells. It is evocative language, calling up memories and feelings.

". . . her voice sweet and hard, like new strawberries . . ." (*Toni Morrison*)

"A mountain of flesh, she lay rather than sat in a rocking chair." (*Toni Morrison*)

With all the cobwebs and glass ceilings in corporate offices, many women decide not to compete for top jobs.

We have forged a great alliance between our countries.

Metaphor—A comparison between two things without using the words *like* or *as*. It can be used for longer comparisons or life situations. For example, writer Susan Sontag has described cancer as a metaphor.

"The road was a ribbon of moonlight . . ." *(Alfred Noyes)*

"My love is a red, red rose . . ." *(Robert Burns)*

You don't have to swallow this propaganda.

Simile—A comparison, using the words *like* or *as*.

He was like a tiger in battle.

The very word is like a bell.

My love is like a red, red rose.

Note: The word *like* when used in everyday speech, especially by teenagers, does not usually introduce a simile.

NOT a simile: She went, like, you know, a bit crazy.

A simile: She went out like a possessed witch.

Allusion—A reference to some well-known person, place, or thing.

Where is your Romeo tonight?

She's so flaky, we call her Lucy in the Sky with Diamonds.

Personification—A comparison of inanimate objects to people in some way.

His car is allergic to her perfume. Whenever she is in it, it coughs and dies.

Exercise 3.2

With a partner, complete the following sentences using imaginative comparisons.

1. When she heard she had won, her eyes _____.

2. The red light on the police cruiser seemed _____.

3. He doesn't think that there is just a gap between men and women. He thinks _____.

4. A true leader will always act _____.

5. The struggle against this disease is _____.

6. The selection process serves as a kind of _____.

7. These people try to make lies sound like truth and murder

    _____.

8. Developing positive images of themselves involves telling children they are _____.

9. If a boy acts like _____, he is called _____.

10. If a girl acts like _____, she is called _____.

Exercise 3.3*

Choose the correct word in its appropriate form for each of the following sentences. All words are taken from the reading.

amass	dainty	rivalry
binge	epidemic	shun
confront	fad	
conviction	hypotheses	

1. Sexy, sparkling, and always dazzling, J. L. is _____ a fortune from her movies and albums.

2. When Cheney was _____ by her roommate's friends, and they refused even to look at her at the party, she knew that her roommate had been spreading lies about her sexual preferences.

3. Lotta Chin is not afraid to _____ opposing forces in design and will show everyone in New York that Canadian designers have great ideas.

4. The daycare centre was closed when many of the children broke out with spots because everyone was afraid of an _____ of chicken pox.

5. Jennifer Lo thinks that having sparkling-silver page boys at a wedding is just a silly _____ and won't last.

6. Because she spends so much time trying to outdo her sister, Judy visited a psychiatrist to learn how to handle the _____ that poisons their relationship.

7. His _____ that his lifestyle was causing his heart palpitations made Laurence give up booze and cigarettes.

8. When performing scientific experiments, it is important to begin with _____.

9. Eating disorders are often associated with the need to _____ and purge.

10. The tiny skirt and over-the-knee boots made Molly look very small, feminine, and _____, even though she was trying to look tall, strong, and gender-bending.

Recall

Try to answer the following questions from memory. Answer in complete sentences, if writing.

1. For how many years have family photos shown Deborah King that she was of normal weight?

2. What do compulsive overeaters do? Why?

3. What are two possible reasons for King's horror of looking fat? Explain the one involving a sibling.

4. What is involved in the practice of shunning and why does King refer to it here?

5. From memory, list four of the diets King tried in her efforts to become a size 5.

6. What declaration made King depressed?

7. What does King mean when she says, "Now the cycle had me in its grasp."?

8. What disease is now considered to be an epidemic? For which group of people in particular?

9. How do eating disorders lag behind alcoholism and drug addiction in health care?

10. What demons must King confront in her attempts to deal with her weight?

Review

Answer the following questions.

1. Why does Deborah King now say that she must fight her battle for weight control on emotional and mental fronts, as well as physical?

2. Why do compulsive overeaters binge? Give King's views and say if you agree or disagree and why.

3. Why did King try every fad diet she could as a teenager?

4. What sort of behaviour did King indulge in at university? Name at least four specific actions.

5. How did King's addiction affect her life once she was married? Explain.

6. In two or three sentences, sum up what King's problem is.

7. Why does King feel guilty now?

8. What does King feel she needs now?

9. "And I'm going to have help reading the map." What does King mean here?

10. Write two sentences defining an eating disorder.

Response

This exercise may be done individually, in pairs, or in small groups. Respond to *one* of the topics listed below in 20 to 30 minutes.

A. Introduce your response, as Deborah King does, with one sentence, a startling statement.

B. Use at least three of the following supporting details:

- an example from the past—elementary school or a family occasion
- a quotation from an expert in the field
- a statistic from a credible-sounding source
- an anecdote about a sibling
- a comment from a boyfriend or girlfriend
- a reference to King's essay

C. End with a metaphor of some kind.

Topics

1. A dangerous response to stress, I/we have observed

2. The strain of having a beautiful/handsome sibling

3. The guilt of an addict

4. Adult-onset diabetes

5. Company health plans—why they should offer support to smokers or compulsive eaters

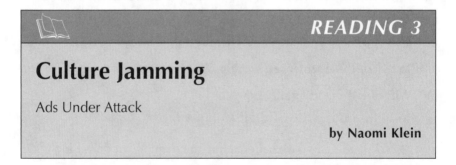

READING 3

Culture Jamming

Ads Under Attack

by Naomi Klein

This excerpt is taken from Naomi Klein's book No Logo. *It is about the economic gaps and cultural divides present in today's global village. Throughout the book she follows her grandfather's advice: "Always look for the dirt behind the shine." In doing so, she exposes the marketing of cool, the brand-bombing, and the brand-based politics that have lead to the rise of anti-corporate activism in many affluent countries.* No Logo *has been a best-seller in Canada, the United States, Britain, and Australia. Naomi Klein lives in Toronto.*

1   It's Sunday morning on the edge of New York's Alphabet City and Jorge Rodriguez de Gerada is perched at the top of a high ladder, ripping the paper off a cigarette billboard. Moments before, the billboard at the corner of Houston and Attorney sported a fun-loving Newport couple jostling over a pretzel. Now it showcases the haunting face of a child, which Rodriguez de Gerada has painted in rust. To finish it off, he pastes up a few hand-torn strips of the old Newport ad, which form a fluorescent green frame around the child's face.

2   When it's done, the installation looks as the thirty-one-year-old artist had intended: as if years of cigarette, beer and car ads had been scraped away to reveal the rusted backing of the billboard. Burned into the metal is the real commodity of the advertising transaction. "After the ads are taken down," he says, "what is left is the impact on the children in the area, staring at these images."

3   Unlike some of the growing legion of New York guerrilla artists, Rodriguez de Gerada refuses to slink around at night like a vandal, choosing instead to make his statements in broad daylight. For that matter, he doesn't much like the phrase "guerrilla art," preferring "citizen art" instead. He wants the dialogue he has been having with the city's billboards for more than ten years to be seen as a normal mode of discourse in a democratic society—not as some edgy vanguard act. While he paints and pastes, he wants kids to stop and watch—as they do on this sunny day, just as an old man offers to help support the ladder.

4   Rodriguez de Gerada even claims to have talked cops out of arresting him on three different occasions. "I say, 'Look, look what's around here, look what's happening. Let me explain to you why I do it.'" He tells the police officer about how poor neighborhoods have a disproportionately high number of billboards selling tobacco and hard liquor products. He talks about how these ads always feature models sailing, skiing or playing golf, making the addictive products they promote particularly glamorous to kids stuck in the ghetto, longing for escape. Unlike the advertisers who pitch and run, he wants his work to be part of a community discussion about the politics of public space.

5   Rodriguez de Gerada is widely recognized as one of the most skilled and creative founders of culture jamming, the practice of parodying advertisements and hijacking billboards in order to drastically alter their messages. Streets are public spaces, adbusters argue, and since most residents can't afford to counter corporate messages by purchasing their own ads, they should have the right to talk back to images they never asked to see. In recent years, this argument has been bolstered by advertising's mounting aggressiveness in the public domain—the ads discussed in "No Space," painted and projected onto sidewalks; reaching around entire buildings and

buses; into schools; onto basketball courts and on the Internet. At the same time, as discussed in "No Choice," the proliferation of the quasi-public "town squares" of malls and superstores has created more and more spaces where commercial messages are the only ones permitted. Adding even greater urgency to their cause is the belief among many jammers that concentration of media ownership has successfully devalued the right to free speech by severing it from the right to be heard.

6   All at once, these forces are coalescing to create a climate of semiotic Robin Hoodism. A growing number of activists believe the time has come for the public to stop asking that some space be left unsponsored, and to begin seizing it back. Culture jamming baldly rejects the idea that marketing—because it buys its way into our public spaces—must be passively accepted as a one-way information flow.

Note: Before looking up unfamiliar words in the Vocabulary or in a dictionary, try to guess what they mean from their location. Some words, like semiotic, *are almost impossible to guess, however. Occasionally Naomi Klein's vocabulary is very sophisticated and fashionable. If you learn the meanings of some of the terms she uses and become aware of them, you will probably notice them all around you in the* discourse *of everyday life; in other words, in the normal mode of discourse.*

Vocabulary

commodity (para. 2): a product; anything that can be used for trade or commercial gain

transaction (para. 2): piece of business

legion (para. 3) a large number of people; originally a large unit of soldiers in the Roman army

guerrilla (para. 3): a member of an independent small revolutionary group fighting for a cause against a larger, more powerful group

dialogue (para. 3): discussion

mode (para. 3): the way something is done

discourse (para. 3): the language used in a particular system of thinking, or particular social institution; the way things in a particular area are talked about

vanguard (para. 3): the leader of a movement; the people out in front; **an edgy vanguard act:** sharp and trendy behaviour; actions giving people a jolt and waking them up

disproportionately (para. 4): out of proportion (*dis*- indicates a negative, a rejection, or a reversal)

culture jamming (para. 5): changing and reworking advertisements or other social messages to make people think more about what they stand for; making people conscious of corporate strategies by mocking them; making people think about where goods are assembled, how the workers are treated, and how they are marketed

parodying (para. 5): making fun of a style or a work; laughing at something like a work of art, a poem, through an amusing imitation

adbusters (para. 5): culture jammers who mock advertisements; people who make fun of an ad—they try to shake up the corporations behind it and make people think about the culture it implies (*Adbusters* is a popular magazine founded by advertising executives based in Vancouver. It aims at making people aware of the role the world of advertising plays in our lives)

to counter (para. 5): to contradict; offer opposition to

bolster (para. 5): offer support

domain (para. 5): area of influence; field of thought or activity

proliferation (para. 5): rapid growth; multiplication

quasi- (para. 5): almost; seeming to be

severing (para. 5): cutting off

coalescing (para. 6): growing together to form one group

semiotic (para. 6): involving signs and symbols; producing meaning through signs. Semiotics is the study of signs, how they are used, and how they produce a particular effect in everything around us, such as advertising, movies, fashion, even cooking and doorways

semiotic Robin Hoodism (para. 6): taking from the rich and giving to the poor through the use of adbusting; using the signs and symbols of the advertising world to create awareness of inequalities

Word Recognition*

From the following list, choose the correct word form for each sentence below. Use appropriate verb forms and tenses, singulars or plurals, nouns, adjectives, or participles. Some words are used more than once.

concentrate	frame	haunt
edge	gorilla	jam
feature	guerrilla	politics

1. Hedwig is afraid that the apartment in Rexdale is _____ because he hears strange moaning noises and buzzing sounds early every morning.

2. Looking over the _____ of his balcony on the 19th floor makes Hedwig dizzy.

3. Nervously, Hedwig bit his lip and _____ towards the duckling stranded on the ledge.

4. If _____ studied the refugee children's faces with _____, they would never forget them, and would surely change their government's policies.

5. Good culture _____ tries to reveal the truth behind an advertising campaign.

6. The way you _____ a picture can add to its appeal.

7. A large fireplace was the one _____ our mother really wanted in her new house.

8. The endangered _____ was shot by mistake by the _____.

9. Pierre decided to go into _____ to work for peace, order, and good government in Canada.

10. In order to avoid a collision, Hedwig _____ on the brakes and skidded to a stop.

11. The convict insisted to his dying day that he had been _____ by members of a rival gang and unjustly accused.

12. Juice made from _____ never seems to taste as good, but it is lighter to carry home.

Exercise 3.4*

Match the words in Column A with the closest antonyms in Column B. Note: There are more words that have an opposite meaning/choices than necessary in Column B.

Column A	Column B
1. activist	a. wasteful
2. public	b. destructive
3. creative	c. totalitarian
4. aggressiveness	d. honour
5. democratic	e. pressure
6. vandal	f. expand
7. devalue	g. passive person
8. reject	h. accept
	i. calmness
	j. creator
	k. private

Recall

Try to answer the following questions from memory.

1. Who is Jorge Rodriguez de Gerada?

2. What was Rodriguez de Gerada doing to the billboard at the corner of Houston and Attorney?

3. What worries Rodriguez de Gerada about what is left after the ads are taken down?

4. What does Rodriguez de Gerada want people to do while he paints and pastes?

5. How often has Rodriguez de Gerada talked the cops out of arresting him?

6. What do poor neighbourhoods have too much of, according to Rodriguez de Gerada?

7. What right should most residents have, according to adbusters?

8. The ads found everywhere, on sidewalks, in schools, on buses, basketball courts, and the Internet, show us what about the advertising industry?

9. What effect is the concentration of media ownership having on free speech?

10. What do more activists think the public should do now?

Review

Answer the following questions.

1. Why does Naomi Klein begin by telling us about Jorge Rodriguez de Gerada and his actions?

2. Why does Rodriguez de Gerada prefer the term "citizen art" to "guerrilla art"?

3. How does Rodriguez de Gerada persuade cops not to arrest him?

4. What does Rodriguez de Gerada want the community to discuss? Why?

5. What does the expression "the politics of public space" mean?

6. Why are culture jammers called adbusters?

7. What sort of messages proliferate in the quasi-public squares of malls? Where else are such messages found more and more?

8. How would you describe the forces that are coming together to create a new attitude to marketing, to create what the writer calls "a climate of semiotic Robin Hoodism"?

9. What do these forces want people to do about public space?

10. What ideas do culture jammers reject? Explain briefly.

Response

In small groups, prepare a brief written comment or an oral presentation on *one* of the topics listed below. (Your teacher may assign different topics to different groups.)

Use references to well-known ads and commercials as much as possible in your response. Be sure to

- begin with a clear statement of your point of view

- support your statement with specific evidence
- conclude by reinforcing your opening statement

Topics

1. Naomi Klein mentions advertising's mounting aggressiveness in the public domain and gives general examples of places where ads can be found. Think of some examples in your neighbourhood or a specific geographic area. What do you think of the way advertising has invaded public space? Why? Give specific reasons for your response.

2. Have you ever drawn a moustache on a poster or defaced an ad in some way? Were you culture jamming or being a vandal, do you think? Pretend to explain what culture jamming is to a group of Grade 11 students. Say what Jorge Rodriguez de Gerada does and why, and then explain your group's response to such behaviour, giving clear reasons for your response.

3. Culture jammers today are more concerned with politics than pranks. One of their targets is tobacco manufacturers, another is factory conditions and sweatshop labour in developing countries, another the fashion and beauty industry. Other people become angry with ads in college washrooms, or logo-jammed clothing.

    What ads or what corporate advertising strategies make you angry? Why? What could be done to help you escape from these ads or strategies? What actions would you suggest? Discuss advertising strategies that upset you and make suggestions for a change in approach.

4. Do you think anything can be done to modify our culture of consumption? How bad is it anyway? (Give examples to prove your answer.) What might modify this culture? Consider the culture of consumerism in today's world.

Summary Writing Exercise

Write a brief summary of the reading from *No Logo* (a half page, double spaced). Before you begin, look again at the Vocabulary definitions and the questions in Recall and Review. Also look at the Steps to Success box on How to Write a Good Summary that appears earlier in this chapter.

Consider the following questions:

1. Think about the reading. What is its title? Who is the writer? What book is the reading from?

2. Will you mention the actual title of the book? Yes. The introductory comment mentions that the book is a best-seller. It must say something people are interested in hearing. What do you think that message is? Look again at the introductory comment, the definitions in the Vocabulary, and the conclusion of the reading itself.

3. What terms occur most frequently in the reading? Will you mention the term *culture jamming* in your summary? Of course you will. Will you mention *advertising, adbusters, billboards*? Yes. What other words or concepts occur often?

4. Is the passage about Jorge Rodriguez de Gerada? Or is it about what he does and what he believes? Why is he mentioned? Will you refer to him in your summary? Why? Yes, you may refer to him in your summary, but only as an example of a creative culture jammer.

Now write your summary, beginning with a statement like

*   In "Culture Jamming: Ads Under Attack," Naomi Klein writes about . . .

*   Naomi Klein explains the attitude of adbusters in her book *No Logo*.

*   In her book *No Logo*, Naomi Klein introduces the idea of culture jamming by . . .

*   Naomi Klein discusses adbusters and their attacks on marketing in *No Logo* by showing us that . . .

Words like *comments on, declares, describes, discusses, examines, explores, explains, highlights, says, introduces, talks about,* and *writes about,* are useful in summary writing.

READING 4

To Die a Martyr's Death

by Ken Wiwa

Ken Wiwa's moving account of the actual day his father was executed is found in his book about his famous father. In it, Wiwa gives an analysis of the back-

ground to the unjust hanging of Ken Saro-Wiwa, a writer, businessman,
father, and a man who devoted his life to fighting for justice for his people,
the Ogoni tribe of Nigeria.

Ken Saro-Wiwa was hanged in Nigeria on November 10, 1995. His wife
and sons fled to London, England. It took Ken, his eldest son, years to come
to terms with his father's death and his life. His efforts to understand his
father led him to talk with Nelson Mandela's daughter, Steve Biko's son, and
Burmese Nobel Prize winner, Aung San Suu Kyi.

Ken Wiwa now lives in Toronto. This account of his father's last hours,
based on eyewitness reports, is taken from the book, In the Shadow of a
Saint: A Son's Journey to Understand His Father's Legacy.

1   On the morning of his execution, my father would have felt conflicting
emotions. He probably had no specific idea that he would be executed that
day, but perhaps he might have had an inkling that it would be his last day
alive. He woke up before dawn—as he had done for most of his life. It was
still dark outside as he began to prepare for whatever the day would bring.
Perhaps he was relieved that his life would soon be over, because he was
exhausted. He was tired of all the speculation, tired of trying to piece
together the conflicting reports, of trying to second-guess what the authori-
ties were going to do with him. He was tired of clinging on for a last-minute
reprieve, especially as he had already convinced himself that death would
absolve him from his labours, would be a merciful release from the aggra-
vations of trying to square the dizzying circles of his life.

2   If anything he was grateful for the last eighteen months he had spent in
detention. He welcomed the solitude, the time to reflect and the chance to
put his mind at rest. He had found solace in religion. He had read the Bible
and studied the Koran. He had been a dedicated agnostic for most, if not all,
of his adult life, but now he was at peace with himself, a state of mind he
had not enjoyed for a while. He smiled at the irony of finding peace of mind
in a filthy, hot, mosquito-infested cell that he had once described as a living
death. He remembered how he had resolved, when he was first sent there,
to endure its deprivations with the cussed determination of a man who had
spent his whole life battling to save a cruel, brutish, brutalizing society from
itself. He even came to enjoy the hardships of his detention, deriving a
perverse pleasure from the squalor around him. As he sat on the damp, cold,
concrete floor of his cell that morning, he reassured himself that he had
played his part. Destiny was at hand. His job was almost done, and his time
had come. He had lived a full life, and he was ready to face death.

3   Something would have been nibbling away at him that morning,
though, a knot of anxiety worming away inside him. He probably turned to
his Bible and offered some prayers for all the people he would soon be leav-

ing behind: his parents, his family and his people. He might have offered a special prayer for my mother, then for his children, hoping we would find it in us to forgive and understand him. He felt pain at how his life had compromised ours, at how his execution would haunt us. He reflected on how his controversial life, the choices he had made, had hurt his family, and how his death would surely pursue his children to their own graves. He thought about all the others who had died in the struggle; the Ogoni who had been imprisoned or killed; the men who had been subject to torture, detention, harassment; the women, many of them young girls, who had been raped by soldiers. All this had been visited on his family and his people largely because *he* had encouraged them to rise up and speak out against injustice. He turned to the Koran, and there, in sura 42, verse 41, was the sentence that offered him reassurance and a lifeline: "All those who fight when oppressed incur no guilt, but Allah shall punish the oppressor." It would have been his final statement to the Auta tribunal.

4   As he finished his prayers and drew himself up from the floor, he took further consolation from the thought that his execution, the sheer injustice of it, would at least draw the world's attention to the discrimination that his people had suffered for so long. He was determined and ready to die a martyr's death. He felt it was a necessary part of the struggle, and as he contemplated the power and symbolism of such a death, he felt at ease again.

5   Later, as the first shafts of daylight crept into his cell, he realized that his mind had been wandering. He had been thinking about all the efforts being made to save his life. He scolded himself for losing his focus, for clinging to that lifeline when he knew it was over. He reminded himself that he no longer had any control over his life. I imagine that my father allowed himself a smile at that. He had always prided himself on being in charge of his destiny. But as he waited for someone else to decide his fate, he realized that circumstances beyond his control had always been conspiring against him, dictating his choices, shepherding him towards his destiny, which was to die for his people.

6   He had reached that conclusion a few months before, and had even had his narrator muse on it in *Lemona's Tale:* "Her story . . . fell into neat little episodes . . . as though it had been carefully laid out by some designer, with one waiting to take the baton from the other. Yes, I was the mere baton. And that was my problem, wasn't it? Everything was happening to me. I did not happen to anything or to anyone. Each time I tried to happen, disaster resulted."

7   Events beyond his control, like the civil war, had changed the shape of his life. Things had happened to him, and not the other way round. But today, he resolved to concentrate on what would be his final act of defiance.

8   He wanted to leave the world with a few words that would not only haunt his oppressors but also inspire future generations to continue the struggle. He rehearsed his last words, trying to imagine the most dramatic and appropriate moment to deliver them. As he considered the various scenarios, he was conscious of the need to guard against the numbing terror of that moment when he heard the clank of the key as the warder opened his cell to allow the soldiers stationed outside to lead him away to be executed. He didn't want to be surprised. He didn't want to react in a way that would betray any anxiety he might be feeling about dying. He realized that the way he reacted at that particular moment would set the tone for the rest of what remained of his life. He would stiffen his resolve, hold his head up high. He wanted history to record that he did not flinch when they came to take him away.

9   They came for him at 11:30 that morning.

Extracted from *In the Shadow of a Saint* by Ken Wiwa, 169–72. Copyright © 2000 by Ken Wiwa. Reprinted by permission of Alfred A. Knopf Canada, a division of Random House of Canada Limited.

Vocabulary

martyr (para. 1): a person suffering torture or death for a belief or cause

inkling (para. 1): a vague idea; a hint or suspicion of something

speculation (para. 1): consideration of something; thoughts and decisions without direct evidence

reprieve (para. 1): temporary postponement of danger, punishment, or death penalty

absolve (para. 1): make free from blame or guilt

solace (para. 2): comfort at a time of sorrow

dedicated (para. 2): devoted; single-minded; showing strong commitment

agnostic (para. 2): a person who claims that the existence of God is not known

cussed (para. 2): stubborn

brutish, brutalizing (para. 2): gross, cruel, and unfeeling; lacking human sensitivity (**brute** (para. 2): a beast lacking reason)

deriving (para. 2): getting

perverse (para. 2): determined to be opposite

squalor (para. 2): a dirty and unpleasant state

compromise (para. 3): expose to danger and suspicion; settling differences by making concessions; meeting halfway

controversial (para. 3): engaging in long arguments; involved in lengthy public disagreements

incur (para. 3): meet with; be subject to

tribunal (para. 3): a group of officials appointed to make a judgment on a specific issue or public problem

consolation (para. 4): comfort at a time of sorrow

symbolism (para. 4): deep meaning or truths suggested by objects or events

shafts (para. 5): rays (of light)

conspiring (para. 5): plotting; making secret plans

narrator (para. 6): person telling a story

episode (para. 6): a part of a story; an incident

baton (para. 6): a short stick used in relay races

Word Recognition

1. In pairs or groups of three, make up a brief story (about three sentences) using at least four of the words, or accepted forms of the words, listed below. Spend no more than 15 to 20 minutes on writing your story. Number or code your story.

2. Pass your story on to another group. Allow at least three other groups to see what you have written.

3. Decide which stories work best. Announce the numbers or codes of the two stories that are clearest and most interesting.

4. On the blackboard, list the numbers or codes of the stories that use the words best.

5. Read out the stories that are most popular.

6. Decide which story is the winner. Find out who wrote this story. Congratulate the writers fulsomely, and/or buy them coffee.

Story Example

The strikingly beautiful star of track and field at Snowflake High, Primrose did not have an *inkling* that she would be *absolved* before the first *shafts* of daylight came into the dormitory. As she sobbed herself to sleep, she was *consoled* by the thought that her enemy in the opposing team had dropped the *baton* in the relay race that afternoon, and Primrose had helped her track team win the city championship.

absolve	consolation	episode	reprieve
aggravation	conspiring	inkling	solace
baton	controversial	martyr	squalor
brutalized	dedicated	narrator	tribunal
conflicting	detention	perverse	

Recall

Try to answer the following questions from memory.

1. When did Ken Saro-Wiwa wake up on the morning of his execution?

2. How did Saro-Wiwa probably feel then?

3. How long had Saro-Wiwa been in detention and how had he found comfort at this time?

4. Choose five words to describe the conditions he was living in at this time.

5. What had Saro-Wiwa spent his whole life doing?

6. List four possible causes for a knot of anxiety "worming away inside him."

7. In your own words, state the meaning of the sentence from the Koran that gave him reassurance.

8. What would Saro-Wiwa's execution show the world?

9. What had changed the shape of Saro-Wiwa's life?

10. What did Saro-Wiwa want history to record about his final moments?

Review

Answer the following questions.

1. Why does Ken Wiwa think that death might seem a merciful release for his father?

2. Why was Ken Saro-Wiwa probably at peace with himself before his execution?

3. Why did Saro-Wiwa think of the Ogoni people at this time?

4. What attitude might Saro-Wiwa have shown to the Auta tribunal? Explain.

5. Why might Saro-Wiwa smile at the thought he no longer had any control over his life?

6. Why does the writer quote from *Lemona's Tale* here?

7. What would be Saro-Wiwa's final act of defiance? Explain briefly what might be the reasons for it.

8. Why does Ken Wiwa use the word "rehearse" and why does he talk about "various scenarios"?

9. What does Saro-Wiwa not want to do at this time? Why do you think he might feel like this?

10. What is this reading about? Explain in three to five sentences, mentioning the place, the situation, and Saro-Wiwa's mental state.

Response

The last words of Sydney Carton, spoken just before he stepped up to the scaffold to have his head chopped off in the French Revolution, are remembered and often quoted: "It is a far, far, better thing that I do, than I have ever done; it is a far, far, better rest that I go to, than I have ever known." Carton is a fictional character who was dying for the woman he loved in Charles Dickens' novel *A Tale of Two Cities*.

Ken Saro-Wiwa was a real person, a husband, a father, a newspaper columnist, an author of 25 books, and a civil-rights leader of the Ogoni people of Nigeria.

His son writes, "He wanted to leave the world with a few words that would not only haunt his oppressors but also inspire future generations to continue the struggle."

What words would you want to leave as your last words, besides messages to your nearest and dearest? What would you want to tell the world before you leave it? Presume you have made your farewells to your family and loved ones, and now wish to address a wider audience.

In small groups, prepare a message of about six sentences to leave behind. You may use questions, if you wish, but not too many.

Ken Saro-Wiwa's Last Words

What sort of country is this that delights in the killing of its illustrious citizens? What have I done that I deserve death, than that I spoke the truth, demanding justice for my poor people of Ogoni? I have always been a man of good ideas, and whether I be killed, my ideas will live forever, and Ogoni, for which I am dying, will one day be emancipated from the shackles of oppression.

Lord take my soul, but the struggle continues.

The readings in this chapter are about the choices people make in their lives. Every day people make choices, some simple and some difficult. Sometimes people get no chance to make a choice.

Writers make choices too, choices of words, of figurative or objective language, choices of details, paragraphing, attitude, and tone.

All summary writers make choices about what is essential or vital to the meaning of a passage, and what can be omitted. Think about what is vital in your own writing and use of language.

REVIEW AND REMEMBER

Summary Writing and Figurative Language

1. Summary writers focus on vital information only, preferring main ideas to supporting details.

2. Supporting data is included in a summary only if it is considered vital to the main idea of a piece of writing.

3. A summary shows how well a reader comprehends an assigned reading.

4. Figurative language, or language with life, uses comparisons and creates pictures with words. This imaginative use of language gives readers a livelier sense of what a writer means. It includes imagery, metaphor, simile, allusion, and personification.

CHAPTER 4

Power Reading

This chapter has four readings for comprehension, analysis, and response.

By now you know how to distinguish fact from opinion, or objective from subjective. You can look carefully at the introduction and conclusion of a piece of expository writing and establish the writer's purpose. You recognize figurative language, and you even use it in your own writing. You have developed your critical thinking skills. Now you can go beyond simple literal comprehension to a thoughtful analysis of a writer's ideas.

By the end of this chapter, you will be able to

- better understand the importance of historical context in the analysis of ideas

- examine a writer's ideas by recognizing the writer's purpose and tone

- examine further how a writer uses language and details to recreate an experience

- connect more easily with the minds and life experiences of other people through their writing

- recognize the place of critical thinking and clear communication in society today and in earlier times, as an instrument for change

Analyzing ideas is not easy. Some subjects can be painful to read about. The suffering of others is always painful. But the censorship of ideas and information causes a different kind of pain. Freedom of information is valued everywhere in the world. It is better to know about the suffering of others than to be ignorant of its existence.

People like to know what is going on in their community and in the world. In these days of media power and freedom of the press, publicity intrudes almost too easily into people's lives. It seems incredible to us, then, that in the past, even today in some places, certain powerful groups and dictators keep important events, such as the suffering of minorities, social changes, and all kinds of horrors, hidden from the public.

Today when the public knows about evil or suffering, people ask questions and speak out. Often something is done.

How can people speak out if they don't know what is happening?

All over the world, for hundreds of years, people have fought for the freedom to present opposing views. Tolerance of dissent is one sign of a free society. In a democracy, the opposition has the right to be heard. It is important, then, to be able to speak out, or to write a letter, to tell people what is going on. As Richard Johnston points out in his essay in this chapter, your words can make a difference.

Confidence in your communication skills will allow you to use language to get your point across and to make a difference in your world, whether personal or professional. Your ability to appeal to logic and reason or shared ethical values through your use of words, your emotional awareness developed through reading and listening, and your critical thinking skills, all will help you succeed in your verbal approach to life. Aren't you happy to be studying English at college, and developing this fine awareness and understanding?

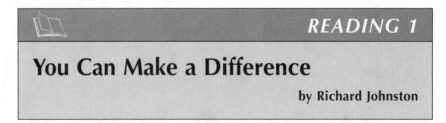

READING 1

You Can Make a Difference

by Richard Johnston

In the following comment, Richard Johnston, president of Centennial College, member of the Ontario Legislature for 11 years, politician, social activist, sheep farmer, husband, and father, gives his views on the place of communication

*skills in our society. His comment here is the introduction to a book that pub-
lished the winning results of a student writing contest at Centennial College.*

1   One of the most common refrains we hear these days, particularly around
election time, is: "What can I do? I'm only one person." It suggests the
powerlessness of an individual in the face of big government and big economic interests.

2   But I can tell you after spending eleven years in the Ontario Legislature that, contrary to popular belief, one person can make a difference. But
only if he or she is equipped with the right skills. And the single most
important attribute to have these days is the ability to communicate—
particularly in writing.

3   A finely crafted letter to the editor in a major newspaper will often
make it into the daily Queen's Park clippings roundup. Ministers and their
handlers have been known to fuss and fret over the contents of a poignant
letter; hands are wrung, the wheels of damage control begin to spin. It is
amazing what a good letter can accomplish—not just in government, but at
the corporate level as well. Articulate your dispute with polish and grace,
and doors will open for you. It is an essential life skill.

4   It is for this reason that I wholly endorse, and strongly encourage students to participate in our annual English writing contest. Writing is less a
talent than a little-known muscle that needs frequent and considerable
workouts. It improves with exercise. Frequently, with practice, you can
learn to say more, and say it better, with fewer words. The works of Ernest
Hemingway serve as good illustrations of this.

5   Fiction and poetry are equally important as instruments of change. For
it is our novelists and poets who first envision and articulate new ideals—
such as a just society—long before they become political mantras. Writers
ignite our collective spirit.

6   I welcome your interest in participating in our contest. Like a Sunday
morning half-marathon, it represents a great opportunity to exercise your
writing muscle. And you shouldn't even break into a sweat.

7   Good luck!

Richard Johnston, "Introduction to Student Writing Contest Winners," from *Celebrating
Student Writing at Centennial College, Volume 1.* (Scarborough, ON: Fall 2000, p. 2.)

Word Recognition

1. Guess what the following words mean from their context in the
    reading before looking them up in the dictionary.

refrain   envision

attribute   fiction

poignant   mantras

dispute   ignite

endorse   collective

2. Use *four* of the above words in sentences that clearly show their meaning.

Exercise 4.1*

Match the synonym (a word or phrase of similar meaning) in the list with each numbered phrase in boldface in the passage below. Modify verb tenses and singular or plural forms as necessary. Note: Not all terms in the list are suitable choices.

a. a means for making a difference

b. anxious attention paid

c. characteristic or quality having the greatest impact

d. concerned and worried

e. executives twisting in the wind

f. important consumer qualities

g. important financial groups

h. in the world of top business employers

i. lines often repeated

j. making quarrelsome sounds

k. opposite to what is usually thought

l. repeated word or phrase

m. separate choruses in the boardroom

n. small gas bubbles

o. special jargon

p. starting interaction to prevent further injury

q. state clearly the reasons for argument

r. with elegance and charm

(1) **Big economic interests** have discovered that, (2) **contrary to popular belief**, emotional intelligence is twice as important as an indicator of success as traditional know-how. (3) **The most important attributes** for top executives are abstract qualities like empathy, creative thinking, self-awareness, an understanding of group dynamics, and relationship-

building skills. These days a (4) **common refrain** heard (5) **at the corporate level** is that soft skills have hard consequences for the bottom line. For example, being able to (6) **articulate your dispute** at a bargaining table and speak (7) **with polish and grace** helps in any power struggle. When (8) **the wheels of damage control** begin to spin, executives need presentation skills, communication skills, and social skills. It's almost (9) **a mantra** in the corporate world that old habits must be replaced with new ones involving soft skills. Research backs up this claim. At the French cosmetic maker, L'Oréal SA, for instance, salespeople chosen more for their emotional smarts than their business knowledge outsold those selected for traditional reasons. The business world is demanding more soft skills. (10) **Hands have been wrung** and many professors and executives have been (11) **fussing and fretting** about the curriculum shift needed. Now Microsoft Corp., Glaxo Wellcome UK Ltd., and Lotus Cars are some of the companies that have signed up employees for workshops in literature because business leaders have become aware that literature is (12) **an instrument for change** in the marketplace. In many places now in Europe, MBA students study Shakespeare as well as information technology.

Recall

Try to answer these questions from memory.

1. What is a common refrain around election time?

2. What does this refrain suggest about the way people feel?

3. After spending 11 years in the Ontario legislature, what does Richard Johnston have to say to people?

4. What does Johnston say is the single most important attribute to have these days?

5. What is a clippings roundup and what is often discussed there?

6. What can make ministers and their handlers anxious?

7. What does Johnston see as an essential life skill?

8. What aspects of writing are also important as instruments of change?

9. What particularly Canadian ideal does Johnston mention as an ideal first envisioned by poets and novelists?

10. What can become political mantras?

Review

Answer the following questions.

1. Why do people often feel powerless at election time?

2. How can one person make a difference? Explain in two or three sentences.

3. According to Richard Johnston, why is the ability to communicate important?

4. What might happen in powerful offices when a letter arouses strong feelings or concerns? Explain.

5. Why does Johnston use the comparison of writing to a muscle?

6. Why does Johnston mention Ernest Hemingway?

7. Why are fiction and poetry important?

8. "Writers ignite our collective spirit." What does this statement mean? Explain in your own words.

9. Why does Johnston welcome interest in a writing contest?

10. What is the purpose of this comment? Explain in two or three sentences.

Response

An *analogy* is a form of figurative language that compares two things that are quite different to make a complicated idea clearer to the reader.

For example, Peer Gynt, in Henrik Ibsen's play of the same name, compares his life to an onion, with many different layers. Each layer represents a stage of his life. When he gets to the middle, he finds there is nothing there. Richard Johnston compares writing to a muscle that needs regular workouts.

1. Prepare an analogy of your own. In small groups, choose *two* of the following subjects and explain each one by comparing it to something else. Choose something ordinary from everyday life, like Peer Gynt did, for your object of comparison. Come up with an extended comparison that will help you explain the subject to the rest of the class.

a college classroom	jogging	root canal
a daycare centre	police on the beat	serial killers
fashion victims	protesters	squabbling siblings
fusspots	road rage	unemployment

2. Do you agree with Richard Johnston about the ability to communicate? Give reasons and examples for your views.

3. Prepare a workout program for exercising writing muscles at college. Be as specific as possible. What would you start with? What reading would you recommend? How much grammar would you study? In your communications workout program, use quotations from Johnston's essay to support your views, as well as anecdotal evidence.

Slave Narratives

Richard Johnston writes about the importance of being able to communicate. "Articulate your dispute with polish and grace, and doors will open for you," he states.

African slaves in the southern United States and the Caribbean did not get much opportunity for dispute, but in spite of all obstacles, many black slaves managed to escape and to let the world know about their suffering. They wrote what has come to be known as "slave narratives."

The tales of ex-slaves about the treatment they suffered and the horrors of bondage spoke for all the silent slaves still in captivity. Slave narratives were very popular in the mid-1800s. *The Narrative of the Life of Frederick Douglass, an American Slave*, published in 1845, sold 5,000 copies in the first months of publication.

At that time, in the United Kingdom and the northern United States, anti-slavery societies were everywhere. People had "itching ears" to hear slave narratives and were fighting for an end to slavery. The stories of slaves went straight to their hearts and inspired them to fight for abolition. It is clear that the ability to communicate made the slave writers leaders in the fight for freedom.

Doors opened for slaves because of literacy. Ishmael Reed wrote in *Flight to Canada* (1976), that the slave who learned to read and write was the first to run away. Being able to read and write means freedom.

Interesting Facts in the History of Slavery

"He who does not know history is destined to remain a child." *Cicero*

1788:   A British parliamentary motion for the abolition of the slave trade carried
1793:   The Upper Canadian Act Against Slavery outlaws the importation of slaves into Upper Canada
1794:   French colonies abolish slavery
1807:   Britain prohibits slave trade
1808:   United States prohibits importing slaves from Africa
1833:   Abolition of slavery in the British Empire
1865:   American Civil War ends
1866:   Ku Klux Klan founded in Tennessee

READING 2

The History of Mary Prince, a West Indian Slave

Related by herself

Mary Prince was born in Bermuda. At the age of 12, after a mostly happy and carefree childhood, she was caring for the child of a neighbour when she was told, "Mary, you will have to go home directly; your master is going to be married, and he means to sell you and two of your sisters to raise money for the wedding."

Many years later in England she told her story. Three excerpts from it are printed here. In one passage, she writes about being a slave to a cruel Mr. D— on Turk's Island, where the harsh treatment she suffered and the unending work in the salt ponds nearly killed her. Later in Antigua she was taught to read by three ladies in the Moravian Church.

When she was taken to England by another cruel master and mistress, she knew she was free there, but alone and impoverished, she was afraid to leave them at first. Three months later she left and sought help from the

Moravian Missionaries. She was also helped in England by Quakers and by the Anti-Slavery Society.

Free at last, she "was unwilling to eat the bread of idleness," as she says, so she worked as a cleaning lady and was paid for her labours for the first time. The following excerpts are from her slave narrative, published in 1831.

1   Oh the horrors of slavery!—How the thought of it pains my heart! But the truth ought to be told of it; and what my eyes have seen I think it is my duty to relate; for few people in England know what slavery is. I have been a slave—I have felt what a slave feels, and I know what a slave knows; and I would have all the good people in England to know it too, that they may break our chains, and set us free.

***

2   I must say something more about this cruel son of a cruel father.—He had no heart—no fear of God; he had been brought up by a bad father in a bad path, and he delighted to follow in the same steps. There was a little old woman among the slaves called Sarah, who was nearly past work; and, Master Dickey being the overseer of the slaves just then, this poor creature, who was subject to several bodily infirmities, and was not quite right in her head, did not wheel the barrow fast enough to please him. He threw her down on the ground, and after beating her severely, he took her up in his arms and flung her among the prickly-pear bushes, which are all covered over with sharp venomous prickles. By this her naked flesh was so grievously wounded, that her body swelled and festered all over, and she died a few days later. In telling my own sorrows, I cannot pass by those of my fellow-slaves—for when I think of my own griefs, I remember theirs.

3   I think it was about ten years I had worked in the salt ponds at Turk's Island, when my master left off business, and retired to a house he had in Bermuda, leaving his son to succeed him in the island. He took me with him to wait upon his daughters; and I was joyful, for I was sick, sick of Turk's Island, and my heart yearned to see my native place again, my mother, and my kindred.

***

4   I am often much vexed, and I feel great sorrow when I hear some people in this country say, that the slaves do not need better usage, and do not want to be free. They believe the foreign people [West Indians], who deceive them, and say slaves are happy. I say, Not so. How can slaves be happy when they have the halter round their neck and the whip upon their back? and are disgraced and thought no more of than beasts?—and are separated from their mothers, and husbands, and children, and sisters, just as cattle are sold and separated? Is it happiness for a driver in the field to take down his wife or sister or child, and strip them, and whip them in such a disgraceful manner?—

women that have had children exposed in the open field to shame! There is no modesty or decency shown by the owner to his slaves; men, women, and children are exposed alike. Since I have been here I have often wondered how English people can go out into the West Indies and act in such a beastly manner. But when they go to the West Indies, they forget God and all feeling of shame, I think, since they can see and do such things. They tie up slaves like hogs—moor them up like cattle, and they lick them, so as hogs, or cattle, or horses never were flogged;—and yet they come home and say, and make some good people believe, that slaves don't want to get out of slavery. But they put a cloak about the truth. It is not so. All slaves want to be free—to be free is very sweet. I will say the truth to English people who may read this history that my good friend, Miss S—, is now writing down for me. I have been a slave myself—and I know what slaves feel—I can tell by myself what other slaves feel, and by what they have told me. The man that says slaves be quite happy in slavery—that they don't want to be free—that man is either ignorant or a lying person. I never heard a slave say so. I never heard a Buckra man say so, till I heard tell of it in England. Such people ought to be ashamed of themselves. They can't do without slaves, they say. What's the reason they can't do without slaves as well in England? No slaves here—no whips—no stocks—no punishment, except for wicked people. They hire servants in England; and if they don't like them, they send them away: they can't lick them. Let them work ever so hard in England, they are far better off than slaves. If they get a bad master, they give warning and go hire to another. They have their liberty. That's just what *we* want. We don't mind hard work, if we had proper treatment, and proper wages like English servants, and proper time given in the week to keep us from breaking the Sabbath. But they won't give it: they will have work—work—work, night and day, sick or well, till we are quite done up; and we must not speak up nor look amiss, however much we be abused. And then when we are quite done up, who cares for us, more than for a lame horse? This is slavery. I tell it, to let English people know the truth; and I hope they will never leave off to pray God, and call loud to the great King of England, till all the poor blacks be given free, and slavery done up for evermore.

Henry Louis Gates, Jr., ed. *The Classic Slave Narratives,* New York: Penguin USA, 1987), 200–15

Vocabulary

lick them (para. 4): beat them; thrash, whip them

moor them up (para. 4): a West Indian phrase meaning to fasten or tie up

Buckra man (para. 4): white man

Word Recognition

Choose the best answer for sets #1 to #7 and respond to #8.

1. A slave narrative is

   a. a tale full of sound and fury

   b. a significant academic analysis of the story of human bondage

   c. an autobiographical account of the experience of a slave

   d. a biographical description of events experienced in "the peculiar institution" of slavery

2. People fighting for Abolition were

   a. begging for forgiveness from church leaders

   b. struggling to give bondage more exposure

   c. desperate to prevent changed attitudes to slavery

   d. eager to eliminate the slave trade and slavery

3. From the context, you would expect the Moravian Church to be

   a. a Protestant church with enlightened views

   b. a church where a Czech dialect is spoken

   c. a Christian sect fighting for freedom in Bratislava

   d. an educational society that trembles at harsh treatment of slaves

4. If you "eat the bread of idleness," you will be likely to

   a. fail courses at college from lack of effort and homework

   b. suffer indigestion in English classes

   c. hallucinate

   d. be admired by your fellow students for your peaceful, happy behaviour

5. If you suffer "bodily infirmities," you will

   a. feel occasional slight tremors on the left side of your body

   b. experience deep feelings in your heart

   c. be gloomy and unresponsive to touch

   d. be subject to physical weakness

6. If you are "vexed," you will

   a. rub yourself with ointment

   b. feel the blood pumping into your heart

   c. be annoyed and irritated

   d. have a sensation of dizziness

7. If you look "amiss," you will

   a. seem to be suffering from fever and inflammation of the skin

   b. be unable to sustain long-term relationships

   c. appear to be out of order, faulty in some way

   d. appear to be in the middle of something

8. The reading presents three short excerpts of Mary Prince's narrative. Each part deals with a separate aspect of her attitude or experience. Write a heading for each part that accurately introduces the excerpt.

Recall

Choose a word or words from the reading that best complete each sentence. Use your own words in sentences 3, 5, 9, and 10. Be sure the words you choose fit the sentence grammatically.

1. In the beginning, Mary Prince says it is her duty to _____ her story.

2. Prince hopes that the people of England, after hearing about slavery, will _____ and _____ .

3. The old woman, Sarah, was not able to work because of _____ and _____ .

4. The wounds made by the prickly pear bushes caused Sarah's body to fester because the bushes are _____ .

5. Prince gives many reasons why no slave can be happy. List three of them.

6. Prince thinks that when English people go to the West Indies, they must _____ and _____ .

7. When Prince says people "put a cloak about the truth," her metaphor means _____ .

8. A person who says slaves are happy in slavery is obviously _____ or _____ .

9. List two reasons why servants are better off in England, according to Prince.

10. Prince points out that no one cares for slaves when they are _____ .

Review

Answer the following questions.

1. Why does Mary Prince tell her story? What is her purpose?

2. What lines would you quote to prove that Prince does not want readers to know only about her own suffering?

3. Why was Prince so happy to leave Turk's Island and return to Bermuda?

4. What are three points Prince makes to people who say that slaves don't want to be free? Which point is the strongest, would you say? Explain briefly your views.

5. Prince mentions many kinds of abuse suffered by slaves. Which ones do you remember most? Why?

6. What response does Prince give to people who say they cannot do without slaves?

7. Faith in God means a lot to Prince. How do you know?

8. What does Prince hope is the result of her narrative? Explain.

Summary Writing Exercise

Write a brief summary (two or three sentences) for each part of Mary Prince's narrative. Write a brief introduction to these summaries, explaining who Mary Prince was and why she told her story. Use your own words.

Response

Respond to *one* of the following topics in small groups.

Topics

1. Mary Prince had no access to business administration or psychology textbooks. She did no research on employment law or on the importance of strong family ties. Yet, the points she makes about these four subjects are as relevant today as they were then. They could come straight out of modern books on these subjects.

    Choose *one* of the subjects mentioned above. State it more precisely. At present, these subjects are suitable for at least one book or a university course. Give your topic a more specific focus.

    You might, for example, choose employment law. Indicate *where, when, what kind of, for what reasons* in your statement of topic. For instance, where and when?: employment law in Canada today. Then ask *what kind of, for what reasons,* and *what about* before choosing your most focused subject. You might end up with a subject like *The position of employees when a company goes bankrupt,* or more specifically, *The Board of Directors at Canada 3000's responsibility towards its employees.*

    a. Quote some of Mary Prince's words on this subject. Quote briefly here; a phrase or a sentence only.

    b. Explain briefly what ideas or subject these words introduce.

    c. State in one sentence whether your group agrees or disagrees with Prince, and indicate why in your statement.

    d. Analyze this. In other words, expand on your last sentence, giving reasons for your group's point of view. Use examples from your own experience, your studies, or the media. Quote from the reading whenever possible to connect your argument to Prince's ideas.

    e. Include your group's ideas on the best way to maintain good relations in the area you are discussing.

    f. Conclude with a comment on the group's emotional reaction to Prince's narrative and mention how it affected at least two members personally, with reasons. Stress the importance of your central argument once more.

g. Before presenting your response in writing or orally, come up with a catchy title for it.

h. Present your response with a smile.

2. Prepare a brief report on the horrors of slavery, mentioning the suffering involved and the attitudes discussed by Mary Prince, but focus on only *one* specific horror in detail. Explain why you have chosen this particular horror. Conclude with a personal reaction to the subject chosen.

READING 3

I Tried to Kill My Pretty Sister

by Hester Lacey

In this essay from The Independent on Sunday, *Hester Lacey writes about siblings and the rivalry associated with that word. She points out that when you're 13, being told you're the brainy one is no compensation for not being the pretty one . . . In her essay, ugly sisters (and brothers), along with a social psychologist and family researcher, speak out about the effects of family attitudes and stereotyping on children.*

1   Seeing Sharon Stone or Claudia Schiffer on screen or catwalk is enough to give most women a twinge of inadequacy. How much worse it must be for their sisters, who have grown with them, seen them blossom into stars, and must know that they will never, ever measure up in the glamour stakes. Poor Kelly Stone and Caroline Schiffer: both pleasant looking women, but doomed for life to being a less perfect version of an acknowledged beauty. Perhaps the worst thing is that they resemble their siblings enough to be recognisably their sisters, but miss out by vital millimetres on their striking good looks.

2   Life is particularly hard for those who want to follow in famous family footsteps. Dee Dee Pfeiffer, Michelle's wanna be sister, blames her former bulimia on trying to achieve film-star slenderness. "Michelle was always the beautiful one, always the one people gave their attention to. I was fat when I was growing up, not attractive at all. And when you don't like yourself, having a sister who is just lovely doesn't help," she told one interviewer wistfully. "In Hollywood they are constantly looking at you, measuring your hips and your thighs—and comparing you to your famous sister."

3   Such rivalry is by no means confined to Hollywood. In many families, sisters are still split into the stereotyped "pretty one" and "clever one" when they are very young—and children tend to value looks over brains. A number of studies have shown that toddlers can distinguish between "beautiful" and "ugly" when shown pictures of different types of people.

4   "I was so jealous of my sister's looks. She had long fair hair and a cute little nose, and I thought she always had the prettiest clothes and the most attention. She was very fragile, while I was a heavy, galumphing child. I hated her so much that I decided to kill her. One day when we had the builders in, I dropped a brick out of a window when she was underneath. Thank God it missed," says one shame-faced near-murderess.

5   "I must have been about 10 at the time, and she'd have been eight. Now we're both in our twenties, and she tells me that she always felt really inadequate following me in school because I did well and she was less academic—but when you're that age, you want attention and compliments and boyfriends, and a string of A grades is no substitute."

6   "I hated parties and family occasions because my older sister Sally was so good in company, so chatty and witty, and I was just this lump sweating nervously in the corner," says another Ugly Sister. "I used to dread anyone talking to me because she made me look so frumpy and boring and lumpen. Looking back, I wasn't that hopeless appearance-wise, but something about Sally just paralysed me and it wasn't until we went away to different universities that I could pull myself together, make my own friends and be myself. I didn't hate her, we got on well together. but I longed desperately to be like her."

7   Sally, the sister in question, is astounded. "I suppose I did exaggerate myself a bit when I was round her, but it wasn't malicious, it was just a bit of showing off."

8   Brothers compete as well, but looks don't seem to be such a bone of contention. "For boys, prettiness is less of an issue—it's more a question of sports and careers, says Dr Arlene Veter, family researcher and therapist at Royal Holloway London college. "It was a question of who did things first—sporty things, physical things—and given that he was older than me and very well built, it was always him," says Tom (now six feet tall and twelve stone). Don Swayze is more concerned with becoming as famous as his older brother than with looking as good as him: "One day I'll step on that pedestal alongside him, and they'll say these are the Swayze brothers, not that I'm just Patrick's little brother."

9   Social psychologists in Britain and the United States are currently concentrating on research into the reasons why siblings can turn out so differently in every way, when they are brought up in the same families and

experience the same background influences. Dr Peter Stratton, director, of Leeds Family Therapy and Research Centre at the University of Leeds, believes that often family attitudes rather than natural advantages are responsible.

10   "Once a child is labelled as attractive, it will dress more attractively, and have an "attractive" self-image," he says. "Children take their parents' word for it—they don't have any alternative. If you are a small child and your parents imply that you're ugly, how will you disprove it? There is lots of evidence to show that when you give a child a label they'll live up to it—or down to it."

11   Such stereotyping, though, is widespread. "Families tend to characterize someone according to a dominant characteristic," explains Royal Holloway's Dr. Veter. "In fact in all social groups there is a tendency to think of people as 'pretty' or 'sporty' without thinking about the context. It can be very liberating and open doors—but it can be very constraining, for example if prettiness is equated with not being very bright." Being lumbered with the "pretty" label or the "studious" label or the "sporty" label is not necessarily a disadvantage, though. It can act as a spur to prick a child into competing ferociously against their sibling. "In a recent interview in the *Face* magazine, Liz Hurley confessed that her sister was always the 'pretty' one and she felt at a disadvantage," observes Dr. Stratton. Or else it can lead to the seeking of excellence in a field where there is no sibling competition. "In many cases, if you are told that your sister is very pretty, then you won't compete, you know she'll win in this particular contest. You'll find something she's not so good at and concentrate on that."

12   But forget becoming a ping-pong champion or expert dahlia grower to sublimate the fact that your sister looks like a supermodel. The best revenge is when the tables are turned in later life. "When we were in our twenties, she was always the good-looking girl-about-town, and I was the staid, dull sister who was studying to be a librarian and preferred reading to partying" says Elizabeth, 35, with barely concealed glee. "Now she's got three children, put on about 20 pounds, hasn't got time or money to do her hair, and is always covered in puréed rusk. I can afford to wear what I like and go out whenever I want. It's not that she's unhappy with her life, or that I feel particularly smug about the way things have changed. I just feel that it's my turn now.'

Hester Lacey, "I Tried to Kill My Pretty Sister," *The Independent on Sunday,* 27 August 1995

Vocabulary

puréed rusk (para. 12): baby food

Word Recognition*

Hester Lacey uses some common figures of speech and idiomatic expressions in her article. From the list of idiomatic expressions below, choose the best one for each of the following spaces. Modify verb forms, pronouns, singulars, and plurals, if necessary. Note: There are more expressions listed than required.

a bone of contention

a twinge of inadequacy

act as a spur

at a disadvantage

blossom into

doomed for life

it can open doors

not malicious

lumbered with

measure up

prick someone into

to sublimate the fact that

Workplace manners are seen as a problem these days. Office workers these days are being (1) _____ communicating more and more with computers only, and working on top of each other in tiny grey cubicles. They may not mean to drive their co-workers crazy, and it's probably (2) _____, but many people at work these days don't pay enough attention to good manners and consideration for others. No one wants to quarrel about it, but certain actions at work do not (3) _____ to standards of acceptable or correct behaviour. Some particular (4) _____ that cause office rage are as follows: making private arrangements loudly on the telephone; barging into other people's workstations; failing to greet fellow workers.

Loud telephone use always seems to (5) _____ for cubicle workers' anger. Who wants to hear someone making a mammogram appointment or sobbing about her cheating man?

Then another way to (6) _____ into a ferocious reaction is assuming that a co-worker wants to talk just because you can see him at his desk, and no walls are keeping you out. Who thinks of calling ahead to see if someone is available?

But it's the simplest things that make you (7) _____ among co-workers, and make them wish you were not a colleague. Workers complain bitterly about others who can't be bothered saying hello, good morning, or please and thank you. Your mother tried to teach you those manners. She hoped you would (8) _____ a charming well-mannered individual, someone people would like to work with. If you didn't listen to her, you will be (9) _____ because today bosses will always give the job to a person who is pleasant to be around. You can feel more than (10) _____ if you know you ignored your mother's teaching and your manners are not socially or professionally appealing.

Recall

Try to answer the following questions from memory.

1. Sharon Stone, Claudia Schiffer, Patrick Swayze, Liz Hurley . . . Who are these people?

2. Who are Dr. Arlene Veter and Dr. Peter Stratton, and what do they do for a living?

3. What is sibling rivalry?

4. What do little girls want to be known for?

5. How do boys usually compete?

6. What are social scientists in Britain and the United States currently researching, according to the article?

7. What is a dominant characteristic?

8. What effect can labelling have?

9. How can a label act as a spur?

10. What is the best revenge for an insecure sibling?

Review

Answer the following questions.

1. Why does Hester Lacey begin this article with references to Sharon Stone and Claudia Schiffer? What do they represent for readers?

2.   What does Lacey expect her readers to know? What sort of people might be reading this article?

3.   Where does Lacey establish the focus of her article?

4.   What kind of rivalry is "by no means confined to Hollywood"?

5.   What do children tend to value over brains? What do they usually value more than A grades?

6.   Who does Lacey quote to bring further analysis and academic credibility to this article? What do they add to her main idea or thesis?

7.   Why are social psychologists in Britain and the United States currently concentrating on the differences between siblings?

8.   How do families affect their children's images of themselves? Explain briefly.

9.   What do you do if you "sublimate" an idea or feeling? Explain why this word is used here.

10. What is Lacey's conclusion?

Response

Answer *one or all* of the following in small groups or individually, as assigned by your teacher.

Topics

1.   How do college students feel about A grades vs. social success? Which do they want? Debate the idea that college students would rather have compliments and attention than straight A's.

2.   What do you think of this article and its ideas? What exactly do you agree or disagree with? Explain using quotations from the essay.

3.   "Families tend to characterize someone according to a dominant characteristic," says Dr. Veter of Royal Holloway London college. Do you agree with her statement? Why? Use examples from your own experience to prove or disprove your views.

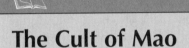

READING 4

The Cult of Mao

by Jung Chang

One of the most popular books of the nineties was Wild Swans, *Jung Chang's story of the lives of her grandmother, mother, and herself in China, from 1909 to 1978. The story of three strong, beautiful women takes readers to just after Chairman Mao's death, when, she says, "China was shedding its Maoist straitjacket."*

Chang writes about the effects of Mao's Cultural Revolution on a population that was then largely illiterate, showing how Mao destroyed much of the country's cultural heritage and left behind him an ugly land with little of its past glory remaining.

During the years of Mao's control, Chang's life involved many unusual experiences, such as learning how to throw hand grenades at the age of 13, and doing eye exercises for 15 minutes every morning because Mao had decided that too many school children were wearing spectacles. The following excerpt tells of another activity demanded at this time.

1   One day in 1965, we were suddenly told to go out and start removing all the grass from the lawns. Mao had instructed that grass, flowers, and pets were bourgeois habits and were to be eliminated. The grass in the lawns at our school was of a type I have not seen anywhere outside China. Its name in Chinese means "bound to the ground." It crawls all over the hard surface of the earth and spreads thousands of roots which drill down into the soil like claws of steel. Underground they open up and produce further roots which shoot out in every direction. In no time there are two networks, one aboveground and one belowground, which intertwine and cling to the earth, like knotted metal wires that have been nailed into the ground. Often the only casualties were my fingers, which always ended up with deep, long cuts. It was only when they were attacked with hoes and spades that some of the root systems went, reluctantly. But any fragment left behind would make a triumphant comeback after even a slight rise in temperature or a gentle drizzle, and we would have to go into battle all over again.

2   Flowers were much easier to deal with, but they went with even more difficulty, because no one wanted to remove them. Mao had attacked flowers and grass several times before, saying that they should be replaced by cabbages and cotton. But only now was he able to generate enough

pressure to get his order implemented—but only up to a point. People loved their plants, and some flowerbeds survived Mao's campaign.

3   I was extremely sad to see the lovely plants go. But I did not resent Mao. On the contrary, I hated myself for feeling miserable. By then I had grown into the habit of "self-criticism" and automatically blamed myself for any instincts that went against Mao's instructions. In fact, such feelings frightened me. It was out of the question to discuss them with anyone. Instead, I tried to suppress them and acquire the correct way of thinking. I lived in a state of constant self-accusation.

4   Such self-examination and self-criticism were a feature of Mao's China. You would become a new and better person, we were told. But all this introspection was really designed to serve no other purpose than to create a people who had no thoughts of their own.

5   The religious aspect of the Mao cult would not have been possible in a traditionally secular society like China had there not been impressive economic achievements. The country had made a stunning recovery from the famine, and the standard of living was improving dramatically. In Chengdu, although rice was still rationed, there was plenty of meat, poultry, and vegetables. Winter melons, turnips, and eggplants were piled up on the pavements outside the shops because there was not enough space to store them. They were left outside overnight, and almost nobody took them; the shops were giving them away for a pittance. Eggs, once so precious, sat rotting in large baskets—there were too many of them. Only a few years before it had been hard to find a single peach—now peach eating was being promoted as "patriotic," and officials went around to people's homes and tried to persuade them to take peaches for next to nothing.

6   There were a number of success stories which boosted the nation's pride. In October 1964 China exploded its first atomic bomb. This was given huge publicity and touted as a demonstration of the country's scientific and industrial achievement, particularly in relation to "standing up to imperialist bullies." The explosion of the atomic bomb coincided with the ousting of Khrushchev, which was presented as proof that Mao was right again. In 1964 France recognized China at full ambassadorial level, the first leading Western nation to do so. This was received with rapture inside China as a major victory over the United States, which was refusing to acknowledge China's rightful place in the world.

7   In addition, there was no general political persecution, and people were relatively content. All the credit was given to Mao. Although the very top leaders knew what Mao's real contribution was, the people were kept completely in the dark. Over the years I composed passionate eulogies thanking Mao for all his achievements and pledging my undying loyalty to him.

Jung Chang, *Wild Swans* (New York: Anchor Books, 1992), 270–71.
Reprinted with the permission of Simon & Schuster. Copyright © 1991 by Global Flair, Ltd.

Word Recognition

Match the words in Column A with the closest synonyms in Column B.

Column A

1. Maoist straitjacket
2. bourgeois habits
3. intertwine
4. casualties
5. generate
6. implemented
7. secular
8. pittance
9. imperialist
10. ousting
11. eulogies

Column B

a. force out; drive from office
b. tributes, speeches of praise
c. practices of a government keen to establish control over other nations
d. produce; bring into being
e. a very small amount of money
f. things or people, injured or hurt
g. conforming to middle-class behaviour
h. twist together
i. garment or situation restricting action
j. not concerned with religious matters
k. put into effect; make happen

Recall

Choose the best answer.

1. The introduction to "The Cult of Mao" indicates to readers that

   a. China was preparing for war since 1949

   b. even in the twentieth century, Chinese women expected to be secondary wives

   c. the history of China in the twentieth century shows how aggressive and militant petit bourgeois non-gardeners can be

   d. a story of life in China in the twentieth century is often tragic, but always compelling

2. Mao decided that grass, flowers, and pets were

   a. signs of outlandish crimes or advanced age

   b. signs that people did not value cabbages and cotton sufficiently

   c. signs of weakness and time wasted

   d. signs of the way politics invaded everyone's lives

3. Some flowerbeds survived Mao's campaign because

   a. people could make a meal from the flowers with cabbages

b. they did not generate any pressure on Mao's beliefs

c. people loved their plants

d. the root systems were too strong to destroy with hoes and spades

4. Jung Chang felt sad often at this time and lived in a constant state of self-accusation because she

   a. was an adolescent and it is essential for adolescents to feel insecure and sad

   b. felt unhappy about any feelings against Mao's teachings

   c. hated eggs and had to eat them every day

   d. was fed up with the persecution of her teachers

5. People in Mao's China were encouraged to be introspective. That means they were expected to

   a. examine their own thoughts and feelings

   b. know and understand Mao's ideas through intuition

   c. eliminate all bourgeois habits

   d. reverse their capitalist position on politics

6. The religious aspect of the Mao cult would not have been possible if

   a. people had no thoughts of their own

   b. people had not known about the ousting of Khrushchev

   c. people had not turned their backs on the sayings of Confucius

   d. the standard of living had been lower

7. In the sixties, China was proudly promoting its scientific and industrial achievements because

   a. the country had eliminated all bourgeois religious practices

   b. young women all over the country were composing passionate tributes to Chairman Mao

   c. China exploded its first atomic bomb and eliminated famine

   d. university students were exiled to faraway areas to do back-breaking farm labour without machinery

8. At this stage, the United States

   a. sent many advisors to observe the thought reform

   b. was following its usual imperialist path in Sichuan

    c. was angry with France for recognizing China

    d. was refusing to acknowledge China's place in the world

9. There was no political persecution in 1965, writes Chang. She means that

    a. many people had been sent to the countryside to be "reformed"

    b. people were not worried about their political beliefs

    c. no one was subjected to harsh treatment for their beliefs

    d. harmful and destructive behaviour was not condoned

10. The Chinese people were kept completely in the dark about

    a. the undying loyalty of the people around Chairman Mao

    b. the medieval elements in Chinese culture

    c. what Chairman Mao was really doing or not doing

    d. Mao's earthquake phobia

Review

Answer the following questions.

1. The deep, long cuts in Jung Chang's fingers caused by pulling out grass could be seen as symbolic of or representing the way she felt about many of her activities at this time. Why? Explain briefly.

2. "People loved their plants, and some flowerbeds survived Mao's campaign." What does this statement show about people?

3. The writer writes about "the religious aspect of the Mao cult." What does she mean? Explain briefly.

4. The signs that the country had made a stunning recovery from famine encouraged people in what way? Explain.

5. Inside China what three events reinforced national pride? Why?

6. At age 13, the writer composed passionate eulogies thanking Mao for

    a. getting rid of all bourgeois habits like flowers, pets, and grass

    b. keeping schoolchildren safe and protecting their eyesight

    c. standing up to imperialist bullies

    d. impressive economic, scientific, and industrial achievements

7. "We can soar to the heaven, and pierce the earth, because our Great
    Leader Chairman Mao is our supreme commander!" was a popular
    Red Guard slogan during the time of Chairman Mao's rule. The
    reading here indicates that everyone took that idea seriously, because
    even in 1965

    a. schoolchildren were told to pierce the earth with hoes and spades
       to remove all grassroots, and to plan to explore space

    b. the people in Chengdu, full of pride in Mao's achievements,
       believed everything was fine in their town, and tried to please Mao

    c. even a slight rise in temperature would mean that piercing the
       earth had not been successful the first time

    d. piercing the earth was a sign of bourgeois hypocrisy

8. Self-examination and self-criticism were a feature of Mao's China
    because

    a. he expected the good service and polite behaviour of pre-revolution
       China to continue

    b. that way he implemented his orders and made things grow
       internally

    c. he wanted people to follow the party line and not think for
       themselves

    d. he felt it was a way to stand up to imperialist bullies in Russia

9. The writer tried to suppress any instincts that went against Mao's
    instructions because

    a. she knew that flowers and pets caused class bitterness

    b. she did not want the grass to make a comeback

    c. she did not want to have to go into battle all over again

    d. she blamed herself for not following the correct way of thinking

10. Why would a whole country be content at this time, do you think?

Response

Your teacher may assign *one or more* of the following topics for a collaborative or individual writing exercise, or for an oral presentation.

Topics

1. "First comes the food. Then come the morals," said German writer Bertolt Brecht. Do you agree? Give reasons. How does this reading from *Wild Swans* reinforce your views? Explain by making clear what your central argument is, and using examples from the reading and from the world around you to reinforce your point of view.

2. How far does an individual go in following orders? We are used to living in a democracy where the majority rules. Are the demands of the group, or the majority, always more important than the rights of the individual? Explain how you feel about individual freedom versus group responsibility.

    Consider this idea in relation to the power of a political philosophy compared to the power of individual wishes. Refer to the reading, history, and society today in making your points.

3. In *Silent Spring,* an environmental book that rocked the world in 1962, Rachel Carson warned the world of the dangers of insecticides. She wrote about a spring when no birds sang, no chicks hatched, and no bees pollinated apple tree blossoms. Jung Chang writes about a time when flowers and plants were being eliminated.

    What kind of world would it be without birds, flowers, and grass? Describe such a world, with attention to specific details about the environment. Say what sort of people might inhabit this world. Focus on one or two types of inhabitants, such as the leaders, schoolchildren, parents, or teachers.

4. "The Cult of Mao" is the title of the chapter where this excerpt is found, where Jung Chang writes about the cult of Mao in China in the sixties. Are we very different in the West today? Do you know any people who worship a celebrity or a political leader? Describe the cultish following of a leader or a set of cultish beliefs in our society today. Focus on one or two specific examples to prove your point, and try to give reasons for it the way Chang does in her writing.

The readings in this chapter show how a writer can make a statement about an experience in a particular society at a particular time. Such writing communicates experiences that would otherwise be denied to you. Reading allows you, then, to gain understanding of the unknown. Making things clear to others is what communication is all about.

REVIEW AND REMEMBER

Power Reading

1. Ask exactly what the writer is making clear to a reader. Note the *what, why, when, where, how,* and *who* behind the reading.

2. Look at the reading's main ideas, and the choice of words and details used to present these ideas.

3. After thinking about the reading, ask yourself what aspect of social experience or social history is now clear to you.

4. Be able to state how and why you reached this deeper level of understanding.

CHAPTER 5

Critical Reading and Thinking

This chapter looks at more challenging essays for comprehension, analysis, and response.

By the end of this chapter, you will be able to

- evaluate the use of specific data in supporting an argument

- gain further practice in the analysis of ideas

- identify details and authoritative evidence that make an argument credible to a reader

- recognize the cultural context that determines the approach a writer takes to a topic

At college, you are often encouraged to study classic texts in English classes to gain some understanding of the cultural background of where you live. Education leads to *acculturation,* which means learning the cultural expectations, discourse, and behaviours of a specific cultural group. By the time you reach college, you know that there is more to culture than diet, dance, and dress. Culture is a way of thinking.

In today's global world, you come across many different cultural responses to experience. You also know that the cultural context affects the experience.

So far in this textbook, you have had the opportunity to read many different voices in English. Some of them are from away, some of them from close to home. Think of the voices you have encountered so far.

You would not respond emotionally to any of the voices, however, if the writers and their writing did not kindle a response. Good writing touches the minds and imaginations of readers. Good writing is clear writing first. It is also correct and coherent. If facts are involved, they are accurate and reliable. Good writers are aware of and use all the resources available to them of language, of information retrieval, of imagination.

The essays and articles in this final chapter of readings often use specific data and facts to support points. Note how the readings gain in credibility from the use of this data. Some of the writing here may be more challenging, but by now you are able to think more analytically. (Keep in mind the reading strategies presented in Chapter 1.)

Analytical thinking is always important. Last century, Winston Churchill said that people were living in an age "of gape and gloat, clatter and buzz." His words are just as resonant today. In an age where facts, reasons, ideas, and analysis are too easily replaced by sitcoms, videos, celebrity gossip, terrorist coverage, and constant muzak, it is as important as ever to have knowledge and understanding, to get over the gaping and gloating, the clatter and buzz, and to look carefully at exactly what is being communicated, to analyze exactly what is being said.

The distinguished Canadian writer John Ralston Saul says that knowledge and understanding are the foundations of consciousness. As conscious citizens of the twenty-first century, please keep reading and thinking.

READING 1

Equipped to Make Her Own Way

by John Stackhouse

John Stackhouse, an award-winning writer, spent 7 years in New Delhi as the first overseas development writer for The Globe and Mail *newspaper. During his time in India and since, he has travelled to more than 40 countries, and has written on the struggles of the world's poor, "carried on in hamlets and slums, on riverbanks and mountainsides, by people who until now have been largely excluded from public decision-making."*

His highly-praised writing about the world's poor, "from East Timor to Timbuktoo," shows that poverty is mostly a direct result of human actions. When people are able to become self-directed, and have some control over their own lives, poverty can be overcome. In the following article, you will read about how some women in India are gaining control over their own lives.

1 Few women face more difficult lives than the women of Koliahi.

2   Born, raised and married in Banda, one of India's poorer districts, they spend their days digging for water, collecting firewood and stooping over rock-strewn fields to sustain their families. They spend their nights cooking, cleaning and keeping an eye out for the bandits who roam the badlands of north-central India.

3   For a girl in Koliahi, going to school is a foreign concept. For a woman, going to a health clinic is a stranger idea still.

4   "Let's say one of them had problems during childbirth," explained Madhavi Kuckreja, a local social worker. "They would have to put her on an ox cart and take her a few kilometres to the nearest road. Then they would put her on a bus to town, where there is a small health centre. But it is closed at night."

5   What would happen to such a woman?

6   "Most likely," Ms. Kuckreja conceded, "she would stay home and die."

7   Into this environment, enter Chamela, a mild-mannered mother of four, riding her battered black bicycle across the broken fields of Banda. Late last year, Chamela asked her husband for something alien: She wanted to leave the village for five months to learn to read and write.

8   To her surprise, he agreed. "I thought she should learn something, like me," said Radesh Shyam, who spends most of the year working on the railway.

9   So, along with 26 other women from the surrounding villages, Chamela left her four young children with her sister and headed to the district's first-ever literacy school for women, organized by the Indian government's Mahila Samakhya program.

10   Apart from a one-month midterm break to help with the winter harvest, the women, aged 14 to 40, would study morning, afternoon and evening. They would draw pictures, sing songs, form letters on paper and eventually write sentences.

11   For five months, they would not be chattels of village life.

12   When Chamela returned home, she wrote a letter to her husband. Uneducated and ignored for most of her life, she even wrote a small story about Ram Mohan Roy, the great 19th century Bengali liberal who fought for women's rights during British rule.

13   "Knowledge," she said, beaming. "I know about things now."

14   Since 1989, the Mahila Samakhya program—literally, "women speaking as equals"—has spread through more than 1,200 villages in the states of Uttar Pradesh, Gujarat and Karnataka.

15   With financial support from the Dutch government and coaching from local social groups, the organization that started as a self-help group has become a movement that was showcased during the World Conference on Women held in Beijing. "We are self-sufficient," said Shiv Kumari, who is Chamela's cousin and, now that she too has gone to literacy camp, exudes self-confidence. "The biggest thing that has happened is, I don't need to build faith in anyone. We have our system. We don't need anyone else."

16   Unlike India's national literacy movement, which merely teaches men and women to sign their names, the Mahila Samakhya movement aims to give women the skills to manage their lives better. They learn how to read repair manuals for hand pumps, write diaries to manage their time, make accounts balance and, in some cases, ride bicycles.

17   They're also encouraged to fight for what rightfully is theirs.

18   "You must understand, this is a long, bitter struggle for these women," said Nishi Mehrotra, director of the program in Uttar Pradesh. "Many of the women are beaten by their husbands before they come, and they still come."

19   "Some problems we can solve," said Ram Koli, a Mahila Samakhya member in Kamiaha. "Everyone knows us now. When we go to the block development office, they give us chairs to sit in."

20   Government officials hope that, once women like Ram Koli, a mother of four, recognize their own rights and power, they will be more inclined to send their daughters to school. But giving rural women a sense of power through literacy cannot overcome all social ills.

21   Many of the women in the villages of Banda still complain about the local bureaucrats. Recently, the local sub-district magistrate demanded the women pay him 5,000 rupees ($220) for a spot at the annual fair.

22   Following years of government handouts, there also remains an ingrained welfare mentality in many villages. When the Mahila Samakhya program first built meeting huts for the women's groups, the modest structures fell apart. Now, each group must build and maintain its own hut.

23   Nonetheless, on many of the feudal fields of northern India, there has been a change in mind, if not matter. In villages such as Koliahi, the men pay more attention to women. They now see them as decision-makers, too.

24   "I used to write my wife letters," said Chamela's husband Radesh Shyam. "Now she writes to me.

John Stackhouse, "Equipped to make her own way," *The Globe and Mail,* September 4 1995, A7.
Reprinted with permission from *The Globe and Mail.*

Vocabulary

foreign concept (para. 3): an idea coming from outside

chattel (para. 11): a movable possession; a piece of personal property

showcase (para. 15): show to advantage

exude (para. 15): ooze with; show freely

ingrained (para. 22): fixed firmly

feudal (para. 23): a system of land control from the Middle Ages (fifth century to fifteenth century) in Europe

Word Recognition

Define *two* of the following expressions in two to five sentences, using examples from the reading and from society today.

chattels of village life

ingrained welfare mentality

feudal fields

self-sufficient

foreign concept

Recall

Try to answer the following questions from memory.

1. Why do the women of Koliahi have a hard life?

2. What are five reasons for the hard lives of these women?

3. How might they react to going to school or a health clinic?

4. What did Chamela ask her husband for and where did she go with 26 other women?

5. What does "Mahila Samakhya" mean?

6. Where does the Mahila Samakhya program exist, and how is it supported?

7. What does this program aim to give women?

8. What are three skills women learn in this program?

9. What are two problems graduates of the Mahila Samakhya program still face?

10. What must each women's group now do with their meeting huts?

Review

Answer each of the following questions in complete sentences, unless asked otherwise.

1. Why would a woman of Koliahi who was having problems giving birth be likely to stay home and die?

2. What is this reading about? Answer in your own words in three to five sentences.

3. "For a girl in Koliahi, going to school is a foreign concept." What does John Stackhouse mean? Explain in one to three sentences.

4. "For five months, they would not be chattels of village life." What does Stackhouse mean? Explain briefly.

5. What is the Mahila Samakhya movement and how did it develop? Explain in two or three sentences.

6. Why is attending the literacy program a long and bitter struggle for many Koliahi women?

7. Why are government officials keen for Koliahi women like Ram Koli to recognize their rights and power?

8. What social ills are still hard to overcome?

9. What change of attitude is now noticeable in many of the feudal fields of northern India?

10. What does the title of the reading mean?

Summary Writing Exercise

Write a short summary, about a half page, explaining *one* of the following topics. Use your own words.

Topics

1. life for women in Koliahi, India

2. the Mahila Samakhya movement

3. how literacy allows rural Indian women gain a sense of power

4. a change in attitude in the feudal fields of northern India

Response

Write a one-page, double-spaced comment on *one* of the following topics.

Topics

1. "I feel a chattel when . . ." Describe a situation.

2. A very important reading experience in my life.

3. A story I will never forget.

4. "I exude confidence when . . ." Explain what gives you self-confidence.

Exercise 5.1

In small groups, discuss a literacy program for college students. What would be involved? Would it resemble the English or Communications program at your college, or would you offer something quite different? Decide what you think is important to encourage greater literacy among college students today.

Prepare a proposal for your literacy program. Begin with a statement of rationale, giving reasons and purpose. Then list recommendations. Be as specific as possible. Conclude with a brief reinforcement of the rationale, showing why literacy is still important in a digital and virtual world.

READING 2

Our Environmental Shame

by David Suzuki

Scientist, writer, and broadcaster David Suzuki is chair of the Vancouver-based Suzuki Foundation. In 2001, he wrote that Canada's proposed endangered species legislation needs to be made stronger before it is too late.

1   Quick, think of a country with a strong environmental reputation. Which one came to mind? You probably didn't think of the United States, and I really doubt you thought of Mexico. But I'll bet you couldn't help thinking of Canada.

2   Yet both the United States and Mexico have legislation to protect endangered species. Canada does not, and the current proposed legislation, following two previous failed attempts, needs crucial changes if we want to start catching up to our neighbours.

3   Internationally, Canada still has something of a Boy Scout reputation when it comes to the environment. We are blessed with an incredible natural heritage, a relatively small population and a huge land base. Visitors cannot help but be awed by our natural splendour—indeed, that's why many come here. We've also played host to international environment conferences that were the impetus for important agreements, such as the Montreal Protocol, to eliminate ozone-depleting substances.

4   But our reputation far exceeds our track record and it has begun to fray, badly. If you followed the climate summit meetings in The Hague last fall, for example, you may have noticed that non-governmental organizations

gave Canada more "Fossil of the Day" awards than any other country for attempting to weaken the Kyoto Protocol on greenhouse gas emissions. Equally glaring is Canada's lack of federal legislation protecting endangered species, which should be a national embarrassment.

5   In recent years, scientists worldwide have recognized how important the variety of life is to the ecosystem and human health. Everything from the largest carnivore to the smallest soil invertebrate has a function within an ecosystem that helps the system maintain itself over time. This diversity of life also drives the "ecosystem services" that sustain human life, everything from maintaining soil fertility to regulating the climate, cleansing our air and water, and absorbing our waste. Whenever we lose a species, we unravel a thread in the fabric of life that binds us all together.

6   Like Canada's international reputation, Earth's life fabric is fraying. In fact, human activities are creating what scientists call the sixth great extinction, because species are going extinct faster now than they have since the dinosaurs died out. Worldwide, thousands disappear every year. In Canada, 364 species are considered at risk, although the actual number is likely much higher.

7   Belatedly, Canada is finally poised to enact endangered species legislation. Unfortunately, the current bill, known as the Species at Risk Act (SARA), is more about politics than it is about protecting endangered species. On paper, it has many possibilities, but it puts far too much power in the hands of politicians, and not enough in the hands of scientists and researchers who, unlike politicians, actually have some knowledge about the animals that need protecting.

8   For example, the No. 1 threat to biodiversity worldwide, and the No. 1 threat to Canada's endangered species, is habitat loss. Yet SARA does not directly protect habitat, where an animal forages for food, breeds and raises its young—it only protects an animal's nest or den. This is absurd. A species cannot exist without habitat—they are inseparable. SARA does not even directly protect the habitat of animals that obviously fall under federal jurisdiction, like migratory birds. Instead, habitat protection is left entirely up to the discretion of cabinet, which "may" or may not actually enforce action, depending on what, if anything, the province involved is already doing. And we all know how cooperative and well-integrated federal-provincial politics are.

9   Strangely, SARA does not even start with the existing list of 364 species at risk identified by the scientific committee that assesses the status of wildlife in Canada. Instead, SARA starts with zero species and requires the same committee to review the existing list.

10   Once that's finished, cabinet gets to pick which ones will be protected under SARA. Again, the final decision is political, not scientific.

11   Canadians overwhelmingly want habitat protection to be mandatory, not discretionary (79 per cent said so in a recent poll). In fact, it's already mandatory in four of the six provinces that do have endangered species legislation. Even industry groups like the Canadian Pulp and Paper Association and the Canadian Mining Association have reached a consensus with environmental groups and are proposing tougher legislation.

12   Canada has an opportunity before us that we must not pass up. Allowing the continual erosion of life's diversity is not an acceptable option. As an international group of scientists recently wrote in the journal *Nature*: "The scientific community and informed citizens should become engaged in conveying to the public, policy makers and land managers the enormity and irreversibility of current rapid changes in biodiversity. Despite convincing scientific evidence, there is a general lack of public awareness that change in biodiversity is a global change with important ecological and societal impacts and that these changes are not amenable to mitigation after they have occurred."

13   In other words, humans depend on a diversity of life. It is suicidal to tear at the web of life that provides our most basic needs—clean air, water, soil and energy. We must take action to conserve this biodiversity, because once it's gone, we can't bring it back. What we can start to reclaim right now is our international reputation and we can begin by strengthening our proposed endangered species legislation to have some teeth.

David Suzuki, "Our Environmental Shame," *The Globe and Mail,* 22 March 2001, A17

Vocabulary

impetus (para. 3) a driving force

Protocol (para. 3) preliminary draft of an agreement; first copy of a treaty before its final acceptance

depleting (para. 3) reducing in size

fossil (para. 4) remains of something pre-historic; completely out of date

glaring (para. 4) obvious to everyone

ecosystem (para. 5) a biological community, an environment of interacting organisms

carnivore (para. 5) :flesh-eating animal or plant

invertebrate (para. 5): having no backbone

sustain (para. 5): support and keep alive

fraying (para. 6): unravelling; wearing out with loose threads

bio- (para. 8): life; of living things (e.g., biodiversity, biology, biography, biopsy)

forage (para. 8): look for food

jurisdiction (para. 8): range of authority or power

mandatory (para. 11): compulsory

discretionary (para. 11): done or used at a person's judgment

consensus (para. 11): general agreement

erosion (para. 12): gradual wearing away

amenable (para. 12): willing to be guided by, open to influence

mitigation (para. 12): made milder, reduced in seriousness

Word Recognition*

Choose a word from the Vocabulary that best reflects the idea of the sentence. *Two* sentences have no connection with the Vocabulary.

Example

The years Rosa spent in the garment industry taught her to see **when a fabric was about to give way and wear out.** *fraying*

1. The island of Borneo, with its lush tropical rain forests and unspoiled beaches, offers biologists **a variety of places to study.**

    _____

2. It was **obvious to everyone** that Monika was destroyed by Jimi's death. _____

3. Even industries that have had poor environmental records in the past are finally in agreement about the need to **protect habitats and keep them alive.** _____

4. What she really wants is a white extra-extra stretch limousine with **a swimming pool and a movie theatre.** _____

5. In Britain, chicken tikka masala **has overtaken** fish and chips as the national dish. _____

6. Margot Franssen, president and partner of The Body Shop Canada, believes that the way to keep business alive and healthy is to be bold, be daring, be different, be caring, and give people **the freedom to make their own choices.** _____

7. The spiritual and psychological healing powers of water meant that Sobia enjoyed the **compulsory** swim program for all employees, even though she had not expected to. _____

8. Portia was not seeking **to reduce the seriousness of her plea,** but she was willing to be guided in a different direction.

    _____

9. Eileen's views on racism and affirmative action took so long to develop that they were **out of date** by the time she voiced them, so many colleagues think she is a little out of touch with present-day reality. _____

10. Because the governing party said there was **a pressing need** and a forceful public demand for the change in student loan legislation, the bill was passed quickly. _____

Recall

Try to answer the following questions from memory.

1. What do Mexico and the United States have that Canada doesn't?

2. What is a "Boy Scout reputation"? Give two reasons for Canada's international Boy Scout reputation.

3. What did non-governmental organizations (NGOs) give Canada at the meetings in The Hague?

4. According to David Suzuki, what should be a national embarrassment in Canada?

5. What is another word of for the variety of life? (Think of the prefix that means life.)

6. What two examples does Suzuki use to show that everything in an ecosystem has a place, no matter what its size?

7. What disappears every year in Canada?

8. What does Suzuki think is wrong with SARA, the Species At Risk Act?

9. What is the biggest threat to endangered species?

10. What does Suzuki think Canada should do right now?

Review

Respond to the following questions.

1. What kind of audience is this article written for? How do you know?

2. Why does David Suzuki say Canada's track record is not as good as its reputation? Explain in two or three sentences.

3. Why did Canada get so many "Fossil of the Day" awards in The Hague?

4. What is the real purpose of Suzuki's criticism of Canada's environmental record? Answer in one sentence.

5. How does biodiversity help sustain human life? Explain and give three examples.

6. Suzuki uses figurative language to help him describe the problems in the environment. Find two of his metaphors and explain how they make the situation clear.

7. Why is the protection of habitat important for endangered species?

8. How does Suzuki know that Canadians want habitat protection to be mandatory? What three points does he give to support his argument?

9. In your own words, summarize the support given by a group of scientists in the journal *Nature* for Suzuki's argument about stopping the erosion of biodiversity.

10. How are clean air, water, soil, and energy threatened in Canada today, according to Suzuki? Explain briefly.

Response

Respond to *one* of the following topics, using as much specific data as possible. Use examples from everyday life, from David Suzuki's article, or from research, if available.

Topics

1. In small groups, decide what you would do to restore Canada's international reputation as an environmental good guy. Prepare a brief policy statement saying what you would do and why you would do it.

2. How would you make the public aware of the importance of biodiversity in sustaining life? Plan an educational program for improving public awareness.

3. Decide what is the best way to give teeth to any environmental legislation so that it works.

4. "Whenever we lose a species, we unravel a thread in the fabric of life that binds us all together." What does Suzuki mean? Explain his comment in your own words. Give examples. Conclude with your ideas about this comment. Do you agree? What do you think and feel about this issue?

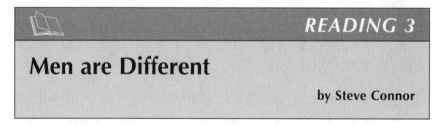

READING 3

Men are Different

by Steve Connor

Are men really from Mars and women from Venus, as the popular book tells us? Or are they different for other reasons and not just for the ones you see when you change a diaper? Steve Connor tells us what research on the brain shows us about the differences between men and women. The reading below is taken from "Landmarks of the Mind" an essay in the Sunday Review of The Independent on Sunday.

(Dear reader: When reading Steve Connor's article, please don't worry too much about remembering specific terminology like cingulate *[**cingulum:** any structure acting like a girdle; a bundle of fibres around the corpus callosum] and* encephalization *[**encephalic:** pertaining to the brain]. Just look up key*

expressions and note how they are used in context. Learn any words that will help you understand the differences between the sexes. Other expressions, like "magnetic resonance imaging scanner" are part of everyday hospital life today.

Warning: The following material may cause discomfort. Reader discretion is advised.

1   Why are men better at darts and women better at chatting? How do we recognise fear in others? What is memory made of?

2   Think about it. Every word in this sentence is causing wave upon wave of electrical storms to rage through your brain. The very act of reading and thinking, such a uniquely human feature, is generating intricate patterns of electrical and chemical activity that are so complex, yet so transient, that they seem beyond the comprehension of the brain itself. Scientists believe this is about to change dramatically, however, now that brain scanners have allowed them to view the vast landscape of the human mind.

3   What do we really know about the workings of our own brains? The answer is that we understand a tiny fraction of what the brain can do, but the potential for finding out more is enormous. This year has seen a remarkable variety of research reports elucidating different aspects of brain function. Scientists have identified, for instance, a region of the brain involved in recognising fear in the faces of others; they have come closer to understanding the cerebral abnormalities that seem to be associated with dyslexia and other reading difficulties; and they have examined with some success an age-old debate centred around the battle of the sexes—do men and women think differently?

4   The apparent differences between the capacities of men and women have been apparent ever since psychologists devised problem-solving tests to assess mental performance. Women are generally better at rapidly matching objects or items in their field of vision, a skill called "perceptual speed". They are more verbally fluent, performing better than men in tests involving words. They are also better at arithmetical skills and recalling landmarks from a route, as well as being better at precision manual tasks, like putting different shaped pegs into holes on a board.

5   Men are good at spatial tasks, such as imagining an object being rotated in space or navigating round an obstacle course. They generally have better mathematical skills that involve reasoning, and are better at what psychologists call "target-directed motor skills"—but what the rest of us call "playing darts".

6   Many people would argue that these attributes are due to upbringing, not to innate biological differences in the brain. Upbringing and the way little boys and girls are treated undoubtedly play their part, but this is not the whole story. Even three-year-old boys are better than girls of the same

age at target skills, so conditioning—in the form of the "male" and "female" sports played in childhood—does not appear to account for the sex differences in the targeting skills of young adults.

7   Doreen Kimura, a professor of psychology at the University of Western Ontario, believes the differences between male and female brains are real. "It has been fashionable to insist that these differences are minimal, the consequence of variations in experience during development. The bulk of the evidence suggests, however, that the effects of sex hormones on brain organisation occur so early in life that, from the start, the environment is acting on differently wired brains in girls and boys."

8   Differences in the way the two sexes process language has been an especially interesting area for brain researchers to investigate, particularly since women tend to "outverbalise" men. It has been known, for instance, that aphasia—speech disorders—are more common in men than in women when the left side of the brain is damaged, say in an accident or after a stroke. Yet Professor Kimura has found that women are more likely than men to suffer aphasia when the front part of the brain is damaged. This clearly indicates that the brains of men and women are organised differently in the way they process speech.

9   Earlier this year, this sort of research received a dramatic boost with publication of a study by a team of scientists led by Bennett and Sally Shaywitz, a husband-and-wife team at Yale University. The researchers took 19 men and 19 women, and placed them in a magnetic resonance imaging scanner that could detect minor changes in blood flow to different parts of their brains while they were asked to match rhyming words. What they found was that many of the women used the right side of their brains more than the men for this very specific task.

10   Another well-known feature of male and female minds is being able to determine the emotion in another person's face. How the brain deals with facial expressions is important because, from a very early age, we recognise the value of reading correctly whether a face is angry, say, or happy.

11   Anecdotal evidence abounds of men being incapable of seeing that someone has upset their partner until they find themselves swimming in a flood of tears. On a more experimental basis, it does seem true that women are far better at determining emotions by facial expressions. In one experiment, women correctly identified sad faces among a set of photographs of men and women nine times out of ten. Men matched that performance only when they had to assess the sadness of male facial expressions. They were significantly worse when it came to assessing sadness in women's faces, getting just seven out of ten correct.

12   Ruben Gur, professor of neuropsychology at the University of Pennsylvania in Philadelphia, has studied emotional differences in men and women,

again with the help of the ubiquitous brain scanner. He took 61 volunteers under 45 years of age, 37 men and 24 women. He measured how fast certain areas of their brains were using up blood glucose when they were resting, but awake. Men were more likely to have activity in the temporal limbic region of the brain, which in evolutionary terms is very old because we share it with most other animals, including reptiles; women were more active in the cingulate region, which is far more recent, being more developed in "higher" animals such as the primates and particularly well-developed in humans.

13   Professor Gur concluded that men tend to deal with emotions on a more basic level, much like a crocodile lashing out aggressively, whereas women "sit down and talk about it"—akin, perhaps to a chattering monkey. "Men often express their emotions through overt aggression. Women deal with theirs more symbolically by talking about their feelings more than men, who often sulk and say 'What's there to talk about?'," Professor Gur says.

14   Brain size alone, however, is not terribly meaningful in terms of measuring intelligence. What distinguishes us most from apes is the degree of "encephalisation," or complexity, within the structure of the brain. Encephalisation is a measure of how many brain cells exist over and above those needed by a body of a certain size. The human brain is as large as might be expected for a far larger primate, whereas an ape's brain is comparatively smaller.

15   Apparent differences in the mental abilities of men and women, evolving over perhaps millions of years, have been particularly intriguing for evolutionary biologists. In prehistory humans lived in relatively small groups of hunter-gatherers where the division of labour between the sexes was quite marked. It is likely that men were responsible for hunting big game, requiring long-distance travel and good navigation skills. They had little need to be great conversationalists, but had to solve tactical problems together and be good at aiming and throwing.

16   Women would have been more involved with child rearing, tending the camp and preparing food and clothing—evolutionary survival was never non-sexist. This would put a premium on women with inherent abilities in short-range navigation (remembering landmarks), dexterity, being emotionally sensitive towards others, especially children, and communicating emotion verbally.

17   This does not mean, however, that we are doomed to our sexual stereotypes as laid down by our evolutionary history. Far from it. The very power of our mental imagination means that our brains have given us the ability to be liberated from our past.

Steve Connor, "Landmarks of the Mind," The Sunday Review of
The Independent on Sunday, 28 May 1995, 82–83

Word Recognition

Look at the way the words and expressions listed below are used in the reading. Use context clues to help you understand their meanings.

Paragraph 2:

> generating intricate patterns
>
> transient

Paragraph 3:

> the potential . . . is enormous
>
> *Lux* means light in Latin. *Lucid* means clear. If you shed light on a subject, or make it clear, what do you do? You can use one word to explain this process. What is the word? Look for a word in paragraph 2 beginning with *e*.
>
> cerebral abnormalities
>
> What part of the body is described as *cerebral*? If you show no *cerebral* activity, what state are you in? Cerebral thinking is concerned with concepts. Limbic thinking [see paragraph 12] is concerned with senses and feelings.
>
> dyslexia
>
> *Alexia* is a disease where people lose the ability to read because of injuries of the brain. The prefix *dys-* means diseased, faulty. You already know the term *dysfunctional:* unable to function normally. People with brain damage may suffer from *dysphasia*, if they cannot coordinate speech. What is a *dystopia*? Would you rather live in a *Dystopia* or a *Utopia*?

Paragraph 4:

> apparent differences
>
> perceptual speed
>
> verbally fluent
>
> manual tasks

Paragraph 5:

spatial tasks

rotated in space

obstacle course

Paragraph 6:

attributes

innate

Paragraph 11:

anecdotal evidence (establishes or reinforces a fact or point through a brief story or short account of some incident)

A word about *anecdotal evidence.* Because anecdotal evidence does not rely on amassing data in a scientific way, through experiments, and control groups, it is not easily measured and is not considered as reliable in establishing proof or for presenting a reason. That is why it is not wise to rely entirely on anecdotal evidence when developing an argument. However, anecdotal evidence does add a human dimension to the development of ideas and helps provide a human picture that people tend to remember more easily than numbers. Do not ignore anecdotal evidence. Just be sure to back it up with other measurable data, where possible, especially if writing a report.

Paragraph 12:

neuropsychology

Neuro- means of the nervous system. A *neuron* is a nerve cell. *Neurology* is a study of the nervous system and its disorders. What is a *neurosis?*

ubiquitous (found everywhere; widespread)

temporal limbic region (the most chemically active part of the brain; the site of the origin of emotions, near the temples of the skull)

Paragraph 13:

overt aggression

Paragraph 14:

primate

Paragraph 15:

particularly intriguing

tactical problems

Paragraph 16:

put a premium on

inherent abilities

dexterity

Exercise 5.2

1. Steve Connor uses figurative language occasionally in his article to help make ideas clear. Some of the expressions he uses are

    chattering monkey

    like a crocodile lashing out aggressively

    swimming in a flood of tears

    the vast landscape of the human mind

    Use *two* of the expressions above and add *one* of your own in a brief comment on EITHER sexual stereotyping you have experienced OR what you have observed about the puzzling way the opposite sex deals with emotions.

2. A definition helps make abstract ideas clear to a reader. A good definition makes references that relate to the culture of the reader and often shows how a writer thinks or feels about the word. Write a three to five sentence definition, including specific examples, for *two* of the following words/expressions:

evolution	large primates
good conversationalist	neuropsychology
hunter-gatherers	pre-history

Recall

Try to answer the following questions from memory.

1. What does the act of reading and thinking do to the brain?

2. What question in paragraph 3 prepares a reader for the essence of this article?

3. What has been obvious since problem-solving tests were started?

4. What are three differences between male and female brain performance?

5. What point is introduced by the words "but this is not the whole story" in paragraph 6?

6. What makes male and female brains so different, according to Professor Doreen Kimura of the University of Western Ontario?

7. If you say that something is "wired," what do you mean?

8. What can a magnetic resonance imaging scanner do?

9. What did Professor Ruben Gur conclude about male and female brains?

10. What skills did men need in pre-history? What skills did women need then?

Summary Writing Exercise

Write a brief summary (one or two sentences) of selected paragraphs. Note the key idea of the paragraph, and focus on answering a question implied or stated in the paragraph.

For example, paragraph 2 begins with "Think about it." The rest of your summary would focus on what the author wants readers to think about, explaining what "it" refers to.

The following questions will help you get started on your paragraph summaries:

Paragraph 3: What question does the paragraph begin with? What is the answer and why is it important to the article?

Paragraphs 4 and 5: What are the apparent differences between male and female brains?

Paragraph 6: Even if social conditioning is important in determining the differences between male and female capacities, why isn't it the whole story?

Paragraph 7: What makes male and female brains so different, according to Doreen Kimura?

Paragraph 8: What are researchers discovering about the differences in the way the two sexes process language?

Paragraph 9: How has the study of Bennett and Sally Shaywitz helped research into the differences between male and female brains?

Now, form your own questions for the other paragraphs you choose to summarize.

Review

Answer the following questions.

1. Why doesn't our evolutionary history doom us to sexual stereotypes?

2   How might the apparent differences in the mental abilities of men and women have evolved? Explain what aspects of hunter-gatherer societies would have encouraged inherent brain differences.

3. What effect does brain size have on determining intelligence? How do you know?

4. What could an evolutionary biologist say about sexism in pre-history?

5. How are women better at determining emotions than men?

6. What do we know about the differences between male and female brains from magnetic resonance imaging scanners?

7. Why do women seem more emotionally sensitive towards others than men? Give at least three reasons in your answer.

8. Why does conditioning not appear to account for the sex differences in the targeting skills of young adults?

9. What is a stroke, and what part of the body is affected by a stroke?

10. What differences in brain activity did Professor Ruben Gur's research pinpoint? What did Professor Gur conclude about these differences?

Response

Answer *one or more* of the following questions, in small groups or individually.

1. What does Steve Connor reveal in this article about the differences in the way men and women respond to emotion? Note carefully who says what and where in your answer.

2. Are we doomed to become sexual stereotypes, in your view? Why or why not?

3. How can we, today, counteract our evolutionary history and social conditioning? Explain.

4. "All I know is, I've dated black men and I've dated white men, and they've all been dogs."

    What do you now know about the way men and women handle emotions that might explain this sorrowful statement from a community college student? Explain.

READING 4

John Kenneth Galbraith's World Tour
by John Kenneth Galbraith

John Kenneth Galbraith, born and educated in Ontario, is one of the most respected and influential economists alive. When he speaks about the state of the world and economic policy, people listen. He taught for over 60 years at Harvard University in Cambridge, Massachusetts, near Boston, and, as his speech shows, is still active in research and writing.

The veteran economist was 90 years old when he gave this speech to the London School of Economics, where he received an honorary doctorate at the end of the twentieth century. Wouldn't it be great if his view of the state of the planet as a place where some inhabitants are gloriously free from toil, while others starve, could be modified before he dies?

1   I was born and reared on a farm in Canada. To this day I never awaken in the morning without a sense of satisfaction that I will not have to spend the

next hours in that monotonous toil. One of the achievements of the century has been the general escape from what Marx, with some exaggeration, called the idiocy of rural life.

2   We have seen a wonderful lengthening of the years of health and enjoyment of life. We have also now the much celebrated technological supplements to human intelligence, including the computer world. This, in some aspects, is serviceable and good, in others contrived and diversionary.

3   More important, there has been an escape from the worst feature of modern existence: hard, tedious, boring toil. This has not yet been eliminated, but one of the greatest accomplishments of the century has been the reduction in the proportion of people so engaged.

4   The word "work" is our most misleading social term. It designates the occupation of those who would be very unhappy without it. And we use the same word for hard, repetitive, even physically painful toil. No word in the English language stretches over such different conditions. There is the further perverse fact that those who most enjoy what is called work are those who are best paid. And they are also allowed the most leisure.

5   Over the 60 years I have been teaching at Harvard, I have often, while crossing Harvard Yard, been stopped by one of my colleagues with the question, "Aren't you working a bit too hard?" Leisure is essential for the affluent and also for those of us for whom work is pleasant, mentally rewarding. For those who must truly toil, however, leisure is an escape from social virtue. Nonetheless, here too there has been progress. In the century past many have graduated from the miseries to the enjoyments of work.

6   In the fortunate countries there has been an enormous increase in the production of goods and services, the wherewithal of life. The measure of the increase, the annual rise in the gross domestic product, has become the prime indicator of all human progress.

7   But this summer thousands of visitors will descend on Florence in Italy. By all modern standards, in its greatest days past it was a city of small, even insignificant income. William Shakespeare was of a country with a very low GDP. Paris in the years of the Impressionists was appreciably less affluent than now. So, also, was the world that gave us Charles Darwin, and no one since has so challenged embodied belief.

8   Success as measured by economic output bears no close relationship to human achievement. The most ardent artistic effort is now devoted not to the arts but to promoting the sale of goods and services. And so also most of our scientific effort. Darwin's successors now concentrate heavily on getting new products for the market.

9   If the history of the arts and of science gives us pause as to the measures of present achievement, there are also problems within economies as well. The most serious is the ancient and unsolved problem of instability—of the enduring sequence of boom and bust. The speculative crash, now called a

correction, has been a basic feature of the system. In the United States we are now having another exercise in speculative optimism after the partial reversal last year. We have far more people selling derivatives, index funds and mutual funds (as we call them) than there is intelligence for the task.

10   When you hear it being said that we've entered a new era of permanent prosperity with prices of financial instruments reflecting that happy fact, you should take cover. This has been the standard justification for speculative excess for several centuries. Let us not assume that the age of slump, recession, depression is past.

11   I come to two pieces of the unfinished business of the century and millennium that have high visibility and urgency. The first is the very large number of the very poor even in the richest of countries and notably in the U.S. Once the impoverished were scattered over the countryside in our case, especially in the rural south. Now everywhere they are in the great cities, melding in with the larger urban mass. In the fortunate lands, poverty, urban poverty, is the most evident and painful of the economic and social legacies from the centuries past.

12   The answer or part of the answer is rather clear: Everybody should be guaranteed a decent basic income. A rich country such as the U.S. can well afford to keep everybody out of poverty. Some, it will be said, will seize upon the income and won't work. So it is now with more limited welfare, as it is called. Let us accept some resort to leisure by the poor as well as by the rich.

13   We have a bizarre problem in the distribution of income—a heavy concentration in the very top income brackets, much less to those below. There is now a stirring discussion of inequality I would like to see intensified. When it is said, as it is, that we should protect the income of the rich, reduce taxes in order to encourage effort, I have an answer. Perhaps we should have a higher marginal rate of taxation to stimulate effort to maintain after-tax income. This is not widely applauded.

14   As we look at the achievements of the century, we must all pay tribute to the end of colonialism. Too often, however, the end of colonial rule has also meant the end of effective government. Particularly in Africa, colonialism frequently gave way to corrupt government or no government at all. Nothing so ensures hardship, poverty and suffering as the absence of a responsible, effective, honest polity. Once this was the result of the earlier escape from colonialism in Latin America. So now in much of Africa and in lesser measure in Asia.

15   In a humane world order, we must have a mechanism to suspend sovereignty when this is necessary to protect against human suffering and disaster. Let there be government by the United Nations to bring about an effective and humane independence. Economic aid is important, but without honest, competent government, it is of little consequence. We have here one of the major unfinished tasks of the century.

16   My emphasis, you will have observed, is on the UN. I believe it should have had the dominant role in the recent tragedy in the Balkans. I am also far from enthusiastic about air power as used there. There was nothing to be said for the Serbian rule of Kosovo. But neither for the basically indiscriminate nature of bombing—of men, women, children and, one should add, foreign embassies.

17   There is one more piece of unfinished business. It is our position on the edge of a total end to civilized existence on the planet, perhaps of life itself. Available are the nuclear weapons which could do precisely this. And there is a strong commitment to keeping and protecting these weapons even though we fully realize the threat. As long as we accept them in the nuclear countries, we are limited in our ability to persuade others to a policy of sanity and survival. When India and Pakistan last year exploded nuclear weaponry, we in the U.S. reacted adversely. They had the natural answer: "What about you?"

18   Thus the greatest unfinished business of the century now ending is the need to eliminate this weaponry. It need only fall into the hands of mentally vulnerable politicians to bring a nuclear exchange which, to repeat, could be the end of all civilized existence and, quite possibly, of all existence.

John Kenneth Galbraith, "John Kenneth Galbraith's world tour,"
The Globe and Mail, 6 July 1999, A13. Reprinted from *The Guardian.*

Word Recognition

John Kenneth Galbraith's talk was given at the London School of Economics (LSE), a world-famous academic institution. Galbraith's audience would have been a highly educated group of young people, their parents, people from the media, economists, and other academics. He would just presume that they understood terms like *polity, gross domestic product,* and *colonialism.*

He would also expect that his audience would know exactly what he was talking about when he mentioned Marx, Harvard, Florence, William Shakespeare, Charles Darwin, the Impressionists and the Balkans. Educated people are accustomed to such references.

Even if you have never read the works of William Shakespeare, Karl Marx, or Charles Darwin, it is a good idea to know what each is famous for, and be able to refer to them occasionally.

What are the following famous for?

William Shakespeare (1564–1616) needs no introduction. Some of his most famous plays, such as *Hamlet, King Lear, Macbeth, Romeo and*

Juliet and *A Midsummer Night's Dream* are constantly quoted, and have given us phrases and expressions that are part of everyday speech.

Karl Marx (1818–1883), a German political philosopher and economist, wrote *The Communist Manifesto* with Friedrich Engels, another philosopher. Later, he wrote *Das Kapital* about wealth, work, workers, and the control of production. Once seen by some people as the source of all evils in communist countries, many people now refer to him as a visionary.

Charles Darwin (1809–1882), a British naturalist whose book *On the Origin of Species by Means of Natural Selection* about evolution astounded the people of his time and caused great controversy.

Florence, the city of art, is in Italy but other countries have named places after it, so Galbraith automatically qualifies his reference with the phrase, "in Italy."

In Florence, visitors can see Michelangelo's *David* at the Accademia; Botticelli's *The Birth of Venus* at the Uffizi Gallery; frescoes by Italian masters; the Pitti Palace; the Duomo, or cathedral, one of the city's architectural marvels; palaces like the Palazzo Vecchio; the Boboli Gardens; and countless other treasures. The city, created by great sculptors, artists, and architects, is known for its Florentine style. Florence, a city of elegance and beauty, on the Arno River, even though it bakes in summer and freezes in winter, attracts thousands of visitors every year, all year round.

The Impressionists were painters who developed their theory and style of painting around the 1870s in France. Impressionists tried to create a sense of reflected light in their paintings and tended to use small strokes of the brush to get the effect they wanted. In their paintings, they tried to convey the direct feelings of people enjoying themselves and the effects of light and shade on colour. Some famous names associated with the Impressionists are Auguste Renoir, Édouard Manet, Claude Monet, Edgar Degas, Alfred Sisley, Berthe Morisot, and Camille Pissaro.

The Balkans is the term used to refer to the countries of the Balkan Peninsula, a region known for its troubled history, hostilities, and frequent wars since the time of Philip of Macedon in the third century BCE.

Vocabulary

economics (introduction): often known as "the dismal science," economics deals with matters of finance and material wealth, with the production, development, and management of wealth creation, and the prosperity of a society, country, or household

idiocy (para. 1): stupid behaviour

diversionary (para. 2): disruptive, distracting; offering an alternative

perverse (para. 4): obstinately doing the opposite of what is expected or considered reasonable

gross domestic product (GDP) (para. 6): the total value of goods and services produced in a country in one year

speculative (para. 9): buying and selling at risk

justification (para. 10): showing sufficient reason for

colonialism (para. 14): the policy of being politically in control of a distant country; settling or conquering distant regions and controlling them

polity (para. 14): an organized society; the form of government belonging to the citizens of a nation

Paraphrasing

A word about *paraphrasing*. When you paraphrase, you restate what the writer has said in different words. You make the same point as the writer, but in your own voice. When writing an essay, you will often paraphrase a passage from your research or a brief quotation because an essay offers *your* views on a topic, not just a parachute drop of quotations from other people. The reader wants to know what *you* think. That's why your words are the most important part of an essay. That's why it is useful to be able to paraphrase another author's comments.

Exercise 5.3

Now for some practice in paraphrasing. Complete the second sentence of each set in as many words as necessary so that it paraphrases the first. Be sure to make the same point, but in your own words.

Example

John Kenneth Galbraith says that one of the greatest achievements of the twentieth century is that fewer people are engaged in hard, tedious, boring toil.

Paraphrased: According to John Kenneth Galbraith, *the reduction of the numbers of people working at repetitive, dull labour is one of the twentieth century's biggest successes.*

1. In some aspects, computers can be seen as serviceable and good, in others, as contrived and diversionary.

    In some ways, people can see computers as _____.

2. It is a perverse fact that the people who actually enjoy their work are the best paid.

    It is a strange contradiction that _____.

3. Nonetheless, here too there has been progress. In the century past many people have graduated from the miseries to the enjoyment of work.

    Progress in the twentieth century is also seen in _____.

4. In today's world, the prime indicator of all human progress has become the GDP.

    The GDP is now _____.

5. Success as measured by economic output bears no close relation to human achievement.

    The greatest cultural achievements of the human race

    _____.

6. John Kenneth Galbraith warns us not to assume that the age of slump, recession, depression is past.

    According to John Kenneth Galbraith, we should not be sure that

    _____.

7. The huge numbers of poor people in the cities of even the richest countries is one of the most visible and urgent problems of today.

    The horrifying extent of urban poverty, found even

    _____.

8. Respected economist John Kenneth Galbraith states clearly that everybody should be guaranteed a decent basic income.

    John Kenneth Galbraith, the reputable economist, says right out that _____.

9. These days the distribution of income is a bizarre problem causing stirring discussions of inequality, discussions which John Kenneth Galbraith would like to see intensified.

    Today, an unusual problem that deserves more discussion is

    _____.

10. There is a strong commitment to keeping these nuclear weapons even though we fully realize the threat.

    On the subject of nuclear weapons, John Kenneth Galbraith worries that _____.

Exercise 5.4*

Select the correct word form for each sentence. Use appropriate verb forms, or singulars and plurals, as required by context.

1. **limit, limited, eliminate, limiting, limitless**

    a. The United Nations plans to _____ all symptoms of beriberi from Ugwaziland by the year 2019.

    b. The disastrous effects resulting from nuclear weapons are

        _____.

    c. As long as a country has nuclear weapons, citizens within that country are _____ in their ability to stop other countries from having them.

    d. Even though retirement will liberate you from career demands, it does not have to _____ your enjoyment of life.

    e. Some retired people find that their aging bodies are more _____ than they would wish.

2. **enjoy, enjoyment, enjoyable, enjoying, enigma**

    a. Joe thought Rhonda's response to the invitation puzzling but delightful, so he continued to see her as a beautiful

        _____.

    b. Many retired professionals are _____ a complete change in lifestyle.

    c. They are not embracing the idea of leisurely "golden years" of mindless recreation, but instead _____ volunteering where they are needed.

   d. These retired people realize that their time helping the poor and the homeless is, in fact, _____.

   e. Their sense of accomplishment offers them more _____ than a dull life of golf, cruises, and endless television.

3. **concentrate, concentration, concentrating, concerted, concerned**

   a. We all know that Herbert's powers of _____ lead to great financial rewards.

   b. We are very _____ though, about his lack of restraint in spending money.

   c. Some mature students returning to school after years of home-making may find it hard to _____ on doing only one task at a time.

   d. When Sheila forgot her lines for the third time that night, the director asked her why she was not _____.

   e. The director reminded her that everyone at the rehearsal was expected to make a _____ effort and focus on the scene on stage, not the scene outside.

4. **optimism, optimistic, optometrist, option, optimist**

   a. The study of the eye and its diseases still fascinates Jon, even after years as an _____.

   b. Some Canadians feel _____ about the Comprehensive Nuclear-Test-Ban Treaty, even though the United States has not signed it.

   c. Because the United States is helping finance a global network for monitoring nuclear action, many Americans have a feeling of _____ about the future.

   d. Most ordinary citizens feel they do not have many _____ when it comes to international treaties.

   e. Nuclear explosions, like the one on the Russian nuclear-powered submarine *Kursk* in the Barents Sea, make most people feel nervous, in spite of all the talk from politicians who tend to be just cockeyed _____.

5. **research, researched, researcher, resign, resigned**

   a. Colleen was relieved to hear that _____ say that garlic will reduce heart disease and stroke, because she loves hummus.

   b. The student knew that he had not _____ the subject thoroughly, so was not surprised by his failing grade.

   c. Even after everyone voted overwhelmingly against him, the Leader of the Opposition refused to _____.

   c. After years of _____, the new drug for arthritis that made Bill's life easier finally came onto the market.

   d. She did not find it easy to become _____ to the idea that her father would never come home again.

Recall

Answer the following questions in your own words.

1. Who is John Kenneth Galbraith and where is he from?

2. What is Galbraith always glad to have escaped from?

3. What sort of people are usually the best paid and enjoy the most leisure in our society?

4. What has become the prime indicator of social progress in fortunate countries?

5. In what direction are the most enthusiastic artistic and scientific efforts often channelled today?

6. What, in Galbraith's view, are the two topics of greatest urgency in the world at this time?

7. What solution does Galbraith propose for the problem of urban poverty?

8. What has the end of colonialism often meant? Explain briefly.

9. According to Galbraith, what could bring an end to civilized existence on the planet?

Review

Answer the following questions.

1. What is the good news about technological advancements, according to John Kenneth Galbraith? What is the bad news?

2. Why does Galbraith refer to the word "work" as "our most misleading social term"?

3. Why does Galbraith refer to Florence, William Shakespeare's country and Paris in the years of the Impressionists? What do these places have in common and why does he mention them?

4. Why does Galbraith see the economic sequence of boom and bust as a problem?

5. What do people do in a period of speculative optimism?

6. What discussion would Galbraith like to see intensified? Why?

7. Galbraith celebrates the end of colonialism but regrets some results. Why?

8. Why does Galbraith say we need "honest, competent government"? Give reasons.

9. What are Galbraith's views on nuclear weapons? Explain in two or three sentences.

10. What message does Galbraith leave with his audience?

Response

In small groups, respond to *one or more* of the following topics.

Topics

1. Think about the messages John Kenneth Galbraith gave to his audience.

    What message would you leave with a group of young graduates? Prepare a convocation message. Follow the author's approach. In other words, begin with a statement of where you came from (choose one from within your group), what you are doing now (use your imagination), and what you see as good and also what you see as disturbing about today's world. Mention some possible approaches to the problems as you see them.

2. Galbraith worries about what might happen if nuclear weaponry falls "into the hands of mentally vulnerable politicians."

    What sort of politicians are mentally vulnerable, in your view? Create a description of such politicians and say what they might actually do and why. Be specific about their vision of the world and about what might incite them to use nuclear weapons.

3. Galbraith uses Marx's expression, "the idiocy of rural life." Think about the tasks and experiences that might have inspired this expression. Obviously, the expression refers to considerable physical labour and toil. Are there jobs in Canada today that still involve "hard, repetitive, even physically painful toil"? What are these jobs?

    Write about a job today that offers little enjoyment and much idiocy. Indicate the labour involved and the repetitive quality of that labour. Use examples to show the work is neither pleasant, nor mentally rewarding. Conclude with suggestions as to how to bring such labour into the twenty-first century.

This is the end of Part 1. You have covered a range of readings in the fields of life-writing (memoirs, personal essays), journalism, and political argument rather than rhetorical modes, such as description, narration, definition, cause and effect, process, and persuasion.

Today's concept of texts or textuality is broader than in the past, but the most important reasons for writing and reading have not changed. Writers write because they want to communicate something. Readers read because they want to know what a writer has to say. At college, readers read to learn and understand. Student readers still need to ask:

- Do I understand what the writer is saying?

- What exactly is the writer saying?

- How is the writer communicating the ideas?

- Do I agree with the writer? Why or why not?

    Your work on the readings in Part 1 has developed your reading skills. You know that there is more to reading than just looking at words on a page.

In Part 1, you have focused on three aspects of reading comprehension.

1. *Your literal comprehension.* This is the basic understanding of a text's main ideas through vocabulary, through skimming, scanning, grasping, and **recalling** the sequence of events.

2. *Your critical comprehension.* This is the ability to recognize a writer's purpose; to note subjective and objective material; to see how a writer supports an idea; and to analyze what is actually being said, through **reviewing.** It's what you understand about the details, concepts, and key points communicated.

3. *Your affective comprehension.* This is your emotional involvement with what you read, how you feel about it and react to it after reading and thinking at the literal and critical levels. It's how you feel about the material communicated, through **responding** to it, after analysis of the language and ideas. You are responding, not at a gut emotional level, but rather with thought, analysis, and imagination.

Congratulations.

REVIEW AND REMEMBER

Part 1

Critical Thinking and Comprehension

1. What does the writer want you to understand? **Subject**
    *   What is the point of the reading?
    *   What subject does the writer introduce at the beginning?
    *   What subject does the writer reinforce at the end?
    *   What facts, examples, specific data does the writer use?
    *   What opinions does the writer voice?
    *   What is the specific subject of the text?
    *   What is it all about, then?

2. Why is the writer writing this text? **Purpose**
    *   How does a clear sense of purpose emerge?
    *   Does the writer wish to persuade, inform, narrate, explain, describe, define, compare, contrast, instruct, or analyze?

- Does the writer have a message? What is it?
- Can you summarize the writer's purpose in your own words in one clear sentence?
- What is the point of it all, then?

It is obviously impossible to get into a writer's head, but the style, the purpose, and the ideas presented will give you an idea of what the writer's purpose might be. *(It may be a problem to state the intention, aesthetic or intellectual, of a work of art. Changes in the cultural environment make it questionable to state a writer's intention. However, most of the readings at this stage gain from a statement of purpose.)*

3. Who is likely to read the material? **Audience**

- What level of education is essential for understanding the text?
- What facts or information is the audience expected to have already?
- Who is going to read this?

Writers write to be read. The language, the style of writing, the ideas, or facts communicated will give you an idea of the possible audience for the prose.

Part 2

Interactive Critical Thinking

Part 2 offers a series of collaborative pre-writing and critical thinking writing tasks designed to help you organize your thoughts and choose specific data to support your ideas.

CHAPTER 6

Getting to the Point

This chapter offers steps to successful, clear communication.

By the end of this chapter, you will be able to

- put your thoughts and ideas in order so an audience can understand them easily

- focus your thoughts so you always begin with a **specific, precise, clear (SPC) subject,** a micro-subject

- make a point about that micro-subject for a topic sentence

- use resources to support your main point effectively

- avoid making vague generalizations

- introduce your main point with impact

- present your ideas convincingly

- conclude carefully

- be convincing

Before you begin to write or speak, you need to sort out your ideas. If you don't, you may come across as confused and unprepared. Learning to put your thoughts in order gives you an advantage in communication.

You want your readers or listeners to trust you. Your readers want to trust you too, but they also do not want to waste their time. People today are in a hurry. They want the information, they want it now, and they want it to be easy to understand. To give people the information they want or need, you must know *what* you are writing about.

Before you even begin to write, you need to ask *why* you are preparing this material and *who* is going to read it. In other words, you should think about your **purpose.** Then, you can design your material to appeal to your **audience.**

First, think about *why.* Why are you writing this paragraph or paper? Why do you want to communicate a specific idea, attitude, thought, subject? Do you want to explain your views on an issue? Do you want to motivate people to do something? Do you want to give the facts of a situation to someone?

Usually you write because you have something to say. You may wish to communicate an idea or make a point. Sometimes you have to describe a place or situation, compare objects, share a discovery, a feeling, or explain an issue. Whatever the reason you write ("for a grade," most students say), you write to communicate with someone else. Who is that someone? Who will read or listen to your words?

Think about *who,* or the audience.

- Who exactly is going to read or listen to your essay?

- What do they know about the topic?

- What do they need to know?

- What will they remember after they have read or listened to your paper?

You want your audience to remember your thoughts and ideas, not muddled points, spelling mistakes, and confusing sentences. That is why it is important to develop the sensible pre-writing and thinking habits suggested in Part 2 of this book. Parts 3 and 4 will focus more specifically on writing.

If you always remember to ask yourself *why* and *who* before you begin to write, you will be well prepared to communicate essential material clearly.

Whatever career you choose, your employer will be pleased if you can communicate clearly. Read on and discover how easy it is to become a clear communicator. Just follow these 11 steps.

Remember: **Clear thinking means clear writing.**

Steps to Becoming a Clear Communicator

Step 1: Think Before You Write, *or* It's the Thought that Counts

Exercise 6.1

In pairs or groups of three, choose at least *two* topics from the following list and discuss them. Find out what your partner or each member of the group thinks about the topic.

smoking	pornography	recycling
terrorists	rock music	your driving
birth control	homosexuality	caffeine
beer	feminism	taxes
winter	death	dancing
seniors	arranged marriages	boxing

Undertake the following tasks for each topic chosen:

1. After your discussion (about 5 minutes on each topic), consider the views you have just heard. Do you feel the same about the topic? Are your views similar to those of your parents? Why or why not? In what ways do you agree with each other? With your parents? How do your views differ? Why? Make a list of points you agree upon and points where you differ.

2. Now is the time to stop and think. Consider the ideas presented on the topic and ask yourself why you think the way you do. Do you have a particular bias? What is the other side of this issue? Are there good points about that view?

3. Ask your partner or group members to state their opinions on the topic again. Take brief notes of that response. Be accurate and note any specific reasons for their views.

    After you have discussed and responded to each topic chosen:

4. Stand and deliver! Tell the class how your partner or group member feels about one of the topics discussed. Represent this person. You might mention if you disagree for the sake of comparison.

5. After listening to all the presentations, ask your partner or group members if they felt fairly represented. Discover why or why not. What would they have liked to hear? What important points, if any, were omitted?

6. With your partner or group members, decide which presentation worked best and decide why. Compare your presentations with others heard in the class.

    Note: It is important to be honest but tactful at this stage. Be sure to say what was good about your partner's or group member's presentation, but be honest, and mention what might be improved next time. Constructive peer evaluation is invaluable. Learning to evaluate is also important in your development as a writer.

Exercise 6.2

In pairs or groups of three, choose *two* of the following topics.

a good car	a good song
a good grandparent	a good teacher
a good high school	obesity
a good movie	the brain drain
a good pet	toll roads
a good photograph	unemployment

For each topic:

1. Narrow the topic so that it's more specific. Try asking *who, where, when, what kind of.* For example, a good movie—for children; a good car—for seniors.

2. Talk about the narrowed subject. Begin by discussing what is good or what is bad in relation to it. Then come up with more sophisticated vocabulary to describe your views. What qualities does a good _X_ have? You might, for example, choose words like

challenging	imaginative	perceptive
comfortable	impressive	skilled
competent	interesting	soothing
dangerous	kind	stimulating
generous	luxurious	thoughtful

    If you choose one of these words, be able to explain why you have chosen it. In your discussion, you might ask

    - Does the topic say or do something in a special way?
    - What makes this something or someone special?
    - Does the topic allow you to escape trivial reality in some way? How?

3. Choose examples or stories to illustrate your ideas on the topic.

4. Write one sentence summing up your ideas about the topic. Include two general points about the topic in your sentence. Choose words that make your points clear.

    Examples

    A good movie for children offers excitement and a world of wonder.

    With exciting activities and good stories, a good Grade 1 teacher can make learning to read fun for kids.

    Stevie Bang's song "Copperhead Choirboy" is a good song because it has cynicism-free lyrics and a hypnotic beat.

5. Prepare a concluding statement to reinforce what you say about your topic. Stress why [your topic] is a good _X_ .

6. Now put all the material together.

    a. Begin with the general statement of #4.

    b. State the name of your specific topic and explain briefly how it fits your general statement (use your ideas from #2).

    c. Use the examples or stories from #3.

    d. Conclude with #5.

Example

With exciting activities and interesting stories, a good Grade 1 teacher can make learning to read fun for kids.

Mrs. Chalmers at Hamilton East Public School knew how to get kids excited about reading. She would read us a story and then get us to act it out. Next, she would help us decode key words and draw pictures with those words underneath. One day I got to be the Gingerbread Man. I'll never forget that jingle, "Run, run, as fast as you can. You can't catch me. I'm the Gingerbread Man." Every kid in that class could read those words by the end of the day. Every day Mrs. Chalmers gave us new stories and new activities. No wonder we were all happy readers by the end of the year.

7. Choose one person to present your material to the class, clearly, slowly, and with a smile.

Step 2: Support Your Views

Readers and listeners want to believe you, but they are suspicious if you don't seem to know what you are talking about. Show them that you do. How? With evidence. With plenty of concrete data. Where do you get that data? From **research.**

You need to know how to find information. Information retrieval is almost a science today. Nobody can know everything. Smart people learn where to go for information. Smart people show they have done research and know how to use it.

Where will you go for the information you need? Information is everywhere today. Students are always being told, "Look it up." Looking it up has never been easier. Today you have the Internet, besides the telephone and the video store, but print sources are still some of the best and most reliable sources of information.

Go to your resource centre, your local public library, any reference library, as well as the Internet. Consult newspapers, magazines, scholarly journals.

Don't forget the experts around you. Ask your boss, your aunt, a professor, the mechanic, the doctor, your friend. Show your audience you know the importance of expert knowledge, as well as real-life experience. Show that you know how to find knowledge and use it.

There are hundreds of sources of information out there. Many of them are not reliable, however. Remember not to trust everything you read when you start to do serious research. You need to discriminate (in the best sense). That is, you have to make a distinction between the good, the bad, and the ugly, or rather, the truthful, the irrelevant, and the incredible. You have to learn to be critical of the information you find, and to use only trustworthy, reputable sources of information. You also have to be cautious, especially when surfing in cyberspace.

How do you become discriminating, in the best sense? You learn to exercise judgment in the selection of your material. Ask yourself

- Who is the writer, the source of this information?

- What is the writer known for?

  (Is the writer an expert in the field or is it some idiot trying to get attention, or make a fast buck? How long has the writer been working in this field? Where does the writer come from? Why would you trust this writer?)

- Where does the information come from? Who put it out?

  (An article written in Canada on health-care providers could be quite different from one written in the United States. A paper written by Greenpeace on the risks of transporting plutonium might give different information from one published by the company keen to get the job of transporting it.)

- When was this information written?

  (An article on essential office equipment written in 1990 is not as relevant today, but a commentary on the Peloponnesian War, a war between Athens and Sparta, 431–404 BCE, [Sparta won], written in 1890 might be the best thing ever written on the subject.)

- Is the information objective or subjective? Why do you say so?
  (See Chapter 2, Objective or Subjective?)

Exercise 6.3

This exercise may be done with a partner who shares similar views, or individually.

Go back to the topics discussed in Exercise 6.1. Decide how you will present your views on *one* of these topics. How can you convince an audience that these views are reasonable and well-thought-out?

1. What evidence could you produce to support your views? Are there any facts, statistics, experiences/anecdotes, examples, or expert ideas you could produce to help prove your point? Where could you find this supporting evidence?

2. Prepare a list of research resources. Use your library or resource centre. Ask for help, if necessary, in finding references on the topic you've chosen. You may also find references through Internet search engines or networks. For example, newspapers and periodicals often can be accessed through Internet search engines and electronic directories. Some of the Internet search engines available are

    www.google.com

    www.yahoo.com

    www.altavista.com

    www.hotbot.com

    www.lycos.com

    Write down the name of at least one electronic source, one periodical, and one other print reference. Underline the titles if writing by hand. Note when and where these references were printed or created, and who created them (writer, editor, or publisher).

3. Find one of these references, and read the part related to the topic. Take notes on how the reference supports or contradicts your point of view. Can you find any statistics, quotations, facts, or other evidence to reinforce your point? Is there evidence that contradicts your point of view?

4. Make a brief presentation (2 to 3 minutes) on your views. Make clear your specific attitude on the topic and the reasons for it. Then explain how the research you have just done supports or contradicts your point of view.

Exercise 6.4*

In pairs or groups of three, decide

- whether you believe the following statements

- where the information might come from; that is, from what sort of person or source

- whether the information is objective or subjective

1. Poached Eggs Mexicana has 345 calories per serving.

2. Idling the engine for more than 10 seconds uses more fuel than restarting the car.

3. An online self-help forum, like ACTalk, is an important place for people to talk anonymously with other people living with HIV/AIDS.

4. There's nothing quite as revitalizing as sea algae, which will help you to unwind and will restore your feeling of well being.

5. It is stressful and dangerous to take an elephant away from her family.

6. Free music on the Internet leads directly to Free Love.

7. Language disturbance, and disturbance of executive functioning (planning, organizing, sequencing, abstracting) are signs of the development of cognitive deficits associated with the dementia of Alzheimer's disease.

8. On the Waccamaw rice plantations, slaves ate the grains, fruit, vegetables, and meat of the New World environment; but to those foodstuffs slave cooks applied an African culinary grammar—methods of cooking, spicing, remembered recipes, ancestral tastes. They added the soul ingredients.

9. You can have your photo taken with the Stanley Cup, watch a movie, see exhibits on the origins of the game, evolution of equipment, women's, minor and minor-pro leagues, then part with your hard-earned cash at the gift shop.

10. Many great cultures, such as those of Japan and India, never had chairs and never missed them.

Sources

Which statements did you believe? Why? Would you trust

1. The Egg Marketing Board of Canada?

2. An article on pollution from the Toronto Environmental Alliance?

3. The AIDS Committee of Toronto?

4. An advertisement for Algemarin shower gel?

5. People for the Ethical Treatment of Animals?

6. An advertisement for Live 365.com?

7. A Handbook from the Ministry of Social Services, Queen's Park, Ontario, on Caring for People with Alzheimer's disease?

8. Charles Joyner, professor, in *Down by the Riverside*, a book about a slave community in South Carolina, published by the University of Illinois Press in 1984?

9. A guide to the Hockey Hall of Fame?

10. An article on ergonomics in the July 2000 issue of the high-tech magazine *Wired*?

Now ask yourselves how you would prove or disprove the statements in this exercise. What facts and figures are needed? Where could you find useful data for your response to one of those statements?

Exercise 6.5

In pairs or groups of three, decide which statement in the following sets sounds most convincing and might provide the basis for a *short* essay or report.

Be able to state why a statement is convincing. It may be useful to ask *so what* or *who cares* to see if the statement offers sustenance for a writer or reader. Note: Does the statement offer the basis for further comment?

You may decide two statements in the same set are convincing. Remember that you should be able to write about three or four pages on the chosen statement after research, if necessary. Be prepared to defend your choice.

1. a. Competing in Olympic distance triathlons is easy.
   b. You have to be strong to compete in Olympic distance triathlons.
   c. Kathy Maj says training for Olympic distance triathlons makes her ravenous.

2. a. The Philippines has imposed a total ban on waste incineration to stop one source of toxic pollution.
   b. Incinerators are the largest producers of dioxins and furans.
   c. Waste incineration should be banned.

3. a. The Detroit Auto Show was first held in 1907 in a beer garden.
   b. The Detroit Auto Show takes place in Detroit.
   c. The Detroit Auto Show is an important showcase for industry achievements.

4. a. Many pet owners worry about their pets' health and treat their animals like humans.
    b. Sheri Bat takes her cat, Wuhan, for acupuncture treatments for his hip dysplasia.
    c. Vancouver veterinarian Mumford Jonze warns pet owners that acupuncture for pets has not been tested in any controlled scientific studies.

5. a. When you get something in your eye, like a speck of dust or onion juice, then extra tears are produced to wash it away.
    b. Sayeeda likes watching sad movies because they make her cry.
    c. Tears are produced all the time by the lacrimal glands.

6. a. Cities in China have served as lines of communication, trade, and industry since 221 BCE.
    b. In choosing sites for their cities, the Chinese have sought to exploit natural advantages, such as a ready supply of water, and protection from invaders and floods.
    c. Some of the best-known cities in China are very nice.

7. a. Ronnie Burkett is Canada's foremost artist in puppet theatre and has performed in Dublin, New York City, and London, England.
    b. Ronnie Burkett has won numerous awards for design and production, including two Dora Mavor Moore Awards, two Chalmers Awards, and one Sterling Award for Outstanding Performance.
    c. Ronnie Burkett is from Alberta and often performs in other countries.

8. a. Every year, hundreds of millions of North American monarch butterflies migrate south.
    b. Every autumn, monarch butterflies create an orange blizzard as they fly south.
    c. Monarch butterflies have a migratory urge.

9. a. In apartments, green plants make living quarters more attractive.
    b. A survey of residents in a public housing development in Scarborough, Ontario, showed that the more greenery people had in their apartments, the stronger their social ties.
    c. Some people have green plants in their apartments.

10. a. Abnormalities in motor development, social behaviour, and mental ability in childhood may be warning signs of schizophrenia.

    b. Schizophrenia usually manifests itself between the ages of 15 and 30.

    c. Schizophrenics suffer delusions.

Congratulations. You have now completed at least two exercises on critical thinking skills and have begun the process of becoming a credible and convincing writer. Read on.

Step 3: Ask Questions and Find Answers

To present a convincing argument on a topic, you have to be sure you understand what the topic is. When you are given an assignment, look closely at the key words used. It may be useful to highlight or underline them. Think about what those key words mean. What does the audience want to know about them? What does the audience want to know, anyway? Decide what your specific subject is going to be. Sometimes you are expected to develop the subject yourself and provide your own focus. When you develop your own topic, always ask yourself

- What exactly will I talk about?

- Who will read my answer?

- What does the audience need to know?

It's very frustrating if you get a low grade and your teacher comments, "Not on the assigned question" or "Off topic." After you've spent hours on research, you do not want to discover you have missed the point of the question. That is why it is important to be sure what the topic is, before you begin research.

Clarify, clarify, clarify. Always ask questions to get to the essence of the topic. You might ask

- What does the audience want to know?

- What are the key words here?

- Who would know about this topic?

- Where would I go to get this expert's opinion?

Decide where to get the information you need. A good researcher is part reference librarian, part investigative reporter, part detective. Sometimes you have to go to the resource centre or the Internet, and sometimes you may have to go to a live person. Sometimes you can rely on your own powers of observation. Sometimes you just have to listen carefully in class and review your notes.

A good researcher knows how to make the most of all sources of information available and how to record the information from those sources accurately. Get into the habit of noting the following information for all research material:

- title
- author
- date
- place published

Exercise 6.6

A good researcher knows how to ask the right questions. Read one of the following:

- a reading in your English textbook
- a recent editorial in a newspaper
- a chapter in a college textbook

After you have read your selection at last twice, answer these questions:

1. What is the title and who is the writer?

   Underline the title of the book if writing in class. Italicize the title of a book if using a computer (underlining is a substitute for italics). However, put the title of a reading or a chapter in quotation marks.

   If you have chosen an editorial, write the editor's name (if known), underline the name of the newspaper (or use italics if using a computer), and give the full date of the edition of the paper.

   Examples

   A reading in your textbook:

   Buuck, Michelle. "Feeling No Pain." *Virtual Readers.*

A recent editorial in a newspaper:

"Herbert Goes to Paris." Editorial, *The Toronto Sunset,* 21 March 2002, A12.

A chapter in a college textbook:

Matthews, M. "Substance Abuse in College Students." *The Psychology of Selfishness.*

2. Is the writer alive today?

    Note any biographical data, if available. Playwright Henrik Ibsen said, "Every man is born with the marks of his time" (women too, as always, but Ibsen was a nineteenth-century writer). Like you, writers are affected by their era, or the historical context. Think about how your ideas have changed as times change. Remember too, that if you misrepresent the ideas of writers, living or dead, you can be sued.

3. What is the reading, editorial, or chapter actually about?
    No lengthy answer is necessary here. Note only key words and ideas.

4. In one sentence, state how the writer *introduces* the topic. Use the writer's first and last name if you know it.

    Example

    Michelle Buuck introduces her essay about reading skills, "Feeling No Pain," with the story of two Centennial College students.

5. In one sentence, state how the writer *concludes* the reading.

    Example

    At the end of her essay, Buuck [note the use of the last name only here] *returns to the two Centennial College students mentioned earlier, to stress how successful they have been at college since they learned how to be active readers.*

6. Is the reading, editorial, or chapter convincing? Why?

    Complete this sentence:

    I found (or I did not find) that [note title or subject and the point you wish to make here . . .] *was convincing because*

    _____.

7. Which words or expressions occur frequently? List them.

8.   Why do you think the words or expressions you listed in #7 are repeated? Comment in one sentence on the use of one or two of these words or expressions.

   Example

   Buuck refers frequently to interactive reading skills and collaborative exercises because she thinks that regular interaction and collaboration help students perform better at college.

9.   Make up three questions that will help other students think critically about the reading. Before you form these questions, look at the list of frequently used words and expressions you put together. Review the notes you have made about the introduction and conclusion. What is the most important idea of the reading? Prepare your questions, avoiding any that will get a simple yes or no answer. A question like "What is the writer's purpose?" might be a useful start.

10.   Try answering the three questions yourself. When you have finished answering them, ask yourself whether the answers reflect the content of the reading. Share your answers with someone else, if possible. Ask this person to tell you what the reading is about. Can this person tell you what the subject of the reading is and what point is made about it? Can your listener tell you immediately? Do you need to offer more explanation? What can your listener tell you? Do you have to read out your summary of the introduction? Your classmate's response will show you how specific you have been in your analysis of the reading.

Exercise 6.7

In pairs or groups of three, respond to *three* of the tasks listed below. For each task chosen

   A. Develop a specific subject. Consider what focus might result from the task (note the key words or ideas in the task). Write down the specific subject, which should be about 6 to 10 words.

   B. Decide what information your response to the subject should offer the audience. List three kinds of data you would present on the subject, such as statistics, statements from experts, examples. You do not have to find the actual data. Ask yourself, What exactly does the audience need to know here?

Remember: All you need to do here is write the clearly focused subject and list the research possibilities.

Tasks

1. Choose an issue that affects student life at your college, and prepare a letter to the president of the college describing this issue, suggesting some possible responses.

2. What is the connection between the program you are enrolled in and the life of ordinary citizens in your province? Explain in a brief essay.

3. "Commercial television, The Youth News Network (YNN), does not encourage students to examine subjects in depth or analyze news at all. It offers a 12-minute news program, two-and a-half minutes of commercials, and a computer lab for the school. Commercial interests thus gain more opportunities to make money from corporate involvement in schools, while schools gain computer labs, and Web access."

   Write a report giving reasons for or against using commercial TV in the high school classroom.

4. Identify and analyze the problems faced by students buying books and supplies at the college bookstore.

5. Prepare a brief report on the need for better sports facilities for an institution, a specific community, or a sport.

6. Explain why ecotourism is important for Canada.

7. Students from China face many pressures: No wonder they often suffer from stress-related illnesses while studying in Canada.

   Discuss possible ways of helping students from China avoid stress-related illnesses.

Exercise 6.8

Interview a classmate on his or her views on *one* of the following topics. Each person interviewed must respond to a different topic. No more than three people can respond to the same topic.

Ask questions eliciting information, not just *yes* or *no* answers. List at least two to four specific points to prove your classmate's views. Ask *what, where, when, why, how,* and other challenging questions.

1. irritating driving habits

2. the origins of life on earth

3. the pleasures or pains of life in small towns

4. the dangers of cellphones

5. shopaholics, or the global gospel of acquisition and what it is doing to us

6. the need for more publicity for the World Environmental Organization to stop the collapse of the ecosystem

7. the importance of family help in times of need

8. a definition of success

9. police on the beat

10. germ warfare and laboratory security

11. the need for more financial aid for Canada's athletes

12. the need for more physical education in schools

13. cloning humans

14. why game shows should be eliminated

15. the causes of terrorism

A. Prepare a statement mentioning the name of the person interviewed, the date he or she was interviewed, and give a one-sentence summary of the person's views on the topic.

B. Follow this statement with the three most convincing reasons offered for that point of view.

C. Conclude by repeating the topic and the one-sentence summary of your classmate's point of view.

Example

On Friday, October 18, 2002, Stacey Simper, a Marketing student at Cantaloupe College, said that she believes Canada's animal-free circus, the Cirque du Soleil, is one of the greatest success stories in the country. Why does she consider the Cirque du Soleil such a success?

1. More than 23 million people worldwide have seen the circus perform since its opening.

2. Sales were more than $420 million this year.

3. This circus loves new talent and new ideas, sending talent scouts all over the globe to find performers for the world's fastest-growing circus.

When asked to define a successful business, Stacey Simper says that Canada's Cirque du Soleil defines success because it is flying high and will continue to jump through all the hoops to stay right at the top with its Big Top.

You may be asked to present your statement to the class or to hand it in. To be sure all information accurately represents your classmate's comments to you, review your notes with him or her. Remember to check that you have spelled his or her name correctly.

Congratulations. You have just completed more exercises in critical questioning skills, another stage in the process of becoming a thoughtful writer. Now it's time to look at avoiding generalizations.

Step 4: Be Specific— Avoid Vague Generalizations

Good writers are very specific. They avoid making generalizations like

- Redheads have bad tempers.
- Headbangers are stupid.
- Cops hate black people.

"To generalize is to be an idiot," said William Blake, the poet and visionary in England, towards the end of the eighteenth century. The same is true in Canada at the beginning of the twenty-first century.

A generalization is a sweeping statement where a comment about a large group is treated as a fact, when it may be true only in one or two cases, if at all. Thoughtful people avoid unsupported generalizations. They check the truth of a statement first or they qualify it. They try to present a precise point, not a general one.

STEPS TO SUCCESS

Avoiding Generalizations

1. Check the truth of a statement.
    *   Who says? Why should you believe it?
    *   What evidence is offered?

2. Choose a specific term instead of a general one.
    *   Instead of "the textbook," choose "*Basics and Beyond.*"
    *   Instead of "the convenience store," choose "7-Eleven."
    *   Instead of "the sport," choose "basketball."

3. Qualify the terms used with a modifying word or phrase.
    *   Instead of "children in the North," say "children in Moose Factory."
    *   Instead of "kids in daycare," say "48 toddlers at the Busybee Daycare Centre in Regina, Saskatchewan."
    *   Instead of "sports cars," say "some Porsche 911s."

Exercise 6.9*

Choose the answer which is the most general in each set. That is, select the answer that includes all the others.

1. a. winter pies
    b. raisin pie
    c. sugar pie
    d. apple pie

2. a. Buick Park Avenue
    b. Chevy Astro Van
    c. fine General Motors cars
    d. Chevrolet Malibu

3. a. pulley
    b. movement
    c. lever
    d. car jack

4. a. Wonder Woman
   b. super heroes
   c. Superman
   d. Indiana Jones

5. a. discus throwing
   b. long jump
   c. pentathlon
   d. Olympic Games

6. a. quality health care
   b. routine gall bladder removal
   c. laser surgery
   d. private-duty nurses

7. a. Alice's Restaurant
   b. eating out
   c. mushrooms with garlic cream on the menu
   d. Harvey's hamburgers

8. a. gasoline
   b. kerosene
   c. oil
   d. liquid fuels

9. a. keratin
   b. brunette
   c. hair follicles
   d. human hair

10. a. vest
    b. clothes
    c. sweater
    d. Levi's

11. a. Brandon, Manitoba
    b. Winnipeg, Manitoba
    c. a province in Canada
    d. Manitoba

12. a. Buffalo treehopper
    b. head louse
    c. wingless insects
    d. hog lice

13. a. Chinese immigrants in Canada
    b. Wo Hen Lee
    c. the Hen Lee trading empire
    d. Chinatown's busy shopkeepers

14. a. zinc
    b. Kitimat, British Columbia
    c. nickel deposits
    d. mineral processing

15. a. failure to proofread
    b. lack of planning
    c. imprecise vocabulary
    d. common student essay faults

16. a. checking for original tires
    b. buying a second-hand car
    c. used business cars
    d. odometer fraud in the second-hand car market

17. a. foreign service careers for women
    b. Canada-U.S. Business Women's Trade Summit
    c. female international development specialists
    d. Canada's female consul general in Kenya

18. a. the need to nurture
    b. the appeal of kittens, babies, dogs in advertisements
    c. advertising appeals to our needs
    d. the need to feel safe

19. a. toxic moulds, high levels of dust, droning machines
    b. nausea, itchy eyes, recurring nosebleeds
    c. biological and chemical contaminants in the workplace
    d. unhealthy work environments

20. a. The Evil House of Cheat, Termpaper.com, The Paper Store
    b. databases for students
    c. essay-writing services on the Web
    d. 12,000 to 25,000 term papers covering every imaginable topic

Exercise 6.10

Decide which of the following sentences are sweeping statements—statements that are too general to be taken seriously. Then, turn those sweeping statements into valid comments by adding your own qualifying phrases. Qualifying words or phrases include *in many cases, sometimes, in small amounts, in springtime.*

Example

General: Wine is bad for you.

Modified: Many health studies show that one or two glasses of red wine a day can be beneficial, but more is bad for your liver.

1. Tempting, tasty, and toxic, sugar is poisonous.

2. Nobody writes letters these days.

3. Cigarette companies are kind to seniors.

4. Teenagers are dangerous drivers.

5. Taking English at college is a waste of time.

6. A grass lawn should be fertilized twice a year.

7. Sorting laundry is really satisfying.

8. All the crazies move to the west coast.

9. Action movies are more appealing than romance movies.

10. Working mothers are too busy to think about their child's cultural development.

Exercise 6.11

Substitute a specific term as quickly as possible for the general term the teacher gives you. When the teacher says, "Don't give me a [general word from list below], give me a [specific name]."

Examples

Teacher: Don't give me a *tree*, give me a _____.

Student: Manitoba maple

Teacher: Don't give me a *dessert*, give me a _____.

Student: Strawberry mousse cheesecake

Teacher: Don't give me a *hockey team*, give me _____.

Student: [You choose. I wouldn't dare.]

General Terms

car	restaurant	bird
woman	man	tree
uncle	aunt	fruit
athlete	store	magazine
furniture	music	musical instrument
song	fuel	food
school	drink	variety store
coin	lake	vegetable
clothing	sport	ocean
rock star	movie	team
palace	bank	running shoe
club	CD	sibling
tire	house	illness
flower	colour	alcoholic beverage
hair style	cosmetic	feeling

Step 5: Find a Focus

Use a zoom lens and move in for a close-up when writing about a subject. To get the best shot, make your subject as limited as possible. Make all subjects **specific, precise, and clear (SPC)**. A good, clear focus does not offer too many possibilities at once. It establishes limits. A convincing paragraph or paper will have an SPC subject, a micro-subject.

According to an old saying, "where there is too much, something is missing." Remember that saying when you decide on your subject. Try not to take on too much.

Keep it simple. Keep it clear. Keep it specific.

Ask *why, where, when, how, so?*

Examples

Instead of: Cycling on Canada's Atlantic Coast is challenging but interesting.

Write: The Cabot Trail in Cape Breton, Nova Scotia, offers some demanding uphill challenges, but many amazing views.

Instead of: Physical activity is good for you.

Write: Daily physical activity helps control weight, reduces depression, and cuts the risk of heart disease and diabetes.

Instead of: The jamming of some improv rockers is worth checking out.

Write: Disco Biscuits' electro-jazz rock, with its love of melodic builds, rhythmic sprawl, and non-linear song structures, really grooves and always draws sold-out crowds in Philadelphia. (Now that's focused.)

Exercise 6.12

In pairs, decide which of the following statements are too broad to be developed in one paragraph. Which statements try to cover too much?

1. Canadians are very creative.

2. Asthma has reached epidemic status in industrialized societies today.

3. "Travel a thousand miles in a train and you are a brute; pedal five hundred on a bicycle and you are basically a bourgeois; paddle a hundred in a canoe and you are already a child of nature." *(Pierre Elliott Trudeau)*

4. More industrial parks are needed out west.

5. Canadians would pay more to drive "green" cars.

6. Computers are good for shopping online.

7. Teenagers love loud techno music and explosions.

8. Ad campaigns from pharmaceutical companies have too much influence.

9. The price of democracy is eternal vigilance.

10. Still waters run deep.

Exercise 6.13

In pairs or small groups, turn *five* of the following general statements into focused statements. Use qualifying words or phrases to clarify meaning.

Example

General: A few years back now, I decided to get my life in order.

Focused: By the end of Grade 11, I had made some important decisions: to study biology, to clean my room every Saturday, and to give up smoking.

1. Children whose parents never read them stories suffer a kind of deprivation.

2. Today's women avoid commitment.

3. Today's men avoid intimacy.

4. Poverty is a crime.

5. Owning an old car is expensive.

6. Students who don't agree with the professor are in trouble.

7. You have to think about your future when you are young.

8. No one can bear being happy all the time.

9. Coming to college is the best thing I ever did.

10. Partying is fun.

11. You should always choose reason over passion.

12. Extreme sports are dangerous.

Step 6: Make a Clear Point about Your SPC Subject

You know how to use a more specific term than a general one. You know it is important to avoid generalizations. Now try to keep the focus when you make a statement and make clear points *about* your specific subject. Use qualifying words and phrases to help you focus your ideas.

Example

Money doesn't bring happiness.

You can recognize that this comment is vague and general. You might wish to qualify it with a word like *sometimes* or *some*.

Sometimes money doesn't bring happiness.

Money doesn't bring some people happiness.

You would make a more convincing point, though, if you could be more specific. If you are writing about the general idea of money not bringing happiness, you might decide to focus on the unhappy situation of a cousin who won Lotto 6/49.

Because my millionaire cousin is now interested only in single malt whisky, fast cars, and strip clubs, I know that money has brought him more spiritual confusion than happiness.

A general statement becomes more interesting and more precise if you continue to ask questions like *why, when, where, how, what kind of.* In your response, use words and expressions like

because	in spite of
although	unless
for	whenever
whereas	even if
for one thing	for another
since	also

Exercise 6.14

Turn *six* of the following general statements into focused statements. Add at least two specific points to your revised statements to make them defined and convincing.

Read your six focused statements to a partner. He or she will select the two that are the most specific, precise, and clear and tell you why.

Examples

General: Students at Snowflake College are getting an inferior education.

Focused: Because they never have homework, because they have a casino in the cafeteria, and because their teachers never give tests, students at Snowflake College are getting a lousy education.

General: Newfoundland is beautiful and fascinating for tourists.

Focused: With its rocky scenery and the world heritage site Gros Morne National Park, Newfoundland is fascinating and beautiful for tourists.

1. Winnipeg is a charming city.

2. Canadians in general are not physically fit.

3. The lyrics of today's pop songs are boring.

4. Movies today are too violent.

5. Cocaine is bad for you.

6. The average Brazilian is more active than the average Canadian.

7. Swimming is good exercise.

8. Sexual harassment is rare on this campus.

9. Television programs are much better this season.

10. Knitting provides an emotional release.

11. We have a lot in common with flies, worms, and mice.

12. Driving enthusiasts love Porsches.

Exercise 6.15*

Choose *two* statements that best support the main sentence of each set.

1. Japanese workers tend to suffer more stress symptoms than Canadian workers.

   a. Fifty-nine per cent of Japanese workers say they feel drained after work compared with 25% of Canadian workers.

   b. Samurai warriors long ago swore loyalty to the death to their feudal lords.

   c. Many Japanese workers drink alcohol to excess rather than admit to feeling stressed.

   d. Self-help books offer good advice to workers in Canada.

2. Ecological insect controls are popular with gardeners now.

   a. The hollyhock, native to China, is a very popular flower of the mallow family.

   b. Mint, geranium, clove, cinnamon, garlic, hot peppers, and citronella are spicing up gardens to repel wasps, hornets, roaches, ants, crickets, and centipedes.

   c. Blue moneywort is a tough, easy-to-grow plant that endures heavy foot traffic.

   d. Garlic is a well-known repellent for caterpillars, whiteflies, aphids, and mosquitoes.

3. Children need to know how to avoid insect stings, in case they have severe reactions.

   a. Pharmacies have kits with a pre-filled syringe of epinephrine.

   b. Children playing outdoors should wear insect repellent.

   c. Caregivers should not allow children to play near food, garbage, insect nests, or trees with fruit on their branches.

   d. Blood pressure drops dangerously in some people after insect stings.

4. Restoring old cars involves a lot of time, effort, and money.

   a. If you're looking for the last word in mechanical serenity, you won't find it with an old car.

   b. Convertible tops come in cloth and vinyl.

   c. Locating the correct materials, finding the necessary hardware, and researching the vehicle's interior for detailing is time-consuming.

   d. Finding the right vinyl or leather for the right year means spending hours and often big bucks to find materials matching in colour, thickness, and grain.

5. Designers of backpacking gear are now trying to create more straightforward equipment.

   a. The Calgary boot has polyurethane cushioning.

   b. The top designers are stripping away all the excess straps, zippers, sunburn alarms, and other doodads on backpacks.

   c. One design keeps the pack-bag and frame separate, but closely connected by a fibreglass rod for comfort and ease.

    d. Most hikers don't bother to adjust all the tensioning straps on their backpacks.

6. British researchers have shown that no drug is more effective than friendship in treating depression.

    a. Women seem to have a stronger emotional reaction than men to potentially hostile stimuli.

    b. People with diabetes are in greater danger of losing their short-term memory as they age.

    c. Seventy-two per cent of a group of chronically depressed women assigned to meet volunteer "befrienders" regularly for chats over coffee experienced a remission in depression.

    d. The friendship prescription, not the drug prescriptions, helped many of the women in the study make a fresh start in their lives.

7. Even in our mechanized, materialistic age, fairy tales still cast a spell on children.

    a. Witches, dragons, talking beasts, flying carpets, wise women, and enchantments are accepted as easily by children as televisions and airplanes.

    b. The sons of Cheops, the pharaoh who commissioned the building of the great pyramid at Giza, took turns entertaining their father with tales.

    c. Society is interested in stories about the agony of breaking through personal limitations.

    d. Today many children around 8 and 9 years old seem most interested in fairy stories about magic; they can't get enough of them.

8. Students at Snowflake College are finding their education there very expensive.

    a. Tuition fees at Snowflake College are nearly $5,000.

    b. Students love the antique fireplace in the main student lounge.

    c. Students stage regular sit-ins and marches to protest against corporate advertising on campus.

    d. Supplies at the college bookstore cost six times more than those at the local discount store.

9. Students at Cantaloupe College take great interest in student politics.

   a. Students at Cantaloupe College always get the highest provincial scores in their professional qualifying exams.

   b. More than 80% of the student population at Cantaloupe College votes in student elections.

   c. Many Cantaloupe College students say there is too much administrative control of faculty.

   d. All the Cantaloupe College students interviewed for this article could name the student association's president and knew when the next students' association meeting would take place.

10. The Louvre in Paris, one of the largest palaces in Europe, is visited by millions of people every year because it has one of the finest collections of art treasures in the world.

    a. Women from Canada and the United States travelling on their own are advised to join one of the English-speaking guided tours to avoid being pestered.

    b. The superb statue of the *Winged Victory of Samothrace,* dating from circa 190 BCE, is splendidly placed on the landing of the eastern staircase as you enter the Louvre, and is one of the greatest Hellenic Greek sculptures.

    c. The Louvre took 666 years to build and many architects were involved in constructing this building of incredible size.

    d. Henri III, the favourite son of Catherine de Medici, often appeared in women's clothes, and he filled the Louvre with his *mignons*, his darlings.

Step 7: Use All Available Resources and Get Plenty of Input

Each member of a team provides a different perspective on the subject under discussion. Multiple perspectives offer new ideas and interpretations. They lead to greater clarity and fresh approaches to topics and issues.

When preparing a collaborative presentation, take advantage of the perspective offered by each group member and work with it, even if you choose to challenge (politely) the ideas involved. Use the input of every person available. Try to transcend individual differences and prepare a reasoned, well-supported argument for your group's point of view.

Exercise 6.16

In small groups, prepare a short oral presentation on one of the topics listed. This collaborative exercise allows you to

- work as a team

- work to a deadline

- encourage all group members to participate

Organize your time. This exercise could take from 15 to 40 minutes. Your teacher will give you your deadline.

Get everyone involved. Learn one another's names. Then give each group member a clear task, such as taking notes, introducing group members, reading out the topic sentence. Make sure everyone participates in contributing and organizing data.

Plan your presentation. Practise pronouncing names and stating key points before you speak to an audience.

Topics

1. teenagers on welfare

2. daily fitness routines

3. why [a particular city or town] is never dull

4. misconceptions about . . . [an ethnic group]

5. attitudes to . . .[a region of the country]

6. why we need student clubs

7. a problem at this college

8. recycling our garbage

Step 8: Introduce Your Topic with Impact

For most short paragraphs, no introduction is necessary. You state your point clearly right at the beginning, and you immediately provide support for your point.

For a longer discussion, you might want to motivate your readers or audience to pay attention to your topic. To do so, use one of the techniques discussed here.

To grab people's attention, what do you usually do? Do you scream or shout? Do you clutch your heart and fall to the ground? Do you smile mysteriously and flutter your eyelashes? Do you ring bells and blow whistles?

Those techniques and many others may work well in some situations, but if you are writing or speaking professionally, they are not possible. Instead, consider the **S3Q3 Formula**. This formula offers six tried-and-true ways of grabbing attention and preparing a reader for what is to come. You can choose the technique that best fits your subject.

> **S3Q3 Formula**
>
> **S3:** *Startle readers.*
>
> Begin with a
>
> - story,
> - statistic, or
> - shocker
>
> **Q3:** *Quicken readers' interest.*
>
> Begin with a
>
> - question,
> - quotation, or
> - quite contrary view

S1: Story. The story or anecdote you choose can be a joke, a personal experience, a case history, a moral fable. It must be

- relevant to your central point
- brief
- inoffensive to any groups

You can tell the story about your grandmother, or about Joe Genetic, even the one about the firefighter, the flight attendant, and the musician, but *only if*

- the story is *brief*
- the story is *relevant*
- the story *prepares* your readers for your central point

S2: Statistic. The statistic must relate clearly to the subject. People like the use of numbers, but not too many.

1. Only one of Canada's 39 national parks is free from ecological stress.

2. Eighty per cent of Cirque du Soleil's revenue comes from the box office.

3. Heart disease and stroke kills approximately 79,000 Canadians each year.

S3: Shocker. Startle your readers. Make readers open their eyes and start thinking.

4. My death has been foretold.

5. I've spent the last 5 years wearing only jeans and a T-shirt.

6. Cola Loca is contributing to climate change.

Q1: Question. This is a favourite way to involve readers and get them thinking.

7. Are you drinking enough water?

8. What makes them so smart?

Q2: Quotation. The quotation could be from your aunt, from an expert on the subject, or from a celebrity in the news. Just be sure it relates to your subject.

9. "Nick rocks—he has a great voice and is just so adorable," says Lisa Gandolfi.

10. Many years ago, actor Peter Ustinov described Toronto as being "like New York run by the Swiss."

11. "It'll all be the same in a hundred years." That's what my grandmother, a very wise woman, always said when I told her my problems.

Q3: Quite Contrary View. Give the opposite point of view before moving gracefully, or seguing (that's a popular word for moving from one point to another) to the real point you wish to make.

12. Caffeine can jolt you into awareness, sharpen your reactions, and heighten your responses.

13. Suits are symbols of wealth, power, and status.

Could you guess what topic each example introduces? Read on to see if you were right.

Topics Introduced by the Sample S3Q3 Sentences

1. the ecological health of Canada's spectacular national parks

2. the success of Canada's Cirque du Soleil

3. health threats to middle-age, with figures from the Heart and Stroke Foundation

4. genetic fingerprints

5. former student faces fashion problems in a new job

6. corporations and the environment

7. bodily fluids

8. the chimpanzees of Uganda

9. the appeal of the Backstreet Boys

10. how Toronto's changed

11. wedding ceremonies for today

12. the dangers of caffeine

13. anti-suit dress codes in some creative industries

Exercise 6.17

In pairs, choose *three* of the following topic sentences and prepare *two* different introductory attention-grabbing sentences for them. Apply a different S3Q3 Formula technique each time.

Read each pair of attention-grabbing sentences to another couple of classmates. They will choose the best of each pair. Read their picks to the class.

Topic Sentences

1. Planning a vacation means we have to consider my partner's love of scuba diving and my love of shopping.

2. No one who knows that when rats ate genetically modified food their stomach walls thickened and their intestines collapsed, would touch the stuff.

3. College is a great place to make new friends.

4. Dating a daredevil can be tiring.

5. Many rap artists go to great lengths to market their overheated dog-eat-dog visions.

6. High grades are not always a good indication of a student's ability.

7. Relationships often fail because the couple does not communicate well.

8. Their father's alcoholism and physical abuse made their childhood a nightmare.

9. Since I began Tae-Bo, I feel fitter, better coordinated, and happier.

10. Comfort and fashion rarely go hand in hand.

11. Car crashes are the leading cause of death among young people today.

12. At this college, even if the classrooms look alike, every student knows that the atmosphere in each one is quite different.

Exercise 6.18

Follow up introductory attention-grabbing sentences with a clear topic sentence. With a partner, choose *five* of the following introductory sentences and prepare a topic sentence stating the main point that could follow each. Note: Topic sentences make clear the idea that will be developed in the paragraph.

Choose the best three out of your five topic sentences and read them to another couple of classmates. They will then select the best one for reading to the class. The class can decide which topic sentences are the best.

1. Babies love vibration, but my sister found that changing baby Jamie's diaper on top of the washing machine on a low spin was not a good idea.

2. If you want to feel more energetic, eat bananas; if you want to be more alert at school, eat high fibre cereal; but if you really want to feel good, eat chocolate.

3. Falling in love is easy.

4. With winter so long and harsh, Canadians like to make the most of the summer months.

5. She is the only vocalist who could take on Mariah Carey in a singing contest and Muhammed Ali's daughter in a fist fight.

6. Charles Chu, 42, of Markham, Ontario, struggled with chronic fatigue syndrome for nearly 4 years.

7. Don't hate me because I'm beautiful.

8. Safe cities are no accident.

9. The most frightening day of Colleen's life began as an ordinary day.

10. We all want Halloween to be a safe and fun time for our little trick-or-treaters.

11. Everyone knows that a rich, single, young man needs a wife.

12. Memories of the past help us make sense of the present.

13. Did you just start college?

14. Kids love the tooth fairy and the Easter bunny.

15. Veronika turned to painkillers as a last resort.

Step 9: Craft Your Conclusion

A conclusion provides the finishing touch. All you need to do is remind your readers what your central point is. That is why you tend to repeat your key idea in your concluding section. Use different words from those in the topic sentence, as much as possible, but review the topic once more.

It is important not to turn off the transmission too abruptly, and leave readers stranded. Round off the paragraph or essay with care. This is no time to startle your readers. Remind them of what you are talking about by reviewing the key point. Never introduce anything new at this stage. Try to end with a statement to remember.

Exercise 6.19

Choose *three* of the topic sentences listed in Exercise 6.17. In pairs, come up with a concluding statement that might be used in an essay on each. Try to make each of your concluding statements short, sharp, and snappy.

Exercise 6.20

What was it about? In pairs or groups of three, choose *five* of the following concluding statements. Decide what the topic might have been.

1. It's taken me a long time to trust my ability to have a healthy relationship, but finally I figured out that the most important person to please is myself.

2. So if you want a job where you get the chance to be an environmentalist, engineer, entrepreneur, CEO, veterinary assistant, financial analyst, heavy machinery operator, and chemist, be a farmer.

3. Taylor does not call herself a traditional believer, but she believes she will meet some special beings, like Rusty, her childhood pet dog, after death.

4. I leave you with this thought: Technology is a tool; creativity is a life-long asset.

5. Surgery or not, nearly everyone eventually needs glasses to read.

6. But then, when you live out in the woods, and your only visitor is the beekeeper, you don't much care.

7. Getting enough water just might buoy your health.

8. If weapon-wielding women are now found in everything from Hollywood movies to Saturday morning cartoons, is it any wonder that women are becoming more violent in everyday life?

9. And so say all of us.

10. So to all of you I say, do the sensible thing: Get out there and vote.

11. Her book isn't something only seniors will appreciate. At any age, people will find her experience moving.

12. It was the performance the crowd had been waiting for.

Exercises for Fun

In pairs, try to guess where some of the following famous opening lines are found. If you recognize them, that's easy. If you don't have a clue where they are from, decide what sort of a book or essay they might introduce.

1. "Where's Papa going with that ax?"

2. Mrs. Rachel Lynde lived just where the Avonlea main road dipped into a little hollow, fringed with alders . . .

3. Whether I turn out to be the hero of my own life, or whether that station will be held by anyone else, these pages must show.

4. When my mother was pregnant with me, she told me later, a party of hooded Ku Klux Klan riders galloped up to our home in Omaha, Nebraska, one night.

5. I was saved from sin when I was going on thirteen. But not really saved.

6. Scarlett O'Hara was not beautiful, but men seldom realized it when caught by her charm as the Tarleton twins were.

7. Far out in the uncharted backwaters of the unfashionable end of the Western Spiral arm of the Galaxy lies a small unregarded yellow sun.

8. Marley was dead to begin with.

9. "Christmas won't be Christmas without presents," grumbled Jo, lying on the rug.

10. All happy families resemble one another, but each unhappy family is unhappy in its own way.

11. Mr. and Mrs. Dursley, of number four, Privet Drive, were proud to say that they were perfectly normal, thank you very much.

12. It was in Burma, a sodden morning of the rains.

Answers

1. E. B. White, *Charlotte's Web.* 2. Lucy Maud Montgomery, *Anne of Green Gables.* 3. Charles Dickens, *David Copperfield.* 4. *The Autobiography of Malcolm X* as told by Alex Haley. 5. Langston Hughes, "Salvation" 6. Margaret Mitchell, *Gone With the Wind.* 7. Douglas Adams, *The Hitchhiker's Guide to the Galaxy.* 8. Charles Dickens, *A Christmas Carol.* 9. Louisa May Alcott, *Little Women.* 10. Leo Tolstoy, *Anna Karenina.* 11. J. K. Rowling, *Harry Potter and the Philosopher's Stone.* 12. George Orwell, "A Hanging."

Famous Last Words

When writing, try to conclude with a memorable statement. Many writers have managed to finish a character's life or end a story with words that have become famous and echo for years in our consciousness.

Look at the following quotations. What situation or story resulted in these famous last words, do you think? If you do not recognize them, decide what subject the book or speech ending with these words might have covered. Answer in at least one sentence.

1. "It is a far, far better thing that I do, than I have ever done; it is a far, far better rest that I go to than I have ever known."

2. "Okay, baby, hold tight," said Zaphod. "We'll take in a quick bite at the Restaurant at the End of the Universe.'"

3. So we beat on, boats against the current, borne back ceaselessly into the past.

4. Wearing my Maple Leafs sweater I went to the church, where I prayed to God; I asked him to send, as quickly as possible, moths that would eat up my Toronto Maple Leafs sweater.

5. But when that dawn will come, of our emancipation, from the fear of bondage and the bondage of fear, why that is secret.

6. I'll think of some way to get him back. After all, tomorrow is another day.

7. It is not often that someone comes along who is a true friend and a good writer. Charlotte was both.

8. The creatures outside looked from pig to man, and from man to pig, and from pig to man again; but already it was impossible to say which was which.

9. But Flopsy, Mopsy, and Cotton-tail had bread and milk and blackberries for supper.

10. Whereof one cannot speak, thereof one must be silent.

Answers

1. *A Tale of Two Cities* by Charles Dickens ends with these lines reflecting the thoughts of Sydney Carton as he went to the guillotine in the French Revolution, so the woman he loved could marry the man she loved.

2. In the book *A Hitchhiker's Guide to the Galaxy* by Douglas Adams, Earthman Arthur Dent, after a dizzy whirl of coping with the end of the world and the right way to behave at such a time, gets this invitation over the intercom.

3. Nick Carraway, the narrator of *The Great Gatsby* by F. Scott Fitzgerald, is brooding on life.

4. Roch Carrier ends his greatly loved Canadian short story *The Hockey Sweater* with this heartfelt prayer from the 10-year-old boy in Quebec.

5. *Cry, The Beloved Country* by Alan Paton, written in 1948, is the powerful story of a Zulu pastor and his son in the troubled country of South Africa.

6. At the end of *Gone With the Wind,* by Margaret Mitchell, Scarlett O'Hara lifts her head and makes plans for the future, in a spirit that makes her one of the best-loved heroines in American fiction.

7. Life in the barn is good for Wilbur at the end of *Charlotte's Web,* by E. B. White, even if Fern is growing up and not visiting him as often, but he will never forget his dearest friend, the spider who saved his life.

8. With these words, George Orwell ends his allegory, *Animal Farm,* a powerful comment on politics and society.

9. At the end of *The Tale of Peter Rabbit,* Beatrix Potter writes how the disgraced Peter is put to bed with chamomile tea, while his siblings, who are good little bunnies, have their favourite food for supper.

10. The philosopher Ludwig Wittgenstein has a message for everyone in his *Tractatus Logico-Philosophicus.*

Step 10. Convince an Audience

Now you have had some practice in being specific. You have also practised these writing tasks:

- getting a focus

- avoiding generalizations

- establishing clear points

- offering evidence

- introducing and concluding

Now it's time to practice convincing an audience that you know what you are talking about.

"Trust me." How often do you hear people say that? Do you trust them? Why? What makes you trust people? What makes you trust a writer?

Mechanical errors can make your readers impatient. People may stop reading if the spelling, punctuation, and sentence structure are full of errors or are confusing to read. They will suffer Irritable Reader Syndrome. But even if the writing is clear and correct, what will keep your audience with you?

Answer: Facts. Details. Examples. Expert evidence. Statistics. References.

A useful marketing slogan to remember is, "The more facts you tell, the more you sell." Facts or faces, fashions or frills, people like specific points, not general statements. The architect, Mies van der Rohe, the designer of Toronto's TD Centre, loved to repeat the saying, "God is in the details." People still remember his fondness for those words, as well as his architectural details.

Try to give your readers, or your listeners, those important details. Convince your audience with evidence. Support your point with information or an informed opinion on a subject. Note: You won't use just any opinion, but one which is supported by evidence. You have to make readers trust you. Find information that will support your opinion or central point.

Find

- facts
- expert opinions
- verifiable data

Remember to select your supporting data carefully.

Exercise 6.21*

Choose the statements that best support the main sentence of each set.

1. In the twenty-first century, air travel will be more unpleasant.

    a. Some airlines are reducing the distance between rows in economy class to just 80 cm.

    b. Business class passengers have access to special lounges to get away from regular travellers.

    c. User fees for airports will increase this century.

2. Smart travellers know how to pack their clothes wisely.

    a. They find out what music festivals are available at their destination.

    b. They pack clothes in the order they intend to wear them.

    c. They pack heavier items like shoes and hair dryers on the bottom of their suitcase.

3. The early activities of Ernest Thompson Seton, the great Canadian writer and illustrator of natural history, helped him become a great teacher and storyteller.

    a. He studied in the Ontario Art School and in the Royal Academy of Arts and Sciences in London.

    b. He changed his name.

    c. He spent many years travelling in the prairies and mountains of Canada.

4. Genetically modified plants are common in Canada.

    a. Consumers are worried about outbreaks of abdominal pain, vomiting, and fever.

    b. The federal government estimates that 57% of the canola crop and 45% of the corn crop are genetically modified.

   c. In Canada, about 40 transgenic crops, crops that are genetically manipulated, are approved by the federal government.

5. Slot-machine attendants at casinos have stress-filled jobs.

   a. Hearing loss is common because of the electronic din from the machines and the blaring pop music.

   b. St. Clair College in Windsor offers gambling studies.

   c. "I've got bruises on my arms from players grabbing me," says one veteran "slottie."

Exercise 6.22

In pairs or groups of three, prepare *three* items of evidence for *three to five* of the statements listed below.

> Note: For this exercise, you may fabricate evidence. That is, you can make up your supporting data. You would **never** fabricate evidence in a written paper for another subject or on the job. This is simply a skill-testing exercise. Have fun, but don't take fabricating evidence seriously. Remember: Phony evidence is illegal.

For this exercise, you might make up

- statistics
- quotations from experts
- historical events
- facts
- case histories or personal stories
- examples

To begin your discussion, try saying, "Yes, I totally agree that . . .," or " No, I don't think that . . .," and then try to think *why*. What will prove your point? Make your data sound credible, but use your imagination freely.

Give names, dates, locations, and times, if appropriate, to establish credibility. Remember that in a written paper, you would need to give the source of your information, and all facts would be verifiable.

1. Hotels in _____ are dreadful.

2. Criminals need to spend more time . . .

3. The Maple Leafs are going to have a great season.

4. Your clothes may define you and betray you.

5. Religion is the cause of most of the world's troubles.

6. Diamonds are a girl's best friend.

7. Writing clearly is hard work.

8. _____ is the most beautiful place on Earth.

9. Canada needs to spend more money on the military.

10. This college needs to improve _____.

Step 11: Plan an Essay

An essay is a form of expression, a vehicle for getting at an idea or at information. Students might think of an essay as a way of speaking to others. An essay is not just a literary genre or a formulaic mode of discourse used by educated elites.

What is an essay, then? An essay is an attempt to present an idea to readers and to convince them. *Essay* originates from the French *essayer,* which means to try. It means the writer is *trying* to get readers to think about a topic. A writer may also wish to persuade readers to do something, or a writer will try to explain something, describe something, or have people think about something in a different way. See Chapter 11 for further discussion on essays.

An essay is not a book, but a short piece of prose in paragraphs. It does not tell a story, but it might use a story to explain an idea.

Essays in college usually follow a formal pattern. That pattern includes an introduction to the controlling idea, or thesis; the thesis; proof of the points in the thesis presented in body paragraphs; and a conclusion reinforcing the thesis.

As they say in the army:

• tell 'em what you are going to say

• say it

• tell 'em what you said

Oral presentations or reports often follow the same format. The following exercises give you some practice in using the essay formula. If you try these exercises, get into the habit of gathering evidence only *after* you have decided on your main point or focus. Get into the habit of stating that focus in one sentence. That sentence will be considered your *thesis*, or controlling idea.

What is a thesis? A thesis is your main idea or central point. A thesis statement expresses that idea. It offers a preview of what you will discuss. Your paper or presentation will then defend and support that idea with clear evidence and explanation. Your thesis will guide and control the development of your points. It is considered to be the controlling idea of your paper.

Exercise 6.23

In small groups, prepare a short presentation on *one* of the following topics.

Try to choose your topic in 2 minutes. Suggested timing for methods of operation are in parentheses. Total preparation time: 25 to 40 minutes.

A. Choose two members of the group to record the material used to support the thesis. Review this record regularly.

B. Choose another member of the group to record the material chosen to introduce and conclude on the topic. (4 minutes)

C. When you have chosen the topic, each group member will prepare two or three questions that he or she would want answered by a presentation on this topic. You may want to ask questions like *how, what, where, when, how many, why, what kind of.*

Or you may decide to be more specific with your questions. Ask probing questions. Pretend you are an investigative reporter. Use these questions to initiate discussion. Be sure each member of the group contributes to the discussion. (6 to 8 minutes)

D. Decide together on the one-sentence statement of your thesis, or main idea. Choose your words wisely. Make sure you have a clear point to prove, to argue about. This sentence gives readers or listeners a PREVIEW of your approach to your topic. Everyone in the group should write down this thesis statement. (4 to 6 minutes)

E. Plan the specific support for this thesis. Use examples, quotations, statistics, expert opinions, case histories, historical, or scientific facts. List the specific data chosen as evidence. (5 to 8 minutes)

F. Prepare the introduction and conclusion. Use the S3Q3 Formula to inspire you. End with a memorable statement. (4 to 6 minutes)

G. Write a brief outline of the material you have gathered (thesis, main points only—in the order of presentation). Review it together critically. Will you convince an audience? Offer feedback. Make any changes necessary. Make sure each person reading from the notes can read them and will not stumble over words. (5 minutes)

H. You or the teacher will choose a group member to present your response to the class.

Topics

1. Rejection research. The ways men differ from women in ending relationships.

2. How to bring up children in the twenty-first century. What you will do or not do differently from your parents.

3. Why the world needs more jocks. The importance of valuing physical activity in society today.

4. A greener future. The need for technology that increases the efficiency and cleanliness of our personal transportation.

5. The credit card trap. What all students need to know about money management.

6. Assisted suicide for the terminally ill. Your views on a person's right to die.

Reports or Commentary on Current Issues

Now it's time to try convincing an audience of your stand on a current social issue. We are surrounded by issues, and they are not just wars, violence, hunger, poverty, environmental decay, and economic disparity. We also all have our own personal issues. Think about the issues you have with your family, your studies, and your life. You often have to explain how you feel and why you feel the way you do about a matter. Then, you have to decide what to do about those feelings.

This also applies to social issues. As a citizen, as an adult, you will often have to argue your point of view on current issues. You have to be able to explain why you feel the way you do. The best argument, the most convincing presentation, will always be the most specific one. It will offer facts, figures, and examples. You will, of course, be even more convincing if the evidence you offer touches the hearts and imaginations of your audience.

Exercise 6.24

In small groups, prepare a presentation on *one* of the following issues, or on another topical issue from your environment that interests you and that is approved by your teacher. At least two members of the group will be responsible for taking clear notes.

A. Decide if you agree with the statement or not. The entire group does not have to have the same view. Opposition helps you develop a stronger argument, but you have to be willing to listen to the other side and to comment on those views.

B. Before you begin your presentation, describe the situation as it is right now. You might use some examples and some specific numbers to describe the situation. (If you are using fake numbers, make them sound credible; e.g., Does $100 million sound like a credible salary for a baseball player?)

C. Turn your chosen topic into a question. (Is $100 million too much . . .?) Then prepare a statement of what your group thinks *ought to be* and say *why* briefly.

D. Prepare evidence for your ideas. Listen to the opposition and prepare evidence that counteracts or counterbalances that view. Use facts, examples, expert opinion, human interest stories, case studies, statistics.

   For this classroom exercise, unless you have easy access to computers or research material, you will probably have to create fictional data. Make it credible. **Remember: For all other papers, readers should be able to check all data and find it is true.** Make a list of your supporting evidence.

E. Decide how you will introduce your topic. Will you use a human interest story from your list of evidence? Statistics? A quotation? A quite contrary view? Or will you stick to the prepared description of the situation?

F. Prepare your conclusion. You may use your introductory material and show how it develops or results, or you may simply sum up your material. End with a short, sharp statement that reinforces your views.

G. Present your findings. *After* your discussion and decisions, make the following choices:

- Choose one member of the group to introduce everyone, with a smile.

- Choose another member of the group to introduce and conclude the topic.

- Choose another member of the group to present the description of the present situation in the field, the way things are now, followed by the evidence for your group's views. This section is the body of the argument.

- When it is your group's turn, stand and deliver to the class, confidently. Speak slowly and clearly, and pause after each important point. Smile at your audience at least once.

Issues

1. Lesbians, bisexuals, homosexuals, and transgendered people need to get more security and respect on campus.

2. Violence on television encourages violence in society.

3. Schools today need metal detectors, book-bag searches, and a police presence on campus.

4. Most criminals suffer from emotional disorders and need therapy, not jail.

5. SUV-choked suburban sprawl shows that people care more about their image than the air we breathe and the water we drink.

6. Eyewitness testimony can be very unreliable.

7. Canadian students need to spend more time learning about traditional native culture.

8. Sports stars get paid far too much.

9. Drunk drivers should lose their licence for life.

10. Terrorism is never about freedom, but always about power.

Exercise 6.25

Choose *one or two* newspaper letters to the editor on a controversial topic, and bring the letter(s) to class. In pairs or groups of three, decide which letter irritates you most. Now, compose a reply to that letter. Plan your reply. Consider the following:

- What facts do you have to support your point of view?

- What evidence will you use?

- What will you say to establish your point of view, so you grab readers' interest and make clear what you are talking about?

- How will you counteract the newspaper letter?

- Can you offer any contrasting points?

- What do you want readers to remember?

- What memorable statement will you conclude with?

Write your reply. Show it to two other groups of students. Ask them

- what they think the letter is about

- how convincing your argument is and why

- what you can do, if necessary, to make your point more convincing

You might like to send your revised and proofread reply to the newspaper, and watch and see if it gets published. If your reply is published, your teacher might reward you in some way.

Exercise 6.26

In small groups, create a proposal on how to solve a problem.

A. Together, identify a problem from the list of possible problems and state it clearly.

B. Ask questions to inspire discussion and a solution. Ask questions like

- How did this problem come up?

- Has this problem come up before?

- If so, how have other people handled it?

- Were their efforts successful? Why or why not?

- What limitations do we have?

- What facts do we need to know before we can begin?
- How will we handle the problem?
- What specifically needs to be done? What tasks?
- What might result from our solution?
- How will we avoid undesirable effects?

C. Consider the results of your discussion. With as much specific data as possible, construct a possible solution to the problem. State your solution in three to five sentences. Anticipate opposition, and prepare your material accordingly.

D. Present your proposal (your response to A, B) to the class. Have each member of the group report on some aspect of the proposal. Ask for feedback from your audience and be prepared to support your recommendations.

The class should try to ask at least two questions in response to each proposal.

Possible Problems

1. the college's parking system

2. the organization of the college bookstore

3. students arriving late for class

4. care of the elderly

5. handling low grades

6. selecting excellent teachers

7. student dropouts

8. encouraging tourism to _____

9. creating a successful shop atmosphere

10. persuading high school students not to smoke

Congratulations. Your presentations will have followed the usual structure of most essays and reports. For each one, you will have created a clear thesis and supported your ideas with convincing evidence. You will have introduced and concluded elegantly and forcefully. You now have had practice in approaching many communication tasks in an organized, thoughtful way. Good luck with your writing.

REVIEW AND REMEMBER

Part 2

Strategies for Communicating Clearly

1. **Think of your audience.** Who are they?

2. **Think before you write.** Why are you writing? Note the expectations. Decide on your purpose.

3. **Support your views with specific evidence.** What will convince people? Use all the sources of information available:

   - yourself
   - other people
   - experts in the field
   - resource centres
   - cyberspace

4. **Ask questions.** What do you need to define, explore, analyze, investigate further? Consider the opposition.

5. **Be specific.** Avoid vague general statements. Check the truth of a statement, use precise terms, and modify them to avoid sweeping generalizations.

6. **Give your main point a clear and obvious focus.** Write about a micro-subject. Limit the scope. Make the subject specific, precise, and clear (SPC).

7. **State your central point briefly.** This point will guide and control the development of your ideas (your thesis or topic sentence).

8. **Introduce and conclude clearly.** At the beginning, motivate your audience to listen. Take off with a zoom. At the end, land gently and smoothly, but also firmly.

9. **Review your evidence.** Have you given your audience clear evidence throughout that you have thought about your subject?

10. **Think of your audience again.** Eliminate any fuzzy logic and unclear points.

Part 3

Practising Paragraphs

Part 3 deals with specific writing skills and approaches to writing. The focus is mostly on paragraph writing, because, as with any skill, it pays to start small and build strength, confidence, and flexibility.

A paragraph is a basic unit of communication. It focuses on one key idea and develops that idea convincingly for readers.

Learning the techniques of paragraph writing has a fortunate side effect. It allows writers to learn about an effective way to organize ideas. Once you grasp the principles of paragraph writing, you can easily transfer those skills to longer writing forms like essays and reports.

CHAPTER 7

Topic Sentences:

The Audience, the Micro-subject, and the Point About It

This chapter looks at the importance of thinking about your audience and providing them with a clear and focused subject.

By the end of this chapter, you will be able to

- prepare for the language and information needs of your readers, or your audience, before you begin to write

- make your subject **specific, precise, and clear (SPC),** a micro-subject that can be easily examined in one paragraph

- understand the form and function of a strong topic sentence

- write a clear topic sentence about your micro-subject

The Audience: Who is going to read your writing?

When you write, you write for a reader or readers. You write to be understood. Unless you are writing creatively, you write to give specific information as clearly, correctly, concisely, coherently, completely, and considerately as possible. That is why you ask, Who is going to read this? What do they need to know? Think of your reader.

Do you speak to your grandparents the same way you do to your friends? Do you address a group of students in the same tone and with the same language as you address a group of senior citizens? Would you explain the subjects you are studying at college to your 8-year-old sister in the same way as you would explain them to a professional at a job placement? No, no, and no.

When you write, you modify your language and your material to suit your audience. All good communicators do that. All good writers consider their audience and prepare their material with vocabulary and references that the audience can relate to.

In the workplace, you write for your boss, colleagues, or your clients. You don't usually write about emotions, romance, intrigue, or espionage. You write to describe, inform, explain, persuade. You want people to take action. That's why you need facts, exact figures, results, and accurate observations.

In college, you write for your teachers. They expect you to follow the rules of clear communication, and they notice if you make mistakes. Your English teachers spend much time labelling those mistakes so you can work on eliminating them. Most other readers won't bother.

Most readers simply have no interest in telling you where you have gone wrong. They just stop reading, or say, "I don't understand this," or often, "Why don't they teach young people to write in school these days?"

Thoughtful writers ask

- How old are my readers?

- How much education do my readers have?

- How much do my readers know about this subject?

- What do I want my readers to remember?

Look at the expressions listed below. Decide who would most likely understand their meaning. Where would you use these expressions?

1. tight hamstrings

2. stock derivatives and options

3. a 2-1 pitch with two out in the eighth inning

4. going quadruple platinum on his major-label debut

5. fresh scat and ripped-apart tree stumps

Sources

1. massage or yoga classes

2. business, stock exchange

3. baseball

4. rapper Marshall Mathers

5. environmentalists noting evidence of a bear at Pickerel Lake

Exercise 7.1

Look at the following paragraphs. Who do you think would be interested in reading them?

1. With a coastline stretching over 1,500 km, the Great Barrier Reef and sunscreen-insistent weather, it's no wonder that Australians use the expression "Going Troppo" for a trip to Queensland, Australia's Sunshine State. Queensland is a place where you can let yourself go. You can take a self-driven adventure to the Outback or hike in the rainforest. You can windsurf on unspoiled beaches or scuba dive into the Technicolor world of the Great Barrier Reef. You won't run out of things to do in Queensland.

2. The findings of the Educational Research Foundation were encouraging, but relatively unsurprising. The children who attended nursery school adapted better to school, and as teenagers were more likely to go into higher education. Other results were far more remarkable. The girls who had been to pre-school had fewer teenage pregnancies; the boys were significantly less likely to get into trouble with the law.

3. Petroleum, or crude oil, is a dark, viscous liquid, usually found at great depths beneath the earth or seabed. It is often found with natural gas, which consists mainly of methane. Petroleum is formed over millions of years by the decomposition of animals and plants under pressure. It is a mixture of hydrocarbons that vary greatly in structure. Many useful products are produced by refining petroleum.

4. Yahoo!'s announcement also sparked a wider rally among companies whose earnings rely on a steady flow of online advertising.

Most Likely Readers

1. tourists planning a vacation; armchair travellers longing for the sun

2. parents interested in pre-school education; educators persuading policy makers to invest more in pre-school education, using the success of the Educational Research Foundation's efforts to cut crime in Michigan

3. students learning or revising chemistry definitions in *The Usborne Illustrated Dictionary of Chemistry*

4. readers of the business pages in a newspaper; investors

The Micro-subject: What exactly are you going to write about?

You know you have to be sensitive to your audience. Just as important, you have to communicate your ideas clearly. Don't beat about the bush. Remember how important it is to be specific. That zoom lens is important in getting close to your subject. A **specific, precise, and clear (SPC)** subject, or a micro-subject, is always easier for readers to understand.

When you write at college or at work, you are not writing a book or an encyclopedia. You don't have the time, and your readers do not want too much information. So there's no need to begin a short paper with words like "Since the beginning of time . . ." Don't even begin to discuss general subjects like crime, transportation, ecology, or business in one paragraph, or in an essay. Whole libraries are devoted to vast subjects like those. You are not yet an expert in your field. So don't attempt the impossible. Limit the scope. Zoom in on a micro-subject.

Make Things Clear

Imagine you are stranded at the cottage with a sprained ankle. You need rest, but you also need food. A distant neighbour can drive your 10-year-old cousin, Tomas, the only other person staying with you, to a big supermarket in the closest town, drop him off there, and collect him on her way home. Tomas will be alone in the supermarket.

You make a list of what you need: milk, eggs, bread, coffee, fruit. It seems clear. But is that list fair for a 10 year old faced with a big, unfamiliar supermarket? Isn't it too general? Try giving Tomas a more precise list.

Did you come up with something like:

1 bag (4L) 2% milk

1 dozen extra large eggs

2 loaves whole-wheat bread

1 can (250 grams) Special Occasion Dark Roast coffee

8 Red Delicious apples

6 nectarines (not bruised)?

Focused, limited subjects are much easier to write about and to research. Get into the habit of zooming in for a close-up of your subject. Create micro-subjects only. In other words, be as specific as possible. Don't try to write a book.

What micro-subject might result from the term *education*, for example? You ask *when, where, what kind of, what exactly, how,* and *why.*

When?	The Middle Ages? The twentieth century? Today?
	(Today is usually the easiest, but think about the scope of the others too. Make them more limited still.)
	Which exact period? In this year? In CE 342? In the sixties?
Where?	The Middle East? Rome? Australia? Scarborough, Ontario?
What kind of?	The education of females today?
	The education of gladiators in Rome in CE 342?
	University education in Australia in the sixties? Pre-school education in Scarborough, Ontario, today?

What exactly?   Education of young adult women in Dubai today.

Gladiatorial training in the Colosseum during the reign of Emperor Commodus in CE 342 in ancient Rome.

Tuition fees for medical students in Australia in the sixties, compared with those today.

The availability of pre-school education for lower-income families in Scarborough, Ontario, today.

More questions can always be asked. Think of those old favourites: compare and contrast, advantages and disadvantages, pros and cons. The most important question to ask is: What do I want my readers to know or think about?

Rudyard Kipling's rhyme is a good one to remember:

I keep six honest serving men
They taught me all I knew
Their names are **What?** and **Why?** and **When?**
And **Where?** and **How?** and **Who?**

Exercise 7.2

In small groups, create a micro-subject for each term in *one* of the sets of subjects listed below. Be creative. Be precise. Choose the two most interesting micro-subjects from your group and share them with the class.

When you have heard all the micro-subjects, decide which three are the best, and be prepared to defend your choice. Cheer the winners.

Subjects

1.	fun	fur	fashion	finance
2.	peace	power	politics	parents
3.	gambling	Greenpeace	gerontology	giants
4.	music	meringues	museums	mice
5.	seafood	science	seasons	school

Exercise 7.3

Decide which subject is the most specific, precise, and clear in each of the following sets.

1. a. serious runners
    b. ten-kilometre races every Sunday
    c. jogging in the park

2. a. student elections at Snowflake College
    b. Snowflake College
    c. the surprising results of the student elections at Snowflake College

3. a. Auntie Mame
    b. relatives
    c. Patrick's aunts

4. a. the joy of graduating
    b. the joy of graduating from high school
    c. graduating from high school

5. a. living through the Depression in the Dirty Thirties
    b. the stock market crash of 1929
    c. the panic in New York on the day of the stock market crash, October 1929

6. a. the effects of malaria on nineteenth-century explorers in Africa
    b. David Livingstone's use of quinine while exploring in Africa
    c. David Livingstone in Africa in the nineteenth century

7. a. playoffs and the Winnipeg Blue Bombers
    b. Winnipeg's beloved Blue Bombers
    c. problems with the record of the Winnipeg Blue Bombers

8. a. the history of New France
    b. the Battle of the Long Sault in New France
    c. battles in New France

9. a. parlour songs for the family in the 1880s
    b. home entertainment in the nineteenth century
    c. family life in the nineteenth century

10. a. hype and sensationalism
    b. members of the press
    c. sensational press coverage of celebrities

Exercise 7.4

A. For *four* of the following general subjects, work out *three* questions for each that will give you a clear focus, and a more specific, precise, and clear subject.

Example

General Subject: cars

Questions: What kind of car?

Which year?

Where was it built?

What are the strengths of the car?

B. Give your list of general subjects and your questions to a partner and see what micro-subjects result.

C. Ask two other students which of these micro-subjects is the clearest and why.

General Subjects

large families	today's divorce rate
teenage crime	the expectations of college students
microwaves	buying a car
small towns	fashion on campus
job requirements	helping the homeless

So, now you know that before you even begin to write, you should consider your readers and focus your verbal sights on a micro-subject.

STEPS TO SUCCESS

Audiences and Micro-subjects

1. Think of your audience. Give your audience what it needs to know in language it can understand.

2. Make the subject you will write about as focused as possible. A micro-subject is Specific, Precise, and Clear (SPC).

3. To form this micro-subject, ask *when, where, what kind of, what exactly, how,* and *why.*

   Ask not what the subject can do for you, but what you can do for the subject.

The Topic Sentence: Stating the Point about Your Subject

You have a good subject. It is a micro-subject. It is focused, limited, specific, precise, and clear. The next step is to say something about it. You need a micro-subject and a point about it.

Micro-subject + Your Point About It = Topic Sentence

The paragraph you write on your micro-subject should make your point clear. You might describe something or seek to explain, prove, clarify, inform, or persuade. Whatever the purpose of your paragraph, your readers need to know what to expect right from the beginning.

First you must make it clear to readers what you have to say about your micro-subject. Readers like to know what to expect. So tell them. Tell them in a topic sentence.

A topic sentence tells readers what the topic is and what approach you will take to it. It establishes the controlling idea or central point of the paragraph. It lets a reader know what to expect in the paragraph that follows.

A paragraph is a group of related sentences that develops the idea stated in the topic sentence. A good paragraph supports and extends the idea stated in the topic sentence. It deals only with the point made in the topic sentence. Keeping to one main point gives the paragraph unity. Unity is very important. Give your paragraph unity with *one* main point only.

Everything in the paragraph relates to the topic sentence. Your paragraph may be short or long, sometimes ranging from one sentence to twenty. Usually paragraphs for English classes are from five to eight sentences. Most readers these days like their paragraphs short. One-liners are used to stress a point or act as a transition.

The first line of a paragraph is usually indented to signal that a new idea or new point is being introduced, and to give readers a visual break. Readers need some white space on a page.

Aim to write about five to eight sentences in your paragraphs, unless told otherwise. A paragraph usually is as long as it needs to be. Your topic sentence will determine how long your paragraph needs to be. It establishes the content. The content is the subject you are discussing. Some subjects need longer discussions than others. Keep to the subject in the topic sentence and stop when you have covered it. You may write 50 to 300 words, depending on what you need to tell readers. Try not to waste words.

For most technical and business writing, be up front. Your topic sentence is, then, the first sentence of the paragraph. Sometimes, though, you may want to begin with a lively introduction (see the S3Q3 Formula in Chapter 6) or some background. In those cases, your topic sentence would come later in the paragraph, but it would still be there, and the rest of your paragraph would support and develop its central point.

Examples of Topic Sentences

Read the following topic sentences. Think about the subject each one is presenting to readers.

1. Canada's greatest drug problem could be a drug prescribed for thousands of children: Ritalin.

2. A few sensible precautions will keep you sneeze-free in allergy season.

3. Many shopaholics suffer from an Impulse Control Disorder that causes real personal and financial harm to others.

4. Online relationships generally intensify more rapidly than real-life relationships.

5. A letter, whether business or personal, will reveal a lot about the writer.

Exercise 7.5

Choose *two* of the micro-subjects you created in Exercise 7.2 or 7.4 and make a point about each one in a complete sentence. The result will be two topic sentences. Ask a partner if he or she could write a paragraph on each of your topic sentences. How would he or she do that? Discuss.

Exercise 7.6

Note the topic and the controlling idea for each of the following sentences. Ask yourself: What is the specific subject? What point is being made about it?

1. Canoeing in Algonquin Park is a great experience.

2. Pasta is one of the quickest, yet healthiest dinners to make.

3. Simon Fraser's explorations were of great importance and interest.

4. Football is a dangerous sport, and many players suffer serious injuries each year.

5. Some wild mushrooms are poisonous.

6. A group of concerned psychologists from McMaster University warns that television violence causes aggressive behaviour in children.

7. Her favourite tree is the Japanese Honeybell tree, which blooms in June with hundreds of fragrant flowers.

8. The Williams Lake courthouse, high and square, was built in the 1920s to dispense justice in British Columbia's Cariboo country.

9. The people of Saskatchewan have been shaped by a sterner physical environment than that of most Canadians.

10. Before indoor plumbing, women had to haul water to the house an average of eight or ten times per day.

Exercise 7.7

In each set, choose the topic sentence that would be most effective for a paragraph of about eight sentences.

1. a. Hume Heaters are a great buy for cottage owners.
    b. Hume Heaters will allow you to enjoy your cottage in winter as well as summer.

    c. With their attractive design, low wattage, and exceptional safety, Hume Heaters are a great buy for cottage owners.

    d. With their spartan use of electricity, Hume Heaters let you enjoy winter as much as summer at your cottage.

2. a. Canadians are funny folk because they love comedy.

    b. With TV shows like *This Hour Has 22 Minutes* and *Royal Canadian Air Farce,* clubs like Yuk Yuk's, and comedians like Jim Carrey and Michael Park, Canadians show they have a great appetite for comedy.

    c. Comedy is a funny business because clubs keep closing.

    d. Independent comics work in clubs.

3. a. Children may be harmed physically and psychologically by specializing in a single sport before adolescence.

    b. Tiger Woods had mastered nine holes of golf by age 3.

    c. Stress fractures and emotional disorders are some risks faced.

    d. Children may not want to play golf or tennis at the age of 2.

4. a. Trucks are selling well in Canada this year.

    b. Figures released by Canada's Big Three automakers show that sales of trucks are setting records this year.

    c. Canadians like to use their vehicles for many purposes.

    d. Ford's overall vehicle sales are down right now, but its truck sales are doing well.

5. a. George Clooney is the best actor.

    b. George Clooney is very convincing.

    c. My mother thinks George Clooney is the best-looking actor.

    d. George Clooney, in his role as a world-weary hero, is very convincing as well as cute.

6. a. The Harry Potter books are popular.

    b. Children love the Harry Potter books.

    c. Clever ideas about magic and social situations make the Harry Potter stories popular with both adults and children.

    d. Both adults and children enjoy the Harry Potter books.

7. a. Many people influence you while you are in college.

    b. You meet lots of people while you are in college.

    c. Some of your peers will encourage you to skip classes while you are in college.

    d. The people who influence you most when you are in college are faculty, counsellors, and your fellow students.

8. a. You are fortunate indeed if you see the northern lights, the *aurora borealis*, light up the skies of northern Canada.
   b. A collision of solar electrons and gases produces the *aurora borealis*.
   c. Pink is produced when nitrogen is hit.
   d. Some people claim to hear sounds when watching the northern lights.

9. a. Most children like linking words together.
   b. Old Mother Goose is a wonderful bird and full of rhymes.
   c. Because rhymes may train the brain, as well as help children get used to sounds and words, reading rhymes aloud to young children offers them an enriched language experience.
   d. Children love Humpty Dumpty and Wee Willie Winkie.

10. a. Ecstasy is the favourite drug on the rave scene.
    b. Ecstasy delivers a short-term high.
    c. Serotonin's exact function in the brain is not known yet.
    d. Researchers at Johns Hopkins University say that the recreational drug, Ecstasy, could deliver worse than a short-term high; it may cause brain damage.

Exercise 7.8*

Decide which of the following sentences *would not* make good topic sentences for a paragraph. Consider whether each sentence is sufficiently limited and whether you would be able to provide sufficient support for it. Try the *so what* test. Also consider how you could develop the paragraph. (This exercise can be done orally.)

1. Children used to begin playing telephone jokes in Grade 6.

2. Veiled, almost motionless, the old woman is dabbing at the wall.

3. That song drives me crazy.

4. Teenagers need space of their own.

5. The Second World War lasted from 1939 to 1945.

6. Retirement does not just mean withdrawal from circulation; it means withdrawal from the boss, tradition, and promotion.

7. Dan spends winter in Australia every year.

8. David took the train to Montreal on Tuesday.

9. Harry begged Sally not to go to the restaurant.

10. The atmosphere in that household depends on the temperament of the mother.

11. The ink is faded and the writing is illegible.

12. Many songs of heavy metal bands signal renewed prejudice against minorities in our society.

13. The impresario made a sweeping gesture with his hand and shattered the coffee pot.

14. A well-chosen video can be a valuable learning experience for a child while daddy is making dinner.

15. The human race has achieved so much in what is, in geological time, a short period.

16. The tusks of the elephant weighed about 200 kg.

17. It is dangerous to use a telescope for looking at the sun.

18. Ninety-five per cent of people who have AIDS live in developing countries.

19. Your library is the cornerstone of literacy and learning in your city.

20. Vogon Jeltz heaved his unpleasant green body around the control bridge.

Exercise 7.9*

The topic sentence of a paragraph is: *Rice is perhaps the most important food crop in the world.* Decide which of the following sentences would destroy the unity of a paragraph on this topic sentence.

1. Rice is eaten daily by at least half the population of the world.

2. From the muddy deltas of Bangladesh and Vietnam to India and China, Indonesia, Sri Lanka, Thailand, Malaysia, Japan, Egypt, Brazil, the United States, southern Europe, and Australia, rice is grown for food.

3. Meat, fish, eggs, and cheese are sources of protein.

4. In the West, people may eat, on average, 4 or 5 kg of rice per year.

5. Some people say Japanese food is not filling.

6. People in Bangladesh, however, eat 0.5 kg of rice per person every day.

7. China produces and exports a lot of green tea.

8. On average, an Indonesian eats 0.4 kg of rice per day.

9. In many countries, rice flour is used to thicken soups and sauces, and to make sweets and noodles.

10. In some developing countries, rice is people's only food.

Exercise 7.10*

Find the topic sentence in each of the following paragraphs, and note the numbers of the sentences which destroy the unity of the paragraph.

1. (1) The young prince had been protected by his father from all knowledge of age, sickness, death, or monkhood. (2) The king, hoping to show the glamour of the royal vocation, provided his son with three palaces and 40,000 dancing girls to keep his mind attached to princely pastimes. (3) He gave his son-in-law many presents. (4) One day, however, the gods decided the time for enlightenment of the prince had come and they brought a monk into his quarters. (5) From that day on, the prince was a different person.

2. (1) Back pain can often be caused by badly chosen office furniture. (2) Careful selection of chairs, desks, and caution about the placing of computers are crucial, especially for employees who work long hours. (3) Office furniture should have adjustable height structure and manoeuvrability. (4) A footstool or telephone book, when necessary, can help provide the correct height. (5) Workers should also consider traditional impact aerobics with routines that are challenging. (6) A backrest at a level near the waistline, for instance, can hold an employee's back in a safe resting position. (7) Knees should be parallel with the hips. (8) More popular versions of word-processing software are being developed as we speak. (9) Severe back pain may come on suddenly, but it could be the result of many years of sitting at badly designed workstations.

3. (1) Dorothy's hands were so white and cold at the football game, her friends made her phone her doctor. (2) It turns out she has a condition called Raynaud's syndrome. (3) This condition is an exaggerated sensitivity to cold. (4) No wonder she has never joined in snowball fights. (5) Raynaud's syndrome, a widespread problem, is not usually serious, but it can make life difficult for sufferers. (6) Nicotine is bad for anyone. (7) People suffering from a typical Raynaud attack complain of coldness, numbness or tingling, and colour changes in the fingers. (8) These colour changes can be dramatic, ranging from extreme whiteness to blueness and redness. (9) Dorothy has decided to learn Spanish. (10) People like Dorothy with Raynaud's syndrome learn to cope with the condition, but the world is a colder place for them.

4. (1) When composer Richard Wagner met the young poet and writer Mathilde Wesendonck, he felt he had found his ideal woman. (2) The fact he was married never prevented him from seeking his ideal woman. (3) Wagner described himself, as a student, as "weak, wild, and lazy." (4) Mathilde Wesendonck was married too. (5) Her husband, although treated badly by the lovers, actually supported and helped Wagner. (6) Mathilde Wesendonck loved the composer deeply, and Wagner later declared that she made his years in Zurich, "my richest flowering time."

5. (1) An identity crisis as a teenager is no bad thing, apparently. (2) If you don't have some kind of identity crisis as a teenager, you might have one at a later stage of life, when people may not be so tolerant, and when you have heavy responsibilities to face. (3) Children have to be encouraged to think of themselves as competent and responsible. (4) Knowledge is not something to be poured like concrete. (5) It is important that, as a teenager, you discover exactly who you are and sort out your personal view of life with your own beliefs and values, and not just those of your parents. (6) Of course, it can even be a good thing if those beliefs and values are considered mysterious, weird, or maddening by your parents. (7) Stumbling around suburbia looking for babes and parties is boring. (8) That way you know you are a person in your own right, with your own world view, your own identity. (9) The emotional separation of parent and child begins then, in those turbulent teen years.

Exercise 7.11

Add qualifying phrases or modifying comments to *five* of the following general sentences to make the subject more Specific, Precise, and Clear.

Example

General Sentence: House league hockey is fun for kids.

Specific, Precise, and Clear Sentence: House league hockey is great for 10 year olds because it is not very competitive and it allows every player on the ice.

1. Hockey is a great game.

2. My dentist is terrific.

3. This town needs more bicycle paths.

4. Alcohol causes more violence than drugs.

5. Teenagers are difficult to live with.

6. Jon's garden is delightful.

7. Granville Island is fun to visit.

8. Many diseases are inherited.

9. Shebib had a successful career.

10. Good communication is important in the office.

Exercise 7.12

In pairs or groups of three, answer *five* of the following questions with a one-sentence answer that would be a strong topic sentence. Each topic sentence should indicate clearly the direction the paragraph will take.

1. How can we reduce the number of road accidents?

2. Why are winter vacations a good idea?

3. Why should high school students wear uniforms?

4. What can students do to solve their negative cash-flow problems?

5. Is universal daycare a good idea?

6. Can politicians ever be considered heroes?

7. Is violence ever justified?

8. Do we really live in a racist (or sexist or ageist or homophobic) society?

9. How can we limit car use in order to reduce greenhouse gas emissions?

10. Why do people become addicted to soap operas?

Exercise 7.13*

In pairs or groups of three, prepare the topic sentence that will introduce and control the rest of the paragraph for *six* of the following paragraphs. Your teacher may assign different paragraphs to different groups. It is a good idea for at least two groups to write topic sentences for the same numbers, so they can compare their results.

A. Read the paragraph. Decide what the *subject* of the paragraph is.

B. Look at the concluding sentence of the paragraph. What point does it reinforce?

C. State what you want to say about the subject to let readers know what to expect.

D. Write a topic sentence that presents a PREVIEW of the ideas in the paragraph.

1. It can appear in childhood or during adulthood. It can worsen gradually or have onset suddenly. Some people may have only one attack in their entire life, but for others, asthma is a chronic condition.

2. The oil and filter must be changed as recommended in the operator's manual. Waiting longer causes wear and may even ruin your engine.

3. It is not difficult to imagine our prehistoric ancestors sleeping in their caves, rumbling and snorting in the flickering light. In fact, according to one theory, present-day snorers are simply re-enacting the primitive instinct of making loud noises at night to protect their sleeping womenfolk.

    Derek S. Lipman, M.D., *Stop Your Husband From Snoring.*

4. Little Denvil does not like the same songs as Grandpa. Auntie Rita does not want to listen to the same sounds as her 19-year-old niece, Ayesha. And does Ayesha want to listen to Raffi all afternoon? Family

get-togethers may be popular, but if everyone keeps asking you to change the record or turn down the volume, it's no fun deciding on background music. One solution is to choose soundtracks from movies like *Forest Gump*, which span the sixties and seventies, or *The Mambo Kings*, which have irresistible Latin dance numbers. Then everyone at the family party will be hopping.

5. She can flash the kind of smile that makes your heart miss three beats. She will primp and flip her hair. She will lean towards you like a plant seeking sunlight. She will put her head on your shoulder. But will she go out with you? No. She is not interested in dating. She just wants to be adored and admired.

6. Both creatures are astonishingly clever and curious, passionate students of life. But within short order the chimpanzee must drop out of school and work for a living, whereas the child—let's be predictable and call her a girl—remains in most cultures in the luxury of the nanny state.

Natalie Angier, *Woman: An Intimate Geography.*

7. In ancient Rome, child-bearing and housekeeping were considered to be only part of a woman's duties; she was also expected to play an active role in the wider business of the family. One result was that her life was less secluded than that of her contemporaries in other countries.

8. Gum wrappers lie on the floor amidst dirty socks and underwear. Down there with the dirty laundry lie covers from various CDs. No Doubt, Supergrass, Funky Green Dogs, De La Soul, Queen Latifah, and Tangerine Dream spill out from a tangle of T-shirts, Gap Worker jeans, an old backpack, Air Nikes, and empty Starburst jellybean packets. Mel Gibson looks fiercely committed on a crumpled *Braveheart* poster, lying on top of what seems to be a faded caftan. *The Divine Ryans* by Wayne Johnston lies on the floor on top of discarded jeans. Photos of his girlfriend are scattered everywhere. What a mess my brother leaves in his bedroom.

9. Ride quality is firmer, but still very comfortable. It has better noise isolation, and fuel economy has also been improved. It accelerates to 100 km/h in just a tick over 4 seconds. The fully independent suspension with stiffer rear leaf springs and revised camber settings

allows the tires to remain flatter on the road for improved grip. This Corvette is one cool car.

10. It may be derived from the old English word *steorling*, meaning coin with a star, for the small stars found on some coins at the time of William II, or it may come from birds on the coins of Edward the Confessor. Some people think it comes from *Easterling,* the medieval name for coiners from east German states. The money they minted was considered reliable because it was always of the same weight and same quality of metal. Other countries have no special name for their money, but all over the world, British money is called *sterling.*

Exercise 7.14*

In pairs or groups of three, consider the points given in each of the following sets.

A. Prepare a topic sentence for at least *three* of the following sets. Decide on a micro-subject. Then use the details given to help you form your topic sentence.

B. Below each topic sentence, list two or three specific and relevant points to support the idea in the topic sentence. Note: Not all the support given is useful. You will have to rearrange, reject, or rephrase details. Be discriminating.

Examples

(See sentence set #1 below.)

Topic Sentence: Blueberries, a summer tradition for Canadians, are more than just a tasty treat, but are full of health-giving nutrients.

Support 1: Anthocyanin, the compound that makes blueberries blue, is very beneficial.

Support 2: Blueberries are high in antioxidants, so they neutralize molecules causing heart disease and cancer.

OR

Topic Sentence: Picking blueberries in the Maritimes may be hard work, but the rewards are great.

Support 1: Harvesting wild blueberries by hand in Nova Scotia and Prince Edward Island is back-breaking work.

Support 2: Blueberries add sweet-sharp flavour to tarts, muffins, pies, salads, jams, and sauces.

1. a. a bundle of fresh herbs on the barbecue to enhance the flavour of grilled foods
    b. anthocyanin, the compound that makes blueberries blue, very beneficial
    c. harvesting wild blueberries in Nova Scotia and Prince Edward Island in August
    d. hard work picking wild blueberries by hand
    e. sweet-sharp flavour popular in tarts, muffins, pies, salads, jams, sauces
    f. research shows that blueberries high in antioxidant activity
    g. antioxidants neutralize molecules causing cancer, heart disease
    h. blueberries versatile and full of flavour
    i. blueberry picking, a summer tradition for many Canadians

2. a. space for kids, sports equipment, picnic gear, maybe even a pine table from St. Jacobs
    b. space, flexibility, crucial extra inches
    c. handling and safety very important, but comfort for the kids not to be overlooked
    d. the hard life of single mums
    e. choosing a family car
    f. state-of-the-art safety features like the inflatable curtain to protect passengers from side impact
    g. vintage clothes, antique dolls, furniture, and collectibles
    h. Air bags equipped with special sensors and whiplash protection
    i. red lights becoming longer

3. a. summer heat and winter cold, drought, fire, and flood
    b. no tractors, cars, computers, trains, roads
    c. hard to leave the warmth of their beds
    d. the tough life of early pioneers in Canada
    e. horses essential
    f. country rough, but beautifully timbered
    g. indescribable discomforts, but with the horse, people able to win through
    h. those early pioneers made the wilderness shine

     i. no lumber and brick for building to be bought at the store

     j. hunters sometimes kill protected migratory birds

4. a. thought humiliating students was clever

     b. could not keep to the point

     c. always referring to hip hop music to be cool

     d. worst high school history teacher

     e. used to leave his cowboy hat and boots in his locker

     f. expected students to memorize petty details about the Canadian Constitution

     g. gazed out the window whenever Ms. Zoldas, the pretty ESL teacher, walked past and lost track of what he was saying

     h. in 1841, the United Province of Canada was Canada East (now Quebec) and Canada West (now Ontario)

     i. had forgotten most students' names in January, after the holidays

     j. would talk to the blackboard as often as to the class

     k. many public opinion polls in Quebec

5. a. Bogdan and Bozena always fighting

     b. having a successful relationship not easy

     c. some common problems of communication in couples

     d. always blaming each other for their problems

     e. couples from Argentina to Australia accusing each other

     f. never come to terms with conflict

     g. keep putting off, avoiding making decisions

     h. follow patterns observed growing up

     i. never cooperate, never compromise

     j. withdraw physically or emotionally or both to show anger

Learning to write a clear topic sentence is very important. A topic sentence shows you have a purpose for your communication. It lets readers know what you intend to discuss or explain. It may lead to action. Your ability to focus and make a point about a specific microscopic subject shows you are ready to develop your ideas further.

REVIEW AND REMEMBER

Topic Sentences

1. Be sure to have a clear micro-subject, an SPC subject, before you decide what to say about it.

2. Think about this micro-subject.

3. Prepare a clear point about the micro-subject.

4. Write down the micro-subject and the point you are making about it in one sentence.

5. Remember that this sentence, **the topic sentence**, tells a reader what to expect in the paragraph. It guides and controls the development of the paragraph.

6. Remember you will be stuck with developing and supporting what you say in this topic sentence. Your paragraph needs *unity*. To achieve unity, keep to the point mentioned in the topic sentence—the whole point and nothing but that point.

CHAPTER 8

Outlines:

The Proof, the Support, and the Way to Convince Your Readers

This chapter looks at how to write convincingly so readers know that you know what you are talking about.

By the end of this chapter, you will be able to

- support the point you have introduced in your topic sentence effectively

- use specific evidence for the key point in the topic sentence

- use relevant and reliable statistics, definitions, anecdotes, facts, examples, case histories, personal stories, historical or scientific information, or comparisons and contrasts as support to prove your point

- integrate quotations and statements from experts into your paragraph to support your point

Your topic sentence acts as a guide to your readers. It controls the development of your paragraph. But how will you develop your paragraph? How can you prove your point to readers?

Details, details, details. That's what it's all about. That's what you need. You have a super-specific micro-subject. You have a great point to make about it in your topic sentence, but you still have work to do. You still have to convince readers that you know what you are talking about.

How will you convince your readers? You provide specific information about it. Specific information gives strength to your argument. It gives support for your point. A strong, well-built paragraph proves its point. It may defend, define, describe. It may classify, clarify, compare, contrast, or complain. It may narrate, nag, or natter. But it must develop the point made in the topic sentence with convincing support.

How? With details. Strong support includes statistics, definitions, anecdotes, facts, examples, statements from experts, case histories, personal stories, historical or scientific information, comparisons, contrasts. Suit the support to the subject.

Outline of Support

It is wise to work out the supporting details you will use before you begin to write a paragraph. Get into the habit of outlining your support by listing key evidence.

Your outline of support might look like this:

Your Topic Sentence: A specific, precise, clear statement about your micro-subject, indicating what you will discuss in your paragraph

Support 1: An example—a human interest story, perhaps

Support 2: A statistic reinforcing the subject of the human interest story

Support 3: A statement by an expert in the field of the statistic and the story

You would conclude with a statement reinforcing the topic sentence.

Examples of Outlines of Support

Look at these topic sentences from Chapter 7, Examples of Topic Sentences. Below each topic sentence is an outline of the kind of support that develops the point clearly and convincingly for readers.

1. Canada's greatest drug problem could be a drug prescribed for thousands of children: Ritalin. *How will you prove that point?*

    a. According to *University of Toronto Magazine,* 95% of the worldwide Ritalin consumption is in North America.

    b. Any chronic stimulant use causes brain changes; compare Ritalin with other psychotropic drugs.

    c. The number of emergency room visits connected with Ritalin misuse in children between ages 10 and 14 jumped from under 50 in 1991 to over 1,000 in 1998, according to *Adbusters.*

    d. Present the case history of Tyler, whose oral therapeutic doses of Ritalin caused reactions similar to those produced by doses of intranasal cocaine.

2. A few sensible precautions will keep you sneeze-free in allergy season. *What precautions?*

    a. Check newspaper, radio, and Lung Association sources for the local pollen count.

    b. Keep away from areas like fields, roadsides, and construction sites, where pollen-rich plants or toxic dust is found.

    c. Shower, or wash one's face and hands after being in a dusty, pollen-filled place.

3. Many shopaholics suffer from an Impulse Control Disorder that causes real personal and financial harm to others. *How do you know?*

    a. Visa reports that every year 32% of joint credit card holders seek to be released from joint responsibility for debt caused by one shopaholic partner.

    b. You have personal knowledge of Imelda. She experiences abnormal excitement and increased tension before buying shoes. Her closet contains 64 pairs of shoes, most of them black.

    c. Imelda's pleasure and gratification last no more than two hours. Then she sinks into a depressed silence that troubles her partner and children. Her family feels neglected and worried.

    d. Social psychologist, Dr. Pepi Lucas, says that feelings of neglect, abandonment, and financial strain were experienced by 92% of the partners of shopaholics studied by the Department of Inland Revenue in 2001 in the Greater Toronto Area.

Outlines, like the ones here, give you a plan to work from. They provide a skeleton for you to flesh out. Select the flesh carefully, so you end up with a beautiful body for your ideas.

Specific Data

Choose as much support as you like to prove your point. Use statistics, definitions, anecdotes, facts, examples, statements from experts, case histories, personal stories, historical or scientific information. It is important to choose very specific data. Be as concrete and precise as possible. Use names, dates, locations. Too often student writing is vague and uninformed. Give your readers something to take away with them, specific data, not airy nothings.

How do you find this specific data? Sometimes you need go no further than your own head, but mostly it is wise to look beyond the personal. Do some research for up-to-date reliable information on your topic in sources such as encyclopedias, textbooks, newspapers, magazines, journals, and Web sites. Find experts your readers will trust. Who those experts are depends on your topic.

Would you believe Paolo's kid sister when she insists soul music is having a big revival? Probably not, unless she works in a music store. If you find that *Rolling Stone, Spin, Word Up!*, as well as *The New York Times* all have articles quoting sales figures about soul groups that are selling thousands of CDs, you are more inclined to believe Paolo's kid sister. Remember that names and sources give credibility. Give the information about your sources clearly to readers and your paragraph will be more convincing.

Signal Phrases for Introducing Quotations

Introducing quoted material clearly and elegantly is not difficult, but many student writers often forget to show readers *why* they have chosen to quote a particular point. Get into the habit of introducing all quotations with what is called a *signal phrase*. It will signal what is coming, and show readers that you have done some research and know how to use that research to help develop your topic. Mention the name of the person you are quoting in your signal phrase.

Examples

According to Dr. Jennifer Mei...

Heathcliff insists . . .

Leela Khurana always says . . .

Professor Denvil Buchanan points out . . .

You might give readers some information about the person or situation you are quoting. People usually remember meeting someone if they are given some details that help them remember that person.

Examples

Percy Parselmouth, the famous snake-charmer, advises all children . . .

Sobia Zeman, television personality and women's rights activist from Saskatchewan, emphasizes . . .

In her lecture on the place of the comma in today's world, Sheila Doherty maintained . . .

Later you will learn to place parenthetical references after each quotation so readers can check the source of information, if they wish to do so.

> For in-class work in English, you *may* be allowed to invent details, but be sure your readers know you are using your imagination. Remember to make all invented support credible. Truth may be stranger than fiction, but will your teacher be convinced by your examples? Is it likely, for example, that solar-powered bicycles are used in the Arctic Circle? Be realistic. Fantasies are out of place in the classroom.

People like to read about people. In today's cold, computerized world, human interest stories still hold readers' attention. Numbers need human connections. Statistics are more forceful if you give them a personal dimension. For example, most people know that 6 million Jews died in the Holocaust. Yet readers will be even more moved by the love story of Holocaust survivors Simon and Cyla Wiesenthal, who lost 89 members of their extended family between them and were left with only each other.

Get into the habit of listing the support you will use to prove your point on paper rather than in your head. It helps to write something down. Whether you try brainstorming, talking to others, doing research, or watching television to get inspired, jot down the support. You may reject some details or expand on others, but you will have some idea of what you are talking about, before you begin to write. Specifically, list any

- statistics
- anecdotes

- facts

- quotes

- examples

- statements from experts

- case histories and personal stories

- historical or scientific evidence

- comparisons and contrasts

What support would you provide?

Look at the following four topic sentences. What support would you provide for each?

Topic Sentence A: *My Uncle Joe believes his kids have shocking social values.*

   PROVE IT!

- *With statistics?* They're no use here.

- *With examples?* Yes, they're essential here.

- *With case histories similar to the topic?* They wouldn't be right for a personal essay; they'd be better for a paper using research.

- *With statements from experts?* Who would be an expert here?

- *With comparisons and contrasts?* Yes, you could use Uncle Joe's ideas.

   Supporting details:

- All three of Uncle Joe's kids demonstrated against daycare cuts in Ontario.

- Mario joined the Anti-Nuclear Power Coalition.

- Danny wears a button that says "Question Authority."

- Rosanna was arrested at a peace march.

- All three kids marched in protest against the World Trade Organization meeting.

- Uncle Joe has quite different views.

Topic Sentence B: *My teachers in college have been an important influence on me.*

PROVE IT!
Supporting details:

- *With personal experience and anecdotes with details.*

- Academic direction—My teachers made suggestions related to my interests, told me what to read, and what to look for when I read. Professor Gavin made suggestions related to my interests and assigned readings in our textbook that stimulated fierce discussions in class and made me think.

- Academic inspiration—My teachers made me want to explore new ideas, go deeper into a subject. Professor Finnigan actually made me want to do the research on management and employee relations for my final paper.

- Academic guidance—My teachers encouraged me and helped me organize my study time. Professor Hustler offered me good advice when I wanted to quit. Because of her interest and guidance, I'm still in college.

Topic Sentence C: *I have learned how to prepare for a job interview in college.*

PROVE IT!
Supporting details:

- I know how to research the organization I am interviewing for.

- I know about common interview techniques.

- I know and have practised answering frequently-asked interview questions.

- I know, through role-playing practice, how to smile and present a positive attitude.

- I know how to evaluate the interview afterward and send a follow-up letter.

Topic Sentence D: *Light beers are popular today.*

PROVE IT!
Supporting details:

- *With statistics, examples, and a statement from an expert.*

- Forty-five per cent of beer sales last year were for light beers, compared to 30% the previous year, according to Embryonics Research in Toronto.

- My friends, Colleen and Dave, like most of their friends, buy only light beers.

- Marvin Grolsch, marketing director of Froshters Breweries in Guelph, says, "We have stopped making two of our stronger brews since sales dropped, and will now concentrate on light beers."

Exercise 8.1

Decide which points could be used to support each topic sentence.

1. Hockey sticks have come a long way.

   a. prime ash wood

   b. wheat stubble

   c. laminated handles

   d. New Year's Day

   e. curved blades

   f. multi-component sticks

   g. plastic inserts

   h. playing in Calgary

2. Pasta is very nutritious.

   a. first produced in China

   b. less than 1% fat content

   c. hundreds of different pasta shapes exist

   d. high in complex carbohydrates

   e. international cuisine

   f. high in minerals and fibre

   g. Canadians are buying more linguine

    h. not enough shelf space for more varieties of pasta

    i. combined with protein, provides a sound meal

    j. old-fashioned supermarket retailers

3. Fabio's new car performs well.

    a. comfortable red leather seats

    b. reasonable price for quality

    c. independent suspension system

    d. Mad Max's automobile

    e. responsive rack-and-pinion steering

    f. low wattage paper fan

    g. super low -0.21 drag coefficient

    h. damage to the ecosystem

4. On the East Coast, fishing boats have become too efficient at killing fish.

    a. better gear

    b. total of 65,000 fishermen looking for cod

    c. technological sophistication on board

    d. the Scotian Shelf

    e. bigger holds

    f. cod, haddock, flounder, hake, herring

    g. faster boats

    h. Californian pilchards

    i. powerful systems using modern electronics

    j. inaccurate estimates

    k. established communities in Newfoundland

Exercise 8.2

Choose the point that does not support the topic sentence in each set.

1. New hospitals are built with special separate corridors and elevators for robotic carts to collect and deliver supplies.

    a. Robots pick up soiled laundry and used trays.

    b. You never see robots in the corridors or elevators.

    c. Population growth is out of control.

2. Many celebrities are looking for some spiritual connection in their lives.

    a. The clove-like scent of carnations fills a room with a natural aroma.

    b. Madonna and Rosanne study kabbalah, an ancient Jewish mysticism.

    c. Richard Gere has turned to Buddhism.

3. Billions of bank notes are printed around the world every year.

    a. English pounds have watermarks and a metallic thread running through the paper.

    b. The Bank of Canada issues about 800 million new bank notes a year.

    c. 12 million bank notes roll off the presses every day at the US Bureau of Engraving and Printing.

4. The Mounties, Canada's celebrated national police force, do many unusual jobs.

    a. Mounties have gone canoeing with Prince Andrew.

    b. Mounties have rappelled out of a helicopter onto a moving ship full of drug smugglers.

    c. Mounties used to carry revolvers, but now they carry semi-automatic pistols.

5. Albums from Japan's popular singers sell in the millions.

    a. The debut album of 17-year-old singer Utada Hikaru became Japan's best-selling album with sales topping 8 million.

    b. DJ music is found everywhere from car commercials to teen pop.

    c. A children's song about three dumplings on a skewer sold 3 million copies in 12 days in Japan.

6. Air conditioners keep Canadians shivering in summer.

    a. To protect her vocal cords, Céline Dion does not have air conditioning.

b. In 1992, about 17% of Canadians had some form of air conditioners, but this number almost doubled to 33% in 1998, according to Statistics Canada.

c. Canadians take sweatshirts to hotels and jackets to the office on even the hottest days.

7. Spandex is everywhere.

a. Nearly 30% of clothes manufactured today contain spandex.

b. With new technology, manufacturers can put from 2% to 5% stretch into fabrics like wool, leather, cotton, and silk.

c. Fashionable teens become obsessed with revealing well-cut triceps, biceps, and glutes at the gym.

8. Patients with heart disease can expect to undergo a variety of tests.

a. Coronary angiography involves the injection of dye into a patient to produce an image of the blood vessels.

b. Elevated cholesterol, smoking, and high blood pressure are risk factors for heart disease.

c. Exercise tests involve being connected to an electrocardiogram machine and walking on a treadmill.

9. St. Ann's, Nova Scotia, was a centre of shipbuilding in the great era of sailing ships.

a. A wealthy Acadian family buried a barrel of gold there.

b. A large brigantine sailing ship, the *Norman,* was built there in 1846.

c. Many vessels built in St. Ann's went trading up and down the Atlantic coast, to Britain, and to the West Indies.

10. The Vancouver International Marathon is truly international.

a. Over the past few years, best men's times were from runners from Germany, Mexico, and Japan.

b. Running through Vancouver on a sunny day is hard to beat.

c. The women's race has runners from Poland, Mexico, Spain, and Japan, as well as Canadians from across the country.

Exercise 8.3*

Read both paragraphs and choose the best answers for the questions below.

1. Ethanol was the drug most frequently implicated and detected (48%) in cases of death due to overdose in the city, studies in Halifax show. Illicit drugs (cocaine and cannabis) were detected in five overdose deaths; however, only two of these deaths had a final medico-legal disposition of death due to overdose of an illicit drug (cocaine). Viewed another way, 62% of all deaths due to overdose in Halifax from 1993 to 1995 involved psychotropic medications often prescribed in the treatment of mental health disorders (antidepressants, benzodiazepines, antipsychotics, hypnotics, and sedatives).

   A. What is the topic of this paragraph?

   i. psychotics and cannabis in Halifax

   ii. death due to overdose in Halifax

   iii.Halifax's drug problems

   iv. illicit drugs in Halifax

   B. What are two specific details used to support this topic?

2. By contrast, men who are high in emotional intelligence are socially poised, outgoing, and cheerful, not prone to fearfulness or worried rumination. They have a notable capacity for commitment to people or causes, for taking responsibility, and for having an ethical outlook; they are sympathetic and caring in their relationships. Their emotional life is rich, but appropriate; they are comfortable with themselves, others, and the social universe they live in.

   Daniel Goleman, *Emotional Intelligence.*

   A. What is the topic of this paragraph?

   B. What are three specific details used to support this topic?

Exercise 8.4

Respond to the following exercise in pairs or groups of three.

   A. Find the topic sentence in *five* of the following paragraphs. Make #4, #7, or #8 one of the paragraphs you choose. Note: The topic sentence is not necessarily the first or the shortest sentence in the paragraph.

B. Write the specific type of support used to develop the topic sentence. Remember, types of support are

- statistics

- anecdotes

- facts

- quotes

- examples

- statements from experts

- case histories and personal stories

- historical or scientific evidence

- comparisons and contrasts

1. In the small town of Pointe Anne, Ontario, the choice between the low pay of its only industry, the cement plant, and the dollars available from the ice rink was an easy one for young Bobby Hull. He had learned to skate before he learned to read. The year he was four, Santa Claus brought him his first pair of skates. By the end of the day he could manoeuvre on his own. "From then on," he remembers, "I was on the ice every day and skated until I was exhausted." This small town Ontario boy eventually became the highest paid player in the NHL in the late sixties.

2. Why does a week have seven days? Days, months, and years measure the time taken for movements of the earth and moon, but a week? We get the week from people who lived 6,000 years ago. They were the Babylonians who decided they needed a division of time, longer than a day, but shorter than a month. They thought that seven was an important number. They thought they saw seven planets in the sky and that seven days was the time it took for the moon to go from new to full and back again. Because seven was so important to the Babylonians, they grouped their days into seven and named each one after a planet.

3. Many Canadians love the prairies. They love the way the wind sets the swaying grasses singing. They love wildflowers like black-eyed Susans, purple coneflowers, queen-of-the-prairie, and big bluestem grass. Maybe Canadians love to be reminded of the continent's wild heritage. At the time of European settlement, approximately 1.4 million acres of North America were covered by tallgrass prairies. The

prairies are fascinating and much more than midwestern mono-chrome to most Canadians.

4. In the last 10 years, the number of female white-collar crimes has risen tremendously. Figures from the Ministry of Justice show that between 1986 and 1996, arrests of women increased 26% for theft, 31% for forgery and counterfeiting, 85% for fraud, and 51% for embezzlement. The women responsible for these crimes vary in their occupational status from top executives to office workers. They have jobs in large corporations, small businesses, and government offices. Some recent examples of arrests illustrate this range. Aphra Benn, feminist and writer, was convicted of stealing government funds provided to launch small businesses. Patrizia Starre pleaded guilty to embezzling $250,000 from a provincial government while serving as a treasury assistant, and Molly Flanders was convicted of defrauding tenants of thousands of dollars rent at a housing project. However, while more women than ever before are cheating employers or consumers, the number of female white-collar criminals is still much lower than that of male white-collar criminals.

5. Our memory allows us to learn from our experiences and make sense of what is happening now. Cognitive psychologists Roger Schwank and Robert Abelson tell us we have scripts in our heads of common experiences, like going into a restaurant, so we know how to act, even if we've never been to that particular restaurant before.

6. The southern region of Brazil, with its 24 million inhabitants, was once famous for the huge herds of cattle driven across the pampas by *gauchos* (cowboys). Now there are endless fields of soybeans and heavy industry instead, encouraged by the cheap electricity from the Itaipú Dam.

7. A poet once described the beauty of Frida Kahlo's art this way: "The art of Frida Kahlo is a ribbon around a bomb." When she was 18, Frida was in a terrible accident in Mexico City. Suffering terrible pain from a broken spine, and shattered pelvis, leg, and foot, she had a nurse bring art supplies to her bed. From then on, painting allowed her to endure the misery of her body, even when she had a foot amputated many years later. Her brush became an outlet for the physical and emotional pain she experienced all her life. In 1985 the Mexican government declared Frida Kahlo's paintings to be a national treasure.

8. Switzerland is considered progressive in its approach to treating inmates. Short-term imprisonment is extremely popular in the Swiss criminal justice system. In 1996, for example, 42% of all custodial sentences and 25% of all unsuspended sentences were 14 days or less. Such sentences are widely used for driving under the influence and other road traffic offences, drug use, and related drug offences. The Swiss Criminal Code allows short prison sentences.

Exercise 8.5

Read the following paragraphs from the book *Emotional Intelligence* by Daniel Goleman, and respond to the questions below.

A. The Neural Tripwire

Most intriguing for understanding the power of emotions in mental life are those moments of impassioned action that we later regret, once the dust has settled; the question is how we so easily become irrational. Take, for example, a young woman who drove two hours to Boston to have brunch and spend the day with her boyfriend. During brunch he gave her a present she'd been wanting for months, a hard-to-find print brought back from Spain. But her delight dissolved the moment she suggested that after brunch they go to a matinee of a movie she'd been wanting to see and her friend stunned her by saying he couldn't spend the day with her because he had softball practice. Hurt and incredulous, she got up in tears, left the café, and on impulse, threw the print in a garbage can. Months later, recounting the incident, it's not walking out she regrets, but the loss of the print.

1. What is the topic of this paragraph? State it in your own words in one sentence.

2. In three to five words, state what Daniel Goleman is trying to prove.

3. What method does the writer use to illustrate his point?

4. Which words would you choose to describe the key emotion of the young woman in the paragraph?

delighted	incredulous	resigned
frustrated	appropriate	impulsive
rational	disbelieving	suspicious
hotheaded	lecherous	hasty

5. Write a sentence, using one or more of the adjectives from #4, reinforcing the topic of the paragraph.

6. What did you think of the young woman's behaviour? Write one sentence stating your views and show it to a partner. Decide whose answer would be easier to prove.

B. The Price of Pessimism

As with depression, there are medical costs to pessimism—and corresponding benefits from optimism. For example, 122 men who had their first heart attack were evaluated on their degree of optimism or pessimism. Eight years later, of the 25 most pessimistic men, 21 had died; of the 25 most optimistic, just 6 had died. Their mental outlook proved to be a better predictor of survival than any medical risk factor, including the amount of damage to the heart in the first attack, artery blockage, cholesterol level or blood pressure. And in other research, patients going into artery bypass surgery who were optimistic had a much faster recovery and fewer medical complications during and after surgery than did more pessimistic patients.

1. What is the topic of this paragraph? State it in your own words in one sentence.

2. What does the writer say about this topic? Answer in a complete sentence.

3. What details are given to support the topic? List at least two.

4. What is the best predictor of survival after a heart attack?

5. Write one sentence explaining the medical advantages of optimism.

Exercise 8.6

A. Interview someone in the class and find out what he or she thinks about *one or two* of the following topic sentences. Ask first, "Do you agree that . . .?" and then "Why?"

B. Write a one- or two-sentence statement on this person's views on each topic covered, and introduce the sentence, saying who said it, when, and where.

Example

Topic Sentence: The Great Apes Project wants apes to receive legal protection of their right to life and freedom because the great primates have a special consciousness.

Response: On Thursday, October 23, 2001, outside the Ontario legislature, Marisa Victor, well-known animal rights activist, told a *Toronto Star* reporter, "I feel it is high time for chimpanzees, gorillas, and all great apes to have some rights protected by law. After all, these great primates deserve protection, just as much as you and me."

Topic Sentences

1. We need laws for noise control because sound at high decibel levels can ruin your health.

2. Slow-cooked food always has more flavour than fast food.

3. Parking is a big problem at this college.

4. The messages sent to men by society, through sports and the media, make it obvious that the real cause of domestic abuse is society itself, not individuals.

5. Canada needs stronger environmental protection laws against the dumping of hazardous waste in our country.

6. It is ridiculous to write nasty things about how fat a baseball player is. Journalists should stick to writing about how well someone plays the game.

7. Children today do not get enough exercise.

8. Celibacy is good for you.

Exercise 8.7

In small groups, invent *three* supporting details to prove *four* of the following topic sentences. You might use one statistic, one quotation, and one human interest story as your support.

Example

Topic Sentence: Many young people today seem to be more interested in shopping than politics.

Support 1: Ninety-eight per cent of Grade 12 students at Snowflake High School could identify more brand logos than politicians.

Support 2: Sissie Snufflump, a 19 year old in the Travel Counsellor program at Cantaloupe College says, "All the politicians I've ever heard of are, like, total knuckleheads and don't speak for me. I'm never going to vote for any of them. I'd rather go to the mall."

Support 3: Sissie and her friends prefer soap operas and shopping to political issues. They sigh and put on their headsets if conversation ever turns to politics.

Topic Sentences

1. Young people today are very involved in environmental issues.

2. Renovating old houses is expensive.

3. The Corvette is still a dream machine.

4. A career-related summer job is a good idea.

5. Mr. Braggart's classes in high school were so boring.

6. That maple tree in the backyard is beautiful, but a lot of work.

7. Living at home is sensible for college students.

8. It is a good idea for college students to live away from home.

9. Camping trips to a provincial park are a great holiday.

10. We are increasingly becoming a world of migrants made up of people from here and there.

Exercise 8.8

Outline possible support for *two* topic sentences of your own subject choice. List *three* specific details, stating the kind of support they are, for each topic sentence. Have you chosen a statistic, anecdote, fact, quote, example, statement from an expert, case history, personal story, piece of historical or scientific evidence, or a comparison or contrast?

Present each outline of support as follows:

Topic Sentence: _____

Support 1: _____

Support Type: _____

Support 2: _____

Support Type: _____

Support 3: _____

Support Type: _____

REVIEW AND REMEMBER

Strong Support Systems

1. A convincing paragraph gives readers specific support that proves the point made in the topic sentence. Strong support is essential.

2. The support used will suit the subject of the paragraph. It may be

   - statistics

   - anecdotes

   - facts

   - quotes

   - examples

   - statements from experts

   - case histories and personal stories

   - historical or scientific evidence

   - comparisons and contrasts

3. A convincing paragraph uses the most reliable sources of information on the subject.

Coherence:

The Reminders, the Glue, and the Ways to Avoid Coming Unstuck

This chapter looks at presenting an argument or discussion logically and coherently. It discusses how to glue your material together so readers do not feel they are being misdirected.

By the end of this chapter, you will be able to

- understand the importance of unity and coherence in clear communication

- achieve coherence in your writing through the use of constant reminders, transitional expressions, and attitudinal markers

You've got great support to prove your topic sentence. Any reader will be convinced you know what you are talking about. But will readers be able to follow your thoughts and see the connections you are making?

You need to keep the ideas flowing. To do that you connect each supporting point clearly to the topic sentence. You "glue" each point to the central idea of the paragraph. A well-glued paragraph, a cohesive paragraph, is a coherent paragraph.

All good paragraphs, reports, essays, and presentations have *unity* and *coherence.*

How do you write with unity?

- Deal with one thing at a time.

- Keep to the point. Don't get distracted and go off track.

How do you write with coherence?

- Glue your points together. Remind readers that every detail you use is relevant and connected to your main idea.

What is coherence? You know when someone is being incoherent. You come across it frequently in your everyday lives. If someone shouts "Bus! Stop! Mother!" at you, what will you think? What interpretations do you come up with? Think about the possible scenarios from those three words.

To avoid confusion and conflicting views in your writing, you need to show the connections between points. Make reading easy for readers. Guide them along the path of your ideas, with connecting signs.

How do you show connections between points?

- Offer *constant reminders* on what your topic is.

- Use *transitional expressions* to move from one idea to another.

- Add *emphasis* to show the importance of your ideas.

Constant Reminders

Parents tend to offer constant reminders to their busy, forgetful children to clean up their rooms. Children seem to need constant reminders. Readers are much the same. They need to be reminded of the key point in the topic sentence so they don't lose sight of it in an untidy mess of data.

Synonyms, words of similar meaning, are often used as reminders. A thesaurus or a good dictionary can help you find useful substitute words. Be careful, though. If you are not familiar with the word, don't use it. It might be wrong in the context.

Pronouns can help keep the topic in view. Pronouns are words that refer to and take the place of previously mentioned nouns. Pronouns such as *this, that, these,* and *those* point to the subject. So do regular pronouns like *it, he, she, they, them,* and *we.* Just be sure the subject referred to is obvious to readers.

Note how the main point in the topic sentence is reviewed and repeated for readers in the following paragraph.

Example

My Uncle Joe believes his kids have **shocking social values.** He was **shocked** when my three cousins were seen on national television in a protest against environmental cutbacks in Ontario. When Mario, the eldest, joined the Anti-Nuclear Power Coalition, he was **horrified.** It is **shameful** to Uncle Joe that Danny, the youngest, wears a button saying "Question Authority," and just **disgraceful** that his adored daughter, Rosanna, was arrested at a peace march. **To upset him further,** all three of his children marched to protest against the World Trade Organization meeting. The lively discussions at the supper table about social issues like AIDS in the community, he considers **nasty and distressing.** He can't understand why his children are not more like him, why they show no interest in fancy cars, power, and prestige. To Uncle Joe, it is **alarming** that his children do not find life perfect right now, and worse, that they even make his friends and neighbours aware of their **shocking social views.**

Transitional Expressions

The paragraph about Uncle Joe's kids could be better coordinated with careful use of transitional expressions. Transitions help readers move smoothly from one point to the next. The word *transition* literally means going across. *Transitions* are words or expressions that go from one idea to another to establish the relationship between one point and the next. They glue points together and help make your paragraph coherent.

What are some transitional expressions? You use them all the time in speech. In writing they offer a marker to readers; they show the link between ideas and prevent your writing from seeming choppy and unconnected.

Transitional Expressions to Glue Points Together

To add an idea:
- first, second, third . . .
- again, also, and, another, in addition, as well as, in the same way, besides, last, likewise, more, moreover, next, similarly, too

To emphasize an idea:
- above all, actually, after all, especially, even more so, more important, most important, indeed, in fact, without a doubt, clearly

To give examples:
- for example, for instance, as follows, as an illustration, as a case in point, in this case, in other words, in particular, namely, such as, that is, to illustrate

To compare and contrast:
- but, even so, however, instead, and yet, nevertheless, on the contrary, on the other hand, still, in contrast, otherwise, conversely

To show time:
- after, afterwards, always, as soon as, eventually, immediately, next, in the meantime, later, soon

To show results:
- accordingly, as a result, consequently, hence, for that reason, therefore, thus, because of this

To conclude:
- finally, in conclusion, as has been noted, in short, in other words, to sum up, clearly, obviously, then, therefore, lastly, at last

Note how a paragraph improves with careful use of transitions, as well as constant reminders.

Example

My Uncle Joe believes his kids have shocking social values. **For instance,** he was shocked when my three cousins were seen on national television in a protest against environmental cutbacks in Ontario. **Moreover,** when Mario, the eldest, joined the Anti-Nuclear Power Coalition, he was horrified. It is **also** shameful to Uncle Joe that Danny, the youngest, wears a button saying "Question Authority," and just disgraceful that his adored daughter, Rosanna, was arrested at a peace march. **In particular,** he was even more upset that all three of his children protested against the World Trade

Organization meeting. **Furthermore,** the lively discussions at the supper table about social issues like AIDS in the community, he considers nasty and distressing. **Indeed** he can't understand why his children are not more like him, why they show no interest in fancy cars, power, and prestige. To Uncle Joe, **without a doubt,** it is alarming that his children do not find life perfect, and worse that they even make his friends and neighbours aware of their shocking social views.

Attitudinal Markers

Sometimes you want to make readers aware of how important your ideas or facts are. You may wish to emphasize your points. To do so, you stress your commitment to the subject. You can use the transitional expressions listed earlier to add emphasis.

You can also use attitudinal markers to strengthen your point. Words like *certainly, assuredly, definitely, undeniably, undoubtedly, clearly, obviously, fortunately, unfortunately, rightly, wrongly,* and *significantly* all show an attitude. In the paragraph about Uncle Joe and his kids, think of the effect of replacing *furthermore* and *indeed* with attitudinal markers.

How can you show commitment, the "C word," in writing? It can be helpful in your personal communications to learn ways of showing commitment.

A Note about the Personal Point of View

Expressions like *in my opinion, I think,* and *I feel* are not really necessary in a paper with your name at the top of the page. Obviously, you are presenting your personal point of view. Why waste words? You don't want to appear to be on an ego trip.

However, today, in our impersonal digital world, some readers want a personal tone. The subject will determine whether you use the pronouns *I* or *we. You* is often just as good. Be cautious with personal pronouns. Many topics, reports, and presentations need to be as impersonal as a tax form. Personal pronouns can show commitment and work well with verbs like *understand, know, consider,* but they can also show self-obsession and should be used sparingly.

Where do you place these constant reminders, transitional expressions, and attitudinal markers? Sometimes the placing comes naturally, but if you are uncertain, place them before or within each new supporting point, to make the connection to the topic sentence obvious.

Example

Topic Sentence: _____

Transition: _____

Support 1: _____

Transition: _____

Support 2: _____

Transition: _____

Support 3 or Conclusion: _____

After a while, you will use constant reminders, transitional expressions, and attitudinal markers instinctively to connect your points. You may find that they are not necessary in certain places. Think of your readers. Coherence keeps them in the communications loop.

Exercise 9.1

What key term or idea is repeated in each of the following paragraphs? Note the number of times this term or idea occurs.

1. Where do the things you dream about come from? You dream about things that happened during the day. You dream about movies you have seen. You dream about stories you have heard. Sometimes you dream that you are someone else. Some people use dreams to help them solve problems. Dreams are your brain's attempts to make sense out of new data.

2. Witches may be part of Halloween's fun now, but for hundreds of years, witches were taken very seriously, indeed. People believed that witches were friends of the evil spirits that wandered about at Halloween. They would wear masks to frighten the witches and evil spirits away.

3. The way a raccoon walks is funny. It will waddle along on its short legs with its back hunched. But don't laugh. A raccoon may fool you

into thinking it is clumsy, but it can run up to 24 km/hr. for a short distance, if it meets an enemy. However, a raccoon will usually climb up a tree to escape a threat.

4. Martin Frobisher was one of England's finest sailors, at a time when England was known for great sailors. Queen Elizabeth I liked this adventure-loving sea captain. When he sailed down the Thames in June 1576, he was admiral of three ships and ready for the adventure of a lifetime.

5. Colourless, odourless, and usually tasteless, a powerful and dangerous drug has caused at least 65 deaths since it first came on the scene. Known as the date rape drug, this drug can cause dizziness, nausea, vomiting, seizures, coma, and death. Just a few drops of gamma-hydroxybutyrate (GBH) stirred into a can of pop, a glass of juice, or an alcoholic drink can cause someone to get high and pass out for several hours, leaving the victim with no memory of what happened. There is no antidote for GBH poisoning. The liquid is often sold illegally in dance clubs by drug dealers.

Exercise 9.2

Find all the transitional expressions and constant reminders that give the following passages coherence.

1. Another thinker of the later years of the nineteenth century also helped to change the way people think about the world. Like Charles Darwin, Sigmund Freud thought of himself as a scientist, not a philosopher.

2. Also, when we first go out, it's great if my date can teach me something new. If we're having a discussion and she can talk about music, politics, video games, even lacrosse, and give me a new perspective on some topic, I'm hooked. Besides, if I pick up a new fact, I like to pass it on to someone who will appreciate it too.

3. Acropolis was the name given to the highest part of cities in ancient Greece. This part was surrounded by fortifications, temples, statues of gods. Most of the towns in ancient Greece, Asia Minor, and southern Italy had an acropolis then.

4. Many beginner skaters find the most difficult part of skating is learning to stop. To avoid another skater, skaters will stop by

bringing both feet together and turning the body in a quick twist to the side. Most of the time, however, skaters stop or slow down by making the skates act as a brake by turning the toes inwards.

5.   Football is a dangerous collision sport that should be banned from college campuses. Indeed, playing football is like going into combat. Every year, promising young men suffer injuries to spines and knees. Quarterbacks tend to suffer most of the serious injuries in the game. Because of the high stakes and violence involved, football produces a war ethic. This war ethic can include chemical warfare too. For instance, Fro Tuffingham, Manitoba Vikings quarterback actually says amphetamines allow players to achieve "a fine plateau of endurance and competitive zeal." All the broken backs, ruptured spleens, bruised kidneys, broken legs, and spinal damage that occur every fall in the legitimized warfare of football show how dangerous it is. Clearly football should be banned before anyone is killed in action.

6.   The discovery in 1856 of how to make an artificial dye from coal tar, the first aniline dye, was a great achievement. How did this come about? The discovery began with the work of a poor, young chemist with an idea. William Perkin, this young chemist, performed experiments alone in his parents' house. For his great discovery, he ran some pure aniline from a pipette into a glass flask and slowly added sulphuric acid. Next he added a few crystals of potassium dichromate and heated it all over a gas burner. From there the experiment continued until a clear purple liquid was produced. Perkin had made the first aniline dye and changed the colours of our lives. The dye changed the young chemist's life too. This artificial man-made dye made Perkin a wealthy man.

Exercise 9.3

Write the word or expression used in each sentence that provides coherence in a paragraph.

1.   Another important factor is the selection of details.

2.   Consequently, the details a writer chooses show what he or she considers important.

3.   These choices of details still cause problems.

4.   The selection of facts will, therefore, reveal something about the writer.

5. Most of all, a writer has to decide what is worth reporting.

6. On the other hand, writers learn that word order and transitional expressions can create emphasis and help slant an argument.

7. In speech, for example, if we say "Socrates was a wise old man," we can stress whichever word we choose.

8. Nevertheless, the greatest problem of all is unmotivated students.

9. Regular feedback from the teacher, however, ensures that students keep on target.

10. It is possible, then, to encourage students to be more analytical about their response to the material.

Exercise 9.4*

In pairs or groups of three, decide whether the italicized words in *two* of the following paragraphs are

a) a constant reminder

b) a transitional expression

c) a pronoun reference to the subject

1. A more immediate worry for Dasgupta and Company is its management problems. *The company* is seen as having inconsistent management. Although *many of its units* are successful, others have problems. *Still,* take Victory, the Internet unit run by Yang Yang Zu. *It* is based in Lawrence Park. *Inside this unit* is a committed dynamic young organization. *Victory* has already won many major contracts. *However*, other parts of Dasgupta and Company are less successful and do not have *the same sense of commitment*. Middle management gets the blame.

2. Although my friend Winona always got A's in school, she has little common sense. *In the past,* she was always the one who forgot important ingredients when cooking. She would *also* go to the beach and forget her bathing suit. *Now* she has a Ph.D. in psychology and is an expert in *intelligence*. She has done important research on *basic notions of intelligence. In particular,* her research shows that there are *many aspects to intelligence*. She says we have to know that there is more to life than analytical *intelligence*. Creative and practical skills are important *too*. I'm glad she realizes *that* now.

3.   Charles Darwin made his first trip to a tropical forest in Brazil in 1832. He was delighted and astounded with *it*. None of his books had prepared him for the magnificence of the Brazilian *rainforest*. Everything about *the forest* filled him with *wonder*—the spectacular plants with their glossy green foliage, the variety of flowers, the unimaginable wildlife. *Filled with awe, he* collected specimens every minute he could. He became *fascinated* by the way both plants and animals were adapted to *their rainforest environment*. There in the *rainforest, Darwin* began to realize that all the species fit together like the pieces of a jigsaw puzzle.

4.   Diagrams and drawings attract attention. *They* are an aid to explanation and help you present information quickly, clearly, and concisely. Consider *them* as an important part of any report, not just as an ornament or a last-minute addition. Use *plans, maps, charts, and drawings* as part of your discussion. *Effective diagrams or illustrations* allow you to use fewer words. *Obviously*, in today's busy world, readers appreciate *fewer words* and more pictures. You should *therefore* always plan to use graphs, diagrams, and illustrations in your report.

Exercise 9.5

In pairs or groups of three, add constant reminders and transitional expressions to *two* of the following paragraphs to make them more coherent.

1.   Nanjing, with its population of nearly 5 million, lies on the southern bank of the Yangtze River. Nanjing is one of China's most attractive cities. The construction work that is spoiling so much of modern China does not seem to have affected Nanjing as much as most of the other eastern cities. It has beautiful broad boulevards lined with trees. The trees give relief from the oppressive heat in summer. Nanjing is known as one of China's "three furnaces."

2.   Training and competing for the love of sport, not for the love of money, is important. The best long distance runners know that. They know that certain inner qualities are essential. Motivation, self-discipline, and effective time management are as important for an athlete as they are for any college student. A coach can provide interest and enthusiasm with a training program, but the motivation, self-discipline, and the time have to come from the athlete.

3.   The Winter Garden Theatre in Toronto is a beautiful place. The Ontario Heritage Foundation paid millions to buy and restore the

theatre complex on Yonge Street. Shows like *Cats* and *Joseph and the Amazing Technicolor Dreamcoat* were very successful there. Lately, it has been empty a lot of the time because operating costs are so steep. The Ontario Heritage Foundation plans to redesign it for more cabaret-style acts, with movable tables and chairs. Food and liquor will be served inside the theatre.

4. When you have a fight with someone, avoid the blame game. Denying your own role in the situation is no way to get others to realize what they have done wrong. Swallow your pride and admit you have made mistakes. The other person is more likely to acknowledge his or her responsibility. Take responsibility for your own actions first. Open the door for the other person to explain. Respect the other person's side and make hassles history.

5. South of Syracuse is the beautiful baroque city, Noto. You pass a chain of beaches where the deep blue of the sea is matched in intensity by the glistening green of the citrus groves. Noto is a few miles from the coast. With decorated church facades, its *piazza*, broad sweeping stairs, the beautiful arcades of the town hall, and magnificent palaces, it is an architectural treasure. It was a shock when people discovered that the slightest earth tremor would make it go down like a house of cards.

REVIEW AND REMEMBER

Coherent Writing

1. Arrange your material so readers can see the connections between points clearly.

2. Use **constant reminders** to keep your topic clear.

3. Use **transitional expressions** to establish relationships between ideas or add emphasis.

4. Use **attitudinal markers** to add emphasis and show commitment, but be cautious with these markers. Don't overdo them.

CHAPTER 10

Other Modes of Discourse:

Some Versions of the Paragraph

This chapter looks at rhetorical modes.

By the end of this chapter, you will be able to

- plan and write the following rhetorical modes:
    - description
    - process
    - comparison and contrast
    - definition
    - classification
    - cause and effect

You are now familiar with the clear thinking, planning, and writing techniques needed to build a strong paragraph or essay. Your organizing techniques will see you through most writing exercises. Sometimes though, your teachers will ask you to write a specific kind of paper: a description, a process paper, a comparison-and-contrast paper. They may ask you to classify some material, define a term, or write about cause and effect.

While each of these rhetorical modes has a different label, the approach to writing them is the same as for the regular expository writing you have been doing in Part 3. You still need a clear focus expressed in a topic sentence or thesis statement, specific supporting data, and a conclusion.

Rhetorical Modes

Description

We all have to describe something at some time. When we talk to a child about what to expect at school or camp, we describe the situation in words a child can understand. When we talk to a friend about our new car, we describe it in a way that shows its appeal. When we first tell a friend about someone who attracts us, we describe that person. Sometimes we say as much about the way this person looks as we do about how the person thinks. We describe the impression the person makes on us.

In the workplace, you often have to describe a specific situation: your travels, a daycare, a client's health status or behaviour, a car's strengths, a procedure, food, clothing, shelter, and more.

To create a clear description, concentrate on *showing* not *telling*.

Begin by looking at whatever you are describing with new eyes. You may pretend you are from another planet, or another culture, age group, or gender. How would you describe a salad spinner to a child from a village in Cameroon? How would you describe getting on and off a streetcar to an old man from Baffin Island? How would you describe a rave to a group of senior citizens? Try seeing what you are describing from another perspective.

Next, undertake a sensory evaluation of the topic. Use your five senses, whichever are appropriate, and choose concrete details to explain how something looks, sounds, tastes, feels, smells. Select details that convey the sense of what you are describing.

Size matters, remember. Think about how big? How small? How high? How low? Think about space and dimension. Is it as small as an ant, or as big as a football? Create a picture for your readers.

Consider the impression you want to leave with readers. What do you want them to remember most? The particular focus or memory you leave behind is sometimes called the *dominant impression.*

Follow these Steps to Success in your description writing.

STEPS TO SUCCESS

Description Techniques

1. Think about what you are describing from another point of view.

2. Show, don't tell. Use some or all of the five senses to help recreate in words what you are describing.

3. Consider the size and shape of what you are describing in specific measurements or in relation to other objects.

4. Use examples and comparisons where possible for clarity.

5. Choose details that will leave readers with a strong, specific impression.

Exercise 10.1

In pairs or groups of three, list all the sensory details in the following descriptive passages. What do you see, hear, touch, smell, or taste in each?

1. The air of the *Place* is filled with the musky scent of those little early Cavaillon melons, and then you become aware of another powerfully conflicting smell—rich, clove-like, spicy. It is the scent of sweet basil, and it is coming from the far end of the market where a solitary wrinkled old man sits on an upturned basket, scores and scores of basil plants ringed around him like a protective hedge.

Elizabeth David, *The Markets of France: Cavaillon.*

2.   Its engine is already one of the silkiest that autodom has to offer. You can almost imagine you are being propelled forward by some external force, like a magnetic field, or the mother of all tailwinds. The engine's sporty snarl is very expressive. Driveability is good with punchy throttle tip-in and a healthy appetite for revs. Add a smooth, sweet cushioned ride, and driving is a no-brainer.

Jeffery Splintok, *Green Light.*

3.   They are curious, these great dark-violet anemones. You may pass them on a grey day, or at evening or early morning, and never see them. But as you come along in full sunshine, they seem to be baying at you with all their throats, baying deep purple into the air. It is because they are hot and wide open now, gulping the sun.

D. H. Lawrence, *"Flowery Tuscany," Selected Essays.*

4.   Now I noticed that the inside of the window was covered with my frosty words which had condensed then frozen the second they hit the windshield. Frost had begun to creep onto the dashboard in shapes of cracked crystals and hairy sticks and was moving towards us like frozen lava as the minutes crept by. Our breath was literally closing in on us.

Catherine Gildiner, *Too Close to the Falls.*

5.   The films could be described as mythological-historical-tragi-comic-musicals. While they went on, there was a great deal of yelling, crying, getting up, singing along—and certainly no one minded the noisy unwrapping of newspaper cones that held *chane jor garam,* flattened chickpeas that had been highly spiced with cumin, red pepper and sour mango powder.

Madhur Jaffery, *A Taste of India.*

6.   Def Dopes' latest album, *All Stuck Up,* is a hit. If you want an experience so kinetic, so fully all-to-your-fingertips good, listen up. Their fuzztone-and-distortion-soaked sound will elevate your blood pressure. My personal fave cut is *Eh?* an infectious psycho-metal extravaganza that's so sweet on the ears, it's a syrup of sound. The poetry of tone in this album sets you floating on a parachute of song.

Malvina Minor, *Soundsright.*

7. In the mornings the heads of nails in the half-finished bedrooms would be white with frost, and the frost on the windowpanes would have to be scraped away with our fingernails or melted by the warmth of breath before the outside world could be seen in its icy stillness.

Alistair MacLeod, *No Great Mischief.*

8. It was the terrible "Triumph of Death" by Breughel, painted on such a massive scale that all the multitude of ghastly figures towered over us in the gloom, those ruthless skeletons ferrying the helpless dead in a fetid moat or pulling a cart of human skulls, beheading an out-stretched corpse or hanging humans from the gallows. A bell tolled over the endless hell of scorched and smoking land, towards which great armies of men came with the hideous mindless march of sol-diers to a massacre.

Anne Rice, *Interview with the Vampire.*

9. The flames leapt up. He thought he heard the hanging man scream, but he was not sure. Sweat was pouring from the hair in his armpits, poured down his sides, over his chest, into his navel and groin. He was lowered again; he was raised again. Now Jesse knew that he heard him scream. The head went back, the mouth wide open, blood bubbling from the mouth; the veins of the neck jumped out; Jesse clung to his father's neck in terror as the cry rolled over the crowd.

James Baldwin, *Going to Meet the Man.*

10. She looked bloated, like a body long submerged in motionless water, and of that pallid hue. Her eyes, lost in the fatty ridges of her face, looked like two small pieces of coal pressed into a lump of dough as they moved from one face to another as the visitors stated their errand.

William Faulkner, *A Rose for Emily.*

Exercise 10.2

Choose a familiar workplace object: a pen, paperclip, computer, coffee mug, binder, anything. Now write a *What am I?* description. Your brief description (five to seven sentences) should hint at the object's function, but not at its name.

Give your description to someone else and see if that person can guess what you have described. If your description is not clear, ask what you need to add to make it more precise.

Exercise 10.3

Write a paragraph describing a frightening experience you had as a child. Begin by establishing your age and the setting. How old were you? Where were you? Capture your fear then and conclude with your feelings now. Include as many sensory details as you can to describe what happened and to express the feelings you had at the time.

Process, or "How to" Instructions

In your job, at home, at school, anywhere you go, you often have to tell someone how to do something. Whether you are explaining how to make a cappuccino, write an incident report, change oil, or fill in a tax form, telling or showing people how to do something is part of everyday life.

The writing of instructions explaining how something is done or how something operates is called *process analysis*. If you want examples of clear process writing, take a look at books like *Weight Training for Dummies* or instructions accompanying prescription drugs. Note how they are written. They have to be clearly written because people of all levels of education and literacy have to understand them.

The first thing to do when you write a process paper is to consider why you are writing it and who is going to read it. In other words, it is the same story for all writing—*purpose* and *audience* need to be clear in the writer's mind before writing begins.

You may decide your audience needs some humour or needs to be told how serious a procedure is. Think why the particular process is important or needs to be learned. Choose your words and approach your subject according to its significance and the audience. Keep your explanation simple. Your audience does not like being confused or feeling dumb.

Then decide what materials readers need to assemble before they begin the project. What ingredients, tools, equipment, safety precautions or attitude do they need? What do they need to do first, second, third?

Run through the steps and materials in your head, or draft them on paper. Are there any specific actions or attitudes readers should avoid? What should readers expect the final result to be? When you have thought about all these points, and made brief notes, you are ready to write.

Follow these Steps to Success in your process writing.

STEPS TO SUCCESS

Process Writing Techniques

1. Write a topic sentence saying what you are going to cover and why. This is your statement of intent.

2. Prepare readers to begin the process. Mention any ingredients, tools, essential materials, safety precautions necessary for the process.

3. List the steps in order. Explain the process, step by step, and make clear what ingredients, tools, and actions are involved in each step.

   Be as specific as possible here. Indicate possible times for each procedure, if necessary. Explain the significance of each step if you have time.

4. Be conscious of safety. It is a good idea to list what to avoid or to be careful of somewhere in your instructions, maybe in a special section.

5. Use transitional expressions consciously and carefully so the connections between each step are obvious.

6. Think of your readers. Use comparisons with familiar procedures or objects to explain a step, wherever possible.

7. Make your instructions look good.
   - Have you listed them in the right order?
   - Is the layout appealing?
   - Have you used plenty of white space?
   - Have you used headings, italics, underlining, or boldface appropriately?

8. Conclude with a brief, positive statement that reinforces the statement of intent. Congratulations may be in order.

9. Review your instructions for accuracy. Could you follow them? Try them out on someone else.

Exercise 10.4*

In pairs or groups of three

> A. Re-order the following scrambled instructions on how to replace the battery in a calculator. (Numbers are enough.)

> B. Write an introductory and concluding statement.

1. Finally, press AC to turn the power on.

2. Wipe the new battery with a soft cloth, before loading it.

3. Continued use of the calculator when the figures on the display screen are dim can result in improper operation.

4. First, press OFF to turn the power off.

5. Replace the battery cover and secure it in place with the two screws you have already removed.

6. Remove the two screws that hold the battery cover in place. Put them in a safe place.

7. Remove the battery cover.

8. Load the battery into the unit with the positive (+) side facing up.

9. Remove the old battery.

Exercise 10.5

Pretend you are Miss Manners. Write a paragraph explaining the correct way to behave at one of the following events or situations:

- a first date
- a hockey game
- a baby's first birthday party
- a rock concert
- a friendly neighbourhood baseball game
- the Molson Indy
- in the cafeteria before a final exam
- a fashionable hairdressing salon

Exercise 10.6

Choose a procedure related to your field of study or your profession. You might choose an intervention technique, measuring blood pressure, installing a dynamometer, changing oil and oil filters, preparing a special recipe. Write instructions for a handbook on the procedure.

Assume your reader has no experience with this procedure. List the significant steps in chronological order. Include diagrams or illustrations if you wish.

Comparison and Contrast

Comparison-and-contrast essays are often assigned. Why? Well, because comparison and contrast is part of everyday communication. Maybe you want to compare Mena Suvari with Minnie Driver or the Beastie Boys with Bad Boy Bill or the Beatles. You may have once compared the mating habits of the male lion with the mating habits of the male moose. The process of comparison and contrast can show advantages and disadvantages. Whenever you compare one friend, teacher, car, or running shoe with another, you are indulging in comparison-and-contrast thinking.

You instinctively use comparison and contrast whenever you try something new or make decisions. Comparison and contrast (often known as C–C) helps you make up your mind. That's why so many teachers choose this mode for writing topics.

You can consider *similarities*. You can consider *differences*.

When writing a comparison-and-contrast paper, be sure that the items you are comparing are from the same category or class. In other words, don't waste time comparing apples and oranges.

Make sure you have a good reason for your comparison and contrast. Readers don't want to be left saying, "So what?" Think of your central purpose and your conclusion before you begin writing.

It is easy to construct a clear topic sentence, or preview statement, for a comparison-and-contrast paragraph. You already have your micro-subjects, and you have some reason to compare them. For example, you may show similarities or differences between A and B, or you may weigh the advantages or disadvantages of A and B. Whatever approach you take, remember to be as specific as possible about what you compare and contrast.

Examples

1. Although cellphones are great for safety reasons when travelling on business, e-mail is better for simple text messages.

2. Lynne's influence on Dick is easier to understand than Hillary's influence on Bill.

3. Healthy-sounding, so-called low-fat, sugar-free snacks can contain as many calories and be as unhealthy as regular ones.

Look at Example 3. You have a choice on how to organize your paper. Will you compare and contrast one snack at a time, or will you compare and contrast the so-called healthy snacks as a group with the regular snacks as a group? You have a choice between the block **One Thing at a Time Approach** or the **Alternating Approach** of looking at one smaller element at a time. The topic determines the approach. The topic sentence of Example 3 lends itself to the One Thing at a Time Approach.

Follow these Steps to Success in your comparison-and-contrast writing.

STEPS TO SUCCESS

Comparison-and-Contrast Techniques

1. Prepare a topic sentence with a clear sense of comparison and contrast. Your sentence should give some indication of which aspects of the subject will be dealt with in your paper.

2. Make clear your reasons for the comparison and contrast.

3. Decide on the order of approach. Will you deal fully with one item at a time, A and then B, or will you alternate A and B throughout? In a longer paper, this choice is more important. Your choice needs careful planning.

Sample Comparison-and-Contrast Structures

One Thing at a Time Approach   Alternating Approach

    Introduction   Introduction

    Aspect A   **Support 1**

    Support 1   Aspect A

Support 2	Aspect B
Support 3	**Support 2**
Aspect B	Aspect A
Support 1	Aspect B
Support 2	**Support 3**
Support 3	Aspect A
Conclusion	Aspect B
	Conclusion

4. Make careful use of transitional expressions and attitudinal markers that indicate the comparison-and-contrast mode. Use words like *similarly, likewise, moreover, in addition, however, conversely, in contrast, yet, although, on the other hand, but,* and *while.*

5. Try to devote equal time to each aspect you compare and contrast.

6. Reach a clear conclusion or make a definite point at the end.

Exercise 10.7

1. In small groups, discuss and make notes on one of the following topics.

   a. your parents' attitude to dating compared to yours

   b. the differences between high school and college

   c. a college diploma versus a university degree

   d. two politicians

   e. two rock groups

   f. life in a small town and life in a big city

2. Consider what you have discussed and prepare a comparison-and-contrast paragraph on this topic. Read out the final result to the class.

3. Vote on which paragraph comes across most clearly. Be prepared to explain your evaluation.

Exercise 10.8

Compare the way you are now with the way you were when you were . . .

Be precise about the age and stage you are comparing yourself with. For instance, you might be interested in the comparison between you as a mature student and you as a teenage dropout; you as an innocent trusting 8 year old and you as a suspicious, doubtful adult; you as a hopeful bride and you as a saddened single parent; or you as an idealistic student at the beginning of your course and you as a more realistic person now.

Exercise 10.9

Compare and contrast *two* attitudes to an environmental issue. Choose a specific environmental issue and a specific place (if possible) for your topic. Focus on the local, not the global.

You might consider two attitudes to water testing, greenhouse-gas emissions, energy consumption, car-sharing, nuclear power, wind energy, extreme weather from climate change, or local garbage. You might compare your mother's attitude to recycling to yours. Make clear in your conclusion what your opinion is.

Definition

Dictionaries define words. Textbooks define professional terms. You define situations and ideas when you explain something to another person. You may define behaviour, something from another culture, a drug reaction, a gourmet dish.

Why would you write a definition?

• You might want to offer a new way of looking at a subject.

• You might want to make a subject clear.

• You might want to communicate the dominant impression made by a subject.

• You might want to prepare people for a change in attitude.

When you write a definition, you usually go beyond a mere dictionary definition and offer an extended explanation to make your point clear. That means your definition will probably include comparisons, opinions, examples, and feelings. When feelings are involved, you need to be especially careful with *diction*, the words you choose for your writing.

A dictionary definition gives the *denotation* of a word. No one gets too excited about a dictionary definition. The connotation is more interesting. That's where feelings are involved. *Connotation* refers to the emotional associations of a word. Connotations can be said to *con* the reader into certain reactions. Think of the difference between the denotative meaning and connotative meaning of the words *bunny, chick,* and *stud.* Sensitive writers are careful about connotations.

Follow these Steps to Success in your definition writing.

STEPS TO SUCCESS

Definition Techniques

1. Decide on the term you will define and why.

2. Consider how much your readers know about the term.

3. Prepare a topic sentence with readers and purpose in mind.

4. Plan specific support to prove your topic sentence. Make your point of view clear with your selection.

Exercise 10.10

In small groups, decide how you would define *one* of the following terms. Come up with *two* examples and *one* anecdote for your definition.

Terms

embarrassment	prejudice
homophobia	processed food
loyalty	religious freedom
materialism	road rage
obesity	sexism

Exercise 10.11

Answer *one* of the following questions. In your definition, imagine you are making your points clear to a visitor from another country. Use local examples for a Canadian perspective. If you know any international examples, use them for comparison.

1. What is a feminist?

2. What is a techno-peasant?

3. What is a trade union?

4. What is a panhandler?

5. What is Tim Horton's?

6. What is a jungle party?

7. What is a daycare centre?

8. What is the CAA?

9. What is compost?

10. What is maple syrup?

Classification

Classification is fun. Like comparison and contrast, you do it all the time and you rely on it every day. When you visit a drugstore, you don't expect to find the skincare lotions with the diapers. You don't expect to find Shania Twain beside Doctor Dre at the record store, or *Dracula* next to *The Little Mermaid* at the video store.

Dividing things into logical groups is called *classification.* It helps us sort things according to certain characteristics. These characteristics are specific qualities. It is important to keep these qualities clear to readers.

Think of all the possible classifications for you and your friends at college. What kind of students are you? What is your program at college? How else can you be divided? For example, are you conscientious workers, Canadian, Chinese, Egyptian, Hungarian, Trinidadian, blind, differently abled, balding, financially challenged, rich, mature, unemployed, digitally dexterous, ambitious, highly motivated?

How would you classify your particular group? What common qualities do you have? How do you differ within your group? Classification helps you understand a subject better by separating it into distinct parts. It helps put things in order, and it helps show the differences within a similar group.

But, be careful. Forcing people into specific groups can lead to stereotyping. Clearly, it is very hard to fit a person into one specific slot only. Think of all the possibilities mentioned above for your group of friends. You can easily apply several adjectives to one person. It may be simple to classify cars, movies, videos, operas, trees, and animals, but not human beings. However, sometimes we have to put people into groups to try to understand them better. Just try not to oversimplify.

Follow these Steps to Success in your classification writing.

STEPS TO SUCCESS

Classification Techniques

Choose a topic that has a common thread.

1. Before you write:
    *   Decide how and why you want to classify the items in your chosen topic.
    *   Choose the working labels of the topic for the categories you use.
    *   Be consistent with your groups and establish clear characteristics for analysis. (Avoid exceptions here.)
    *   List the specific points that show how each group fits your categories.
    *   Consider offering comparisons for clarity.

2. Write your classification seriously or humorously, depending on your audience.

Exercise 10.12

In pairs or groups of three, choose *two* of the following topics. Work out *three* possible classifications for each topic chosen.

Examples

Topic: health hazards of the holiday season

1. tired feet

2. weight gain

3. depressed spirits

Topic: biological weapons

1. Rift Valley Fever virus

2. anthrax

3. botulism

Topics

accounting	fashion
automotive technology	health sciences
computer science	movies
corrections	music
engineering	supermodels
family sedans	visual arts

Exercise 10.13

Choose *one* of the following topics for a classification paper, describing each category and stating a preference for one. Narrow the topic further, if necessary.

Begin with a statement telling readers *how many* and *what* categories you will consider. For one paragraph, attempt two or, at the most, three categories. Use the same number of specific details to support each category. Choose vivid supporting details.

Topics

allergies	jeans
college teachers	perfume
hamburgers	portable CD players
high school students	sport utility vehicles
ice cream	television commercials

Cause and Effect

Your friend can't keep a job. No wonder. She is late most days and does not smile at customers. Her bosses won't put up with her attitude. She gets fired from one donut shop after another. She says she doesn't understand why, but you do. One thing leads to another, as your mother always told you.

English teachers refer to analyzing actions and results as cause and effect, or *causal analysis*. Cause and effect means looking at how one thing caused another to happen. It asks *why, what caused X,* and *what were the consequences.*

If you leave the oven on high, the cookies will burn. If you unplug the VCR, the videotape won't play. That's simple. Life is not always so simple though. Why have homicide rates dropped in Canada, and not in Britain? Why does your brother eat red meat, and you don't touch it? Cause-and-effect reasoning can be complex. If you are dealing with social and political issues, it is essential to do some research so you know what you are talking about.

When writing a cause-and-effect paper, start with *why*. Be aware that if the topic is complicated, you may not reach a firm conclusion. You may have to qualify your concluding remarks in some way.

Follow these Steps to Success in your cause-and-effect writing.

STEPS TO SUCCESS

Cause-and-Effect Techniques

1. Narrow the topic so you don't attempt to write a book.

2. Do research. Learn as much as possible about the topic.

3. Think about the conclusion you will come to. Sometimes you have to use cautious language, like *seems, appears.*

4. Decide whether to concentrate mainly on causes or effects. List them in order.

5. Prepare a topic sentence that makes clear why you are writing this analysis.

6. Use transitional expressions to show cause and effect. Words like *due to, therefore,* and *because* help indicate developments and connections. Take readers with you.

7. In your conclusion, remind readers of your reasons for the discussion.

Exercise 10.14

In small groups, discuss *one* of the following questions. Come up with reasons for your answers to the question.

A. Make a list in two columns (Causes and Effects) and indicate the relationship between each cause and effect with lines or colours.

B. Prepare an introductory and a concluding statement. Prepare two or three questions that lead to the topic indicated in the introduction.

C. Allot the presentation tasks below only after you have covered A and B.

Questions for Discussion

1.   Why do so many relationships fall apart?
2.   Why do some people who never go hunting for food own guns?
3.   Why do teachers get upset when students are late for class?
4.   Why should people be forbidden to chop down healthy trees?
5.   Why are women in Canada at greater risk of developing breast cancer than women in Thailand?
6.   Why do many marriages work?
7.   Why should children get free dental care?
8.   Why do so many people eat bland food?
9.   Why do many wealthy people suffer from insomnia and depression?
10. Why are good communication skills important?

Presentation Tasks

A. On the blackboard, one member of the group will write up the Causes list, another the Effects list.

B. Another member of the group will introduce the topic by asking two or three questions about it and then presenting the prepared introductory statement.

C. Another member of the group will talk about the lists on the blackboard and show how they support the introductory statement.

D. The classmate who introduced the topic (in B here) will then try to answer the questions he or she asked at the beginning, and will end with a concluding statement.

E. The class will point out any errors in logic.

Exercise 10.15

Write a paragraph examining the cause and effect for *one* of the following topics.

1. Why many students dislike giving presentations.

2. Why I chose my course at college.

3. Why I do not intend to have children.

4. Why we need to support the CBC.

5. Why married men live longer than single men.

6. Why motorcycles are dangerous.

7. Why marijuana should be legalized.

8. Why my parents are great role models (or not).

9. Why we need noise pollution laws.

10. Why I love _____ .

Most writing for professional reasons uses a mixture of definition, analysis, description, cause and effect, and comparison and contrast, but sometimes you will focus more on a specific type of writing. Then, you might use one of the traditional modes of development described in this chapter.

REVIEW AND REMEMBER

Rhetorical Modes

1. **Description** shows readers what something is like.

2. **Process** tells readers how to do something or how something works.

3. **Comparison and contrast** shows how things are alike or how things differ.

4. **Definition** makes clear the meaning of a term or expresses a point of view about the meaning of the term.

5. **Classification** divides things into logical groups.

6. **Cause and effect** shows the reasons things happen.

CHAPTER 11

Essays

This chapter moves from the totally convincing paragraph to the Formula Five Essay, with a brief look at conclusions, research, and documentation.

By the end of this chapter, you will be able to

- understand the term *expository writing*

- know how to conclude with style and certainty

- organize paragraphs in an **I**-frame format

- understand the role of a strong thesis statement

- know the Formula Five approach to essay writing

- integrate and acknowledge reference material to support your thesis

- document sources correctly

You have now covered most of the steps involved in writing clearly and coherently. You have even had the chance to prepare an oral presentation in essay format. Mostly, though, you have been concentrating on writing a convincing paragraph. In fact, all the skills you have been developing are those used in writing any expository prose.

What is expository prose? *Prose* is the term used for ordinary, regular writing that is not poetry. *Expository prose* is the sort of writing that informs or explains something. Most of the writing you do is expository. For example, a paragraph is a short unit of expository writing.

What is an essay? You looked at this subject briefly in Step 11: Prepare an Essay in Chapter 6. You know that an essay is an attempt to explain an idea in more depth than one paragraph. In an essay you try to make a point, just as you do in a paragraph.

In college, some teachers like essays of only five paragraphs. A five-paragraph essay allows one paragraph for the introduction, one for the conclusion and three for the middle, or central body, of the essay.

Note: An essay or report may have four or many more paragraphs. Nowhere is it written in stone that all essays must have five paragraphs, even though many generations of students have learned how to write a Five Paragraph Formula essay. What generations of students have really learned is

- how to focus

- how to prove a point

- how to present that point coherently and convincingly

The five-paragraph essay is simply a useful formula for learning these skills. It works, so it's worth learning.

So far in this textbook, most of what you have been writing are strong body paragraphs, suitable for the central section, or body, of a five-paragraph essay. You have also learned techniques for introducing a topic that can be applied to any introduction, anywhere. As well, you can write to convince your readers that you know what you are talking about. Therefore, you already know the basic techniques for essay and report writing.

STEPS TO SUCCESS

Expository Writing

1. Choose your subject and make it as specific, precise, and clear (SPC) as possible. Limit the topic until it is a micro-subject.

2. Ask yourself who is going to read your paper, what you want readers to remember, and how you will reach these readers. Think about your audience.

3. Make a point about your micro-subject and construct a clear topic sentence presenting that point.

4. Prove the point stated in your topic sentence with strong support: statistics, definitions, anecdotes, facts, examples, statements from experts, case histories, personal stories, historical or scientific information, comparisons and contrasts, all relating to your point, and only that point, so your discussion has **unity.**

5. Develop the support with **coherence,** with careful use of constant reminders, transitional expressions, and attitudinal markers.

6. Conclude effectively. Show your readers clearly that you have come to the end.

Now it is time to land. You don't want to leave your readers up in the air. You do want to reinforce your key point. Think about the impression you want to leave with your readers. When you conclude: be brief, be clear, be conclusive.

STEPS TO SUCCESS

Conclusions

1. Restate and reinforce the topic sentence using different words.

2. Stress, if you wish, your strongest argument for the point in the topic sentence.

3. Return, if you wish, to the idea of your opening remark, and make some point about it that is appropriate.

4. Pull everything together in one conclusive, interesting statement.

5. Make sure you have reviewed your topic satisfactorily.

Note: You *never* introduce a new idea in a conclusion.

The I-Frame

Look at the paragraph on Uncle Joe's children in Constant Reminders in Chapter 9. Note how the topic sentence is reinforced at the end. That is considered a REVIEW statement. The topic sentence offers readers a PREVIEW. The specific support offers a clear VIEW.

Aim for an **I** with your paragraph.

THE I-FRAME FOR A PARAGRAPH

PREVIEW: Topic sentence

VIEW:

- Specific support
- Specific support
- Specific support
  (whatever is needed)

REVIEW: Concluding statement

Example

```
PREVIEW:
Fabio's new car is very comfortable to ride in.


VIEW:

   • The drivetrain is smooth.

   • It has multi-adjustable seats
     with lumbar supports.

   • It has automatic seat-belt
     presenters


REVIEW:
With its smooth ride, comfortable seats, and easy
seat-belt use, Fabio's new car is cushy and restful.
```

To read some examples of paragraphs written with an **I**-frame, see Sample **I**-Frame Paragraphs at the end of this chapter.

Exercise 11.1

Write a concluding sentence for *four* of the following paragraphs. Choose *three* paragraphs of different lengths. Review the Steps to Success box on Conclusions before beginning. Note the topic sentence in each paragraph.

1.   A Yale psychologist says that there are three types of intelligence: academic, creative, and practical. Most of us have a combination of all three. We may not have had straight A's in school, but we may be smarter than we think. Most of us can absorb and retain information, find unusual solutions to problems, and also show common sense.

2.   The biggest challenge in most Canadian hotels is staffing. Employers have real problems finding, training, and keeping good staff. Sales people, computer technologists, and controllers have the highest turnover rates because the demand for them is high everywhere. Then, many employees head south for warmer weather and more flexibility, leaving their employers with a headache. They know that

finding good employees for hotels is not easy. In order to recruit the right applicants, the hospitality industry is now targeting post-secondary institutions for bright, young people, and community centres for mature, stable workers.

3. The advertising industry comes up with some great ideas, but it can also create ads that are really dumb. In the same year that Molson's rant from Joe, that 60 seconds of pure maple syrup, touched Canadians' hearts, and The Breast Cancer Society of Canada's Cam Exam was one of the most requested spots on a US Web site, advertisers also gave us a Microsoft commercial of a guy sitting on the john, scribbling on the wall, forgetting to flush when he asks his boss to admire his work. That ad got the Smelliest Ad of the Year Award. Then there was a Carlsberg commercial of a woman talking about her boyfriend, waving her hands in a lewd way that offended many viewers.

4. My sister's mood swings are really scary. One minute she is a ray of sunshine, the next she is a thunderstorm. You never know when her mood will change. She will be planning an outing with the family, all smiles and laughter, and then, suddenly, she takes offence to some-thing. Boy, watch the skies darken. The thunderclaps start with a torrent of words, lightning flashes from her eyes, and high tension crackles in the air before she subsides into a dark cloud of sulks.

5. Parents who raise happy children talk to their children a lot. They listen when their children talk about Peter Rabbit and who they don't like to sit near in school. They let their children chatter about their favourite colour and why they hate Brussels sprouts. They talk with them about what they plan to do together, and who they will meet. They do not criticize their children's responses or become impatient. Parents who care about communication will ask questions and listen to the answers.

6. Domestic accidents actually kill and injure more people than accidents on roads. In the safety of their own home, people trip on loose carpets and bunched underlays, they fall down stairs, they slide on wet floors, and they burn themselves with their irons or hot coffee. Sewing needles, vacuum cleaners, and food mixers are also the cause of many injuries. People should be more careful at home. They need to know that furniture, fixtures, and fittings in the home are often hazardous.

7. Seeing the Rockies by three trains was an experience I will never forget. In Edmonton, I boarded the shining, stylish train *The Canadian*

and saw the prairies along the banks of the North Saskatchewan River, before arriving in Jasper. I left that beautiful place two days later from Williams Lake on a train called *The Cariboo Prospector,* riding in comfort through the hills of Cariboo country into the Fraser Canyon, climbing mountains and running along lake shores without moving from my comfortable seat. The scenery was spectacular, but the most impressive scenery of all was viewed with ease from the wide windows of the famous *Rocky Mountaineer,* travelling from Banff to Vancouver.

Exercise 11.2

In pairs or groups of three, try restating *five* of the following topic sentences in a different and conclusive way. Make your concluding statement reflect some aspect of a paragraph that might have been written on the topic.

1. *A* grades are not always a good indication of a student's ability.

2. Many business people prefer short assignments overseas to gain a new perspective and to avoid uprooting their families.

3. Because of his alcoholism, Uncle Egbert was not good at providing for his children.

4. Theresa tries hard to carry her religion into all her other dealings in life.

5. Good social relationships, not material goods, are what give meaning to our lives.

6. It is important to wear safety glasses when operating a cutter head.

7. Her enthusiasm for life, her interest in politics, and her love of music and dance make my 90-year-old Aunt Gladys fun to visit.

8. Most Canadians have no idea that the industrial use of coal is actually increasing.

9. A good routine and clear career goals lead to success in college.

10. Tears are an excellent way to release emotions.

Now it's time to write some totally convincing paragraphs of your own. Think of the paragraph you write as part of an essay, the *body paragraph* as it is sometimes called. Build your body paragraph strongly. First, outline what you will do.

Exercise 11.3

Respond to this exercise in pairs or groups of three.

A. Organize the relevant material in each of the following sets into an I-frame.

B. Eliminate any points that do not support the topic sentence.

C. Restate the topic sentence in your own words for the REVIEW that will create a firm conclusion.

1. When you are making a puppet it is always fun creating the head.

   a. fabric choice for clothes can be anything from lace to feathers

   b. choosing eyes, nose, and mouth

   c. special effects can be achieved with fur, raffia, or string

   d. exaggerating facial features helps create a particular impression

   e. choosing paint colours for makeup

2. Children with AIDS need to be treated sensitively in school.

   a. caring, open teachers needed

   b. children do not want to die among strangers

   c. the school peers' parents have to know about the disease

   d. children often must go through extreme medical treatments

   e. other children at school easily learn accepting attitudes

3. Women gain many physical and social benefits from weightlifting.

   a. meet many new friends

   b. cigarette smoking and hypertension cause the most problems

   c. make lungs function more efficiently

   d. learn a more disciplined approach to work

   e. daily moisturizer soothes dry skin

   f. gain greater control over cardiovascular condition

4. The Galapagos Islands deserve conservation because of their historical background.

   a. mountains, ridges, valleys, plateaus, and craters interesting to study

   b. renegades and buccaneers used them as a refuge and a base for raids in the eighteenth century

    c. Charles Darwin developed his theory of evolution there

    d. Darwin's ideas caused a shift in thinking

    e. discovered in 1535 by the bishop of Panama, but not on any map until 1570

5.   Fabio's car costs very little to run.

    a. good fuel economy

    b. washes away dirt, road film, insects, and other contaminants regularly

    c. simple routine maintenance so far

    d. responsive rack-and-pinion steering

    e. low service costs

    f. enough muscle to rival any V8

6.   Good looks in holiday snapshots are easy to achieve if you take some candid advice.

    a. make sure the camera is not lower than you are

    b. keep your mouth closed when you chew

    c. relax, and try tilting your head slightly to accentuate your bone structure

    d. lots of people suffer from holiday blues

    e. avoid loud prints and bright colours

    f. look up at the camera with your neck stretched

    g. spray yourself with a fresh cologne so you smell nice for the photo

Exercise 11.4

Choose *one* of the following topics and prepare an **I**-frame for it. In other words, prepare the

    A. PREVIEW (topic sentence)

    B. VIEW (list of supporting details)—Use one quote, one example, one statistic

    C. REVIEW (reinforcement of topic sentence)

Topics

1. If I had $50,000 to spend in 1 week, I would . . .(give reasons for the expenditure)

2. What really bugs me about [a friend, a politician, a singer] is . . .

3. One of my worst habits is . . .

4. The best thing about my car is . . .

5. Winter is especially difficult for the physically challenged because . . .

6. The pastime I most enjoy is . . .

7. Shoplifting is a major social problem because . . .

Exercise 11.5

Decide which constant reminders, transitional expressions, or attitudinal markers you will use to create coherence, and write the complete paragraph from the **I**-frame you created in Exercise 11.4.

Congratulations. You have prepared a totally convincing paragraph on a topic. You have prepared

- a clear topic sentence,

- an outline for your support, and

- the coherent presentation of material in your final written version.

You have had time, though, to focus only on *one* approach to your topic. For example, you might have written:

One of my worst habits is not concentrating when I study.

OR

If I had $50,000 to spend in 1 week, I would donate every cent of it to the Salvation Army.

OR

If I had $50,000 to spend in 1 week, I would take a luxury 7-day Pharaoh Cruise in the Pacific Ocean with my lover.

The Formula Five Essay

Consider now what you would say if you had time to expand on one of the previous topics and had to find more key points. You need to discuss three key points in what can be called a Formula Five Essay—the five-paragraph essay. You might come up with two more bad habits that will not help you get straight A's in college:

- talking on the telephone for hours
- not telling your boss that you need to cut your hours at work

Or, you might come up with three reasons for supporting the Salvation Army or for taking a cruise in the Pacific Ocean.

For each point you must still provide a topic sentence, specific support, transitional expressions, and a concluding comment. The three resulting paragraphs will then be the central body of a Formula Five First-Year Essay.

You still have to come up with the other two paragraphs: the first and the last. You have to think about how to introduce your points and conclude strongly. That's the easy part. You have had plenty of practice introducing topics in Part 2. You know how to review your key points in a conclusion. How do you write an introductory paragraph?

Your introductory paragraph will use an attention-getting device (S3Q3 Formula), an introduction to the micro-subject itself, and a sentence that establishes the three key points you will discuss. That sentence, usually the final sentence in the introductory paragraph of a Formula Five Essay, is called the *thesis statement* (see Chapter 6, Step 11: Prepare and Essay).

What is a thesis statement?

The term *thesis* was originally associated with academic papers presenting an argument and involving considerable research. The term *thesis statement* has come to mean the sentence that presents the key points to be discussed and proved in an essay. It implies that you will argue for your ideas about the subject of the essay. For a Formula Five Essay on the previous topics, a thesis statement could be:

> Three reasons for my disappointing grades in college are not concentrating when I study, talking on the telephone for hours, and not telling my boss I need to cut my hours at work.

OR

If I had $50,000 to spend in one week, I would donate every cent of it to the Salvation Army because I admire their organizational skills, their attitude to the homeless, and their support of musical talent.

A thesis statement presents points to prove. It begins with a micro-subject and makes a point about it. In a Formula Five Essay, a thesis statement presents three key points about the specific, precise, and clear subject (**SPC + 1,2,3**). It provides the basis for an argument, not simple facts. It does not ask a question, but it allows questions to be answered.

Poor Thesis Statements

Man first landed on the moon on July 20, 1969.

My brother has brown eyes.

Why do I attend Snowflake College?

Better Thesis Statements

Man first landed on the moon in 1969, even though at that time many of the Earth's oceans were still unexplored, and millions of people lacked good medical care.

My brother's brown eyes have a devastating effect on young women, old women, and dogs.

I attend Snowflake College because it is near my home, it has a good program in computer studies, and it never gives grades below B.

The possible thesis statements above allow for an argument. They will allow an answer to *so what* or *prove it!* Most people agree that Apollo 11 landed on the moon in July 1969. Some flaky types might still believe that it really happened in a back lot at Universal Studios, but most people accept the fact. So what's to be discussed?

No one will contradict you when you tell them your brother has brown eyes (unless you don't have a brother), but why are you telling them? The question about Snowflake College demands an answer. Your answer gives you the basis for an essay.

Remember, an essay can make one or more points, but for essays at college, many teachers like three key points. If they want a Formula Five Essay, give it to them.

Exercise 11.6

A strong thesis statement has a specific, precise, clear subject, and makes two or more specific points about that subject.

Decide which of the following statements would be suitable for an essay. Ask if the subject is SPC and if this micro-subject has a clear focus. Ask if you could prove it. Try the *so what* test.

1. Some drugs prescribed to prevent social anxiety are not well tolerated.

2. People who dash out for a cigarette just as the entree is served, people who expect extra special care, and people who book large tables then come late or forget to cancel will not be welcomed back to a restaurant.

3. Why was that moment a milestone in my life?

4. Sun, stress, and pollution can make a healthy skin dull and lifeless.

5. Great ingredients are raspberry, parmesan, and lemon grass.

6. Your listening habits and your environment have to be considered when making a decision.

7. Because she hates the dust, dirt, hair, and common allergens that accumulate in her house, my sister spends all her spare time at the mall.

8. Employers today want people who excel at teamwork, problem solving, and applying technology to business issues.

9. The Canadian Dental Association asks you to brush your teeth twice a day with fluoride toothpaste, to floss daily, and to see your dentist regularly.

10. The Columbine Camp in the Rockies gives inner-city adolescents a memorable opportunity to learn map-reading skills and environmentally friendly camping techniques.

Exercise 11.7

How would you support each point in *two* of the acceptable thesis statements in Exercise 11.6? Try coming up with stories or examples to support each of the key points mentioned in these thesis statements. Use the sample outline format below as a model.

Example

My New and Improved Study Habits

I. Concentrating When I Study

   A. switch off my telephone and music systems

   B. follow active reading habits learned from *Basics and Beyond*

II. Not Talking to Friends on the Telephone for Hours

   A. tell my friends that I cannot be reached between 8:00 p.m. and 11:30 p.m.

   B. limit telephone conversations during the week to 10 minutes

III. Telling My Boss I Need to Cut My Hours at Work

   A. tell Mr. Warbucks that I am not available beyond 10 hours per week

   B. get Call Display so I don't answer the telephone when my boss calls to beg me to work extra hours to get him out of difficulty

Exercise 11.8

In pairs or groups of three, plan an essay on *one* of the following topics.

   A. Prepare a thesis statement with two or three key points for your essay.

   B. List *two* different kinds of support (statistics, anecdotes, facts, quotes, examples, statements from experts, case histories and personal stories, historical or scientific evident, or comparisons and contrasts) for each key point.

   C. Write one sentence for each paragraph beginning with "According to _____," and quote from a member of your group. Indicate the occupation, study program, or age of your group member when you give his or her name. Comment on the quotation.

Topics

1. the best way to evaluate students in the _____ course

2. stories remembered from kindergarten

3. a commercial that really works

4. what teachers need to know about students today

5. a fashion trend that is fun

6. a pet peeve about this college

Exercise 11.9

Using the S3Q3 Formula for creating introductions, prepare an introductory paragraph for the topic chosen in Exercise 11.8. End the paragraph with your thesis statement.

Exercise 11.10

In pairs or groups of three, answer *three* of the following questions.

After a brief discussion of the answers, prepare a thesis statement suitable for a Formula Five Essay on *one or two* of the topics. In other words, prepare a statement with three key points to prove about a focused microsubject, after brainstorming.

1. Are computers a wise investment for college students?

2. What are the major causes of stress in a college student's life?

3. Why do so many live hip-hop concerts attract violence?

4. What can schools do to prevent cheating?

5. How can a student create a quiet environment for study?

6. Why do students buy cars?

7. Is an increased lifespan a good thing?

8. Why should everyone eat garlic?

9. What sort of movies appeal to teenagers?

10. What is the biggest problem in our world right now?

Exercise 11.11

Using specific support that indicates sound, movement, or emotion, write a short essay about a favourite song, singer, or group, making it clear why this particular song, singer, or group appeals to you.

Quoting for Support

So far in this textbook, most of the writing you have worked on has asked for a personal response or support from personal experience. But your teachers, supervisors, bosses usually want to know more than just what *you* feel about a subject. They want facts, details, specialized knowledge, reference to the latest research so your discussion is convincing. They want you to go beyond personal experience.

Chapters 6 and 8 look at the place of research in supporting an idea. You know that other people offer an interesting perspective on most topics, so in many of your paragraphs, you use quotations from other people. You might decide to quote Great Uncle Hugo's views on single parents, or you might quote Dr. David Kent on Christina Georgina Rossetti's poetry. You will be careful to quote exactly what the person said, or to *paraphrase* it; that is, put it in your own words without changing the original meaning.

You always keep a record of the following:

- name of the person you are quoting

- title of the book, magazine, or other research material

- page or place you found the quotation

- date of publication

- the city and the publisher

Presenting quotations gracefully is important. Introduce your quotation so readers understand why you are quoting. Remember the signal phrases referred to in Chapter 8, Signal Phrases for Introducing Quotations. Use them to integrate your quotations into your writing.

Suppose, for example, you are writing about single-parent families today:

> Single-parent families are more common now than when my parents were young. People accustomed to the suburban realities of the past, when Dad worked, and Mum stayed home to care for the 2.5 children and the dog, sometimes find it hard to accept the idea of a single working woman with children managing perfectly well on her own. When he hears about unmarried women with children, my Great Uncle Hugo snorts in disbelief, "Should never be allowed. Women can't raise kids alone."

OR

My generation accepts that single-parent families are a normal occurrence today, but some of my older relatives find the idea strange. For example, my friend Angela says, "I'm happier bringing up my children alone," whereas my Great Uncle Hugo snaps, "Who is your young friend fooling? She can't manage two kids on her own. Shouldn't be allowed by the government."

Using Research Material

Outside sources can expand your knowledge and give you new insights. At college you are developing the ability to understand, interpret, and evaluate new material. You are not only gaining information, you are also learning how to find it and use it. You know that employers today like "knowledge workers"; that is, people who know what is out there and can access it.

You probably have a good idea by now of how and where to find out what you need to know, and what research materials work best for you. Work on becoming comfortable with information-retrieval networks, like Google at **www.google.com**.

Whether you consult live human beings, magazines, newspapers, books, film, audiotapes, videotapes, television, CD-ROMs, or the Internet, your research will show readers that you know what you are talking about, and that you know where to find information on a topic.

You have to know how to present the results of your research gracefully and accurately. Presenting names, dates, places of origin, and other bibliographical information shows you are smart enough to do research. It shows the strength and credibility of your material. It also means you cannot be accused of the literary crime of plagiarism (see page 314).

STEPS TO SUCCESS

Quoting within a Paragraph

1. Introduce the name of the person you are quoting in a signal phrase ending with a comma (see Chapter 8, Signal Phrases).

   Jon Redfern, the Canadian mystery writer, says, ". . .

2. Place quotation marks around the exact words of the quotation.

3. Keep the quotation brief. A word, a phrase, or a sentence is usually sufficient within one paragraph.

4. Omit the comma if you use the word *that*.

> Professor Bill O'Sullivan always says that "the road to hell is paved with good intentions and faulty spelling."

5. If you use longer quotations (more than four lines),

- begin on a new line

- indent the quotation

- introduce the quotation by a statement ending in a colon

  > In her book, Kerry Bigelow says she found peace in the Himalayas:
  >
  > > I think India is still the best place in the world to find spiritual contentment. In Ananda my shattered nerves were restored to calm. I stayed in the palace of a maharaja, a believer in the Himalayan way to health and happiness. It is a huge health spa, smelling of incense, aromatherapy oils, and the scent of floral displays, and offering Ayurvedic or conventional treatments.

6. Provide text references in parentheses, if required, at the end of the quotation. This form of acknowledging research material is known as a *text citation,* or a *parenthetical reference.*

   > "I think India is still the best place in the world to find spiritual contentment" (Bigelow 42).

Note:

- For APA style, give the last name of the author and the date of publication at the end of the quotation: (Lipschutz 2002).

- For MLA style, give the last name of the author and the page number (no comma goes after the author's name) at the end of the quotation: (Lipschutz 125).

7. If you have already mentioned the full name of the author and/or the title of the work cited in your introductory remarks, all you have to note in parentheses is the page number where you found the quotation.

   > As Kerry Bigelow says, "I think India is still the best place in the world to find spiritual contentment" (42).

A Note about Plagiarism

What is plagiarism? It is the use of another person's *words* or *ideas* without giving that person credit. It is considered theft because it steals another person's intellectual property. To avoid being accused of plagiarism, always indicate where you found the research material you are using, and whether you are quoting the exact words or simply referring to the ideas.

How will you show where the words or ideas you are using came from?

Consult the style guide recommended by your professional field. In the social sciences and health sciences, you will probably follow the APA (American Psychological Association) style. In the humanities, subjects such as philosophy, history, and English, you will probably follow the MLA (Modern Language Association) style.

At this stage of your studies, a small college style sheet will be sufficient for documenting your research material correctly. The word used for giving proper credit for borrowed material is *documentation*. Documentation conventions (aka *style*) add clarity and order to a mass of data, so try to become familiar with the conventions for the use of research material. That means, watch your style.

Readers can find further information about the source of a quotation at the end of a research paper in the Works Cited or References page. Either name refers to the list of sources used in preparing the paper. That list can also be called a *bibliography*.

Today, when people sometimes do not consult books at all in their research, they tend not to use the term *bibliography* (from the Greek *biblion*, for book) as the heading for their list of references. But that doesn't mean to say that books are no longer used as sources. Try not to ignore the good old-fashioned **book** in your studies and research. The reviewing, editing, and research processes involved in publishing a book make print a respected and reliable source of information and ideas. Books are also portable, affordable, durable, and need no batteries, so they are here to stay.

Exercise 11.12

In small groups, introduce *five* of the following quotations with a signal phrase that would integrate the remark gracefully into an essay. Try ending with a parenthetical reference where possible. Be creative and vary your introductions.

Example

As Charles Wadsworth once observed, "By the time a man realizes his father was right, he has a son who thinks he's wrong." **(Wadsworth 49)**

1. "Of all the things I've lost, I miss my mind the most." Ozzy Osbourne.

2. "For these societies the land is alive, a dynamic force to be embraced and transformed by the human imagination."

   Vancouver-born explorer and writer Wade Davis in his essay, "A dead end for humanity." *The Globe and Mail* 28 December 2000: A15.

3. "To remove all the useless material baggage from a man's heritage is, at the same time, to free his mind from petty preoccupations, calculations and memories."

   Pierre Elliott Trudeau reveals his philosophy of self-denial and self-discipline in his first published essay, "Exhaustion and Fulfilment: The Ascetic in a Canoe."

4. "Happiness is good health and a bad memory." Ingrid Bergman. 1962.

5. "I want them to realize that hatred will confine you but love can set you free."

   Denzel Washington talks about the values he wants to pass on to his children in *First for Women* Volume 12 Issue 33 August 14, 2000.

6. "It must have been his little-boy-lost demeanour that attracted me to Dylan."

   Caitlin Thomas, p. 93 of *Double Drink Story: My Life with Dylan Thomas.* Viking 1997.

7. "Mr. Right's coming, but he's in Africa and he's walking." Oprah Winfrey when asked about finding a husband, September 1999.

8. "Time is scarce."

   Jan Pronk, the Dutch Minister of the Environment in a speech to delegates at the summit on global warming in The Hague, November 2000.

9. "Teachers need to watch for students using abusive language as a way of testing limits." Staff Handbook at Heathrow Collegiate Institute.

10. "If you listen to it you will notice that rap then was more of a truthful story."

Lolita Shanté Gooden in "Roxanne's Revenge Is the Sweetest Yet," an article by Phil Johnson in *Culture* p. 8, 27 August 2000.

A Word about the Web

If you decide to do electronic research, remember that more than 900 million Web sites exist. The Internet offers advantages of speed and up-to-the-minute information, but has many limitations: no peer review for assessment and control of data; link rot or increasing numbers of pointless hits; limited search methods; and case sensitivity.

Because there are hordes of semi-literate idiots without a life spewing mindless drivel into cyberspace, researchers need to be careful. They need to be critical about the source of information. They also need to be able to narrow their subjects and be as specific, precise, and clear as possible. Does that sound familiar?

Many of the same questions used for print searches apply to the Internet:

- Who wrote it?
- Where does the material come from? who sponsors the site? For example, is it from a cult or a university?
- When was it installed? Is the site current?
- Is the site well presented, free of errors, and well designed?
- Does the source indicate knowledge of other work on this subject?
- Is documentation supplied? From where? What date? Which writer?
- Can the facts be checked? Are sources given?

If you use the Internet for information, be sure to print out part of every source you consult. You never know what you might need, and you never know if you will be able to access the same material again in the same place. Online material is notoriously unstable.

Whether you crawl, navigate, browse, explore, seek, or surf, take a few cyber trips somewhere, and become comfortable with the research options available on the Internet. However, be cautious, be critical, and check for reliability before using material. For example, the Web site extension **.edu** may signify an educational institution, but does it mean that student papers from that institution are reliable? Think about the time and effort you put into some of your papers. No matter what the source, government (**.gov**), non-profit organizations (**.org**), commercial sites (**.com, .net**), be cautious. Always record the URL (uniform resource locator), or the Web site address, and the dates of posting, revision, and access. You will need the information for the Works Cited page of your paper.

Documenting Electronic Resources

Consult a style guide for more information on documenting electronic resources. Visit the MLA Web site at **www.mla.org** and the APA Web site at **www.apastyle.org**. At these sites, you can find electronic referencing style tips.

Online Article in a Journal (MLA style):

Author's last name, first name. "Title of Article." *Title of Journal*
    volume. issue (year) : number of pages or paragraphs. date of
    access <URL>

Example: Kersey, Bonita. "Laugh Lines" *Motherlore* 4.3 (2001) : 2
    pages. 21 Feb. 2002 <http://www.mumsonline.com:202>

Web Site (APA style):

Author's last name, first initial. (date of posting or revision). *Title
    of Page*. Retrieved date from World Wide Web, from URL

Example: Nadel, L. (2002). *Sixth Sense*. Retrieved April 1, 2002,
    from http://www.neuro-psych.org/mp.html

Exercise 11.13

Research using the Internet.

A. Choose one of the Web directories below for your research on a
    general subject related to your field of study.

B. Through this Web site, find a link to a more specialized site for
    your general subject. Note the name of this site. Browse this site
    and narrow down your initial topic. Be specific, precise, and clear.

C. Write down your SPC subject and decide what you want to learn
    about it.

D. Using keywords or synonyms, continue your search. Find two
    sources of factual information on your subject and note what
    they are. Note

   • author or sponsor of site

- date of installation or revision of site
- presentation of material—is it free from spelling and grammatical errors?
- two facts about your topic

Web Sites

1. Yahoo! at **ca.yahoo.com**

2. e.big.com at **www.ebig.com**

3. National Library of Canada at **www.nlc-bnc.ca**

4. Department of Justice Canada at **canada.justice.gc.ca**

5. Statistics Canada at **www.statcan.ca**

6. INFOMINE at **infomine.ucr.edu**

7. Humbul Humanities Hub at **users.ox.ac.uk/~humbul**

8. Environment Canada at **www.ec.gc.ca**

9. Best Environmental Directories at **www.ulb.ac.be/ceese/meta/cds.html**

10. HR Zone at **www.hrzone.com**

11. Altavista at **www.altavista.com**

12. Maple Square (Canada's Internet Directory) at **www.maplesquare.com**

Exercise 11.14

Encyclopedias give only a general view of a topic, but can be useful for introducing you to a topic. They often have useful facts too. (Remember the old marketing slogan: *The more **facts** you tell, the more you sell.*)

A. In pairs or groups of three, choose *two* of the topics listed below and find *two* encyclopedias that comment on these topics.

B. Write down *one* fact on both topics from each encyclopedia.

C. Note the *name* of the encyclopedia, *where* it was published, and *when* it was published. (For an encyclopedia, the dictionary, the Qur'an, the Bible, or a one-page article, you do not need to give a page reference.)

D. Prepare a topic sentence that introduces each topic.

E. Present the facts from the encyclopedias next, incorporating them gracefully into your presentation. In other words, introduce each one with a signal phrase, or a transitional expression, or both. Acknowledge the source in some way.

F. Conclude with a restatement of the topic sentence.

G. Present your material orally to the class.

Topics

diamonds	Marilyn Bell
diesel	penicillin
Ernest Rutherford	public relations
F. R. Scott	Réné Levesque
fibre optics	snails
Grand Marnier	the Avro Arrow
Hans Selye	the cardiovascular system
hydrogeology	Tom Longboat
Lucy Maud Montgomery	waste management

Exercise 11.15

Using at least two references to one or more sources, write a paragraph on *one* of the following topics. Narrow it down to a micro-subject, if you can.

Topics

a dream house	stealing cars
a source of stress	tainted meat
characteristics of baseball managers	teenage ethics
collectibles	the Euro Cup
home-schooling	trading in salt
seat belts	Vaseline

REVIEW AND REMEMBER

Part 3

A Strong Paragraph or Essay:

1. has a clear micro-subject

2. establishes one or more specific points about the subject in a topic sentence or thesis statement that states only what you will discuss in your paragraph or essay

3. uses a pre-writing plan of the evidence needed to prove, defend, develop, and explain the points established

4. keeps to the point, just the point, and nothing but the point established in the topic sentence to give each paragraph *unity*

5. gains strength from supporting evidence: statistics, anecdotes, facts, quotes, examples, statements from experts, case histories and personal stories, historical or scientific evidence, or comparisons and contrasts

6. is as long as it needs to be

7. keeps your ideas connected and flowing with transitional expressions, constant reminders, and attitudinal markers for *coherence*

8. follows an **I**-frame for structure, with a PREVIEW, VIEW, and REVIEW of the topic

9. documents correctly the source of any research material in order to add credibility

10. is clear and correct

Sample Student I-Frame Paragraphs

Below are some sample student paragraphs that use an **I**-frame approach. The student writers write convincingly on their topics. Note how the following paragraphs from first-year students

- establish a topic clearly

- support it with details

- reinforce the conclusion

The student writers use an I-frame approach to build convincing paragraphs that PREVIEW, VIEW, and REVIEW their topics.

The Escape Route of Alcohol

by Shawna

Some people choose to muzzle their emotions by consuming alcohol. Do they know that the sense of escape and well-being they experience for the moment can destroy them eventually? The adverse effects of alcohol cause permanent damage to the body and mind. Alcohol causes damage to the liver because it interrupts the filtering of blood and cellular waste. Since alcohol penetrates the bloodstream, it also causes damage to the brain cells. Dr. John Smith at the Heiho Clinic reports, "Thousands of brain cells are destroyed by one bottle of wine." He cautions that alcohol makes the heart work harder and a higher heart rate results in higher blood pressure leading to heart attacks and strokes. When alcohol consumption is taken beyond moderation, the adverse effects result in permanent damage to the heart, liver, and brain. In conclusion, people trying to escape their problems by turning to alcohol should think twice about its adverse physiological effects before turning to the bottle after a hard day at work.

Food for Thought

by Clare

Everyone deals with their emotions differently. One method of dealing with emotions is overeating. Some people will stuff cookies down their throats in order to suppress tears. Others will reach deep into the fridge searching desperately for a hidden treat behind the apples, simply because they have nothing better to do. It is unfortunate that all the best foods seem to have a ton of calories and fat and are also cheaper than the healthy foods at the grocery store, because it all adds up to one thing . . . obesity. Being overweight is one of the worst crimes in Canada because everyone blames you for it and no one will forgive you for it. If someone is anorexic or bulimic, oh dear, it's not their fault; society, their peers, or the advertising industry did it to them. Well, I don't see society or peers sticking a finger down a bulimic's throat, but people will rally to help the bulimic. An anorexic person will be put into hospital and covered under OHIP. A person who is obese, on the other hand, has no chance of getting help for free. When people are overweight they have low self-esteem, and society is quite willing to leave it low with accusing glances and rude comments. An obese person has less of a chance of getting a job than a person of normal weight. An obese person also has major health risks, such as diabetes and heart attacks. Chairs in theatres, or on buses and airplanes are too small for them. Being overweight is embarrassing every day. No wonder it is so hard to stop overeating. You eat because you are sad, embarrassed, and depressed. It's a Catch-22 because being overweight causes you to eat more. Then you cry because you are obese and nobody loves you, so you reach for the cookies again.

Washrooms in Poland

by Barbara

Canadian travellers who are planning to visit Poland probably will find some differences and difficulties in adapting to new circumstances, especially with washrooms. Since 1989 when Poland became a democratic country, these differences rapidly decreased, but in the "toilet area" there still exists a deep gap. Visitors must be prepared that in many cases they will spend a great deal of time looking for a public washroom when travelling on roads across the country. The same problem comes up in small restaurants or snack bars. All tourists can eat there, but they either have to forget about their dirty hands or just imagine a beautiful washroom with paper towels. Travellers in Poland should always carry in a pocket or purse a piece of toilet paper for their convenience. They should not be surprised that it is missing or limited in many washrooms. Also, they have to remember to pay for using the toilet. So be prepared and take a few rolls of toilet paper on your trip. Then you can enjoy the differences there more.

Maisie and William

by Kim

My 9-year-old daughter Maisie and my 7-year-old son William can be contrasted in terms of their interests. Maisie is an active girl who loves to participate in all programs at school, from track and field to swimming competitions, from folk dance to playing violin. She even joined Girl Guides after school. It is surprising that William is a boy because he always stays calm and quiet; he seldom plays rough games as some of his classmates do. When we encouraged him to join the swimming class 2 years ago, it was such a big job to get him into the pool. People used to say that boys should be rough and tough, and girls should be quiet and calm. If the saying is right, then my two kids probably have to change over in their stages of growing sometime in the future. Right now they are such contrasts.

This is the end of Part 3. You have focused on organizing your ideas for writing. You should now be more aware of how to organize your thoughts for clarity, how to use specific data to be convincing, and how to link your ideas for coherence. You know the importance of the PREVIEW, VIEW, and REVIEW of ideas. There is a lot more to communication than an I-frame, but knowing how to use an I-frame sure helps prop up the prose for most writing tasks. Good luck with future prose efforts.

Part 4

Celebrating the Sentence and other Grammatical Necessities

Part 4 focuses on how to avoid accidents in writing. While the previous parts looked at the essences of writing, these final chapters offer guidelines or rules for clear expression. They deal with the nitty-gritty. You need to be aware of how to keep your writing free from the nits and the grits that can disturb readers. That's what grammar errors are: nits and grit. They irritate readers.

You don't want to cause IRS (Irritable Reader Syndrome, in Canada), because IRS causes loss of interest, fatigue, failure to comprehend, confusion, and neural numbness. No writer wants to cause these symptoms. That's why you need to know how to eliminate errors in sentence structure, verb forms, pronoun reference, spelling, punctuation, and mechanics.

No book or teacher can turn you into a great writer. But books and teachers can help you plan and proofread, so you become a clear, correct, coherent writer. Isn't that what you will need for your writing on the job?

CHAPTER 12

Clear Sentences:

The Basics

This chapter looks at the basics of sentence structure: subjects, verbs, and subject-verb agreement.

By the end of this chapter, you will be able to

- identify the essential ingredients of a sentence

- understand the rules of subject-verb agreement

Read the following statements:

> The funnel cloud roaring over the fields.

> Roaring twisters!

> When the twisters roar again.

> If a tornado comes, I'll scream.

> Although twisters roar loudly . . .

> I hate twisters.

Which of the above statements makes sense? Why? What is needed to make a jumble of words into a sentence?

First, you need to talk about something: a subject. Second, you need to say something about that subject. Third, you have to make sense.

Three things are essential to form a sentence:

- a *subject*
- a *verb*
- a *complete thought*

It's easy enough to say what makes sense. A complete thought can stand on its own. But what are subjects and verbs?

Identifying subjects and verbs can be tricky, but if you can do so, you will avoid confusing your readers with these errors:

- subject-verb agreement errors
- sentence fragments
- run-on sentences
- dangling or misplaced modifiers
- faulty parallel structure
- pronoun reference problems

Try saying the above list of errors very fast. Phew. Who wouldn't want to know how to avoid them? In fact, occasionally even experienced writers may make some of these mistakes, but basic errors like those listed above confuse readers and create the wrong impression.

It is, you see, a matter of image. You wouldn't go for a job interview with bits of your breakfast staining your clothes or makeup smears on your face. What would the interviewer think?

Errors in writing create a similar reaction. Sloppy looks don't stop you from doing your job. You might be very good at it. Looking funny at a job interview does not mean you don't know what you are talking about. But will people listen to you when they are distracted by stains or smears?

Writing errors distract readers. Irritable readers may not be able to say exactly what is wrong with your writing, but they know it doesn't sound right, and they don't quite understand what you have written.

Writing errors make readers wonder if you know what you are doing.

You want to create a good impression and be clear. Study Part 4 to learn more about the basics of clear communication.

Clear communication begins with basic sentence structure: subjects, verbs, and complete thoughts.

Subjects

Every sentence has a *subject*. The subject is the focus of the sentence.

STEPS TO SUCCESS

Subjects

1. A subject answers the question: *Who* or *what* is the sentence about?

Heppner sings.	*Who* sings?	Subject: **Heppner**
Birds fly.	*What* fly?	Subject: **Birds**
Joseph wept.	*Who* wept?	Subject: **Joseph**

2. The sentences above are simple sentences, very simple sentences. The subject does not change, though, even if other words or qualifying phrases are added. A *phrase* is a group of words without a subject or a verb.

    Ben **Heppner**, *born in Canada*, often sings in New York.

    In autumn, most **birds** fly south.

    Upset at his son's fate, **Joseph** wept.

3. The subject of a sentence is *never* in a prepositional phrase. Prepositional phrases often begin with *of*.

    Either *of them* is coming tonight.

    One *of the thieves* was saved.

    In the middle of the island stands a **museum**.

Prepositional phrases usually show the *position* of something. They begin with little words called prepositions: *beside* the lake, *beneath* the trees, *up* your nose, *around* the corner, *in* your face, *of* the teacher. The noun following the preposition is never the subject. Note where the subject is in the following verse.

> On top of Old Smokey
> All covered with snow
> I lost my true lover
> Through courtin' too slow.

4. In sentences beginning with *there is* and *there are,* the subject follows.

    The English language is always changing. In the twentieth century students were taught to change the verb according to the subject in *there is, there are* expressions. Students were taught to say and write *There **are** many reasons for this change.*

    In the twenty-first century, many people say and write ***there is** many reasons for this change,* and no one cares. (The French have been using *il y a,* the singular form for years, whether the subject is singular or plural.) Many English language users are now using *there's* all the time now, as in ***there's** lots of changes all the time.* However, if your reader prefers twentieth-century style, and many readers do, be aware that *there is* may read strangely to some people.

5. Subjects follow the verb (the action or state of being) in most questions, or come between parts of verbs.

    > What *are* **you** *doing* tonight?
    >
    > Where *are* **you** *going*?
    >
    > What *are* **they** *looking* at?
    >
    > *Did* **he** really *say* that?
    >
    > *Will* **your mother** *pay* for your ticket?

6. A sentence may have more than one subject. These subjects are called compound subjects. Compound subjects are joined by *and* or *or.*

    > **Peter** *and* his **sister** have always agreed about that.
    >
    > **Jomo** *or* **Jenn** is giving the presentation.

7. A subject may be understood or implied. **You** are being addressed, but not expressed. (*You* is understood.)

    > Please stop whistling.
    >
    > Go home at once!

Exercise 12.1*

Note the subject that appears in each of the following sentences. Number 1 is already done for you.

1. Joe Dobson will try to do more housework in one day than a woman in two. **Subject:** *Joe Dobson*

2. Away went Joe to milk the cow.

3. His business was about to begin.

4. She tossed the pail and kicked his leg.

5. The blood ran down his shin.

6. Next to boil the pot he went.

7. He forgot to build the fire.

8. Away went Joe to wash the clothes.

9. The water scalded his hands.

10. He went to hang the clothes to dry.

11. It was a lovely day.

12. But, oh alas! A magpie came and stole his wig away.

Exercise 12.2

Who or what is each of the following sentences about? Write the subject that appears in each sentence. Note: Two sentences have two subjects.

1. Baseball players often know very little about baseball.

2. They may know all about the suicide squeeze, the hit-and-run play, even the infield rule, but they are usually ignorant of the rich history of the game.

3. Few, if any, can tell you about the legendary players of the past, and they probably do not know anything about the most famous moments of the game.

4. Sure, most ballplayers will have heard of Babe Ruth, and also Cy Young because of his award.

5. But will they be able to identify Honus Wagner or Al Simmons or Lefty Grove?

6. Most of the current ballplayers have never heard of Jackie Robinson, even.

7. Do ballplayers ever listen to old-timers talk about the game?

8. No, they are too busy talking to their agents.

Exercise 12.3

Write down each prepositional phrase and each subject found in these famous verses of Robert Service, from his poem *The Cremation of Sam McGee*. (Used by permission of the Estate of Robert Service.)

> There are strange things done in the midnight sun
> By the men who moil for gold;
> The Arctic trails have their secret tales
> That would make your blood run cold;
> The Northern Lights have seen queer sights,
> But the queerest they ever did see
> Was that night on the marge of Lake Lebarge
> I cremated Sam McGee.
>
> Now Sam McGee was from Tennessee
> where the cotton blooms and blows.
> Why he left his home in the South to roam 'round the Pole,
> God only knows.
> He was always cold, but the land of gold seemed to hold him
> like a spell;
> Though he'd often say in his homely way that
> "he'd sooner live in hell."

Verbs

A *verb* is the backbone of a sentence. It keeps a sentence straight up and clear. Every sentence has one.

STEPS TO SUCCESS

Verbs

1. A verb expresses action or helps make a statement.

    I **love** it.

    It **seems** small.

    You **wish.**

    They **looked** weird.

2. The most common verb in any language is the verb *to be*. (Shakespeare knew all about that. The most popular quotation from Shakespeare is Hamlet's *To be or not to be.*)

    When identifying the verb in a sentence, go straight to the parts of the verb *to be* and see how they are used. The verb *to be* never functions as anything other than as a verb. If you become familiar with the verb *to be* parts, you will be more confident about recognizing verbs.

    To be

was	has been	am	will be
were	have been	is	will have been
		are	had been

3. Some verbs are called *linking* or *helping* verbs. They help keep the action going, help make a statement, or link verb parts together.

    Linking Verbs

appear	has	shall
become	have	should
can	look	smell
could	may	sound
did	might	stay
do	must	taste
does	ought	will
grow	remain	would
had	seem	

4. Verbs are not always one word. Linking verbs count as part of the complete verb.

> Orlando **was sitting** in a corner. He **had been swimming** all night. He **could understand** the old woman's reaction to him. He knew he must look weird. He **was** happy, though, that he **had been able** to escape from bondage.

5. Words like *not, just, only, always, quite, never* may interrupt a verb sequence to modify the meaning. They do not count as verbs.

> This **is** *only* your brother **speaking.** I *just* **want** to make it clear that we **are** *not* **going** to leave until I **have been able** to hear my favourite song.

6. Verbs are limited. They are finite and focused, not floating out of control in infinity. They are grounded by three things:

    *   tense

    *   number

    *   person

In other words, verbs, like all of us, are controlled by time, people, and amount.

Tense

A verb changes according to its time zone.

> **Past**
> Yesterday you **seemed** so far away.
> She **has been** further away before.
> They **had thought** of going further.

> **Present**
> Today you **seem** closer.
> She **is** closer today.
> They **think** they **are** very close now.

> **Future**
> Tomorrow you **will seem** so far away.
> She **will be** further away.
> They **are going to be** miles away by tomorrow.

Number

One or more than one? A verb is either *singular* or *plural,* depending on whether you are concerned with one single entity or more.

Singular	Plural
I **think.**	We **think.**
It **sneezes.**	They **sneeze.**
The baby **cried.**	The babies **cried.**

Note: Names of things (nouns) end in *-s* to form the plural (e.g., one toy; two toys). But verbs do the opposite (e.g., one girl dance**s**; many girls dance). Add *-s* to the end of a *singular* verb, present tense. Do not add *-s* to the end of a *plural* verb.

Person

A verb changes according to the type of pronoun that controls it. A pronoun is a word that stands in for a specific noun. A pronoun comes in first person (*I, we*), second person (*you*), and third person (*he, she, it, they*). For more information on pronouns, see Pronoun References in Chapter 14.

Note: The person, place, or thing controlling the verb is the *subject* of the verb. The subject determines the form of the verb used (*she* dance*s*; *they* dance), so it is important to know what subject controls a verb. Subjects and verbs must match in number and person.

Verbs change according to the person and number, as well as tense.

	Singular	Plural
First Person:	I **love** you.	We **love** you.
Second Person:	You **love** me.	You **love** me.
Third Person:	He, she, it **loves** everyone.	They **love** everyone.
First Person:	I **was** happy.	We **were** happy.
Second Person:	You **were** happy.	You **were** happy.
Third Person:	He, she, it **is** happy.	They **are** happy.

Note: Which form of a verb has an *-s* added to it? Third-person singular only.

To find a verb, try the verb test. Ask yourself, Is this word changed by tense, person, number? For example: Can it be *yesterday?* Can it be *I* or *they?* Can it be *one* or *more than one?*

Which one is clearly the verb?

scream versus ice cream

I scream? Yesterday they screamed?

I ice cream? Yesterday they ice creamed?

7. Don't be fooled by **infinitives**. They are the basis for all verbs; that is, the stem, or seed, from which all verbs grow, the verbal embryo. But infinitives do not count as verbs. They are verbal phrases. They are, indeed, infinite, not limited by person, tense, or number. Infinitives always stay the same no matter who, no matter when, no matter how many. Look for the tell-tale *to*.

   Infinitives

to be	to die	to sleep
to dream	to sing	to sniff
to say	to love	to leave
to live	to lose	to dance
to think	to play	to do

8. Watch for participles. These words play many *parts* (get it?). Sometimes they play the *part* of a noun or an adjective. Sometimes they are *part* of a verb. No wonder they are called *participles*. They count as verbs only when accompanied by a linking (helping) verb. They can also be called *verbals* or *modifiers*. Regular participles end in *-ing* or *-ed*.

   Acting as Nouns:

   Voula loves **dancing** and chocolate.

   Controlling it will be difficult tonight.

   Smashing Pumpkins is a great group.

   Acting as Adjectives:

   Her **dancing** eyes gave her away.

   His **controlling** behaviour is destructive.

   He is wearing a **smashing** jacket.

   Acting as Part of the Verb:

   Voula **was dancing** all night.

   She could **have danced** all night.

   He **has** always **controlled** his feelings.

   Dave **is smashing** pumpkins again.

   That **has torn** it.

9. In *either . . . or, neither . . . nor, both . . . and* constructions, choose the verb form according to the noun closer to the verb.

> *Either* the astronauts *or* the robot **has taken** control.
>
> *Neither* the robot *nor* the astronauts **have taken** control.

10. **Regular verbs** are, as the name implies, the regular forms of a verb.

Past	Present	Future
I loved.	I love.	I will love.
I have loved.	I am loving.	
I was loving.	I do love.	
Have I loved?	Do I love?	

When children say things like, "I bringed the teacher an apple," or "I never throwed it," they are using the logical regular forms of verbs, but not all verbs are regular.

Parents and caregivers will kindly say to children, "You *brought* the teacher an apple?" or "You never *threw* it?" stressing the correct form. Children instinctively record the correct form to be used next time. If you have some faulty verb habits, you will need to record correct forms too.

Exercise 12.4*

Decide which of the following words can function as verbs. Note: Many words can act as both nouns and verbs. The way the word is used in a sentence determines its grammatical label.

Try the tense, number, person test. Try asking:

- Can the word change tense? Does it change for yesterday, today, tomorrow?

- Can the word change based on number? (singular, plural)

- Can the word take a person, a pronoun? (*I, we, you, he, she, it, they*)

address	fear	pale
announce	fight	peel
announcement	finally	raspberry
catch	flash	sentence
clever	fuse	strip

concern	garden	talk
convert	inspiration	together
dance	music	Tuesday
extract	opinion	waste

Exercise 12.5

Choose the complete verb or verbs in each of the following statements. Remember, participles on their own are not complete verbs.

1. There was a little fellow once, and Harry was his name.

2. Many a naughty trick had he—I tell it to his shame.

3. One most cruel trick of his, was that of catching fish.

4. Many a little fish he caught, and pleased was he to look, to see them writhe in agony, and struggle on the hook.

5. At last when having caught enough, he hastened home.

6. He intended to put all the little fish on a shelf there.

7. But as he jumped to reach a dish, to put his fish within—

8. A large meat-hook that hung close by, did catch him on the chin.

9. Poor Harry kicked and called aloud, and screamed and cried and roared.

10. While from his wound the crimson blood in dreadful torrents poured.

Exercise 12.6*

Choose the correct verb form in parentheses in the following paragraph.

Cancer Care Ontario *(grows, is growing)* _____ fast to meet the expanding need for new cancer services. The number of people living with cancer *(continues, continued, continue)* _____ to *(growed, grow, growing)* _____. New centres are *(planning, planned, plan)* _____, and others *(are expanding, have expand, expanding)* _____ to serve people better in their regions. Patients *(is assessed, assess, are assessed, are assess)* _____ and *(treat, treated, will have been treated)* _____ by multidisciplinary teams. Cancer Care Ontario *(made up of, are made up of, is made up of, makes up)* _____ many talented people. These people *(has, have, will have had, have been)* _____ expertise in cancer prevention and early detection. They *(offers, offered, offer)* _____ many supportive care services.

Exercise 12.7

Make a list of each verb and its subject from the following story.

After losing the game, the boys were on their way home. Each of them was boasting of better results and great achievements. Adidas started with his story.

"A month ago, I went on a 200-k run at Climax. There were 20 of us and I won by 6 minutes. I got a gold medal and a set of Waterford crystal glasses. My mother thinks they are terrific and she is very proud of me."

"That's nothing," Rebok said. "Why, when I shot that goal in North Battleford, the mayor presented me with two gold medals and two sets of crystal glasses."

"I don't think much of that," sniffed Nike. "In Brandon one time, in one day, I got five gold medals, three sets of crystal glasses, and two Rolex watches."

"Yes," said Adidas, "and the judge called it breaking and entering."

Exercise 12.8*

Decide which of the following sentences have incorrect verbs. Correct any errors.

1. After Vijay went to the School of High Performance Driving in Arizona, he begun to drive more carefully.

2. While he was there, he drove on acres of sunburned desert.

3. The School of High Performance Driving is having a fleet of 120 Mustangs and 30 Formula-One-style Fords.

4. Vijay had wrote to them to find out when he could come.

5. He was booked into the 3-day Mustang class.

6. He had never took any advice from his father about driving.

7. After a heavy dose of classroom theory, he choosed a bright yellow latest model.

8. All the students pushed their vehicles to the max on the racetrack.

9. Vijay could have drove all day out there around the track.

10. Tanya wished she could have went with him, he had such fun.

Exercise 12.9*

Choose the correct verb from the list given below.

My friend, Radhu, (1) _____ and no longer (2) _____ next door. The new people who (3) _____ in have had no contact with us yet. Today, across the fence, I (4) _____ a young woman, the daughter, probably. She (5) _____ very pretty. She (6) _____ morning tea at the late hour of 10. This young woman (7) _____ a lot. Her mother and father also (8) _____ frequently. They always (9) _____ happy. I wonder what sorts of things they (10) _____ about and why they (11) _____. Their lives (12) _____ obviously (13) _____ full of fun, because I (14) _____ them laughing all day long. It (15) _____ great to laugh so much.

Verbs

1. have moved, has been transferred, will leave, have gone

2. live, was living, has been living, lives

3. has moved, have moved, are moving, will move

4. has seen, will have seen, saw, seen, have been seeing

5. look, are, think, seem, is looking, is, can be, was

6. was drinking, drinks, is drinking, has drunk, drank

7. has laughed, are laughing, is laughing, will laugh, laughs,
   has been laughing

8. laughs, was laughing, have been laughing, laugh, will laugh

9. are looking, is looking, have been looking, looked, look, will look

10. is talking, talks, have been talking, talked, talk, was talking

11. have never laughed, are not laughing, have often laughed, are always
    laughing, never will laugh

12. is, must have been, could of been, must, should have, has

13 been, be, being, known, laugh

14. has heard, will have heard, used to, hears, hear

15. is not, should be, cannot be, does, must be, is being

Exercise 12.10*

Add the *-ed* ending or the correct verb form where necessary in the following sentences.

1. Lennox was not suppose to become a boxer. His mother want him to be a schoolteacher. She had decide that he had brains, but his father decide that his son had a great left jab.

2. Lennox was not interest in school work anyway. He prefer to go down to the gym where he use to watch his big neighbour practising his punching range. The man who open the gym took an interest in Lennox and he arrange for him to take boxing lessons.

3. When Lennox live at home, his mother straighten out her confuse son, and made sure he got plenty of good food and sleep. She refuse to let him spend hours at the gym, but tell him he could nurture his talent doing his homework.

4. Lennox has always be a great physical specimen who never change his mind about boxing being his life. He could have beat anyone who got in his way, but he was as gentle as a lamb outside the ring.

5. Lennox said he never suffer from nerves before a fight, but he was always glad when a fight was over. In the past he mostly walk away uninjure and a winner. In interviews after a fight he has never make excuses.

6. He says he is in boxing for the long haul and he never get depress or start thinking of retirement. The world has not see him at his peak yet.

7. While other boxers often show aggression, Lennox has always show willpower and courage. He is well know for punching hard.

8. Strip down and ready for battle, he is huge. He is much bigger than Mike Tyson. In many fights he dwarf his opponent.

9. After his divorce he got marry again. His new wife is call Latifah. She has warn Lennox that he must cut back on caffeine. She was amaze to learn that he drinks nearly 10 cups of coffee a day.

10. Lennox is a champ. He has develop enormous skill and boxing smarts. He has try to give back to the boxing community and has donate large sums of money to young boxers. He has never turn down an honour.

Exercise 12.11*

Choose the correct form of the verb in parentheses in the following story from East Africa.

Think carefully about your choice of tense. The story begins in the past. Follow the logical tense sequence. Number 1 is already done for you.

1. Sunguru, the hare, *(be)* <u>was</u> out in his garden all morning.

2. When he *(come)* _____ back to his house, he *(see)* _____ some strange-looking tracks in the dust.

3. It looked as if some huge animal had *(go)* _____ inside.

4. Sunguru had never *(see)* _____ such tracks before. He was quite convinced that some monster *(be)* _____ in his house.

5. He *(call)* _____out in a shaky voice, "Hodi, who is inside my house?"

6. A big voice *(reply)* _____,"I am the warrior son of the long one.

7. I can *(crush)* _____ the mighty rhinoceros to earth and the elephant *(tremble)* _____ at my voice. Beware!"

8. Sunguru was frightened. He *(shudder)* _____ at the thought of any creature who could make such tracks, could crush a rhinoceros, and could make an elephant tremble.

9. He *(decide)* _____ to get help from some of his friends.

10. He *(go)* _____ off into the bush and there he *(meet)* _____ the jackal, Mbweha.

11. "Oh clever Mbweha," he cried. "Please *(help)* _____ me. Some strange, strong animal is in my house and *(refuse)* _____ to come out."

12. But after talking to the long one, Mbweha *(be)* _____ as frightened as his friend.

13. "He *(sound)* _____ very ferocious, Sunguru. I think we better go away and leave him."

14. So the hare and the jackal *(trot)* _____ into the bush.

15. There, they *(ask)* _____ Chui, the leopard, to help them.

16. After talking to the long one, the jackal and the leopard *(run)* _____ into the bush leaving the disappointed hare looking sadly at his house.

17. Tembo, the elephant, said he had never *(hear)* _____ of a creature who could crush the mighty rhinoceros and make an elephant tremble. He told Sunguru to find another house.

18. When Sunguru was *(sob)* _____ in the bush, Chura, the frog, *(come)* _____ to his rescue.

19. He *(go)* _____ with Sunguru to his house and called to the intruder, "I am a leaper. If you don't leave the house of my friend, I will leap upon you."

20. When Nyodu, the caterpillar, *(crawl)* _____ out of the house, Sunguru could not believe his eyes. Chura, the frog, laughed and said, "I have *(learn)* _____ never to believe a thief. If you remember that, you *(save)* _____ yourself a lot of trouble."

Exercise 12.12*

Correct any errors in verb forms in the following paragraph.

Suhail join the Ukelele Freedom Front when he was in high school. He has always remember hearing a speaker from Hawaii talked about his prize ukelele collection. The man from Hawaii tell about how nobody give the instrument proper respect, and how important it is to end six-string domination. "There was a huge ukelele revival going on right now," Suhail say. He try to convince everyone to learned how to play ukeleles, but not too many of his classmates in college is convince that he have a point.

Exercise 12.13

Correct any errors in verb forms in the following paragraph.

When Jodi is a little girl at summer camp, her friends dare her to jump off a bridge, into the lake. Look down at the water terrifyingly far below, she learns something about herself. "When someone say I can't do something, I immediately wants to do it." She jump off the bridge, breaked both her legs, and suffer internal injuries. However, she made a good recovery, and, older and wiser, she now take part in Eco Challenges. One year she goes to

Morocco where she endure hypothermia, dehydration, and sleep deprivation. With three male teammates, she spent 7 days sea-kayaking through violent surf, descend sheer rock faces, and come through 500 km of mountain on foot. The next year she and her teammates was head for Patagonia. Jodi say, "For me, things has to be really hard."

Subject-Verb Agreement

Subjects and verbs must agree in number, always. Verbs must also agree in tense. What does that mean?

It means you *do not* write

The pictures here is wonderful.

The car are very expensive.

One are silly.

He went out and buys poison for the rats.

You would not write those statements anyway, would you? But what if something comes between the subject and the verb? Aha. It is important to know about subjects and verbs, so they always agree.

What will you write now?

The pictures at the Exhibition in the palace at St. Petersburg _____ wonderful.

The car, with the roll-bar cage, gas-tank protection, and tuned suspension _____ very expensive.

One of her reasons for not liking him at all _____ silly.

He went out and, after thinking about it, _____ poison for the rats.

STEPS TO SUCCESS

Subject-Verb Agreement

1. A verb agrees in number with its subject.

it **is**	NOT	it **are**
they **are**	NOT	they **is**

Singular	**Plural**
The child **is** playing.	The children **are** playing.
Only one **is** left.	Hundreds **are** left.
No one **likes** that player.	Many **like** his style.
The Trojan woman **is** tall.	The Trojan women **are** tall.

2. Compound (more than one) subjects joined by *and* take a plural verb. (One thing is singular; more than one is plural.)

   Noisemakers *and* ears **make** it easier for some insects to find mates.

   Nadia *and* Billy Bob **are** going to the concert together.

3. A sentence may have more than one verb.

   The wasp **found** the spider, **paralyzed** it, and **hauled** it back to its nest.

4. A prepositional phrase, or an expression like *as well as, together with, in addition to, including,* does not affect the subject. The verb agrees with the subject only.

   That **book,** *as well as the videos and the tapes,* **does not belong** to Luke.

   Lucy, *together with Dorothy and Colleen,* **likes** Renaissance drama.

5. *Each, every, either, neither, nobody, no one, anybody, anyone, everybody, somebody, someone* are singular and take a singular verb.

   Each of us **was expected** to bring her flowers. (each one)

   Everybody **was invited** to the party. (every single body)

   Someone **is knocking** at my wee small door. (one person)

6. *Many, few, both, several* are plural.

   Many **are cold.**

   Few **are frozen.**

> *Both* **are tired** of snow.
>
> *Several* **have moved** south.

7. *Some, any, all, most, half* may be either singular or plural. The context makes it clear whether to use singular or plural.

> *Some* of my friends **like** symphony concerts.
>
> *Some* of the program **sounds** interesting.
>
> **Have** *any* of them ever been to a rock concert?
>
> **Has** *any* of it been eaten?
>
> *All* of her CDs **were** stolen.
>
> *All* of her furniture **was** broken.

8. Collective nouns may be singular or plural, depending on whether you are thinking of the collection as distinct individuals or as one unit. Collective nouns name groups. Some collective nouns are *audience, army, crowd, committee, club, class, faculty, group, team.*

> The *committee* **was** surprised by the response. (one unit)
>
> The *committee* **were** not in agreement. (separate individuals)
>
> That *group* **is** always on time. (one unit)
>
> That *group* **arrive** at different times. (You might add "members of that", if you prefer.)

9. Words showing amounts of time, money, measurement, weight, volume, fractions are singular.

> Ten minutes **is** too long to wait.
>
> Ten dollars **is** too much to ask.
>
> Ten km **is** too far to go.
>
> Ten kg **is** too heavy to lift.
>
> Ten-twentieths **is** one half.

10. The title of a book, even if it seems plural, takes a singular verb.

> *The Best Short Stories of the Modern Age* **was** first recommended to me by Carol Baxter.

11. *Mumps, measles, mathematics, news* are considered singular. *Scissors, trousers, tidings* are considered plural. *Politics, economics, statistics, gymnastics, athletics* are singular when considered as one unit; they are plural when they are opinions, activities, qualities.

> The *scissors* **are** always in that drawer.
>
> *Politics* **is** often boring.
>
> The *politics* at that college **are** amazing.
>
> *Economics* with Professor Cumming **is** fascinating.

12. The verb agrees with the antecedent of the relative pronouns like *who, which, that.* (An *antecedent* is the noun the pronoun stands for.)

She is one of those *people* **who are** never satisfied.

Exercise 12.14

What is the subject and what is the verb in the following sentences? Correct any verb that does not agree with its subject.

1. Apparently a migrant mosquito from Asia are now spreading through North America.

2. This imported insect bites aggressively.

3. In the Eastern hemisphere, this mosquito transmit debilitating and sometimes fatal diseases.

4. It might serve as a carrier for dengue fever and other infectious diseases.

5. So far, nearly every effort to eradicate these resilient intruders have failed.

6. Workers has been burying used-tire piles and eliminating standing water areas.

7. No obvious results have been noticed, except that no deaths has been recorded as a result of this Asian mosquito.

8. Scientists are trying to keep track of the mosquito's progress.

9. The need for vaccines are keeping many highly trained minds busy.

10. The health of millions of babies and children is on their minds.

Exercise 12.15*

Choose the correct verb in parentheses in the following sentences.

1. Politics (*is, are*) _____ always active in the forest.

2. When there (*is, are*) _____ no water to be found anywhere, a committee (*is, are*) _____ formed to decide what to do.

3. The lion, the bear, the wolf, the monkey, the fox, and even the rabbit (*is, are*) _____ at the meeting in the forest.

4. "Today," said the lion, "all of us (*is, are*) _____ going to think of a plan."

5. The committee (*has, have*) _____ many different ideas about what to do.

6. Eventually the animals (*decides, decide*) _____ to dig a well, and everybody (*is, are*) _____ going to help.

7. Everybody, except the rabbit, (*thinks, think*) _____ the well is a great idea.

8. Neither the fox nor the bear (*is, are*) _____ pleased with the rabbit.

9. "Very well, Mr. Rabbit," say the animals, "each of us (*is, are*) _____ going to have a drink from the well, but you cannot have one drop of water."

10. The audience of listening animals (*nods, nod*) _____ in agreement.

11. In the middle of them all, (*laugh, laughs*) _____ the rabbit.

12. "That news (*is, are*) _____ not frightening to me," says the rabbit, smart as ever.

13. "You go ahead and dig your well. I'm not afraid. You will find that many ways to get a drink (*is, are*) _____ available to me."

14. Sure enough, what the animals find at the well the next day (*is, are*) _____ the rabbit's footprints.

Exercise 12.16*

Select the correct verb.

1. Neither the store nor the mills in that part of Cape Breton (*was, were*) _____ owned by John Munro at the time.

2. Owning the store and the mills (*was, were*) _____ what Giant McAskill did.

3. One of the best-known pioneers in St. Ann's (*was, were*) _____ the Nova Scotian Giant.

4. There (*was, were*) _____ nothing freakish and strange about Giant McAskill except his height and his strength.

5. A looming 7 feet 9 inches (*was, were*) _____ his height in the days before metric.

6. Exactly 425 lbs (*was, were*) _____ his weight then.

7. Unlike the brains of most giants, his (*was, were*) _____ a good brain.

8. Everyone in Cape Breton at that time (*was, were*) _____ aware of his good humour.

9. This man, together with many of his compatriots, (*was, were*) _____ very kind-hearted too.

10. Each member of the community at St. Ann's (*was, were*) _____ also impressed with the business sense of Giant McAskill.

Exercise 12.17*

Decide which of the following sentences are correct. Make the corrections needed where there is an error.

1. One February day some years ago, a team of NASA scientists observing the Earth's northern hemisphere discover something shocking.

2. The ozone layer—nature's security blanket protecting the planet from harmful ultraviolet radiation—is showing signs of depletion.

3. This finding of signs of trouble in the atmosphere send the scientific community into a buzz.

4.   A stratosphere without its protective layers of ozone result in the sun's UV rays causing terrible damage on earth.

5.   Life as we know it, scientists tell us, could change radically.

6.   People foolish enough to go outside without protection from the sun in the daytime is going to suffer terribly.

7.   Already we know that various forms of skin cancer, as well as cataracts, is caused by the sun.

8.   Immune systems will weaken, so individuals going without sun protection is more susceptible to infection.

9.   The photosynthesis process, essential for crop yields, are affected so drastically that reduced crop yields will result.

10. The amount of phytoplankton, the mainstay of the ocean's food chain, are diminished.

Exercise 12.18*

Add the expression given in parentheses at the place indicated by the asterisk (*) in each sentence. Then correct the form of the verb in italics, if necessary. This exercise will show how comfortable you are with subject-verb agreement.

Example

A medal * *was* awarded to the most improved student in English. (and a cheque)

Revised: A medal ***and a cheque were*** awarded to the most improved student in English.

1.   Maxine Hong Kingston * *has* eaten raccoons, skunks, hawks, garden snails, and snakes. (together with her family)

2.   Her mother * *tells* stories about what the emperors in China used to eat. (as well as her mother's sister)

3.   * those plants and other strange herbs *are* still important for flavour in cooking. (Every one of)

4.   * stories about emperors' banquets *were* sure to give her nightmares. (Some of the)

5.   * those women in her house *cook* fabulous meals for visitors. (Either of)

6. A shortage of food * *was* never a problem in their house. (and a fear of starvation)

7. A warm, friendly atmosphere * *does* not cost money. (or a welcoming smile)

8. The price of food * *keeps* going up these days. (and wine)

9. Many of those customs * *seem* strange to people of other cultures. (of our childhood)

10. * different cultural customs *are* always interesting to observe. (All kinds of)

Exercise 12.19*

Choose the correct present tense form of the verb in parentheses in the following passage.

Example

See how the story begins—Atalanta *(to be)* <u>*is*</u> determined never to marry. Only the man who *(to run)* <u>*runs*</u> faster . . .

The great maiden hunter, Atalanta, *(to be)* _____ determined never to marry. Only the man who *(to run)* _____ faster than she *(to do)* _____ will be her husband. If she runs faster than a suitor, he *(to lose)* _____ his life. Each of the princes who *(to dare)* _____ to try for her hand *(to leave)* _____ his head to decorate the finishing post.

Her cousin, Melanion, *(to fall)* _____ in love with her. Knowing that he could not run faster than Atalanta, he *(to pray)* _____ to the immortal queen of love, Aphrodite. The goddess, like many Greek goddesses, *(to be)* _____ angry that a beautiful young woman *(to refuse)* _____ to marry. Aphrodite, eager to encourage love and marriage, *(to decide)* _____ to help the young man. Neither Atalanta nor her other suitors *(to expect)* _____ Melanion to beat Atalanta. None of the others suitors ever *(to pray)* _____ to Aphrodite.

The race *(to begin)* _____. Atalanta, confident after all the other races, *(to know)* _____ she will win. But the golden apples given to Melanion by the goddess *(to tempt)* _____ Atalanta. Speed and temptation *(to do)* _____ not mix. Atalanta *(to stop)* _____ to pick up the golden apples dropped by Melanion. At the sight of the beauty of the golden apples, Atalanta *(to forget)* _____ everything else. Of course, Melanion *(to reach)* _____ the winning post a moment before Atalanta, so he *(to win)* _____ her for his wife. In a little while they, as king and queen of Tegea *(to live)* _____ happily ever after, so the story *(to go)* _____.

Picking up golden apples *(to seem)* _____ to happen quite a lot in stories from ancient Greece. These apples, found in many a story, often *(to cause)* _____ a hero a lot of grief. No record from that time *(to tell)* _____ how Melanion really felt after he married Atalanta.

Exercise 12.20*

Eliminate any verb errors in the following paragraph.

Almost nine out of ten Canadians lives in the southern part of Canada. To the north lie a huge wilderness. Farley Mowat says that for most Canadians, the North is "a weird and terrible land, where nothing is as it may seem." He say most Canadians shuns the North. In fact, the men who faces the reality and explored the High North in the first place was mostly British, French, Scandinavian, German, American, and Portuguese. Today nature lovers, looking for adventure, as well as polar bears and the region's other wildlife, goes to the north and explores the mountain ranges, glaciers, and lakes. Neither the winter blizzards nor the worst weather the North produces are as bad as people believe. Tourists from Europe and Asia arriving in this ancient land loves to see the wildlife. Everyone always love to discover the birds, the flowering plants of the tundra, as well as the whales, seals, walruses, and polar bears. It is time more people in the southern part of Canada, in "the banana belt," learns to look at the beauty and wildlife found in the North.

Exercise 12.21

Correct all verb errors in the following paragraph.

Each of us have not usually chose our name, but someday we could got the chance to chose the name for our child. Naming children are very stressful, my sister tell me, after she have her first child, a boy. When the time come, she and her partner reads name books, and they looks all over the world it seem, to find a name that would fit into all kinds of societies. They wants a name that will fit their kid, whether he decide to be an aerospace engineer or join a wrestling team. They was not interested in fashionable names, because my sister got tired of being one of about five Lisa's in all her classes at school. They decides against a New Age name like River or Peace. They finally names their son after her partner's father. My nephew is now call Edgar Alexander.

CHAPTER 13

More about Sentence Structure

This chapter examines sentence structure in more depth, with a look at how to avoid sentence fragments and run-on sentences.

By the end of this chapter, you will be able to

- identify phrases

- identify independent and dependent clauses

- identify and correct sentence fragments

- identify and correct run-on sentences

You can now recognize subjects and verbs. You know how to make subjects and verbs agree. But what about the other sentence errors listed in Chapter 12? This chapter will look at sentence fragments and run-on sentences.

Sentence Fragments

There is more to a sentence than a subject, a verb, and a complete thought. Most sentences pack a lot more information into them than just the three essential ingredients. Most sentences go beyond *The cat sat on the mat* and *See Spot run.*

Sometimes when writing becomes more complicated, writers forget the complete thought. Then they end up with a *sentence fragment.* Sometimes writers forget to stop at the end of their complete thought. Then they end up with a *run-on sentence.* Both are to be avoided in writing at college and at work.

To understand how to avoid such grammatical irritations, it helps to know how to identify phrases and clauses. You know about phrases.

A phrase is a group of words without a subject and a verb.

There are prepositional phrases *(up your nose, around the corner, in your face)* and verbal phrases *(to die, to sleep, to dream).* Phrases are no problem, but what are clauses?

A clause is a group of words with a subject and a verb.

Sounds like a sentence, doesn't it? But what if there's no complete thought?

There are two main types of clauses: independent and dependent.

An *independent clause* expresses a complete thought and can stand on its own. If no more information is attached, the group of words with a verb is known as a sentence. If the group of words is attached to others, it is considered an independent clause.

What is really important is: Does this group of words with a subject and a verb make sense? If it does, no worries. It is independent.

A *dependent clause* expresses an incomplete thought and cannot stand on its own. Some people call this kind of clause *subordinate.* It is under (sub) the influence of the main (independent) clause.

Some professional writers use sentence fragments for effect in their writing. However, they are established writers. It is sensible to wait until you have had a few books published before you use fragments freely.

You don't want to upset your readers. One reader, looking at the paragraph on rap in Exercise 13.6, became very irritated (Irritable Reader

Syndrome, or IRS). "I can't be bothered with stuff written like that," he said. "It makes me crazy. Forget it."

Try not to make your readers crazy. Learn how to avoid fragments.

STEPS TO SUCCESS

Clauses

1. A clause is a group of words containing a subject and a verb.

    Social bees live together.

    Bees which live on their own . . .

    They are called olivary bees.

2. A clause that makes sense on its own is a sentence. When it is accompanied by more clauses, it is called an *independent clause,* or main clause.

    Bees are a flower's best friend. (sentence)

    When bees live together in groups (dependent clause), they are called social bees. (independent clause)

3. A clause that cannot stand alone is a *dependent clause,* or subordinate clause. It depends on the independent clause to express a complete thought.

    Because bumblebees live in large groups (dependent clause), they are social bees. (independent clause)

4. A dependent clause begins with a subordinating conjunction to join it to the rest of the sentence, or a relative pronoun to attach it to a noun.

Relative Pronouns	Subordinating Conjunctions	
who	after	although
whose	as	as if
whom	because	before
which	in order that	if
that	as long as	since
	though	until
	wherever	whenever
	while	so that

STEPS TO SUCCESS

Avoiding Sentence Fragments

1. A sentence fragment is not a complete thought. Sentence fragments are often dependent clauses or phrases involving a participle (*-ing*) or an infinitive, or explanatory expressions beginning with *especially* or *such as*.

    Sentence Fragment: Because it started to snow heavily.

    Sentence Fragment: Running to his English class.

    Sentence Fragment: To learn ballet.

    Sentence Fragment: Especially in Schumacher.

2. Add an independent clause to a sentence fragment and it expresses a complete thought.

    We left early because it started to snow heavily.

    Running to his English class, Leroy smiled in happy anticipation.

    Leroy suddenly decided to learn ballet.

    They breed them tough in the North, especially in Schumacher.

3. When checking sentence structure in your writing, get into the habit of asking yourself the three sentence-searching questions:

    *   Does it have a subject?

    *   Does it have a verb?

    *   Does it have a complete thought?

    If the answer to all three is *yes*, then you have a sentence, and it will make sense. When checking your writing for complete sentences, it is a good idea to work from back to front. Watch for clauses beginning with subordinating conjunctions or relative pronouns. They cannot be left alone.

Also, to avoid sentence fragments, put a comma before *especially* and *such as*.

Exercise 13.1*

Decide whether each of the following clauses is dependent or independent.

1. Reggae music is played in Toronto, Te Aroha, Tokyo, and Timbukto.

2. Because Jamaica is the source of the men and women.

3. Who make reggae music.

4. This is the music of messiahs and messengers.

5. It digs into Jamaica's rich heritage.

6. Where nobody has boldly gone before.

7. From the guzzomen and obeahmen to today's reggae, there is a direct line.

8. How Revival and Rastafari have shaped the sound.

9. Reggae music reflects local black pride.

10. Even under the brutal plantation system in the early years of European domination in Jamaica.

Exercise 13.2*

Which essential ingredient is missing here? Decide whether the subject or the verb is missing in the following sentences.

1. Went into the North Pacific to document the death toll of driftnets.

2. The fine mesh nylon of driftnets, thousands of marine mammals, birds, and fish each year.

3. The United Nations to ban driftnets by 1992.

4. Disrupts the complex North Pacific ecosystem.

5. Some birds like the laysan albatross, only on a few small islands.

6. Were found dead in these floating cemeteries for seabirds.

7. People coming from such countries as Denmark, New Zealand, Japan, and Canada as crew.

8. A united desire to save our planet.

Exercise 13.3*

Decide which of the following sentences are sentence fragments.

1. Long-stem roses are the way to her heart.

2. A vamp naked beneath a transparent lace dress.

3. She may be dressing like the traditional bimbo, but this feminist is in charge.

4. Not the traditional standards of feminism at all.

5. Though her intellectual grasp of feminism is slippery.

6. No one can discount the impact of her image.

7. Now that she has children, she has changed.

8. Does not want little Lourdes and Rocco to be brats.

9. She refuses to spoil her children.

10. Hard to be the child of a celebrity.

Exercise 13.4*

Correct all sentence fragments.

1. The beach is a great place for a holiday.

2. Some famous beaches, however, on the Atlantic coast, and along the Mediterranean.

3. They are more famous for raw sewage, tar balls, and used syringes than golden sands.

4. When dead and dying dolphins appeared.

5. Their skin falling off, lesions all over their bodies, as if they had been dipped in acid.

6. Hundreds of dolphins from New Jersey to Florida.

7. Dead dolphins and ones floundering in a mysterious brown slime have been reported everywhere.

8. Scientists concerned about dolphin conservation.

9. Dolphins are in trouble in many parts of the world.

10. Creamy-white beluga whales in the St. Lawrence River riddled with toxic substances.

Exercise 13.5

The following sentence fragments are from student essays. Decide what is missing or what caused the fragments, and how you would correct them.

1. To have more confidence and to really feel good about what I am trying to get across to the group.

2. My last reason is most important to me. To have a career I can really enjoy and look forward to each day.

3. I get a feeling of happiness when I am able to teach young children something new. Like how to write their names or recognize a colour.

4. The scenery an old film of vegetation taken in the 1990s, with a tape of birdsong played in the background.

5. The disposal sites are full. Too many non-biodegradable materials.

6. As I have already made my way here to college.

7. These personal problems can cause the nurse to have an attitude. For the rest of the day.

8. Winter is also full of beauty. The snow covering everything in sight in a soft white blanket.

9. With grass growing and the harvest crops glowing in a golden light.

10. We cannot avoid exposure to radiation. Which causes cancer and other health problems.

Exercise 13.6*

Correct all sentence fragments in this passage from a student writer. Remember, it caused IRS as it is.

The protest songs of the 1990s were rap songs. Where the only militant messages in the pop charts were heard. Rappers, describing themselves as "radical" were determined. To rap about serious ideas. Urban debates on race, education, drugs, and crime. That's what listeners heard in the rap songs of the nineties. The message heard was varied. A mixture of penetrating insights, paranoia, resistance. The rappers were African-Americans. They saw themselves as victims. Of kidnapping through the slave trade. Theft through their labour. Brainwashing through their lack of educational opportunities. And genocide through crack, AIDS, and murder. They urged change. Brand Nubian said. "Black mothers need sons, not children that's been killed by guns."

Exercise 13.7*

Eliminate the sentence fragments in this passage.

Everyone loves a sports car. A simple two-seater with style. Driving around town with the top down. Is always fun. Listening to the turbocharged engines make whispery, whooshing sound. Music to the ears of any sportscar lover. The lusty song of a power-plant engine.

These days people seem to want. A good cargo space, as well as a cushy ride. Tuned for city driving. For older drivers a good sportscar has to be civilized. Able to work as day-to-day transportation. But younger drivers. Like a more nervous, sensitive car. With structural rigidity and slick handling.

Exercise 13.8*

Identify the sentence fragments in this passage and remove them.

Did you know that enough radioactive waste exists in Canada? To cover the Trans-Canada Highway 2-m deep from Halifax to Vancouver? As radioactive waste lasts for 80,000 years. The risk to human health and the environment is frightening. Northern Saskatchewan and other northern regions are becoming. Radioactive wastelands. It is miners and native people in those regions. Who are the first victims. They cannot avoid exposure to radiation. Which causes cancer and other health problems.

Exercise 13.9

Correct the sentence fragments in this passage.

Tea is still a popular beverage. Despite the pleasing flavours and glamorous competition from trendy mineral waters, juice spritzers, and classic colas. The first tea drinkers were the Chinese. Who drank their first cup around 2700 BCE The English have always had a reputation. For being great tea drinkers, but tea did not become England's national drink. Until the nineteenth century. When a rust blight destroyed the Ceylon coffee crop in the 1870s.

Next to water, tea is the most popular drink on the world. Especially for Southerners in the United States. Who find iced tea more refreshing. Than other drinks in summer. Sodas are syrupy. So they make you thirsty again. Iced tea is more refreshing. Because it gives you that little lift with caffeine. Especially without sugar. A spiced orange tea. Is especially popular in the South. When served with fresh mint in season.

The St. Louis World's Fair in 1904 is supposed to be the place. Where iced tea first became popular. Apparently Indian tea merchants set up a booth there, but did not realize. That the summer heat in the Midwest can be as hot as a day in New Delhi. Thirsty fair-goers did not want the hot brew. Until an enterprising Englishman at the booth began pouring the tea. Into glasses filled with ice. Even now, iced tea is often served on the rocks. Hot tea is Russia's national drink, but Americans drink 36 billion glasses of iced tea. As compared to 10 billion cups of hot tea, every year.

Run-on Sentences

Sentence fragments can make your writing seem disjointed and jerky. Run-on sentences make readers gasp for breath. They do not give readers a chance to stop and think. Can you follow this description of a trip to a spa?

> It was this birthday gift token from my aunt, she's a dermatologist, she goes to spas a lot, not just to get rid of her wrinkles and grey hairs, but for her neck muscles, she gets a cramped neck, so I go to this one called Splash, I get breakfast, then I see a dermatologist, she asks me if I want a shot of botox, I ask her what that is, she says it fills out the face, but then I remember it's those killer microbes, you know they cause botulism, we learned about them in food services, I say, no thanks, I'm only 20.

Your mother was right, wasn't she, when she told you, "Know when to stop." Try not to join sentences with a comma. A period is not only more forceful, it is also correct. You know that readers want clear, correct, coherent writing.

There are worse grammatical crimes than run-on sentences. One or two may not confuse readers, but they will make your prose seem agitated and feverish. Run-on sentences are still seen as incorrect writing. Keep your readers calm with careful, correct punctuation.

STEPS TO SUCCESS

Avoiding Run-on Sentences

1. A run-on sentence runs over logical grammatical limits. It is also called a *run-together sentence, fused sentence,* or a *comma splice* (if using a comma).

    > **Run-on Sentence:** Leroy loves English classes he also loves wrestling.

    > **Run-on Sentence:** It started to snow heavily, we went home.

    > **Run-on Sentence:** Many Australians like beer, they like good wine too.

2. After a complete sentence, come to a full stop. Use a period, question mark, or exclamation mark, whichever is appropriate, at the end of the sentence.

3. A comma *cannot* join statements.

4. Note the three ways to avoid run-on sentences:

    a. Use a period and a capital letter

    > It started to snow heavily. *We* went home.

    > Leroy loves English classes. *He* also loves wrestling.

    > Many Australians like beer. *They* like good wine too.

    b. Add a conjunction. Conjunctions can be coordinating conjunctions or subordinating conjunctions.

    > **Coordinating Conjunctions:** *but, or, yet, for, and, nor, so* (BOYFANS)

    > **Subordinating Conjunctions:** *after, although, because, as long as, as, as if, before, if, so that, unless, when, in order that, since, though, while, whenever, wherever*

    > It started to snow heavily, *so* we went home.

    > *Because* it started to snow heavily, we went home.

    > Leroy loves English classes, *and* he also loves wrestling.

    > Many Australians like beer, *but* they like good wine too.

    c. Use a semicolon instead of a comma for longer statements closely connected in meaning.

    > As soon as the test began, it started to snow heavily; with classes cancelled for the rest of the day, we went home.

Leroy, that big tough guy in the corner, loves English classes; studying poetry is not his only love though; he also loves wrestling.

Many Australians, keeping up old traditions, drink a lot of beer; nowadays they like good wine too, especially shiraz, pinot noir, and sauvignon blanc.

3. Use a semicolon followed by a conjunctive adverb (transitional expression) to add coherence. Conjunctive adverbs do not join statements on their own. That is why they are sometimes referred to as *fake conjunctions*. Use them followed by a comma.

It started to snow heavily; *therefore*, we went home.

Leroy loves English classes; *however*, he also loves wrestling.

Many Aussies drink a lot of beer; *nevertheless*, they like good wine too.

**Transitional Expressions
(aka Fake Conjunctions)**

accordingly	meanwhile
consequently	moreover
for example	nevertheless
for instance	next
furthermore	otherwise
however	that is
in fact	then
instead	therefore
likewise	thus

Remember the three ways to avoid run-on sentences when you do the following exercises.

Exercise 13.10*

Put a period followed by a capital letter in the places where a comma CANNOT join statements.

Example

His hair was weedy, his beard was long.

Possible Revision: His hair was weedy. His beard was long.

Possible Revision: His hair was weedy, and his beard was long.

Possible Revision: His hair was weedy; his beard was long.

1. The king was sick, his cheek was red, but his eyes were clear and bright.

2. He ate and drank with kingly zest, he peacefully snored at night.

3. But he said he was sick, and a king should know.

4. Doctors came by the score, they did not cure him.

5. He cut off their heads, and sent to the schools for more.

6. One was poor as a rat, he had passed his time in studious toil, and never found time to grow fat.

7. The other had never looked in a book, his patients gave him no trouble.

8. If they recovered, they paid him well.

9. If they died, his heirs paid double.

10. He was one of those small, misguided creatures, who, although their intellects are dim, are always ahead of their teachers.

Exercise 13.11*

Identify and correct each run-on sentence and sentence fragment.

1. Jeff Gibbs found a national alliance of youth environmental clubs.

2. After he had been on a high school trip to the Queen Charlotte Islands.

3. He has also been on an expedition. To the Amazon rain forest with David Suzuki.

4. Dana discovered that several schools in her area already had environmental clubs, others were intending to form their own soon.

5. These high school clubs work hard. Raising money and concern for protection of the environment.

6. Even though the teenagers involved are often fighting huge corporations, they learn that they can make difference.

7. "We have only one Earth," they declare, "we must protect it."

8. They do not let themselves get discouraged.

9. Though the apathetic attitude of some of their fellow students can be discouraging.

10. "We must educate our peers," they say. "Think globally, act locally, environmental protection begins in our own backyard."

Exercise 13.12*

Do you know where to stop?

A. Decide if the statement in Column B should be part of the word group in Column A.

B. If the statements can make one sentence, put a comma between them.

C. If each statement can stand alone, put a period and capital letter between them.

Example

Column A		*Column B*
After the young man saw the rare ibis in the wetlands	,	he called his girlfriend to tell her about it.

Column A		**Column B**
1. When Aloo Gosht and Suki Cilantro decided to go camping	___	they decided to go to Gros Morne National Park.
2. There they had a wonderful opportunity	___	to see the divide between the Cambrian and Ordovician periods in the cliffs by the campground.
3. An indentation in the cliffs runs from the crest to the bluff	___	in it there are ripple marks that show it has been an ocean bottom.

4. Aloo and Suki pitched their tent in a ____   with plenty of room
   beautiful setting   for their equipment
                                                        and their car.

5. Peace in a natural setting with   ____   without the
   birdsong and gentle water sounds   unnatural noises of
                                                        the city was what they
                                                        wanted.

6. The spot they chose with no one   ____   made a real
   in sight and no one to be heard   change from their
                                                        high-rise
                                                        apartment in Rexdale.

7. In the twilight they would hear   ____   these thumps came
   thumps and small explosions of   from numerous
   noise   varying hares who
                                                        have earned their
                                                        name from their ability
                                                        to change colour with
                                                        the seasons.

8. In the morning they would awake   ____   to birds singing "I love
                                                        Canada, Canada,
                                                        Canada."

9. White-throated sparrows would   ____   when there was
   start singing this patriotic song   only enough light
                                                        to see that it was
                                                        just after 4:00 a.m.

10. At a nearby campsite Aloo and   ____   they had come from
    Suki met Helmut and Heidi   Germany to enjoy
                                                        Canada's wilderness.

11. Many German visitors come   ____   they love the
    every year, attracted by Canada's   wilderness, but do
    unspoiled parks   not want any
                                                        unpleasant
                                                        surprises in the bush.

12. At the end of a path near   ____   for hanging food
    the campsite, Helmut and Heidi   out of a bear's way.
    were alarmed to see a metal
    contraption

Exercise 13.13*

Use a semicolon and conjunctive adverbs ("fake conjunctions") to correct and create coherence in the following run-on sentences.

A. Put a semicolon at the end of the first sentence.

B. Choose a suitable conjunctive adverb to add coherence.

C. Follow the conjunctive adverb with a comma.

Example

Not: Barbados offers many stately homes, afternoon tea, and cricket, *it* also has beautiful beaches and that charming economist, Aurelia Best.

But: Barbados offers many stately homes, afternoon tea, and cricket; *in addition,* it also has beautiful beaches and that charming economist, Aurelia Best.

1. There are three islands in the Dutch Windward Islands, one of them is just as lively as the French island of St. Martin.

2. This island is St. Maarten, with its beautiful mountains and beaches, it also offers plenty of amusements: tennis, horseback riding, golf, sailing, diving, windsurfing, casinos.

3. Saba and St. Eustatius, the other islands of the Dutch trio, are tranquil, St. Maarten is bustling with resorts, shops, and restaurants.

4. Saba has a new marine park, it protects the entire coast, and provides great scuba diving.

5. Some scuba divers attempt to do too much, the Royal Netherlands Navy has donated a compression chamber to the harbour at Saba.

6. St. Eustatius has an extinct volcano, visitors can walk to its summit through a rain forest.

7. On St. Eustatius, tourists can visit a museum, an eighteenth-century fort and church, and the ruins of an old synagogue, it is a great place for history buffs.

8. Recently on this island, Dutch archaeologists excavated pre-Colombian sites, a research team also investigated more historical locations.

9. Outstanding scuba diving is also available on St. Eustatius, some of the Caribbean's best shipwreck diving is found here.

10. Tropical fish and coral reefs are fantastic in the Caribbean, for those who love diving, a natural paradise is waiting there.

Exercise 13.14

Turn this run-on sentence into 11 sentences.

Some years ago now, when Khalid was a business student at college, he was impressed with the pedicabs he saw when he was on vacation in Los Angeles, when he returned to Toronto, he asked around to find out if such a business existed in the city, he found that there was one company operating, but it was about to fold, five vehicles and five employees were involved, it seemed like a good business though for a summer job, so Khalid bought the vehicles, today he has 30 vehicles and 180 people employed, he thinks his pedicab business is a success, most of the employees are students, one is a runner, hoping to make it to the Olympics, the hours are flexible, and the workers are outside during the summer months, the business is also environment-friendly, Khalid has graduated now, and has two more companies.

Exercise 13.15*

Decide which sentences are correct and which are run-on sentences. Correct the run-on sentences with the appropriate punctuation.

1. Women these days hear a lot about gender roles, many books and articles are available for them on sex and gender.

2. But how many boys learn about "manliness" and how to be macho, are boys encouraged to read books about the way they get their notions of masculinity?

3. Many cultures seem to regard manhood as a prize to be won after much struggle through trials of skill and endurance.

4. Boys are told to "be a man," or "act like a man," they are told "boys don't cry," girls seldom hear, "be a little girl."

5. It seems to me that boys suffer as much from gender stereotypes as girls, who are now encouraged to participate in weight lifting and martial arts.

6. Some societies recognize a third sex, the Cheyenne have the *bedache*, while the Omani have the *xanith*, and the Tahitians have the *mahu*.

7. These are androgynous genders, individuals choosing to be the third sex must make a life choice and stick to it.

8. When I was at high school, we were convinced that our teachers were mostly the third sex, I went to a girls' school where our teachers seemed androgynous, long before RuPaul came on the scene.

9. Women today are encouraged to be independent and free, men, however, still have to pass initiation tests and be indoctrinated.

10. On one South Pacific island, men are obsessed with their masculinity, to maintain their macho image they must risk their lives, fight in brawls, drink to excess, and have many sexual conquests, sound familiar?

Exercise 13.16

Fix it! Use all three ways to correct run-on sentences in this passage.

Crispo never made it out of the parking lot, he was stabbed in the heart and died in a dark corner of the lobby in his office building, when two colleagues walked into the parking lot later, they saw Crispo's car with its doors open, the inside light was on, they called police. who, with the others, supposedly searched the building, no one checked the corner of the lobby.

They called his home, they received no reply, they checked his usual restaurants, they received negative responses, they closed the car door and gave up, then they all went home, at midnight, a security guard found Crispo's body, he had apparently staggered into the lobby seeking help.

Investigations turned up no evidence, some witnesses reported seeing someone suspicious in the area, one witness, who had been in the parking lot at the time, said he had seen a man running away, running very fast, he thought he must have seen the murderer.

The media and the public have been very critical about the lack of evidence, they think the police are not trying very hard, after all, Crispo who did a lot of work consulting for the government, wrote critically about their economic policies, and about corruption in various departments, perhaps police are afraid to investigate further, they might be afraid of what could emerge, maybe someone in authority is trying to prevent further investigation.

CHAPTER 14

The Sick Sentence

This chapter looks at errors that are a major cause of Irritable Reader Syndrome: modifier problems, faulty parallel structure, and pronoun reference errors.

By the end of this chapter, you will be able to

- identify and correct dangling or misplaced modifiers

- identify and correct faulty parallel structure

- identify and correct pronoun reference errors

Some sentences are sick. They stagger and lurch along, with pieces dangling, out of order, or unclear. Sick sentences leave readers confused and worried, or worse, they make readers laugh. No one likes having to read something twice to get its meaning. No one wants people to laugh at what is meant to be serious writing.

Some of the writing errors that cause reader-confusion are modifier problems; that is, dangling modifiers and misplaced modifiers, faulty parallel structure, and incorrect pronoun reference.

Errors with modifiers, parallel structure, and pronoun reference can cause a sentence to sound sick and uncertain. Sickly (diseased, dyspeptic, delirious) sentences are hard for readers to digest. You have to work at keeping them in shape.

Modifiers

Modifier problems can also cause mirth. Most of us prefer to have people laughing *with* us, not *at* us, so it is good to be aware of modifiers and make them behave, so readers won't laugh in the wrong place.

Even professional writers have to watch their modifiers. A recent letter to one of Canada's national newspapers mocked mirthful modifier misuse in the sports pages. The letter writer quoted the sentence, "Shannon Stewart lost a ball in the sun that hit him on the head in the third inning," concluding, "I hate it when the sun hits me on the head too." Note the rules for correct modifier use in order to avoid such mockery.

What is a modifier? A *modifier* simply tells *more* about something. In the following sentences, the italicized words and expressions are modifiers.

> He *almost* made it.

> My dentist wears *purple rubber* gloves *on Wednesdays.*

> *Sobbing,* Farida waved goodbye.

> *Enchanted by the rules of grammar,* college students *always* enjoy English class.

In order to avoid mirthful modifier misuse, learn the rules about modifiers.

STEPS TO SUCCESS

Modifiers

1. Place modifiers as close as possible to the words they modify.

    I saw the *boy* **with red hair** on rollerblades.

    Not: I saw the *boy* on rollerblades **with red hair.**

2. Modifiers placed in the wrong place are called *misplaced modifiers.*

    Misplaced Modifier: Whirring and wriggling, Steve was tormented by *the cockroach* in his ear.

    Correct: Steve was tormented by *the cockroach* **whirring and wriggling** in his ear.

3. Clauses following relative pronouns *(who, which, that)* directly follow the word they modify (their antecedent).

    This is the *house* **that Jack built.**

    Where is the *diamond* **that my mother gave you?**

4. Place one-word modifiers like *almost, every, just, merely, nearly, only, scarcely* before the word they modify, if possible.

    Only *Fabio* baked the cake. (Joe and Danny didn't help.)

    Fabio **only** *baked* the cake. (Joe and Danny did the shopping and cleaning.)

    Fabio baked **only** *the cake.* (Joe and Danny made the appetizers, salad, chicken, green beans, and garlic potatoes.)

5. Make sure modifiers have a specific word or expression to modify. Modifiers with no clear point of reference are called *dangling modifiers.*

    Whirring and wriggling, Steve was tormented.

    Sitting at the back, the words on the blackboard were all blurry.

    (What is whirring and wriggling? Who is sitting at the back?)

6. Modifiers at the beginning of a sentence modify the subject.

    Sitting at the back, *Fabio* could not read the words on the blackboard.

    Whirring and wriggling, *the cockroach* in his ear tormented Steve.

Exercise 14.1*

Decide whether the following sentences have a misplaced modifier or dangling modifier. Hint: If the italicized expression has nothing clear to relate to, the sentence has a dangling modifier.

Example

Lucy refused to eat the chicken *thinking about battery farm conditions.* (*misplaced modifier*)

1. A plane flew over the classroom *with red wings.*

2. *Fed up with his unpleasant green body,* the control panel was annoying.

3. He told his co-pilot he wanted a year on a beach *with glowing eyes.*

4. *On the way home,* lightning flashed and thunder crashed.

5. When Mary arrived in Dublin she was met by Tim *wearing her new Armani dress.*

6. The passengers saw a number of guided missiles *talking among themselves.*

7. Hemingway tried to shoot himself after writing a farewell note *with a shotgun.*

8. *In the media spotlight suddenly,* photographers were everywhere.

9. *By repeating it constantly,* the French Revolution came to mean Liberty, Equality, Fraternity.

10. Michael decided to move back to Lethbridge after his partner was sent to jail *to live with relatives.*

Exercise 14.2

Insert the modifier in parentheses in as many places as possible in each sentence. Be prepared to explain the change in meaning, if there is one.

1. (*just*) The freaky waiter served the chicken soup, not the main course.

2. (*only*) The doctor's report said that the teenager's hearing loss was the result of exposure to noise levels.

3. *(almost)* Sixty applications have been registered for the tae kwon do classes.

4. *(only)* You can get lunch on weekdays at Le Cirque restaurant, if you don't book in advance.

5. *(usually)* Substance abuse develops from psychological and environmental influences.

Exercise 14.3*

Find the misplaced modifiers in the following passage. Note: Some sentences are correct.

Example

Wearing pink pyjamas, the train carried the Girl Guides round the mountain. **Misplaced Modifier:** *Wearing pink pyjamas*

Waving frantically and shouting, the rescue launch came close to the survivors on the life raft. They were exhausted and happy to have coffee in the cabin that smelled delicious. The captain came in and only talked to the men in the group.

They all seemed confused and frightened to him. The day grew even colder and the fog came rolling in spreading far and wide. The survivors took warm drinks from the sailors in brown pottery mugs. A clear ringing sound floated across the water from the bell on the island. The bell had an unearthly sound from the old church floating across the water. One of the survivors found a gold chain in a pocket that he had lost. He gave this gold chain to a sailor that was a valuable memento of the brave and daring rescue from the wild seas.

Exercise 14.4*

Decide which sentences use modifiers correctly. Fix the sentences where the modifier is used incorrectly.

1. At an early age, Beatrice was taken to the Factory Theatre Lab by her drama-loving dad.

2. Watching the moon for some time, the positions of the craters became clear.

3. Only his Grade 6 teacher could get Peter to sit still.

4. The restaurant is advertising for a man to wash dishes and two waiters.

5. Minnie and Matta were furious when he announced that he was a specialist in women and other diseases.

6. My aunt promised to serve me tea in a bag just like mother.

7. They want to sell their boat which has had one owner freshly painted blue.

8. Conrad and his friends are selling newspapers that are blind.

9. Disturbed by the beautiful stranger, he felt all his strength desert him.

10. Pyramids were constructed by hands reaching up to 500 m.

Exercise 14.5

Correct all modifier problems in this story from Indonesia.

Pamudjo, a man who lived on the bank of the Malang River heard that a rich neighbour, Keromo, one day upstream was giving a feast from another neighbour, for all the people on this part of the river who wanted to eat at his banquet.

"It's a long while since I've had enough to eat." Pamudjo said to his wife who sounded angry. "Being so stingy with food, I never feel satisfied. You go visit your mother. I'll eat with rich Keromo."

Dressed in his finest sarong, the boat steered upstream. Pamudjo met other men in boats on the river. Noticing they were all paddling downstream, all the people were in great spirits. Pamudjo called out to them, "Why are you going downstream?"

A man replied, "A big feast is being held today, at the house of Muchmud." Pamudjo thought to himself, "Muchmud is richer and more generous than Keromo."

Turning his boat around, his paddles moved fast. He wanted to be one of the first to arrive badly. Noticing after a while, many boats were going upstream filled with laughing, waving people.

"Why are you so excited all?" asked Pamudjo.

"We are going to Keromo's. He is serving a cow and two calves today."

Slowing down, the cow and two calves sounded good.

Paddling upstream again to catch all the boats that had passed him, a boat going downstream came close and the man in it asked, "Why so fast are you rowing upstream?"

Pamudjo told him about Keromo's cow and two calves licking his lips.

The man shouted back to him, "I'm going to have a feast and receive a gift of money that Muchmud is giving to everyone in bags."

Turning his boat around again and paddling downstream once more, his boat was finally pulled on to the beach by Muchmud's house. Arriving at last in his finest sarong, the people called out to Pamudjo, "Why are you so late? The feast is over. The money bags have all been given out."

Back on the beach the boat was shoved into the water. Pamudjo paddled to Keromo's landing as fast as he could. At Keromo's lying back and chatting, with full stomachs after the huge feast, Pamudjo learned that the food was finished.

Back to his boat again and paddling home, the house was empty.

"Oh that woman! Always running off to her mother's," he complained. "Leaving only a small piece of dried fish to eat here."

While sitting down at the edge of the river with a bottle of wine, the bottle fell into the river. Jumping up, the dried fish dropped and Pamudjo watched a hungry dog run off with it.

The people of Java say indecision will leave you hungry.

Parallel Structure

Make a Commitment: Avoid Shifting Tenses or Persons

Readers want consistency. They want you to keep verb tenses and pronoun references clear and consistent. They don't want any unnecessary shift in time or person. Such shifts leave them confused.

Readers don't want you to mix grammatical apples and oranges. They want you to keep points coordinated. They want all lists and line-ups of ideas in the same grammatical shape for easy reading.

In writing, keeping points in similar grammatical shape is called keeping them *parallel*. That means ideas that are similar are expressed in similar form.

Example

Not: All her friends are impressed with Geri's emotional resilience, her indestructible vitality, her decorating skills, and she knows so much about soap operas.

But: All her friends are impressed with Geri's emotional resilience, her indestructible vitality, her decorating skills, and her knowledge of soap operas.

Items that are not parallel are said to have faulty parallel structure.

STEPS TO SUCCESS

Avoiding Faulty Parallel Structure

1. Keep equal groups of words and clauses in the same matching form.

> **Faulty:** Leroy loves wrestling, skydiving, and to crochet.
>
> **Correct:** Leroy loves wrestling, skydiving, and crocheting.
>
> **Faulty:** Although Francie was happy to see her sister in Toronto, and receiving the emeralds from her, she was surprised.
>
> **Correct:** Although Francie was happy to see her sister in Toronto, and to receive the emeralds from her, she was surprised.

2. Always use parallel structure in lists and clauses joined with *and, but, or.*

> **Faulty:** Tracey intends to spend time reviewing her notes, re-reading her textbook, and to smile at the teacher before the test.
>
> **Correct:** Tracey intends to spend time reviewing her notes, re-reading her textbook, and smiling at the teacher before the test.

3. It is useful to think of items as being in a real list or a simple sum.

Cecil loves	Gladys loves
1 digging for clams	1 writing songs
+2 cooking clams	+2 singing songs
+3 eating clams	+3 listening to songs

4. Use parallel structure with the correlative conjunctions *either . . . or, neither . . . nor, both . . . and, not only . . . but also.*

> *Both* the hard work of the social service workers *and* the fundraising of the automotive technicians were mentioned in the local newspaper.
>
> Josie never liked *either* his haircut *or* his mannerisms.

5. Be consistent with tenses. Do not change time zones unnecessarily.

> **Not:** She goes, yes, and decided to go out with him.
>
> **But:** She goes, yes, and decides to go out with him. (or both in past tense)

6. Keep to the same person. Do not change partners mid-project. (This is not such a silly rule . . .)

> **Not:** At Cheticamp you can eat delicious Acadian food, but they will not find any at St. Ann's.

> **But:** At Cheticamp you can eat delicious Acadian food, but you will not find any at St. Ann's.

Exercise 14.6

Make a list of the parallel word groups in the following sentences.

Example

My parents always enjoy

1. meeting new people

2. visiting new places

3. buying new appliances

1. The company badly needs personnel to operate, direct, and maintain the new condominiums.

2. The professor did not want his students to know that he had been born in Philadelphia, that he was a close friend of RuPaul, that he had studied for the priesthood, and that he had been married three times.

3. If you buy a Great Dane, remember that it needs a lot of space, a lot of food, and a lot of exercise.

4. On our visit to Rome we plan to visit the ruins of the Temple of Minerva, to view Filippino Lippi's beautiful frescoes, and to dine at Prefetti's.

5. Victory depended on destroying the supplies, cutting off the rein-forcements, and exterminating the horses.

6. There was a little girl so proud,
    She talked so fast and laughed so loud,
    That those who came with her to play,
    Were always glad to go away.

7. It was the best of times, it was the worst of times, it was the age of wisdom, it was the age of foolishness—in short the period was like the present period.

8. If we can cross the interstellar distance in 1 second, and if we can generate infinite improbability, we won't feel like failures.

9. She was beautiful, charming, intelligent, and I had her to myself.

10. Wuhan would neither attack the creature, nor resist it.

Exercise 14.7*

Some of the following sentences are not correct. Identify any faulty parallel structure, and make the word groups parallel.

1. Professor O'Rourke's lectures are always interesting and a challenge.

2. He is good-looking with brown hair, intelligent, and a Lexus.

3. He has done much work on the diagnosis and treatment of genetic diseases.

4. He has investigated the "jumping gene" where a stable gene jumps from one place in the genome to another.

5. Scientists involved in such work watch for petunias that change from white to pink, and changing in colour from a violet colour to red.

6. They genetically manipulate plants to change colour.

7. Marking papers, preparing classes, teaching, and to meet with students keep Professor O'Rourke busy these days.

8. He comes into class on time and asked questions immediately.

9. He is always happy to meet with students after class, and discussing the material covered.

10. A course in genetic research is not offered at our college, so students enrolled today did not learn about manipulating genes.

Exercise 14.8*

Complete the following sentences with appropriate words or constructions that are parallel in form.

1. Shy people are often misinterpreted because they avoid eye contact and _____.

2.   You will be served more frequently in big stores if you carry packages from another store or _____.

3.   Great leaders are not always nice people; people who accomplish great feats are often stubborn, disagreeable, and _____.

4.   Caregivers of ill or _____ people have to help them adjust to pain, _____, and _____.

5.   Iguanas make good pets because they are quieter and _____ than a cat or a dog.

6.   When your life is fast-paced and hectic, juggling work, _____, and _____ can be difficult.

7.   If your boss refuses to listen and _____, then you should consider getting another job.

8.   My sister thinks that her boyfriend is the most intelligent man in the world and that _____.

9.   Whether she decides to give more money to the homeless or _____, people will criticize her choice.

10. Travelling to other countries gives you the chance not only to see new places, but also _____.

Exercise 14.9

Note the use of parallel construction in the following famous passages.

1.   "Observe the rhythm of his native woodnotes wild: I'm willing to tell you, I'm wanting to tell you, I'm waiting to tell you."

George Bernard Shaw, *Pygmalion*.

2.   We shall defend our island, whatever the cost may be,
     We shall fight on the beaches, we shall fight on the landing grounds,
     We shall fight in the fields, and in the streets,
     We shall fight in the hills;
     We shall never surrender.

Winston Churchill, Speech in House of Commons, Westminster, 1940.

3.   "Age, I do abhor thee, youth, I do adore thee."

William Shakespeare, *The Passionate Pilgrim*.

4. "To lose one parent, Mr. Worthing, may be regarded as a misfortune; to lose both looks like carelessness."

Oscar Wilde, *The Importance of Being Earnest*.

5. "I see one third of a nation ill-housed, ill-clad, ill-nourished."

Franklin D. Roosevelt, Second Inaugural Address, 1937.

6. I said it in Hebrew—I said it in Dutch
   I said it in German and Greek
   But I wholly forgot (and it vexes me much)
   That English is what you speak.

Lewis Carroll, *Through the Looking Glass*.

7. "No sooner met but they looked; no sooner looked but they loved; no sooner loved but they sighed; no sooner sighed but they asked one another the reason; no sooner knew the reason but they sought the remedy."

William Shakespeare, *As You Like It*.

8. When I was a lad I served a term
   As office-boy to an Attorney's firm;
   I cleaned the windows and I swept the floor
   And I polished up the handle of the big front door.
   I polished up the handle so successfullee
   That now I am the Ruler of the Queen's Navee!

Sir W. S. Gilbert, *H.M.S. Pinafore*.

9. "From this day you must be a stranger to one of your parents. Your mother will never see you again if you do *not* marry Mr. Collins, and I will never see you again if you *do*."

Jane Austen, *Pride and Prejudice*.

10. "Man with all his noble qualities, with sympathy that feels for the most debased, with benevolence that extends not only to other men but to the humblest living creature, with his god-like intellect which has penetrated into the movements and constitution of the solar system—with all these exalted powers—still bears in his bodily frame the indelible stamp of his lowly origin."

Charles Darwin, *The Descent of Man*.

Pronoun Reference

Pronoun reference can be a problem for writers. Errors with pronouns do not just irritate readers; they can cause legal repercussions. In a workplace incident report, for example, if pronoun reference is not clear, a report can be misunderstood.

> The supervisor saw her throw the wrench at *her* foot right at the beginning of *her* shift.

Whose foot? Whose shift?

Make sure that all pronouns clearly refer to a specific noun and you will avoid legal tangles.

Remember this saying: Where there's a pronoun, there must be a noun.

That's obvious really, isn't it? A pronoun stands for a noun, after all. It's a bit like saying: Where there's a doorknob, there must be a door.

What are all these pronouns you have to watch? Most personal pronouns come in subject and object form, in singular and plural.

Subject pronouns direct and limit the verb:

	Singular	Plural
First Person:	I	we
Second Person:	you	you
Third Person:	he, she, it	they

Object pronouns are on the receiving end of the verb:

	Singular	Plural
First Person:	me	us
Second Person:	you	you
Third Person:	him, her, it	them

Object pronouns follow a preposition: *between them, for us, with me, by themselves.* Note: There are no such words as *hisself, their selfs, themselfs.*

Relative pronouns (*who, whose, whom, which, that*) you know about already. They like their relatives. Remember, they directly follow their auntie, their antecedent. (Auntie Cedent, get it?)

When the pronouns *who, whose, whom, which* ask questions, they do not have antecedents. (They are then called *interrogative pronouns,* but as interrogatives never cause grammatical trouble, you need not worry about them.)

Indefinite Pronouns

Indefinite pronouns do not refer to anything specific or definite. Examples of indefinite pronouns are:

anyone	anybody	anything
everyone	everybody	everything
either	neither	one
no one	nobody	nothing
none	many	several
someone	somebody	something
whoever	whatever	each

STEPS TO SUCCESS

Avoiding Pronoun Problems

1. Where there's a pronoun, there must be a noun.

    Not: *Ruth* told *Sarah* that **she** had been diagnosed as having a borderline personality disorder.

    But: *Ruth* said that *Sarah* had been diagnosed as having a borderline personality disorder.

    Be especially careful with *it* and *this*. (Some people consider *it* to be a dirty word. Always give *it* a clear reference, so you will not offend people.)

    Not: It's better in the Bahamas

    But: *Scuba diving* is better in the Bahamas.

    Not: Windsurfers do it standing up.

    But: *Windsurfing* is done standing up.

2. Pronouns must agree with the noun they refer to (their antecedent).

    Not: The *student* was late, but then **they** are late every Monday.

    But: The *students* were late, but then **they** are late every Monday.

    Not: All the *women* were there, and **it** did not make a happy crowd.

    But: All the *women* were there, and **they** did not make a happy crowd.

3. Relative pronouns directly follow their antecedent.

> Where is the *boy* **who** looks after the sheep?

4. After *than,* use the form of the pronoun that you would use if the construction were complete.

> Mama did more for Sugantha *than* **I** (did for her).

> Mama did more for Sugantha *than* **me** (she did for me).

5. Use plural verb forms after *many, few, several, both.*

> **Many** *are* cold, but **few** *are* frozen.

6. *Some, any, none, all* may be singular or plural.

7. Avoid *his/her* constructions after nouns and after indefinite pronouns like *everyone, nobody, somebody.* In today's non-sexist world, people tend to prefer the gender-free plural pronoun *they.* Make constructions plural or use a plural pronoun.

> **Not:** A *driver* should be serious about having **his or her** eyesight checked regularly.

> **But:** *Drivers* should be serious about having **their** eyesight checked regularly.

> **Not:** *Everyone* liked hearing **his or her** favourite singer.

> **But:** *Everyone* liked hearing **their** favourite singer.

A super-correct, singular way to avoid his/her constructions is to use the pronoun for your own gender in the sentence.

> A *driver* should have **her** eyesight checked
> regularly.

Exercise 14.10*

Choose the sentences where the pronoun is used incorrectly.

1. Witi told Maui that his canoe had a hole in it.

2. Witi heard his brother laughing after he looked at his boat.

3. All the brothers found Maui a nuisance because of his tricks.

4. When Maui was told to stay behind, it annoyed him.

5. He left the beach sadly, and wondered if he could make a special fish hook to catch more fish.

6.   He remembered a special ancestor of his living in the underworld.

7.   She was dead on one side and alive on the other; everyone was afraid of her.

8.   In the underworld, they live in dark and frightening caverns.

9.   Maui told her hisself that he needed a bone from her jaw.

10. Maui's father was a god, so he knew how to make a magic fish hook.

Exercise 14.11*

Choose the correct form of the pronoun in parentheses in the following sentences.

1.   Carmen and *(he, him)*_____ received the highest mark in *(they're, their)* _____ nutrition test.

2.   After the test, Mr. Pitt invited *(us, we)* _____ students to a party in his house.

3.   I wanted him to take Carmen and *(I, me)* _____ in his car.

4.   *(Us, We)* _____ two ended up taking the bus.

5.   Carmen and *(I, me)* _____ always do our homework together, but I never do as well as *(her, she)* _____.

6.   I don't know if *(she, her)* _____ is as smart as the rest of her family.

7.   She never told any of *(we, us)* _____ how well-known her mother is.

8.   Her mother, Maria, is so clever; *(she, her)* _____ won a mathematics contest once in Venezuela.

9.   When she and *(I, me)* _____ reached the party, I knew it would be fun for Carmen and *(I, me)* _____.

10. No matter when *(they, him or her)* _____ arrived, Mr. Pitt met everyone, including *(we, us)* _____ at the door.

Exercise 14.12*

Choose the appropriate pronoun for the following sentences. Do not use the pronoun *you*.

1.   _____ and David make a good team.

2. _____ played tennis yesterday against Dorothy and Ken.

3. Naomi was upset about the result. She argued with _____ about the score.

4. She says _____ will not play against Dorothy and Ken again.

5. In fact, they played well and everyone at the club knows _____ have been practising for weeks.

6. Maybe instead Naomi should follow David's suggestion that _____ all go on a picnic together.

7. Naomi does not know that David _____ really prefers to play golf or go hiking.

8. Neither Naomi nor _____ are on the social committee of the golf club, though.

9. Ken actually dislikes _____, but he finds David good company.

10. Most people like both of _____, because they are kind and fun to be with.

Exercise 14.13*

Decide which sentences have pronouns without a clear antecedent.

1. Anti-drug forces are showing tremendous courage about it these days.

2. As long as the demand for cocaine is high, drug trafficking continues, so they have little chance of success.

3. Many drug traffickers in Colombia have flaunted their wealth from cocaine and have done incredible things with it.

4. Carlos Lehder had a nude statue of John Lennon, complete with a bullet hole through his heart.

5. Several cocaine traffickers bought soccer teams and they distributed it among the poor of Medellin.

6. Medellin is very violent and at one time they were reporting as many as 12 murders a day.

7. This city owes its wealth to the drug trade and for which it will do anything.

8. Pablo Escobar, who began his career stealing tombstones, built housing there for the poor.

9. The drug traffickers will harm anyone who opposes it.

10. Once it even invaded the Palace of Justice to destroy files in which related to the drug trade.

Exercise 14.14

Find the faulty pronouns in the following passage and correct them.

Everyone was happy in Lycia until a terrible monster came and then we were afraid. No one knew what the fearful creature was or where they came from. Men called it the *Chimera* and wherever it went, it destroyed everything in which was in their way. Many brave heroes went out against it, but it carried off they bodies alive. Then one day there came to the court in Lycia a splendid young man, who's name was Mr. B. He brought with hisself a letter from the King of Argos. He did not know what it said so was unaware that it said he should be put to death. The King of Lycia thought Mr. B. looked brave, so he told him about the Chimera and the sorrow in which it brought. "The gods have sent such a great hero to rid the land of this terrible beast. Will you do this for us?" said the crafty king. Mr. B. went out, destroyed the monster after a frightening struggle and won the praise of the kingdom for doing it.

Exercise 14.15*

Choose the correct pronoun in parentheses in the following passage.

Our immune system is like an army and *(its, their)* _____ soldiers have to fight lethal attacks from *(its, their)* _____ enemies. We need to know how it works. *(Its, Their)* _____ primary duty is to destroy the body's own cells when *(it, they)* _____ may have gone wrong. Our bodies have killer cells that seek out tumour cells and other cells that have been attacked by foreign agents. Every killer cell does *(its, their)* _____ job with great efficiency. First *(it, they)* _____ will bind tightly to the renegade cells, doing something vicious to *(it, they, them)* _____, while at the same time sparing innocent cells. Each killer cell must identify *(its, their, your)* _____ target, in order for *(it, them, you)* _____ to bind tightly to the target cell. Once this close contact is established, *(it, they, them)* _____ will begin the deadly process.

Investigators knew about The Attack of the Killer Cells for many years, but *(it, they, you, we)* _____ did not understand the nature of the killing process. Now *(they, it, we)* _____ have been able to dissect *(them, it)* _____ and at last, *(you, we, they, it)* _____ can describe the terminal stage of cell death to the rest of *(them, us, you)* _____.

Exercise 14.16

Seek and destroy all incorrect verbs and pronouns in the following passage.

Sick and tired of pop concerts, Boniface and Byrd decided to try the opera. After all, Kiri being telling them for years that opera represent the highest form of artistic achievement in it. She told them stories from long ago about *castrati*. That's plural for those boys who had their gender-specific parts removed so they can sing high. Boniface and Byrd are a bit concerned about it, but she tells him not to worry, because they are too old now to become *castrati* (that are the plural form for the two of them). She say that their voices was never good enough for it anyway.

The *castrati* is very popular in Italy in the eighteenth century, but it isn't around today. Boniface and Byrd found the idea of this here *castrati* guys quite upsetting, but Kiri eventually persuade they to go to the opera, *The Barber of Seville*. Boniface like the title, because he is a hairdresser. Him and Byrd enjoyed the opera so much that now, when you visit them, all we hears is arias, that's songs sung by famous tenors and sopranos. Byrd's favourite soprano is Greek and when you hear one sung by she, we get goosebumps.

Boniface and Byrd turn up the sound so loud that their neighbours complains. One man sent a card with a quotation from John Cage, a modern composer. They said, "The music I prefer, even to my own or anybody else's, is what we are hearing if we are just quiet." Boniface was angry with it. Him and Byrd just cannot seem to understand the message.

CHAPTER 15

Mainly Mechanics

This chapter looks at punctuation, spelling, and word confusions (aka homonym horrors).

By the end of this chapter, you will be able to

- identify and correct errors in punctuation and spelling

People moan a lot about the decline of literacy. They have been doing so for hundreds of years, in fact. What people usually mean today, when they moan, is that standards of spelling and punctuation are slipping. That's why it's important to know how to write without any basic errors in spelling and punctuation. Readers get upset and irritated when writing is hard to follow because the mechanics (spelling and punctuation) are not correct. Try to avoid causing Irritable Reader Syndrome (IRS). To prevent chronic IRS, learn the rules for correct spelling and punctuation.

You have to remember that writers cannot rely on body language to get their points across. No grunts, winks, shrugs, gasps, or smiles come off the page. When you are writing, you have to use words and writing skills to communicate ideas effectively and clearly.

The bad news is basic errors ruin your image as a communicator. The good news is basic errors are easily eliminated. The rules are easy to learn. All you have to do is apply the rules and proofread. Some basic rules for punctuation and spelling follow in this chapter.

Punctuation

Punctuation offers readers road signs on the route of your ideas. They are the signs that give your readers a chance to stop and take a breath, or to pause and think. They can be seen as the traffic signs on your thought tracks.

OVERVIEW OF PUNCTUATION

1. A comma allows readers to pause. It does not join statements.

2. An apostrophe shows possession or contraction.

3. A capital letter is used for the first word of a sentence, a name, the pronoun *I*, a personal title, deity, organization, institution, special event, and the key words in titles.

4. A semicolon is neither a period nor a comma. It comes between statements that are connected, but complete.

5. A colon introduces a useful point already mentioned, or a list already named.

6. A dash indicates a break in thought.

7. A hyphen connects words to make them function as one. It is used for compound words, fractions, spelled-out numbers from twenty-one to ninety-nine, and to separate syllables at the end of a line of print. (Apostrophes and hyphens may be considered endangered species, but educated people use them.)

8. Quotation marks are used for quotations. They also indicate titles of poems, songs, short stories, essays, lectures, or parts of a whole work. They may also show you are using a word in a particular way, as in *the semicolon is "connected."* Don't overdo this usage. (It can make your work look as startled as a "pulled matron." That is a face-lifted woman with a permanent look of surprise.)

    Commas and periods are placed inside quotation marks. Colons and semicolons are placed outside quotation marks.

    Question marks and exclamation marks are placed inside or outside quotation marks, depending on whether they are part of the quoted statement or not.

9. Italics are used to set off titles of books, magazines, movies, newspapers, miniseries, foreign words, or anything that needs emphasis. (Words can be easily italicized by word processors.)

    In handwriting, all the titles mentioned above are usually underlined. Underline these titles if your teacher asks you to do so.

10. Parentheses (round brackets) enclose additional, supplementary material that could be omitted. The material enclosed will be non-essential, but explanatory.

11. An ellipsis (three dots) shows that material has been omitted or indicates a hesitant pause . . . in other words, some uncertainty.

The Comma

Readers like little pauses. A comma offers readers the chance to take a breath, to pause for refreshment. Good writers avoid Comma Overload. They use commas as an ideal stopover on the autoroute of expression.

STEPS TO SUCCESS

The Comma

The **I**'s have it for commas. Use commas for

1. Items in a series
2. Introductions
3. Interruptions
4. Independent clauses (after the first)
5. In Speech

Where to Use a Comma

1. Items in a Series

Separate items in a series with a comma.

> As he grew up, Peter wanted to be a fireman, an astronaut, a spy, a truck driver, a stuntman, and a detective.

Note: The comma before the *and* in a series of three or more items is optional. If all items are joined by *and* or *or*, no comma is needed.

> Bishop and abbott and prior were there.

> Britney wears jeans with tons of patches or wild belts or funky hats and lots of velvet.

In dates and addresses, items are set off with commas.

> Thursday, November 10, is my love's birthday.

> She lives on Baddeck Street, Fort McMurray, Alberta.

2. Introductions

After an introductory group of words or a dependent clause, use a comma where readers might want to take a breath. A brief introduction may not need a comma.

> Suddenly, Byron changed his mind.

> **Better:** Suddenly Byron changed his mind.

> According to the Canadian Contraceptive Study, about half of all sexually active teenage girls have mistaken ideas about birth control.

Because many young people find it difficult to discuss contraception with their partners, they need good sex education and access to contraception.

3. Interruptions

Surround any expressions that interrupt a sentence with commas.

You will, I hope, be on time tonight.

Their children, to tell the truth, are noisy, rude, and selfish.

If a word, group of words, or dependent clause *is not essential* to the sentence's meaning, set it off with commas. If you could pick out the expression and throw it away without altering the meaning of the sentence, use commas to set it apart.

Her favourite movie, *Men at Work,* was written and directed by his brother.

Braque, the artist, liked to wear blue overalls.

Karen, who is a real dynamo, will run the Planned Parenthood meeting next week.

However, if an expression is *essential* to the meaning of the sentence, if it *restricts* the meaning of a word in any way, *do not* use commas.

All customers paying cash receive Canadian Tire money.

The students who skip class will fail the course.

But: The students, who are a lively group this year, keep Ms Fudge busy.

4. Independent Clauses (After the First)

Use a comma after the first independent clause to allow readers to take a mental breath.

Keats gazed in admiration at Fanny, and then he took a step towards her, but she ran back to her mother.

Ostriches are the largest flightless birds, but their wings are not useless. They are spread out to help the birds cool down when they are hot from running, and they are often used as weapons to attack threatening animals.

5. Speech

Use a comma to separate direct quotations.

"You're crazy," she said.

"I believe," he replied with dignity, "that you are mistaken."

Extra useful rule: Use a comma before the expressions, *especially* and *such as.*

Chatwin loved desolate places, such as Patagonia.

Where Not to Use a Comma

1. between a subject and a verb, when one follows the other

   Chinch bugs reproduce rapidly.

   Not: Chinch bugs, reproduce rapidly.

2. between the verb and the first item in a series

   Squash bugs damage squash, pumpkins, gourds.

   Not: Squash bugs damage, squash, pumpkins, gourds.

3. to join statements

   Ambush bugs will lie concealed in flowers; from there they will grasp any visiting insect.

   Not: Ambush bugs will lie concealed in flowers, from there they will grasp any visiting insect.

   Remember always: A comma cannot join.

FOR FUN

Q. What's the difference between a cat and a comma?
A. A cat has paws at the end of its claws. A comma is a pause at the end of a clause.

Think about the importance of punctuation in our lives as you read this sexist joke.

An English teacher wrote on the blackboard, "Woman without her man is nothing."

She asked the class to punctuate the statement correctly.

The men wrote, "Woman, without her man, is nothing."

The women wrote, "Woman! Without her, man is nothing."

Exercise 15.1*

Add commas as required in the following sentences. Commas are needed here for items in a series, introductions, and interruptions.

1. The Pure and Bright Festival Ch'ing Ming is the Chinese celebration of the coming of spring.

2. When the branches of the willow begin to show buds and green leaves it is a sign of spring.

3. Soon the swallows returning from the south build their nests.

4. The time to celebrate Ch'ing Ming is exactly 106 days after the winter solstice has arrived.

5. Early in the morning of this great spring festival the people of China honour the dead.

6. Each grave or family receives willow sprigs two white papers representing paper money and offerings of food.

7. Whether rich or poor all people make their offerings to the souls of departed family members in *even* numbers.

8. When they make offerings to the gods they make them in *odd* numbers.

9. The principle of yin and yang gods are yang souls of people are yin must never be ignored.

10. After honouring the dead the people celebrate the rest of the day joyously.

Exercise 15.2*

Insert commas where necessary in the following sentences. Decide which sentences use commas correctly.

1. When choosing books for children to read it is important to avoid ones that are in any way racist or sexist.

2. In order to counteract racism and sexism in children's books we have to be aware just how bias is reflected in some picture books.

3. Simple as this sounds it is not easy.

4.   Developing country activists feminists the disabled ethnic minorities all have perspectives that are frequently overlooked by children's book editors.

5.   In the marketplace unfortunately stereotypes are popular.

6.   After all books reflect the values of our society.

7.   If we rely on commercial publishers to be more sensitive we are making a mistake.

8.   In our local communities we have to begin to consider the values transmitted by those little books found in the supermarket.

9.   Parents as well as caregivers and early childhood education teachers have to take responsibility for selecting books that give positive images to all children.

10.   If we the adults don't bother how can we expect stereotypes and misconceptions to disappear?

Exercise 15.3

Insert commas where necessary in the following passage.

My aunt Vida loves gardens especially her own near Sissyhurst but she has never visited Butchart Gardens 20 km from Victoria BC. She doesn't know what she is missing. The gardens especially beautiful in spring and summer are a beautiful place to visit. When young Jenny Butchart started these gardens years ago in 1904 she hardly knew a daisy from a daffodil. Faced with an ugly scar after her husband had quarried limestone she decided to create a sunken garden. "You'll never do it" friends said knowing her ignorance of gardening. "Of course I will. After all" she replied defiantly "where there's a will there's a way."

First she had to collect rocks into piles for her raised flower beds and then she had tons of topsoil carted in from neighbouring farms. Now visitors are entranced by Italian and Japanese gardens, not to mention the wonderful rose garden. Open all seasons no matter what the weather the gardens are especially romantic illuminated by hundreds of hidden lights on summer evenings. April with the hyacinths tulips rhododendrons and 550 cherry trees is my favourite time.

The Apostrophe

Sometimes students get very worried about apostrophes and throw them everywhere they see an -*s*, in regular plurals, even in verbs. That's a mistake. This mistake is sometimes known as *the shopkeeper's apostrophe.* Why? Because nervous shopkeepers want to be correct, but don't know the rules, so they throw in an apostrophe to be on the safe side. Then you get signs like *Passport Photo's in Five Minute's.*

There's no need to worry about apostrophes. Why? First, apostrophes are an endangered species on the autoroute of clear expression. Only Germanic-based languages require them, and in a digital global world of expression, they are seriously underused. By the year 2052, you may not have to bother about them.

Second, there are only two key rules to worry about. Omitting an apostrophe usually does not affect meaning, so when in doubt, leave it out. Still, educated people know how to use apostrophes. Learn the rules, apply them, and fret no more.

STEPS TO SUCCESS

The Apostrophe

1. An apostrophe indicates ownership. One rule covers all for the owner's apostrophe: **The apostrophe comes after the owner.** Ask yourself who or what owns it, them, whatever. Who or what does it, they, whatever belong to?

    Who owns it?

    The student's lockers = lockers belonging to one student

    The students' lockers = lockers belonging to more than one student

    Ulysses' adventures = the adventures of Ulysses

    Women's rights = the rights of women

    Children's laughter = the laughter of children

    If a noun already ends in -*s*, and -'*s* makes the possessive sound awkward, just put an apostrophe after the -*s*.

    Ladies' shoes

    The sausages' smell

    The Joneses' snowmobile

It helps sometimes if you use the expression *of* or *of the* in your head before placing the apostrophe.

> The kindness of strangers—the strangers' kindness
>
> The smoking of the tenant—the tenant's smoking

2. An apostrophe indicates the omission of a letter or letters. In contractions, the apostrophe replaces the omitted letter or letters.

> does not = doesn't
>
> I am = I'm
>
> it is = it's
>
> they are = they're
>
> who is = who's

Contractions like *wouldn't* and *isn't* are not favoured in formal writing. For reports, use the full expression, unless a light, informal tone is required.

3. Often, an apostrophe is used to form the plural of numbers, letters, words, and signs referred to as units.

> Britney's lowest grade was in the 80's.
>
> There are two *r*'s and two *s*'s in embarrass.
>
> Too many no's and not enough yes's, I'm afraid.
>
> She has six +'s and four -'s.

The plural of a number may simply have an *-s* added to it.

> The temperature was in the 30s all the time.

A number written has no apostrophe.

> It was all sixes and sevens.

An apostrophe is not necessary for the plural of a year.

> The Dirty Thirties means the 1930s, not Uncle Romeo's age.
>
> The sixties did not end until 1974.

Note: *it's* stands for *it is* only. The possessive *its* has no apostrophe ever. It is like *his, hers, ours, yours, theirs.* (When in doubt, leave it out.)

Exercise 15.4*

Use apostrophes as necessary in the following sentences. They are taken randomly, with apologies to George Sims, from his affecting ballad, *Billy's Rose*, a best-seller in 1879.

1. Billys dead and gone to glory—so is Billys sister, Nell.

2. Theres a tale I know about them; were I poet, I would tell.

3. In that vile and filthy alley, long ago one winters day.

4. While beside him sat his sister in the garrets dismal gloom.

5. Cheering with her gentle presence, Billys pathway to the tomb.

6. This was Nells idea of Heaven.

7. Oh the children look so happy and theyre all so strong and well.

8. Let us run away and join them if theres room for me and you.

9. Where a drunken fathers curses and a drunken fathers blows.

10. Drove her forth into the gutter, from the days dawn to its close.

Exercise 15.5*

Give both the singular and plural possessive form of the following words in italics.

Example

the *company* policy

Singular: company's

Plural: companies'

1. the *youth* name/s

2. the *hero* leg/s

3. the *community* centre/s

4. the *parent* expectations

5. the *mouse* hole/s

6. the *bus* route/s

7. the *woman* money

8. her/their *life* work

9. the *taxi* driver/s

10. the *baby* bottle/s

Exercise 15.6*

Write the possessive using an apostrophe for each of the following expressions.

1. the leather jackets of Bruno

2. the anti-gang police squad of Metro Toronto

3. the revenge of Daniel bar Jamin

4. the people of Inuvik

5. the students of the wizards

6. the rumpus of Max

7. the books of Maurice Sendak

8. the sentiments of Lucretia Mott

9. the children of today

10. the attitude of society

Exercise 15.7

Choose the word in parentheses that students should have used in these sentences from student papers.

1. If *(dog's, dogs, dogs')* _____ are a *(man's, mans', mans)* _____ best friend, then a golden retriever is surely the best of those best friends.

2. She first heard *(voice's, voices', voices)* _____ from Iran trying to contact her at *(Guses, Gus's, Guses')* _____ seance.

3. In *(todays, today's, todays')* _____ society, with women like Margaret Atwood around, a man has to be able to justify his conduct.

4. After a *(weeks, week's, weeks')* _____ hard work, I finally began to understand the *(bodys, bodies, body's)* _____ reactions he had been talking about all semester.

5. In those days they had *(girls, girl's, girls')* _____ entrances and separate ones for *(boy's, boys, boys')* _____.

6. The humming noise sounded like *(thousand's, thousands, thousands')* _____ of bees.

7. Women have to teach men how to be human, but *(whose, who's, whos')* _____ going to teach them first, I'd like to know.

8. If their *(actions', action's, actions)* _____ are as good as their *(word's, words, words')* _____, they will make great improvements in our environment.

9. Many of *(Orwells, Orwell's, Orwells')* _____ bleakest ideas about *(society's, societies' societies)* _____ future are just accepted as normal today.

10. Because his sense of *(humours, humour's, humours')* _____ so strange, many people overlook his kind heart.

Exercise 15.8

Correct the apostrophe use in the following passage.

Its not surprising really, that one former Surgeon General in America is on record as saying that its the height of hypocrisy for the United States to export tobacco, when the United States wants foreign government's to stop the export of cocaine. In one year in the United States, 2,000 people died from cocaine use; however, that same year, cigarettes' killed over half a million. At the time, the Surgeon Generals comment's on these figure's received little new's coverage. Instead, the American network's broadcast 163 cocaine-related story's after a presidents speech denouncing drug use.

For 20 year's, Thailand has had a successful anti-smoking campaign, but it's proposal for a total ban on cigarette consumption upset the major tobacco company's. To find new addicts' the tobacco industry need's 2.5 million new smoker's a year. Its making an effort to do just that in Asia. Whats new about the United States tobacco industries quest for addicts, anyway? In the nineteenth century, the British exported 11,000 ton's of opium a year into China to keep the Chinese quiet.

Capitalization

Capitals are important because people often notice if you don't use them correctly.

STEPS TO SUCCESS

Capitalization

1. Capitalize the name of a particular person, place, or thing.

    King Bruno the Questionable

    Chief Dan George

    Tickle Cove Creek

    the Far North

    Wu-Tang Clan

2. Capitalize brand names, languages, titles, races, nationalities, specific courses, specific institutions, religions, famous religious writings, days of the week, months, specific holidays.

    Whiteout toothpaste

    English

    Mayor Christy Crawford

    Chinese

    Canadian

    Psychology 101

    Keewatin District Health Centre

    Buddhism

    Qur'an

    Thursday

    November

    Thanksgiving

3. Capitalize the first word of a sentence, of the close of a letter, of a direct quotation.

    Sometimes students do not concentrate.

    Sincerely yours,

    She yelled after him, "Liar, liar, pants on fire."

4. *Do not* capitalize generic terms, seasons of the year, regular stuff.

    Go west, young man.

    If winter comes, can spring be far behind?

    Their grandfather never went to school.

    He was admitted to hospital that afternoon.

Exercise 15.9*

Capitalize where required in the following paragraph.

It took many years before african-americans were seen on television. although television was the technological wonder at the 1939 new york world's fair, it did not come into many North American households until early in the fifties. then it was not until 1957 with the nat king cole show that african-americans were finally given an honest image and a black host for a show. previously black people had been cast as servants or buffoons. later roots, the miniseries, was a runaway hit. in fact, three of its episodes rank among television's top shows of all time. nearly 100 million viewers saw the last episode. now with stars like bill cosby, oprah winfrey and will smith, african-americans continue to make a big impression on the small screen.

Exercise 15.10

Correct capitalization where necessary in the following passage.

One of the hottest stocks on the Market Today is Naipaul neighbours corporation. Naipaul neighbours corporation has introduced a Special Wall Unit guaranteed to soundproof any Wall. The Company insists that $800 is a Reasonable Price to pay to keep out the noise of your neighbours' Tv, Stereo, quarrels, crying babies, or parties. Sunil Naipaul, Chairman of the Company, was clear at a Press Conference at the scarborough town centre that we all need our privacy.

"the biggest need any Human Being has is privacy," he said. "if we have to live in each other's pockets, then let us at least live in Soundproof Pockets. My special wall unit, the Trinidad Trammel, has Sound-deadening Devices built in. Sound Waves from an adjacent wall do not affect It. It comes in two sizes, Large and Small."

Mr. Naipaul who studied Data Processing and Fluid Power courses at a College in ontario is happy with the success of the trinidad trammel. So are his Customers. Residents of an Apartment Building in don mills all agree that they have felt reduced stress and better social adjustment since the trinidad Trammel was installed in their walls as an experiment. The Collective Behaviour of the residents in this Building is one of the reasons that stock in naipaul neighbours corporation is booming.

Semicolons and Colons

A semicolon ties closely related thoughts together. A colon lets readers know that a piece of related information will follow.

STEPS TO SUCCESS

Semicolons and Colons

1. A semicolon may be used between two independent clauses (complete statements). Use a semicolon if the clauses are closely connected in meaning, and if used with conjunctive adverbs (transitional expressions).

> On Mondays Ms Fudge is tired from the weekend; however, you should see her on Tuesdays.

> As soon as he received the assignment, Tommy began his research; consequently, he was not affected by the flood in the library.

2. Use a semicolon in a wordy list where each item is long, or has a comma in it already.

> When Sappho went to Delphi she took with her many distractions: the new recording of *Let Love Rule*; some of her friend Corinna's poems; a copy of Diotima's works; and the essay she was writing for her Mythology course with Dorothy.

3. A colon introduces information. It comes *before*

> a. a list where the subject of the list is named

> Chatwin visited many *continents*: Africa, Asia, Australia, South America.

> b. a long quotation

> In her editorial, Beatrice writes: "It is time to give caregivers, homemakers, and pensioners a say in the decision making too. They know better than anyone the need for tough legislation enforcing occupational health and safety standards."

> c. the minutes, when dividing hours and minutes

> 4:30, 2:15

4. But, use colons *after*

> d. the expressions *as follows, the following*

> On his way to Mars, Zaphod saw the following: his half-cousin, two white mice, three coffee cups, and a partridge in a pear tree.

> e. the salutation in a business letter

> Dear Ms Hustler:

Note: *Do not* put a colon directly after the verb *to be*.

> **Not:** There are: roots, leaves, flowers for eyewashes.
>
> **But:** There are roots, leaves, flowers for eyewashes.
>
> **Or:** There are many plant sources for eyewashes: roots, leaves, flowers.

Exercise 15.11

Add semicolons, commas, and apostrophes where necessary in the following sentences from student papers.

1. In many ways their school system is similar to ours both systems expect high standards in math but not in language skills.

2. Perhaps with AIDS and STDs destroying todays young people there will be a return to sexual puritanism there might even be a whole new puritan cult coming soon.

3. In todays society peoples opinions are formed more by television than by newspapers we may have mass circulation but how many people go beyond the headlines and sports results?

4. Freezing temperatures in Floridas citrus orchards mean higher prices in Canadas supermarkets however Canadians will still want to drink orange or grapefruit juice every morning, they need Vitamin C for the winter.

5. Hundreds of boxers suffer from brain damage they may not have been born stupid, now however some of them don't even know their own phone numbers.

6. They don't think at all about the trouble people are going to have with a machine like that, instead all they think about is selling as many as possible.

7. With food delivered through grills in the wall at anyones command nobody would starve nobody would enjoy eating much either.

8. With one famine after another crops dying people starving most of the country has lost hope, funny though that all essential aid and free medicine come from developed countries, not from all the rich people living there already.

9. If people would just be less selfish, for example turn off their engine while waiting, set their thermostat one degree lower in winter the air would stay cleaner.

10. It is very difficult to understand such patterns of behaviour especially the behaviour in cities people behave strangely right in front of you in cities like Toronto.

Review the Overview of Punctuation box at the beginning of this chapter, if necessary, and try the following exercises.

Exercise 15.12*

Decide which of the following sentences are correct. Correct the sentences with errors.

1. One of the most famous sailors in history was a tall good-looking farm boy who's first job was selling groceries, this country lad was James Cook, his voyages of discovery would make him famous.

2. James Cook circled the globe three times he mapped islands in the pacific that no european had ever seen he found a way to prevent the disease of scurvy.

3. Over six feet tall with brown hair and dark eyes, James was much taller and stronger than the other apprentices on his first voyage.

4. He quickly became a good sailor: learning to climb the rigging to hoist anchor; and to steer the ship.

5. When he wasn't working at sea, he was reading and studying mathematics; at sea he studied charts and learned how to use a compass.

6. The life of a sailor in the British Navy was far from pleasant at that time. A sailor could expect terrible working conditions. bad pay; a poor diet the chance of falling ill with scurvy.

7. It was a surprising decision; therefore, when James Cook at the age of 27 turned down the command of a merchant vessel; and joined the British Navy.

8. His first mission; as master of a new 64-gun ship, the pembroke, was to take soldiers to canada where at the mouth of the St. lawrence river; he was to undertake a dangerous assignment.

9. The English wanted to capture an important fort at the edge of the river; Cook was told to make charts of the river and find the location

of hidden rocks. With a carefully chosen group of men, he measured the waters secretly night after night, within range of the French guns.

10. The charts he made were absolutely accurate, when the british sailed large ships up the st. lawrence; not one ship ran aground.

Exercise 15.13

Insert quotation marks and correct punctuation where necessary in the following paragraph.

Some merchants went to an Eastern sovereign and asked him would you like to buy some very fine horses the ruler said he would. you know he announced and he gave the merchants a bag of gold I would like some more horses like these. Not long after the sovereign ordered his highest officer, the vizier, to make out a list of all the fools in his kingdom. When the sovereign saw his own name at the head of the list he yelled Why is my name there? Because replied the vizier you entrusted a bag of gold to men you dont know. these men he said will never come back. but said the king suppose they do come back? in that case sighed the vizier i shall erase your name and insert theirs.

Exercise 15.14

Correct any punctuation errors in the following passage.

In 1931 the chicago herald tribune knew just what was needed a police adventure comic strip. chester gould using both realism and exaggeration created dick tracy. dick tracy is a detective in a big city. the city is anonymous but easily recognized as chicago honest with unshakable integrity dick tracy is the terror of gangster's swindler's spies and other troublemaker's. not even his sweetheart tess trueheart his superior chief brandon nor bribes offered by his enemies can ever shake tracys sense of duty. he battle's corruption in the big city assisted by faithful helpers like pat patton.

comic books introduced fantasy and variety into everyday monotonous lives they allowed their readers to meet an amazing bunch of people like superman, batman the human torch wonder woman the flash.

back in the thirties the code of the comics magazine association of america insisted on the following

respect for parents the moral code and for honorable behaviour.

policemen judges government officials and respected institutions shall never be presented in such a way as to create disrespect for established authority in every instance good shall triumph over evil and the criminal shall be punished for his misdeeds

It is interesting to note today that as violence rose in our culture so too did it rise in comic books the early ones' are now seen as examples of youthful innocence.

Spelling

With spell checker available, many people feel that their spelling worries are over, and so they are—mostly. If you use spell checker, you are now able to spell *convenient* or *visibility* correctly. But what about the homonym horrors and word confusions that can make people laugh or worse, think you don't know what you are doing?

Some grammar checkers will point out if you have a problem, but they won't be able to tell you if you are using the correct form in your paper. That's why it's wise to learn which word goes where to avoid word confusions.

It's also wise to learn a few basic spelling rules and their exceptions. You know the difference between *rapping* and *raping*, between *hopping* and *hoping*, but do you know what the rule is? If you do, then you will never be guilty of placing the zombie word *writting* on your pages.

STEPS TO SUCCESS

Spelling

1. Keep a notebook of your personal spelling difficulties and review about three words a day.

2. Write down each word in several different ways, highlighting the spot that gives you trouble.

3. Look closely at each word, noting the syllables.

ath*letic*	*LIBRA*ry
BUS*iness*	ligh*tning*
*bu*SINess	*mis*CHIEV*ous*
can*did*ates	pro*BAB*ly
film	sur*prise*

4. Say the word aloud, pronouncing it correctly. (Not li*berry,* but lib*RARY;* not *Feberry, but* Feb*RUARY.)*

5. Use sayings as memory aids.

> There's a *lie* in the middle of be*lie*ve.
>
> There's a *rat* in sepa*rat*e.
>
> You *hear* with your *ear.*
>
> De*finitely* is *finite.*
>
> *Emma* is in a dil*emma.*
>
> There are four *s's* in *possess.*
>
> There is only one *e* in *argument.*
>
> *Stationery* is pap*er.*
>
> *Rain* is part of *weather.*

6. Use a dictionary often. Carry one with you; print or electronic, it doesn't matter. Don't leave home without it.

7. Proofread everything you write. Use spell checker as well.

8. Stop saying, "I've never been able to spell," and smiling.

9. Learn some spelling rules and their exceptions.

SPELLING RULES

1. *I* before *e*
Except after *c*
Or when sounding like *ay*
As in *neighbour* and *weigh.*

bel*ie*ve	*ei*ght	rec*ei*pt	sl*ei*gh
c*ei*ling	fr*ei*ght	rec*ei*ve	v*ei*l
conc*ei*t	gr*ie*f	rel*ie*f	v*ei*n
dec*ei*ve	p*ie*ce	shr*ie*k	y*ie*ld

Exceptions

an*cie*nt	*ei*ther	h*ei*r	spe*cie*s
cod*ei*ne	finan*cie*r	l*ei*sure	s*ei*ze
cons*cie*nce	for*ei*gn	n*ei*ther	w*ei*rd

Make up ways of remembering the exceptions. Try sentences like: The foreign financier seized the codeine formula. Those ancient species liked weird leisure activities without hygiene.

2. When adding *-ing* or *-ed* to a verb

> a. If the word ends in *-e*, drop it.

boring	dancing
coming	writing

> b. If a verb ends in *-y*, keep it.

flying	playing	studying

> c. If a verb ends with a short vowel and a consonant, double it.

beginning	omitted	rapping
hopping	planning	stripping
kidding	preferred	

3. **Watch plurals.** Most nouns add *-s* to create the plural form.

> Sharon has one cat. Jobi has three cats.
>
> BUT
>
> a. When a plural means an extra syllable, add *-es*.

birches	businesses	glasses
boxes	churches	kisses
buses	dresses	
bushes	foxes	

> b. When a noun ends in *-y*, change the final *-y* to *-i* and add *-es*.

baby/babies	family/families
company/companies	sky/skies
country/countries	

> c. Some nouns ending in *-f* change to *-ves* in the plural.

calf/calves	life/lives	wharf/wharves
knife/knives	loaf/loaves	wife/wives

> **Exceptions**

chief/chiefs	dwarf/dwarfs	roof/roofs

d. Many nouns ending in -*o*, add -*es*.

echo/echoes   potato/potatoes

hero/heroes   tomato/tomatoes

Exceptions

piano/pianos   soprano/sopranos

radio/radios   studio/studios

e. Words from Latin and Greek origin may form their plurals according to rules of those languages.

alumnus/alumni	datum/data
analysis/analyses	hypothesis/hypotheses
antenna/antennae	index/indices
appendix/appendices	medium/media
bacillus/bacilli	oasis/oases
crisis/crises	parenthesis/parentheses
criterion/criteria	phenomenon/phenomena

Exercise 15.15*

Supply the missing letters, *ie* or *ei*, in the following words.

1. ach___ve	8. for__gn	15. n__ce
2. agenc__s	9. fr__ght	16. rec__ve
3. anxiet__s	10. fr__nd	17. retr__ve
4. bel__ve	11. identit__s	18. s___ge
5. ch__f	12. interv__w	19. v__l
6. cod__ne	13. l__sure	20. w__gh
7. dec__ved	14. misch__f	

Exercise 15.16*

Decide which of the following words are spelled correctly. Write the correct version of any misspelled words. Try to do this exercise in 3 minutes.

1. beginer
2. conscious
3. convience
4. decibel
5. desparate
6. discription
7. enviroment
8. exagerate
9. expences
10. loneliness

11. maintenance
12. medecine
13. personel
14. precentage
15. proffessor
16. resourses
17. secetary
18. summery
19. technique
20. tommorrow

Exercise 15.17

Choose the correct version of the word in each of the following sets.

1. (a) buisness (b) business (c) bussiness
2. (a) definatly (b) definitly (c) definitely
3. (a) unecessary (b) unnecessary (c) unecessry
4. (a) thirtieth (b) thirtyeth (c) thirtyth
5. (a) conscious (b) conscous (c) conscientous
6. (a) controled (b) controlled (c) conntrolled
7. (a) predjudice (b) prejudism (c) prejudice
8. (a) lonliness (b) lonlieness (c) loneliness
9. (a) radios (b) radioes (c) radiios
10. (a) separate (b) seperate (c) sepperate
11. (a) exxagerate (b) exagerate (c) exaggerate

12. (a) goverment (b) government (c) governement

13. (a) mischievous (b) mischievious (c) misschievous

14. (a) comittee (b) comitee (c) committee

15. (a) truely (b) trully (c) truly

16. (a) occassionally (b) occasionaly (c) occasionally

17. (a) privilege (b) privelege (c) priviledge

18. (a) acomodate (b) accommodate (c) accomodate

19. (a) appearence (b) appearance (c) apparence

20. (a) acheivment (b) achievment (c) achievement

Word Confusions

These are the real troublemakers. Spelling *convenient* and *visibility* correctly is not enough. You must avoid word confusions. While you probably wouldn't confuse *fissure* and *fisher*, or *clause* and *claws*, what if you slip up with *your* and *you're*, *who's* and *whose*? Study the common word confusions that follow.

accept, except

> Mitsou accepted the roses graciously.
>
> If they except the cost of transportation, those figures are fine.
>
> Everyone except Luigi wore a golf chain.
>
> *accept:* (verb) to receive
>
> *except:* (verb) to leave out; (preposition) excluding, like *ex-wife*, *ex-lover*

advice, advise

> Be nice, and take that free advice.
>
> I don't advise that small size.
>
> *advice:* (noun) a recommendation for a course of action (like *ice*, *advice* is a noun)
>
> *advise:* (verb) to suggest; to recommend

affect, effect

Mitsou's singing affected him deeply.

The new leader effected many changes.

The special effects in that movie were terrific.

affect: (verb) to influence. Affect is **always** an **action** and never has an article *(a, the)* nearby, but effect can be a noun and a verb

effect: (verb) to accomplish; bring about; (noun) the result

allusion, illusion

Proton did not understand Dolly's allusion to *Paradise Lost* when she talked about her childhood in Owen Sound.

Dolly, luckily, had no illusions about Proton's literary background.

allusion: (noun) indirect reference

illusion: (noun) mistaken idea

aloud, allowed

Dolly actually told him that aloud.

You are not allowed to smoke there.

aloud: (adverb) spoken, or in a loud voice

allowed: (verb) permitted; approved (two *l*'s, two *t*'s, two *p*'s)

already, all ready

The race was not over, but Dolly already knew that she had won.

The children were all ready and waiting patiently.

already: (adverb) previously; before

all ready: (adjective) all = entirely; ready = prepared

altogether, all together

She looks altogether different since her facelift.

When we are all together, we are happy.

altogether: (adverb) completely

all together: (adverb) in a group

beside, besides

Proton promised Dolly. "I'll walk beside you through life's darkest hours."

Sunnybrook Hospital offers many rehabilitation programs besides the Heart Program.

beside: (preposition) near

besides: (preposition) in addition to

choose, chose

Will Dolly choose shoes or a rose?

I do not choose to go with him.

Dolly chose a rose.

choose: (verb) to select; to pick out; to want to do something

chose: (verb) past tense of *choose*

compliment, complement

Otto blushed when Gladys complimented him.

That red carpet really complements the majesty of the staircase.

compliment: (verb) an expression of praise

complement: (verb) to complete

conscious, conscience

Hermann was conscious of the pain.

"Thus conscience doth make cowards of us all." *(William Shakespeare)*

Let conscience be your guide.

conscious: (adjective) aware; able to respond

conscience: (noun) literally, "with knowledge," from Latin (*con* = with and *scientia* = knowledge; conscience = the knowledge of right and wrong)

council, counsel

The city council voted in favour of banning prostitution.

Her counsel was wise.

Dolly's psychiatrist counselled her to change her mind.

council: (noun) group of people

counsel: (noun) advice; (verb) to consult, give guidance

course, coarse

In college, Proton tried to choose easy courses.

That fabric is too coarse for Dolly's delicate skin.

course: (noun) route taken

coarse: (adjective) crass; lacking in delicacy; vulgar

fewer, less

The fewer the English teachers, the less the literacy.

Fewer: (adjective) concerned with countable amount

Less: (adjective) concerned with quantity

Can you count the subject?

If yes, use *fewer.* If no, use *less.*

You can count chairs, but not furniture: *fewer* chairs.

You can count minutes, but not time: *less* time.

For units of time with *than,* use *less:*

We have *less than* three days left of vacation.

Less than 30 years ago, I was a star athlete.

formerly, formally

Formerly, she wrote her novels on a battered old typewriter.

The Queen greeted Proton formally on the steps of Buckingham Palace.

formerly: (adverb) earlier in time; once

formally: (adverb) done with ceremony; showing a sense of form

forth, fourth

We shall go forth together into the sunset.

Dolly placed Proton fourth on her list.

forth: (adverb) forward

fourth: (adjective) describing four

handicap, handicapped

It can be a handicap not being able to spell.

Proton was always handicapped by his spelling.

handicap: (noun) disability

handicapped: (adjective) hindered by

hole, whole

Alice fell down the hole.

On the whole, our time in Timbuktu was worth it.

Gogol read the whole book before he bought the film rights.

hole: (noun) cavity

whole: (noun) having all its parts; (adjective) complete

its, it's

The cow chewed its cud.

It's really silly not to realize that a letter has been left out.

its: (possessive adjective) belonging to it

it's: (contraction) it is

knew, new

Jacob said he knew Sarah well.

Have you seen the new Porches?

knew: (verb) past tense of *know* (to have knowledge of)

new: (adjective) recent

loose, lose

Good heavens, the goose is loose.

Aline hoped Jean would not lose the election.

loose: (adjective) not tied up; free

lose: (verb) to fail; not able to find; be defeated

moral, morale

Don't trust Moloch; he has no morals.

Ben's low morale caused his defeat.

moral: (noun) concern with good or bad behaviour

morale: (noun) state of mind

no, know

It's a no-no not to know the difference.

no: (adjective) negative, not

know: (noun) to have knowledge

past, passed

All that is past and best forgotten.

The Jaguar passed the Jetta on the hill.

past: (adverb) earlier in time

passed: (verb) past tense of *pass*

patience, patients

Mimi showed surprising patience with the patients.

patience: (noun) the virtue

patients: (noun) the people

peace, piece

We hope there will be peace in our time.

What I need is a piece of cake.

peace: (noun) period of calm without hostilities

piece: (noun) part of

personal, personnel

Gogol took a personal interest in the lower depths of the production.

The Human Resources Department is in charge of personnel at the college.

personal: (adjective) relating to a person

personnel: (noun) a number of persons in an organization, company, or service

presents, presence

"Christmas won't be Christmas without presents," Jo sighed.

Dolly could always make her presence felt.

presents: (noun) gifts

presence: (noun) being there; ability to be in charge

principal, principle

Make sure Proton repays Dolly the principal of the loan, at least, and worry about the interest later.

The principal of my high school could not handle the Untouchables.

The principal reason Proton stayed at that high school was Dolly.

Proton found it easy to explain the principles of the binary tree.

Gambling was against his principles.

principal: (noun) sum of money; head of a school;

(adjective) main; chief

principle: (noun) code of conduct; rule

quite, quiet

My Grade 4 teacher was quite determined to have a quiet classroom.

quite: (adverb) really, truly; entirely

quiet: (adjective) little or no noise (two syllables, like quiet)

rap, wrap

Proton likes to rap about social problems.

Dolly likes to wrap up warmly.

Both can be connected with parties, but with a *w* you'd be *w*armer. After all, you might have finished making a movie, so you'd be *w*armed by your achievement.

rap: a sharp blow; a rhythmic rhyme to rocking rhythm

wrap: (noun) soft covering; (verb) cover, finish something

right, write

Free speech is considered a constitutional right in this country.

Down Under they do not drive on the right.

We all learned how to write, but he never did learn how to spell.

right: (noun) a just claim; (adjective) not the left

write: (verb) hand-eye coordination is involved

site, sight, cite

The site of the attack was chosen for its economic power.

What a sight! You look a fright!

Jon cited Struthers as an important influence.

site: (noun) place or location

sight: (noun) the ability to be able to see; something worth seeing

cite: (verb) mention; quote with respect

tents, tense

Campers shouldn't leave food in their tents.

I'm always tense when I look down from the CN Tower.

tents: (noun) shelters, usually canvas or some other fabric

tense: (adjective) not relaxed

their, there, they're

Their espressos are on the table.

There they are.

There was once a place called Tiflis.

They're in love.

their: (possessive adjective) possessive of they, remember the *I*. "I" am a person; "the*i*r" relates to people.

there: (adverb) in that place; introduces statements; similar to *here*

they're: (contraction) they are (write in full, if easily confused)

then, than

Then Sydney Carton stepped up to the scaffold.

"It is a far, far, better thing I do, than I have ever done," he said.

then: (adverb) at a particular time in the past

than: (conjunction) for comparative statements

thorough, through, threw

Dolly was thorough in her preparations for the party.

She roared through the crowd.

They threw the baby out with the baby water.

thorough: (adjective) fully finished

through: (preposition) in one end and out the other

threw: (verb) past tense of *throw*, to project something with force

to, too, two

To err is human, to forgive divine.

She took the train to Toronto.

Think of the dove who thought he was an owl.

To-whit, to-whoo, too silly to coo.

She ordered tea for two.

to: (preposition) shows position, progression, arrival, or introduces the infinitive part of a verb

too: (adverb) to a greater extent than is desired; in addition

two: (noun) the answer to 1 + 1

we're, where, wear

We're wondering where to wear our spangles.

we're: (contraction) we are

where: (adverb) in or at which place

wear: (verb) have on, as clothing

weather, whether

The greenhouse effect seems to be affecting the weather.

With the greenhouse effect, I can't decide whether to invest in a ski resort or a golf course.

weather: (noun) the conditions of climate that affect us

whether: (conjunction) introducing alternatives

Write this rhyme out very quickly and see whether you weather all the weathers:

Whether the weather be fine

Or whether the weather be not

We'll weather the weather

Whatever the weather

Whether we like it or not.

whose, who's

I don't know whose car it is.

Who's he with tonight?

Who's been sitting on my *chaise longue*?

whose: (adjective) possessive of who

who's: (contraction) who is or who has

woman, women

"What does a woman want?" asked Sigmund.

"Women want you to take out the garbage," replied Germaine.

"Women understand men; few men understand women." (read it backwards, word by word)

woman: (noun) one adult female

women: (noun) two or more adult females

Note: one *man,* but two or more *men.*

write, right, rite

Dolly will write to Proton with an explanation.

She knew her results were not right.

Graduation is seen as a rite of passage.

write: (verb) forming shapes, symbols to communicate to readers

right: (noun) correct; morally fair; not left

rite: (noun) solemn ritual or event marking a special stage in life

your, you're

You'll get your wish at midnight.

"You're crazy," Dolly told Proton.

your: (possessive adjective) of or belonging to you

you're: (contraction) you are

yours, yaws

Did you get yours today?

The unsightly infection yaws is contracted near the Equator.

yours: (possessive pronoun) belonging to you

yaws: (noun) a contagious tropical skin disease (actually, this last one is never a problem in Canada, but it's best to be prepared these days)

Then there are:

aunt/ant	horde/hoard	soul/sole
bread/bred	lien/lean	throne/thrown
decent/descent	malt/moult	told/tolled
dessert/desert	mousse/moose	toxin/tocsin
dyeing/dying	phial/file	veil/vale
flare/flair	prey/pray	which/witch

and many, many more.

Proofreading Exercises

Proofreading is an essential writing habit. Why? It prevents IRS. It also allows you to eliminate the basic errors that not only upset readers, but also make them stop reading.

When you speak, you have no way of changing your words once spoken. Your body language, your apologies, your excuses may help you when you have made a mistake, but words once spoken cannot be changed.

When you write, however, you have the chance to review, revise, rewrite, and proofread. Sensible writers do all these activities to be kind to their readers. Sensible writers look at their words and sentences and check them for accuracy and correctness. They literally clean up their act. In the exercises that follow, you get the chance to practise this kind of grammar checking and word-cleaning. Happy proofreading.

Exercise 15.18*

Choose the correct word in parentheses in the following sentences.

1. *(It's, its)* _____ *(to, too, two)* bad that the *(plain, plane)* _____ is not about to take *(off, of, off of)* _____ right *(know, now)* _____ because *(its, it's)* _____ a beautiful *(site, cite, sight)* _____.

2. *(It's, its)* _____ an OB-70 and *(it's, its)* _____ structure has *(flair, flare)* _____ because it is complex and exciting.

3. Supercomputers played a *(cuticle, critical)* _____ role in *(it's, its)* _____ design.

4. The OB-70 entered service 3 years after *(it's, its)* _____ rival, the Strato J. Parkes, and the design was criticized for adding to the *(wait, wake, weight)* _____ of the *(plain, plane)* _____ and *(it's, its)* _____ cost.

5. *(It's, Its)* _____ a response to the *(advice, advise)* _____ of the *(bored, board)* _____ for more fuel-efficient aircraft.

6. The OB-70 was *(past, passed)* _____ over to the production team, who needed a boost in *(morals, morale, morales)* _____.

7. The *(personal, personnel, personel)* _____ *(there, their, they're)* _____ did a great job.

8. *(It's, Its)* _____ a *(simular, similiar, similar)* _____ design in many ways to *(its, it's)* _____ predecessor, but exactly *(whose, who's)* _____ responsible, *(you're, your, youre)* _____ not to *(know, now)* _____.

9. The *(principal, principle)* _____ of the design team is never to state *(aloud, allowed, alowd)* _____ the name of the person *(who's, whose, whos)* _____ responsible for most of the work.

10. The engines *(then, than)* _____ are mounted in front of the wing, to avoid adding to the *(wait, weight)* _____ of the *(plain, plane)* _____ and *(it's, its)* _____ cost.

Exercise 15.19

Choose the correct word in parentheses in the following passage.

The most *(effective, affective)* _____ teacher I ever had for history in high school was my Aunt Sharon's husband, Eldon J. *(Quiet, Quite)* _____ a *(quiet, quite)* _____, even shy, person, he was always enthusiastic about his subject and encouraged active rather than *(pasive, passive)* _____ *(learning, leaning)* _____.

None of his students ever felt that *(they, he, she, he or she)* _____ had taken Eldon J.'s *(course, coarse)* _____ in *(vain, vein)* _____. I *(rember, remeber, remember)* _____ going to class the first week in Grade 12. Some of the boys were very rowdy and clearly *(conscience, contientious, conscious)* _____ that summer was over for *(an other, another)* _____ year, *(due to the fact that, because)* _____ school had begun. Eldon J. showed *(patience, patients)* _____ with *(there, their, they're)* _____ behaviour and settled them down without *(incident, incidence)* _____. He *(must of, must have)* _____ *(knowen, known)* _____ what it was like to face winter and weekly tests in a *(prarie, prairie)* _____ classroom.

I *(know, now, knew)* _____ Eldon J. *(then, than)* _____ handed out a list of books and *(articles, articals)* _____. I *(rember, remeber, remember)* _____ that <u>Ten Lost Years</u> and <u>That Scatterbrain Bookie</u> were on it. He told us *(it would be necessary to, to)* _____ find out about the Depression in Canada. We had to do research *(to, in such a manner as to)* _____ become *(familiar, familar, familier)* _____ with the Depression and to discover how complex the *(courses, causes)* _____ of people's suffering *(were, where)* _____.

(On account of, Because of) _____ Eldon J.'s creative approach to the teaching of history, we all became *(realy, really)* _____ involved with the subject ourselves *(meaning that, with the result that, so)* _____, many of the students from my Grade 12 class went on to study history *(farther, further)* _____, and one boy from the class, Walter, *(could not help but, could not avoid)* _____ researching the history of the Keewatin District. He published a book and *(recieved, received)* _____ many *(compliments, complements)* _____ for his work. Another of my classmates, Stewart, with his sister Ruthie, *(who's, whose)* _____ work on the *(pionneers, poineers, pioneers)* _____ in New France was translated into three *(languages, langages)* _____, was awarded the ECW Medal by Maude Barlow. *(It's, Its)* _____ wonderful the *(effect, affect)* _____ a good teacher has.

Exercise 15.20*

Choose the correct word in parentheses in the following passage.

My *(favorite, favourite)* _____ comic-book hero has always been Batman. *(Your, You're)* _____ sure that this *(capped, caped)* _____ crusader will clean up the dirt and make everything *(right, write)* _____. Batman *(whose, who'se)* _____ motive is, as every Batfan *(knoes, nose, knows)* _____, to avenge his *(parent's, parents')* _____ death, is a creature of the *(knight, night)* _____. He's *(quite, quiet)* _____ scary; he's a bat, an avenger of evil. Superman is a *(regular, reglar, regaler)* _____ guy, all-powerful and brightly *(coloured, colored)* _____, but Batman is dark and *(mysterous, mysterious)* _____. Still, this *(weird, wierd)* _____ figure of the dark is more man *(then, than)* _____ god, and the boy Robin helped us *(too, two, to)* _____ see him as *(human, humane)* _____.

Batman fights many foes. The Joker is a psychopath *(who's, whose)* _____ weapons include razor-sharp playing cards and rictus-inducing poisons. At present he is in an asylum, but as he's the most successful of Batman's *(adversarys, adversaries)* _____, he's sure to escape soon. The Riddler, with his brilliant mind, loves crimes involving riddles and *(dedly, deadly)* _____ traps. His *(principle, principal)* _____ ambition is to outwit Batman. Two-face, with his split personality, gets into *(alot, a lot)* _____ of evil situations. He kills when the *(scared, scarred)* _____ side of his face comes up at the flip of a coin.

Nowadays the evil forces that Batman is *(conscience, conscious)* _____ of are more likely to be savage mutant punks or terrorists *(then, than)* _____ aliens, but Batman *(who's, whose)* _____ been around for 50 years, still fights The Joker and other forces of darkness, even though he is perhaps a bit less popular now *(then, than)* _____ he used to be.

Exercise 15.21*

Choose the correct word in parentheses in the following passage.

If you want to *(apprehend, comprehend)* _____ the *(allusions, illusions)* _____ people often make in *(conversation, conversions)* _____, *(it's, its)* _____ a good idea to become *(familar, familiar)* _____ with some of the old Greek myths. Not only are these *(storys, stories, storeys)* _____ a *(sauce, source)* _____ of entertainment, they can also help you interpret paintings and sculptures, as well as family behaviour. Some of the *(storeys, stories, storys)* _____ are *(quite, quiet)* _____ sensational. Reading them will make you *(conscience, conscious)* _____ of how many of the ideas in our culture have *(developped, developed)* _____. In some versions, lurid details are omitted on *(morale, moral)* _____ grounds, but the *(storys, stories, storeys)* _____ still reveal the spiritual dimensions of our *(existance, existence, existants)* _____. Myth, as C. S. Lewis said, partially lifts the *(vale, veil, vaile)* _____ from the *(mysteris, mysterys, mysteries)* _____ of life through the *(medium, media)* _____ of story. If *(theres, theirs, there's)* _____ a *(lesson, lessen)* _____ to be learned from reading Greek myths, it is that these *(storys, storeys, stories)* _____ of *(ancient, anceint)* _____ times may reflect different ideas about the structure of the universe. After all, the Greeks *(believed, beleived)* _____ the Earth to be flat. No matter what the *(belief, beleif)* _____, human behaviour has always contained the seeds of joy and *(tragedy, tradegy)* _____, and the same dilemmas *(where, were)* _____ present *(than, then)* _____ in the human spirit.

Exercise 15.22

Correct the 24 spelling errors in the following passage.

A beatiful nymph, Echo, had one fault: She talked to much. That's no exageration. In chat or arguement she had to have the last word. One day Juno was searching for her husband who liked to amuse himself amoung the nymphs. Echo kept her talking untill the nymphs escaped. When Juno discovered she had been decieved, she took vengance by mutering this sentence: "You have cheated me. Now you shall forfiet the use of that tongue, accept for that one purpose you are so fond of, reply. You shall still have the last word, but know power to speak first."

Echo fell in love with the hansome youth, Narcissus, who went hunting in the mountains. She longed to make his aquaintance. One day, seperated from his companions, he shouted allowed, "Whose here?"

Echo replied, "Here."

Narcissus called, "Come."

Echo ansered, "Come."

As no one came, Narcissus called again, "Why do you shun me?"

Echo repeated the question.

"Let us join one another," called Narcissus.

Echo replied with all her heart, in the same words.

When she hurryed out, ready to fall into his arms, Narcissus backed away. "Hands off!" he snaped. "I would rather dye then you should have me!"

"Have me," she said in vein.

Narcissus left her and she hid in shame deep in the woods. From that time fourth, she lived in caves and mountain cliffs. She faded away with grief, till at last she shrank to nothing and her bones were changed into rocks. Their was nothing left of her but her voice. With that, she is still ready to reply to anyone who calls her, and she still has the last word.

Exercise 15.23

Find and eliminate all errors in the following passage.

Nucular power is suppose to be clean and safe, but names like Three Mile Island and Chernobyl does not inspire confidents in the pubic. Many experts now very well that the ellaborate safety devises and the bakeup systems of the plants theirselfs is evidence enough of how dangerous nucuar power plants is considered to be. Radioactive wastes, they knows, remains dangerous for thousands' of years. How many poeple live that long?

Officals and experts in the power plants claim's that they have taken all precautions nessary, they say accidents can be foreseen and prevented. But who predict accidents? Accidents are allways supprises by defanition, if they are foreseen they do not hapen.

Nucular experts and plant employees are expected to act with perfect competance in handelling a accident, however poeple in power plant are human bean's and are just as likely to panick and blunder as people anywhere else: they might even falsify or withold information nessecary to pubic health and safety, theirs alot to worry about when its a matter of nuclular power and the safety of the planet.

Exercise 15.24

Seek and destroy all errors in the following passage.

A magazine artical I read resently sited reasons for the brakedown of relationahips. Its very important for poeple to be conscience of these reasons. I found it intresting that the principle reason given for brakedown was failure to communicate. Appparantly some couples can balance there frequent arguements with alot of love and passion, so they stick together thru thick and thin. Others, tho, do not manage to balance there conflict with any posative action. They waist there time arguing, criticizing, and complaning, so they loose patients with each other. The results are disasterous. If they spent more time touching, smiling, paying complements, joking and laughing, for instance, they would avoid all the negativity and tention that create the downward spiral in there relationship. They are suppose to concentrate more on good things. If my friends, Patsy and Liam had of chose to discuss there financial problems, instead of insulting one another and shreiking abuse all the time they might of been together still. There relationship began well, but began to self-destruct to soon. They should of gone to a guidance councillor as soon as they started all the yelling and repeeting silly accusations over and over. They certainly failed to communicate clearly and correctly. Do they no what their missing now, I wonder?

Exercise 15.25

Proofread and correct all errors in the following passage.

Retail is detail says Dorothy Kelleher, president of Radways Reatail. The huge Vancouver-based discount store. Shes the first women president in the history of radways its a significant feet other female executives tell her their counting on her to do well, some male subordinates have had difficulty in the passed working with a women in such a high profile job but know shes been president for four year, she feels the fact shes a women is a non issue.

Her husband ken say shes given the position because of the abilitys she showen in the passed. And the results she generated in her years at The Bay and Sears in Toronto. Dorothy dosent want to spend alot of time talking about gender poeple are no longer suuprise in the twentyfist century she says to find woman in senior positions, she think any body with a retail background administrative abilty and good poeple skill could do her job. Studing literature and drama at university help her develop poeple skill.

Other Chief Operating Officers agrees that a liberal arts background is invaluable for sucess in buisness. They say that they can find people with technicle skill but not with poepe skill. They want more student to study the humanities in college. Josef Penninger in Toronto, one of the youngest of the worlds celebrate scientist, and one of the most exicting medical reserchers in the world, thinks that it is very sad that more students do not read Plato. He says that he would not be wear he is know, if he had not studied Plato and Socrates in high school in Austria. Penninger might win a Noble price one day.

Dorothy Kelleher agree with him. I will never regret the hours I spent at my liberal arts studys she says.

REVIEW AND REMEMBER

Part 4

Syntax and Mechanics

1. Clear sentences always have at least one subject, verb, and complete thought. Phrases and clauses add extra excitement, meaning, and interest to plain statements.

2. Sentence fragments and run-on sentences distract readers, so should be avoided, and used only very occasionally for special effects.

3. Clear verb use is essential to avoid confusions in tense and number.

4. Modifiers need to come as close as possible to whatever they are modifying.

5. Pronouns need clear and consistent references.

6. Parallel structure keeps grammatical parts equal in form and importance.

7. Correct use of commas, apostrophes, capitals, semicolons, and colons keeps readers happy and relaxed on the highway of communication.

8. Correct spelling avoids confusion and creates a good impression.

9. Sensible writers plan and proofread carefully in order to achieve a clear, correct, coherent final version of their paper.

Works Cited

Chapter 1

Campbell, Joe. "Seared meat, smoke and status." *The Globe and Mail,* 24 May 1999, A22.

Filosa, Michael. "After Breathalyzer, a Sleepalyzer?" In *Wellness Options,* February & March 2001, Volume 1 No. 2, 32. Adapted from *Journal of Sleep Research* 9 (2000): 233 in *Occupational and Environmental Medicine* 57 (2000): 649.

Fitzgerald, John, ed. "Summer Barbecues." *Gusto* 1.4, Summer 1995.

Goleman, Daniel. *Emotional Intelligence.* New York: Bantam Books, 1995.

Greenpeace. "Looking Back on the Exxon Valdez." *Greenlink* 7: 2 Spring/Summer 1999, 3.

Chapter 2

Angelou, Maya. "A New Path For Annie." From *Wouldn't Take Nothing for My Journey Now.* New York: Random House, 1993.

Carey, John, ed. *The Faber Book of Reportage.* London: Faber and Faber, 1987.

Facey, A. B. *A Fortunate Life.* Victoria, Aus.: Penguin Books, 1981.

Gildiner, Catherine. *Too Close to the Falls.* Toronto: ECW Press, 1999.

Chapter 3

De Santis, Solange. "On the Line." *Chatelaine* June 1999, 67–70.

King, Deborah. "Resolving a Weighty Matter." *The Globe and Mail* 19 May 1998, A20.

Klein, Naomi. *No Logo.* Toronto: Knopf Canada, 2000.

Wiwa, Ken. *In the Shadow of a Saint.* Toronto: Knopf Canada, 2000.

Chapter 4

Chang, Jung. *Wild Swans.* New York: Anchor Books, 1992.

Gates, Henry Louis Jr., ed. *The Classic Slave Narratives.* New York: Penguin USA, 1987.

Johnston, Richard. "Introduction to Student Writing Contest Winners." From *Celebrating Student Writing at Centennial College,* Volume 1. Scarborough, ON: Fall 2000, p. 2.

Lacey, Hester. "I Tried to Kill My Pretty Sister." *The Independent on Sunday* 27 August 1995.

Chapter 5

Connor, Steve. "Landmarks of the Mind." The Sunday Review of *The Independent on Sunday* 28 May 1995, 82–83.

Galbraith, John Kenneth. "John Kenneth Galbraith's World Tour." *The Globe and Mail* 6 July 1999, A13. Reprinted from *The Guardian.*

Stackhouse, John. "Equipped to make her own way." *The Globe and Mail* 4 September 1995, A7.

Suzuki, David. "Our Environmental Shame." *The Globe and Mail* 22 March 2001, A17.

Chapter 6

Adams, Douglas. *The Hitchhiker's Guide to the Galaxy.* New York: Harmony Books, 1989.

Alcott, Louisa May. *Little Women.* London: The Heirloom Library, 1957.

Carrier, Roch. *The Hockey Sweater and Other Stories.* Toronto: House of Anansi Press, 1979.

Dickens, Charles. *A Christmas Carol: in prose, being a ghost story for Christmas.* London: J.M. Dent, 1963.

Dickens, Charles. *A Tale of Two Cities.* London: Oxford University Press, 1903.

Dickens, Charles. *David Copperfield.* New York: P.F. Collier, 1917.

Fitzgerald, F. Scott. *The Great Gatsby.* New York: Scribner, 1953.

Haley, Alex. *The Autobiography of Malcolm X.* New York: Ballantine Books, 1992.

Hughes, Langston. "Salvation." in *The Big Sea: An Autobiography.* New York: Hill and Wang, 1940.

Mitchell, Margaret. *Gone With the Wind.* New York: Macmillan, 1936.

Montgomery, Lucy Maud. *Anne of Green Gables.* New York: Ballantine Books, 1987.

Orwell, George. "A Hanging." in *Shooting an Elephant and Other Essays.* London: Secker and Werburg, 1950.

Orwell, George. *Animal Farm.* New York: Harcourt Brace, 1946.

Paton, Alan. *Cry, The Beloved Country.* New York: Simon & Schuster, 1995.

Potter, Beatrix. *The Tale of Peter Rabbit and Other Stories.* New York: A.A. Knopf, 1988.

Rowling, J. K. *Harry Potter and the Philosopher's Stone.* Vancouver: Raincoast Books, 1997.

Tolstoy, Leo. *Anna Karenina.* Oxford: Oxford University Press, 1995.

White, E. B. *Charlotte's Web.* New York: Harper, 1952.

Wittgenstein, Ludwig. *Tractatus Logico-Philosophicus.* London: Routledge and Kegan Paul, 1975.

Chapter 7

Angier, Natalie. *Woman: An Intimate Geography.* Boston: Houghton Mifflin, 1999.

Lipman, Derek S., M.D. *Stop Your Husband From Snoring.* Portland, Oregon: Spencer Press, 1998.

Chapter 8

Goleman, Daniel. *Emotional Intelligence* New York: Bantam Books, 1995.

Chapter 10

Baldwin, James. "Going to Meet the Man." In *Going to Meet the Man.* New York: Dell Publishing, 1965.

David, Elizabeth. "The Markets of France: Cavaillon." *An Omelette and a Glass of Wine.* Middlesex, England: Penguin, 1986.

Faulkner, William. "A Rose for Emily." In *Selected Short Stories of William Faulkner.* New York: Random House, 1993.

Gildiner, Catherine. *Too Close to the Falls.* Toronto: ECW Press, 1999

Jaffery, Madhur. *A Taste of India.* London: Michael Joseph, 1985.

Lawrence, D. H. "Flowery Tuscany." *Selected Essays.* Middlesex, England: Penguin, 1950.

MacLeod, Alistair. *No Great Mischief.* Toronto: McClelland & Stewart, 1999.

Rice, Anne. *Interview with the Vampire.* New York: Ballantine Books, 1977.

Chapter 11

Davis, Wade. "A Dead End for Humanity." *The Globe and Mail* 28 December 2000, A15.

Johnson, Phil. "Roxanne's Revenge Is the Sweetest Yet." *Culture* 27 August 2000, 8.

Thomas, Caitlin. *Double Drink Story: My Life with Dylan Thomas.* London: Virago, 1999.

Trudeau, Pierre Elliott. "Exhaustion and Fulfilment: The Ascetic in a Canoe." In Borden Spears, ed., *Wilderness Canada.* Toronto: Clarke Irwin & Co. Ltd., 1970.

Chapter 12

Service, Robert. *The Cremation of Sam McGee.* Toronto: KidsCan Press, 1986.

Chapter 14

Austen, Jane. *Pride and Prejudice.* London: Oxford University Press, 1970.

Carroll, Lewis. *Alice's Adventures in Wonderland; and Through the Looking-Glass and what Alice Found There.* London: Oxford University Press, 1971.

Churchill, Sir Winston. Speech to House of Commons, 4 June 1940.

Courlander, Harold. *Kantchil's Lime Pit and other Stories from Indonesia.* New York: Harcourt Brace, 1980.

Darwin, Charles. *The Descent of Man, and Selections in Relation to Sex.* Princeton, New Jersey: Princeton University Press, 1981.

Gilbert, Sir W. S. *H.M.S. Pinafore, and other plays.* New York: Modern Library, 1925.

Roosevelt, Franklin D. Second Inaugural Address, 20 January 1937.

Shakespeare, William. *As You Like It.* Harmondsworth: Penguin Books, 1966.

Shakespeare, William. *The Passionate Pilgrim.* New York: Scribner, 1940.

Shaw, George Bernard. *Androcles and the Lion: Overruled; Pygmalion.* London: Constable, 1916.

Wilde, Oscar. *The Importance of Being Earnest: A Trivial Comedy, for Serious People.* London: Benn, 1980.

Chapter 15

Sims, George. "Billy's Rose," in Michael Turner, ed., *Victorian Parlour Poetry: An Annotated Anthology.* New York: Dover Publications, 1992.

Answer Key

Not all exercises have answers; those that do are marked with an asterisk (*) in the text. In some exercises, only odd or even numbers have answers.

Chapter Three

READING 2: "Resolving a Weighty Matter" by Deborah King
EXERCISE 3.3 (p. 87)
1. amassing 2. shunned 3. confront 4. epidemic 5. fad 6. rivalry 7. conviction
8. hypothesis 9. binge 10. dainty

READING 3 : "Culture Jamming: Ads Under Attack" by Naomi Klein
WORD RECOGNITION (p. 94)
1. haunted 2. edge 3. edged 4. politicians, concentration 5. jamming 6. frame 7. feature 8. gorilla, guerilla 9. politics 10. jammed 11. framed 12. concentrate

EXERCISE 3.4 (p. 95)
activist/passive person; public/private; creative/destructive; aggressiveness/calmness; democratic/ totalitarian; vandal/creator; devalue/expand; reject/accept

Chapter Four

READING 1: "You Can Make a Difference" by Richard Johnston
EXERCISE 4.1 (p. 110)
1. (g) important financial groups 2. (k) opposite to what is usually thought
3. (c) characteristic or quality having the greatest impact 4. (i) lines often repeated
5. (h) in the world of top business employers 6. (q) state clearly the reasons for
argument 7. (r) with elegance and charm 8. (p) starting interaction to prevent further injury 9. (l) repeated word or phrase 10. (b) anxious attention paid 11. (d) concerned and worried 12. (a) a means for making a difference

READING 3: "I Tried to Kill My Pretty Sister" by Hester Lacey
WORD RECOGNITION (p. 124)

1. being lumbered with 2. it's not malicious 3. measure up 4. a bone of contention
5. act as a spur 6. prick someone into 7. doomed for life 8. blossom into 9. at a disadvantage 10. a twinge of inadequacy

Chapter Five

READING 2: "Our Environmental Shame" by David Suzuki
WORD RECOGNITION (p. 145)

1. ecosystems 2. glaring 3.sustain 4. *no connection* 5. *no connection* 6. discretionary
7. mandatory 8. mitigation 9. fossil 10. impetus

READING 4: "John Kenneth Galbraith's World Tour"
EXERCISE 5.4 (p. 164)

1. a) eliminate   b) limitless   c) limited   d) limit   e) limiting
2. a) enigma   b) enjoying   c) enjoy   d) enjoyable   e) enjoyment
3. a) concentration b) concerned   c) concentrate d) concentrating e) concerted
4. a) optometrist   b) optimistic   c) optimism   d) options   e) optimists
5. a) researcher   b) researched   c) resign   d) research   e) resigned

Chapter 6

EXERCISE 6.4 (p.179)

Sources

1. The Egg Marketing Board of Canada 2. an article on pollution from the Toronto Environmental Alliance 3. the AIDS Committee of Toronto 4. an advertisement for Algemarin shower gel 5. People for the Ethical Treatment of Animals (PETA) 6. an advertisement for Live365.com 7. a Handbook from the Ministry of Social Services, Queen's Park, Ontario, on caring for people with Alzheimer's disease 8. Professor Charles Joyner in *Down By the Riverside,* a book about a slave community in South Carolina, published by the University of Illinois Press in 1984 9.Guide to the Hockey Hall of Fame 10. an article on ergonomics in the July 2000 issue of the high-tech magazine *Wired*

EXERCISE 6.9 (p. 190)

1. a 2. c 3. b 4. b 5. d 6. a 7. b 8. d 9. d 10. b 11. c 12. c 13. a 14. d 15. d 16. b 17. a
18. c 19. d 20. b

EXERCISE 6.15 (p. 198)

2. b,d 4. c,d 6. c,d 8. a,d 10. b,c

EXERCISE 6.21 (p. 213)

1. a,c 2. b,c 3. a,c 4. b,c 5. a,c

Chapter Seven

EXERCISE 7.8 (p. 236)

Sentences 1, 2, 5, 7, 8, 9, 11, 13, 15, 16, and 20 would *not* make good topic sentences.

EXERCISE 7.9 (p. 237)

Sentences 3, 5, and 7 would destroy the unity of a paragraph on the topic sentence.

EXERCISE 7.10 (p. 238)

1. 3 2. 5,8 3. 6,9 4. 3 5. 3,4,7

EXERCISE 7.13 (p. 241)

1. Asthma affects people in different ways.
2. When oil begins to wear out, it can't protect your engine.
3. Snoring has been disturbing human sleep for thousands of years.
4. Selecting the right music for a family reunion can be tricky.
5. Guys, watch out for flirts who enjoy mating games but have no intention of following through.
6. For the first two or three years of life, a human child is not that different from a chimpanzee.
7. As elsewhere in the ancient world, wives in Roman times were expected to take care of the house, but with one difference.
8. My brother's room is a mess.
9. The new Corvette is the quickest and coolest of them all.
10. The origin of the word *sterling* for British money is not certain.

EXERCISE 7.14 (p. 243)

Your topic sentences may be quite different, but must clearly prepare a reader for your selected support.

2. *Topic Sentence:* Choosing a family car means considering space, comfort and safety.
   Support: a, c, f, h
3. *Topic Sentence:* The early pioneers in Canada had a tough life with no technology, but with the help of horses they made the wilderness shine.
   Support: b, e, g, i

Chapter 8

EXERCISE 8.3 (p. 258)

Expression of support may vary slightly.

1.   A. ii)

B. only 5 overdose deaths from illicit drugs; 62% of overdose deaths involved prescription psychotropic drugs

2.   A. **Topic:**   the social advantages of high emotional intelligence in males

or   the social universe for men high in emotional intelligence

B. **Support:** commitment to people or causes; ability to take responsibility; ethical outlook

or show sympathy and caring in relationships; comfortable with themselves and others; rich emotional life

Chapter 9

EXERCISE 9.4 (p. 274)

1.   *company*: a; *many of its units*: a; *Still*: b; *It*: c; *Inside this unit*: a; *However*: b; *the same sense of commitment*: a

2.   *In the past*: b; *also*: b; *Now*: b; *intelligence*: a; *basic notions of intelligence*: a; *In particular*: b; *many aspects to intelligence*: a; *intelligence*: a; *too*: b; *that*: c

3.   *it*: c; *rainforest*: a; *wonder*: a; *Filled with awe,he*: a and c; *fascinated*: a; *their rainforest environment*: a; *rainforest, Darwin*: a

4.   *They*: c; *them*: c; *plans, maps, charts, and drawings*: a; *Effective diagrams or illustrations*: a; *Obviously*: b; *fewer words*: a; *therefore*: b

Chapter 10

EXERCISE 10.4 (p. 284)

Opening and concluding statements will vary. #3 may come at the end of the beginning.

Replacing the battery in your calculator is easy. Just follow these steps:
1. 4 2. 6 3. 7 4. 9 5. 2 6. 8 7.5 8. 1 9. 3

Congratulations. With your new battery installed, you now have many hours of accurate calculation at your fingertips.

Chapter Twelve

EXERCISE 12.1 (p. 330)

2. Joe 4. She 6. he 8. Joe 10. He 12. a magpie

EXERCISE 12.2 (p. 330)
1. Baseball players 3. Few, they 5. they 7. ball players

EXERCISE 12.4 (p. 336)
Did you "V" 17 of the words?

EXERCISE 12.6 (p. 337)
Cancer Care Ontario *is growing…*
…number of people living with cancer *continues* to *grow*
New centres are *planned…* others *are expanding*
Patients *are assessed* and *treated…*
is made up of…
These people *have …*
They *offer…*

EXERCISE 12.8 (p. 338)
1. X, began 3. X, has 4. X, written 6. X, taken 7. X, chose 9. X, driven 10. X, gone

EXERCISE 12.9 (p. 339)
1. has been transferred 2. lives 3. have moved 4. saw 5. is 6. was drinking 7. laughs
8. laugh 9. look 10. talk 11. are always laughing 12. must 13. be 14. hear 15. must be

EXERCISE 12.10 (p. 340)
1.   supposed ,wanted, decided, decided
3.   lived, straightened, confused, refused, told
5.   suffered, walked, uninjured, made
7.   has always shown, known
9.   married, called, warned, amazed

EXERCISE 12.11 (p. 341)
2. came, saw 4. seen, was 6. replied 8. shuddered 10. went, met 12. was 14. trotted
16. ran 18. sobbing, came 20. crawled, learned, save

EXERCISE 12.12 (p. 342)
Suhail *joined…*
He has always *remembered* hearing a speaker from Hawaii *talk…*
The man from Hawaii *told* about how nobody *gives…*
"There *is* … " Suhail *says.*
He *tries* to convince everyone *to learn* … not too many of his classmates in college
are convinced that he *has* a point.

EXERCISE 12.15 (p. 347)
1. is 3. are 5. are 7. thinks 9. is 11. laughs 13. are

EXERCISE 12.16 (p. 348)
2. was 4. was 6. was 8. was 10. was

EXERCISE 12.17 (p. 348)
1. ...a team of NASA scientists... *discovers*... 3. This finding... *sends*...4. A stratosphere... *results*... 6. People... *are going* to suffer terribly. 7. ... *are* caused by the sun. 8. ... individuals going without sun protection *are*.. 9. The photosynthesis process... *is affected*... 10. The amount of...*is* diminished

EXERCISE 12.18 (p. 349)
1. *no change* 3. is 5. cooks 7. *no change* 9. *no change*

EXERCISE 12.19 (p. 350)
is; runs; loses; dares; leaves; falls; prays; is; refuses; decides; expect; prays; begins; knows; tempt; do; stops; forgets; reaches; wins; live; goes; seems; cause; tells

EXERCISE 12.20 (p. 351)
live in the southern part...
To the north *lies*...
He *says* most Canadians *shun*...
In fact, the men who *faced* the reality and explored the High North in the first place, *were*...
Today nature lovers... *go* to the north *and explore*...
... nor the worst weather the North produces *is*...
Tourists .. arriving in this ancient land *love* to see the wildlife.
Everyone always *loves*...
...more people in the southern part of Canada... *learn*

Chapter Thirteen

EXERCISE 13.1 (p. 356)
IC = independent clause; DC = dependent clause

1.	IC	6.	DC
2.	DC	7.	IC
3.	DC	8.	DC
4.	IC	9.	IC
5.	IC	10.	DC

EXERCISE 13.2 (p. 356)

S = subject; V = verb

1.	S	5.	V
2.	V	6.	S
3.	V	7.	V
4.	V	8.	V

EXERCISE 13.3 (p. 357)

Numbers 1, 3, 6, 7, and 9 are sentence fragments.

EXERCISE 13.4 (p. 357)

Numbers 2, 4, 5, 6, 8, and 10 are sentence fragments.

EXERCISE 13.6 (p. 358)

Correct versions may differ. Some writers prefer semi-colons between independent clauses, while others prefer conjunctions.

The protest songs of the 1990s were rap songs where the only militant messages in the pop charts were heard. Rappers describing themselves as "radical," were determined
i) to rap about serious ideas: urban debates on race, education, drugs and crime. That's what ...
ii) to rap about serious ideas. Urban debates on race, education, drugs and crime, that's what listeners heard in the rap songs of the Nineties.
iii) about serious ideas, and so urban debates on race, education, drugs and crime, were what listeners heard...
The message heard was varied: a message of penetrating insights, paranoia, resistance. The rappers were African-Americans. They saw themselves as victims of kidnapping through the slave trade; theft through their labour; brainwashing through their lack of educational opportunities; and genocide through crack, AIDS, and murder. They urged change. Brand Nubian said, " Black mothers need sons, not children that's been killed by guns."

EXERCISE 13.7 (p. 359)

Everyone loves a sports car, a simple two-seater with style. Driving around town with the top down is always fun. Listening to the turbocharged engines make whispery, whooshing sounds is music to the ears of any sportscar lover. Everyone loves the lusty song of a powerplant engine.

These days people seem to want a good cargo space, as well as a cushy ride. For older drivers a good sportscar has to be civilized, able to work as day-to-day transportation, but younger drivers like a more nervous, sensitive car, with structural rigidity and slick handling.

EXERCISE 13.8 (p. 359)

Did you know that enough radioactive waste exists in Canada to cover the Trans-Canada highway two metres deep from Halifax to Vancouver? As radioactive waste lasts for 80, 000 years, the risk to human health and the environment is frightenening. Northern Saskatchewan and other northern regions are becoming radioactive waste-lands. It is miners and native people in those regions who are the first victims. They cannot avoid exposure to radiation which causes cancer and other health problems.

EXERCISE 13.10 (p. 362)

2.   zest. He snored...

4.   score. They did not...

6.   a rat. He had passed...

EXERCISE 13.11 (p. 363)

1. **and** 2. Jeff Gibbs found an alliance of youth environmental groups, after he had been on a high school trip to the Queen Charlotte Islands.

3. He has also been on an expedition to the Amazon rain forest with David Suzuki.

4. Dana discovered that several schools in her area already had environmental clubs; other were intending to form their own soon.

5. *OK*

6. *OK*

7. " We have only one Earth," they declare. " We must protect it."

8. **and** 9. They do not let themselves get discouraged, though the apathetic attitude of some of their fellow students can be discouraging.

10. "we must educate our peers, they say. "Think globally. Act locally. Environmental protection begins in our own back yard."

EXERCISE 13.12 (p. 364)

1. ...camping, they decided to go to Gros Morne National Park.

3. ...the bluff. In it there are ripple marks...

5. ... water sounds, without the unnatural noises...

7. ... small explosions of noise. These thumps came from...

9. ... this patriotic song, when there was only enough light...

11. ...unspoiled parks. They love the wilderness...

EXERCISE 13.13 (p. 366)

2.   ...beaches; furthermore, it also offers

4.   ...a new marine park; in fact, it protects

6.   ...extinct volcano; indeed, visitors can

8.   ... pre-Colombian sites; moreover, a research team

10.   ...in the Caribbean; therefore, for those who love diving,

EXERCISE 13.15 (p. 367)

RO = run-on

1. RO— roles; many books...
2. RO—macho? Are boys...
4. RO— like a man." They are told "boys don't cry;" girls seldom hear...
6. RO— third sex. The Cheyenne...
7. RO— genders. Individuals...
8. RO— the third sex. I went...
9. RO—indpendent and free; men however, ...
10. RO— masculinity. To maintain their macho image... sexual conquests. Sound familiar?

Chapter Fourteen

EXERCISE 14.1 (p. 372)

MM = misplaced modifier; DM = dangling modifier

1. MM 2. DM 3. MM 4. DM 5. MM 6. MM 7. MM 8. DM 9. DM 10. MM

EXERCISE 14.3 (p. 373)

Waving frantically and shouting
that smelled delicious
only talked
in brown pottery mugs
floating across the water
that he had lost
that was a valuable memento

EXERCISE 14.4 (p. 373)

The following sentences have been corrected.

2. Watching the moon for some time, the students on the telescope noticed...
4. The restaurant is advertising for two waiters and a man to wash dishes.
5. ... when he announced that he was a specialist in certain diseases, as well as in women's problems.
6. My aunt promised to be just like mother and to serve me tea in a bag.
7. They want to sell their freshly painted blue boat which has had one owner.
8. Conrad and his friends that are blind are selling newspapers.
10. Pyramids reaching up to five hundred metres were constructed by hand.

EXERCISE 14.7 (p. 378)

The following sentences have been corrected.

1.   ... are always interesting and challenging.
2.   He is good-looking, with brown hair, an intelligent mind, and a Lexus. *OR*
      He is good-looking, brown-haired, and intelligent. He also owns a Lexus.
5.   ... that change from white to red, and from violet to red.
7.   Marking papers, preparing classes and meeting with students keep...
8.   ...comes to class... and asks...
9.   ... to meet with students after class, and to discuss...

EXERCISE 14.8 (p. 378)

2.   ... another store, or look expensively dressed.
4.   Caregivers of ill or old (disabled) people have to help them adjust to depen-
      dency and to an altered lifestyle.
6.   ... juggling work, studies, and a social life
8.   ... the most intelligent man in the world and that he is also the cutest.
10.   ... but also to see how different cultures live.

EXERCISE 14.10 (p. 383)

ref = faulty pronoun reference

1. ref 2. ref 4. ref 8. ref 9. ref

EXERCISE 14.11 (p. 384)

1. he, their 3. me 5. I, she 7. us 9. I, me

EXERCISE 14.12 (p. 384)

1. She 2. They 3. them 4. she 5. they 6. they 7. himself 8. he 9. her 10. them

EXERCISE 14.13 (p. 385)

Sentences 1, 2, 3, 5, 6, 7, 9, and 10 have pronouns without clear antecedents.

EXERCISE 14.15 (p. 386)

its; their; Their; they; its; it; them; its; it; it
they; they; it; they; us

Chapter Fifteen

EXERCISE 15.1 (p. 394)

1. Festival, Ch'ing Ming, 2. green leaves, 3. Soon, *(optional)* 4. *no commas needed*
5. festival, *(optional)* 6. willowsprigs, paper money, *(optional)* 7. poor, 8. gods,

9. The principles of Yin and Yang, gods are Yang, souls of people are Yin, must never be ignored. *(Some people might prefer dashes to separate— gods are Yang, souls of people are Yin—)* 10. After honouring the dead, the people...

EXERCISE 15.2 (p. 394)

1. ...for children to read, 2. in children's books, 3. as this sounds,
4. Third World activists, feminists, the disabled, ethnic minorities, all have...
5. In the marketplace, unfortunately, stereotypes are popular.
6. After all,... 7. ... more sensitive, 8. local communities,9. Parents, as well as caregivers and early education teachers,... 10. ...don't bother,...

EXERCISE 15.4 (p. 397)

1. Billy's dead and gone to glory—so is Billy's sister, Nell.
2. There's a tale I know about them;
3. ... one winter's day.
4. in the garret's dismal gloom.
5. ... Billy's pathway
6. Nell's idea of heaven
7. ... and they're all so strong and well.
8. ... if there's room
9. ... father's curses, and a drunken father's blows
10. ... from the day's dawn to its close.

EXERCISE 15.5 (p. 398)

1. youth's name; the youths' name
2. hero's leg; the heroes' legs
3. community's center; comunities' centres
4. parent's exectations; parents' expectations
5. mouse's hole; mice's holes
6. bus's route; buses' routes
7. woman's money; women's money
8. her life's work; their lives' work
9. taxi's driver; taxis' drivers
10. baby's bottle; babies' bottles

EXERCISE 15.6 (p. 399)

1. Bruno's leather jackets 3. Daniel bar Jamin's revenge 5. the wizards' students 7. Maurice Sendak's books 9. today's children

EXERCISE 15.9 (p. 402)

It took many years before African-Americans were seen on television. Although tv (TV) was the technological wonder at the 1939 New York World's Fair, it did not come into many North American households until early in the fifties (Fifties). Then it was not until 1957 with *The Nat King Cole Show* that African-Americans were finally given an honest image and a black host for a show. Previously black people had been cast as servants or buffoons. Later *Roots*, the miniseries, was a runaway hit. In fact, three of its episodes rank among tv's (TV's) top shows of all time. Nearly 100 million viewers saw the last episode. Now with stars like Bill Cosby, Oprah Winfrey and Will Smith, African-Americans continue to make a big impression on the little screen.

EXERCISE 15.12 (p. 405)

Numbers 3, 5, and 9 are correct.

1. One of the most famous sailors in history was a tall, good-looking farm boy, whose first job was selling groceries. This country lad was James Cook. His voyages of discovery would make him famous.

2. James Cook circled the globe three times; (.He) he mapped islands in the Pacific that no European had ever seen; (.He) he found a way to prevent the disease of scurvy.

4. He quickly became a good sailor, learning to climb the rigging, to hoist anchor and to steer the ship.

6. The life of a sailor in the British Navy was far from pleasant at that time. A sailor could expect terrible working conditions, (:) bad pay, a poor diet, the chance of falling ill with scurvy.

7. It was a surprising decision, therefore, when James Cook, at the age of 27, turned down the command of a merchant vessel, and joined the British Navy.

8. His first mission as master of a new 64-gun ship, *The Pembroke*, was to take soldiers to Canada where, at the mouth of the St. Lawrence River, he was to undertake a dangerous assignment.

10. The charts he made were absolutely accurate. When the British sailed large ships up the St. Lawrence, not one ship ran aground.

EXERCISE 15.15 (p. 410)

1. achieve 2. agencies 3. anxieties 4. believe 5. chief 6. codeine 7. deceived 8. foreign 9. freight 10. friend 11. identities 12. interview 13. leisure 14. mischief 15. niece 16. receive 17. retrieve 18. seige 19. veil 20. weigh

EXERCISE 15.16 (p. 411)

Did you change the following?

1. beginner 3. convenience 5.desperate 6.description 7. environment 8. exaggerate 9. expenses 12. medicine 13. personnel 14. percentage 15. professor 16. resources 17. secretary 18. summary 20. tomorrow

EXERCISE 15.18 (p. 423)

1. It's too; plane; now; it's; sight 2. It's; flair 3. critical; its 4. its; weight; its 5. It's; advice; Board 6. passed; morale 7. personnel there 8. It's; similar; its; who's; you're; know 9. principle; aloud; who's 10. then; weight; plane; its

EXERCISE 15.20 (p. 425)

favourite; You're; caped; right; whose; knows; parents'; night; quiet; regular; coloured; mysterious; weird; than; to; human

whose; adversaries; deadly; principal; a lot; where

conscious; than; who's; than

EXERCISE 15.21 (p. 425)

If you want to comprehend the allusions people often make in conversation, it's a good idea to become familiar with some of the old Greek myths. Not only are these stories a source of entertainment, they can also help you interpret paintings and sculptures, as well as family behaviour.

Some of the stories are quite sensational. Reading them will make you conscious of how many ideas in our culture have developed. In some versions, lurid details are omitted on moral grounds, but the stories still reveal the spiritual dimensions of our existence. Myth, as C. S. Lewis said, partially lifts the veil from the mysteries of life through the medium of story.

If there's a lesson to be learned from reading Greek myths, it is that these stories of ancient times may reflect different ideas about the structure of the universe—the Greeks believed the earth to be flat—but human behaviour has always contained the seeds of joy and tragedy and the same dilemmas were present then in the human spirit.

Index

Abolition of slavery, 113
Acculturation, 136
Active Reader Program, 5, 72
Adams, Douglas, 210, 211
Adbusters, 93
African-American, 48
Adjective, 335
Agreement
    pronoun, 381
    subject-verb, 343–350
"After Breathalyzer, A Sleepalyzer?", 22
Alcott, Louisa May, 210
Allen, Ted, 57
Allusion, 86, 413
Altavista.com (electronic search engine),
    179
Analogy, 112
Analytical thinking, 8, 108, 136
Anecdotal evidence, 150, 153
Angelou, Maya, 41
Antecedent, 346, 371, 382, 383
Antonym, 95
APA (American Psychological
    Association) style, 313, 314
Apostrophe, 396
Attitudinal markers, 266, 270
Audience, 70, 170, 173, 224–227, 232
    convincing an, 212
Author citations. *See* citations

BAC (Blood Alcohol Concentration), 22
Baldwin, James, 281
Be
    no colons with, 404
    verb, 332
Bethune, Norman, 57
Bible, 99
Bibliography, 314

Biographical data, 185
Brecht, Bertolt, 133

Campbell, Joe, 11
Capitalization, 400–402
Caribbean, 113
Carroll, Lewis, 380
Carson, Rachel, 133
Cause and effect, 292
Censorship, 108
Chang, Jung, 127
Chatelaine, 65, 78
Churchill, Winston, 136, 379
Citations, 313
Clarity, 183, 314, 323
Classification, 290
Clause
    dependent, 354
    independent, 354
Clear, making things, 228
Coherence, 266–276, 298, 362
Collaborative writing, 1–3
Collective nouns, 345
Colon, 403
Comma, 390–395, 429
Comma Overload, 390
Comma splice, 361
Commonly confused words, 412
Comparison and contrast, 285
Comprehension, 4
    affective, 169
    critical, 169
    literal, 169
Conclusion, 207, 298
Conjunction, 355
    coordinating, 361
    subordinating, 361
Conjunctive adverb, 362

Connotation, 289
Controlling idea, 215–216
Context, 43–44
Context and comprehension, 32
Co-ordinating conjunctions, 361
Critical reading and thinking, 8, 135
Culture, as a way of thinking, 136
"Culture Jamming: Ads Under Attack", 91
Culture jamming, 91–93
Cultural Revolution, the, 127
"Cult of Mao, The", 127
Current issues, commenting on, 217
Cyberspace, caution in, 178

Darwin, Charles, 158, 161, 380
David, Elizabeth, *The Markets of France,*
   279
Dash, 390
Deadlines, 2, 3
Definition, 154, 288
Denotation, 289
Details, 212, 251
   as support, 248, 265
De Santis, Solange, 75
Description, 278
Details, 212, 248
Dickens, Charles, 210, 211
Diction, 289
"Dining Out", 11
Discourse, 91, 92
   modes of, 277
Dissent, tolerance of, 108
Documentation, 314
   of electronic sources, 317
Dominant impression, 279
Double consonants, and spelling, 409

Ecosystem, 28, 144
Electronic directories, 179, 318
Electronic sources, documenting, 317
   caution using, 316
Ellipsis, 390
Either/or, using verbs with, 336
Encyclopedias, use of, 318
"Equipped to Make Her Own Way", 137
Essay, 215, 296
   Formula Five, 297, 306–323
   planning, 215

Etymology, 14
Evaluation, 175
Examples, as content development, 250
Expository prose and expository writing,
   278, 297–98

Facey, A.B., 49
Famous last words, 210
Fascist, 58, 59
Faulkner, William, 281
Figurative language, 86, 106
Figures of speech, 86, 106
Filosa, Michael, 22
First lines, famous, 209
Fitzgerald, John, 8
Florence, Italy, 161
Focus
   on the essentials, 72
   finding a focus, 194
Formula Five Essay format, 296–7,
   306–310
Fortunate Life, A, 49
Fragment, sentence, 355–360
Fused sentence, 361

Galbraith, John Kenneth, 157
Gates Jr., Henry Louis, 48, 116
Generalizations, 189–194
Gildiner, Catherine, 65, 280
Goleman, Daniel, 20 , 258, 261
Google search, 179, 312
Grammar errors, 325
Gross Domestic Product (GDP), 158,
   162

Haley, Alex, 210
Hamlet, 332
Harvard, 157, 158
Helping verbs, 332
"History of Mary Prince, The", 114
Homonym horrors (aka word
   confusions), 412–426
Hotbot.com (electronic search engine),
   179
"How to" instructions, 282
Hubris, 38
Hughes, Langston, 210
Hyphen, 390

Ibsen, Henrik, 112, 185
Ie and *ei* words, 408
I-frame format, 299
Imagery, 86
Impressionists, 158, 161
India, 137, 313
    A Taste of , 280
Indefinite pronouns, 382
    verb agreement, 344
Indenting long quotations, 313
Independent clause, 353
Infinitives, 335
Information retrieval, 177–8, 312, 316–8
Intellectual property, 314
Interactive critical thinking, 171–222
Internet, 177, 178,179, 312, 316–318
Interrogative pronouns, 381
Interruptions, 392
In the Shadow of a Saint, 98
Introductions, 203
Issues, commenting on, 217
Irritable Reader Syndrome, 212, 325, 389
Italics, 390
"I Tried to Kill My Pretty Sister", 121

Jaffrey, Madhur, 280
"John Kenneth Galbraith's World Tour",
    157
Johnston, Richard, 108

Kent, David, 311
King, Deborah, 82
Kipling, Rudyard, 229
Klein, Naomi, 90
"Know Thyself", 20
Koran, 99, 100

Lacey, Hester, 121
Language and social attitudes, 48
Language with life, 85
Last words, famous, 210
Lawrence, David Herbert, 280
Link rot, 316
Linking verbs, 332
Literally, writing, 85
Loach, Ken, 65
"Looking Back on the Exxon Valdez", 27
Lycos.com (electronic search engine), 179

MacLeod, Alistair, 281
Mao, Chairman, 127
Malcolm X, 210
Marx, Karl, 158, 161
Memory aids for spelling, 408
"Men Are Different", 148
Metaphor, 86
Micro-subject, 172, 194, 224, 227–232,
    298
Mitchell, Margaret, 210, 211
MLA (Modern Language Association)
    style, 313, 314
Model paragraphs, 269, 321-323
Modifiers, 370
    misplaced, 371
    dangling, 371
Modifying phrase, 190
Montgomery, Lucy Maud, 210
Motivators for introductions, 203–5
Multiple perspectives, 201
"Mum's Snake", 49
"My Family Life", 65

Narratives, personal, 32
        slave, 113
Narrowing a topic, 175, 228
"New Directions", 41
Nigeria, Ogoni people of, 99
Nine-Step Program for Active Reading, 5
No Logo, 90
Nouns, 335

Objective, 40, 70
Opposition, 18, 108, 218
"On the Line", 75
Orwell, George, 56, 210, 211
"Our Environmental Shame", 142
Outlines, 247

Paragraphs, 223–300
    coherence in, 266
    I-frame, 299
    introducing, 233
    concluding, 298
    outlining support in, 248
    strong, 320
    student examples, 320
Parallel structure, 369, 375–380

Paraphrasing, 162, 311
Parentheses, 390
Parenthetical reference, 313
Parliamentary procedure, 1, 3
Participle, 335, 355
Peer Gynt, 112
Personification, 86
Personal point of view, 270
Phrase, 328–9, 353
  signal, 250, 312
Plagiarism, 314
Plurals, spelling of, 409
Potter
  Harry, 209, 210
  Beatrix, 212
Power Reading, 107, 134
Point
  getting to the, 172
  making a clear, 196
  about the micro-subject, 232
Point of view, personal, 270
P3SE Formula, reading, 6
Prefix, 14
Prepositional phrases, 329, 353
Prewriting, 171–222
Prince, Mary, 114
Process analysis, 282
Process, efficient, 3
Pronouns, 334, 381
  for coherence, 268
  object, 381
  relative, 354, 381
  subject, 381
Pronoun reference, 381–387
Pronoun shift, 377
Prose, 297
Proofreading, 359, 367, 374, 387, 426–8
Punctuation, 388–407
Purpose, 7, 70, 72, 169

Qualifying words or phrases, 193
  modifying, 190
Questioning, critical, 183
Question marks, placing with quotation
  marks, 390
Quotation marks, 390
Quoting, 250, 311
Qur'an, 401

Reader Program, Active, 5
Reading strategies, 5–8
  critical, 135–170
Reference, pronoun, 381
  research, 312–314
Relative pronouns, 354
Remembering assigned reading, 31
Reminders for coherence, 267
Repetition for coherence. *See* reminders
Research, 177–179
  using, 312–4
"Resolving A Weighty Matter", 82
Resources, using available, 201
Restrictive expressions, 392
Rhetorical modes, 277–295
Root, of word, 14
Rosie the Riveter, 75, 79
Rowling, J.K., 210
Run-on sentence, 360

SARA (Species At Risk Act), 143
Saro-Wiwa, Ken, death of, 98
  last words, 105
sample student paragraphs, 321–323
Saul, John Ralston, 136
Semi-colons, 403–406
Semiotics, 93
Sentence
  essential ingredients, 326–343
  sentence fragment, 353–360
  run-on, 360–368
Service, Robert, 331
Shakespeare, William, 160, 379, 380
Simile, 86
Signal phrases, 250, 311
Slang, 78
Slave narratives, 113
Slavery, historical facts, 114
Sources of information, reliable, 178
Spanish Civil War, 57
Specific data, 250
SPC subject (Specific, Precise, Clear),
  172, 194
Spelling, 43, 407–428
  American or Canadian, 43
Statements by experts, 178, 311
S3Q3 Formula for introductions with
  impact, 203–5, 306

Statistics, use of, 179, 259
Stackhouse, John, 137
Status quo, 39
Stereotyping, 291
Strategies for clear communication, 222
Subject, 169
Subjects, 328–331
Subject-verb agreement, 343–351
Subjective, 40–1, 70
Subordinating conjunction, 354
Suffix, 14
Summary, 72–75, 106
"Summer Barbecues", 8
Support, 247–265
    outline of, 248
    quoting for, 311
    systems, 179, 265
Suzuki, David, 142
Synonym, 67, 110, 267
Syntax, 428
Synthesizing, information presented, 73

Tense
    verb, 333
    shift in, 376
Text citation, 313
Text, 7
    textuality, today's concept, 168
Thesaurus, 267
Thesis, 215–216
Thesis statement, 306–308
Titanic, the, 34
    "A Fireman's Story", 34
    "From A Lifeboat", 36
Titles
    verb agreement with, 345
    punctuation of, 390
Than constructions, 383
Tolstoy, Leo, 210
"To Die a Martyr's Death", 98
Too Close to the Falls, 65, 280
Topic sentences, 206, 224–46
    examples of, 233

Toronto Dominion Centre, 212
Transitional expressions, 266, 269–70

Underlining, in titles, 390
URL (uniform resource locator), 317
Unity, 246, 266–272
Using research material, 312

van der Rohe, Mies, 212
Verbs, 332–351
    to be, 332
    agreement with subject, 343
    finite, 333
    helping or linking, 332–3
    number, 333
    person, 333
    regular, 336
    tense, 333
Vital information and vital language, 71

West Indian, 114
White, E.B., 210, 211
Wild Swans, 127
Wittgenstein, Ludwig, 212
Wiwa, Ken, 98
Words
    confusions, 412
    connotations and denotations, 289
    from Latin and Greek, plurals, 410
Working together, 1
Works Cited, 314
World Wide Web, 316–318
    sites, 318
"Wounded by a Fascist Sniper, 20 May
    1937", 56
Writing, effective, 1–429
    expository, 296–8

Y into *i,* spelling rule, 409
Yahoo.com (electronic search engine), 179
"You Can Make A Difference", 108

Zen master, 20